Desert Dreams

POLITICS AND CULTURE IN MODERN AMERICA

Series Editors: Keisha N. Blain, Margot Canaday, Matthew Lassiter, Stephen Pitti, Thomas J. Sugrue

Volumes in the series narrate and analyze political and social change in the broadest dimensions from 1865 to the present, including ideas about the ways people have sought and wielded power in the public sphere and the language and institutions of politics at all levels—local, national, and transnational. The series is motivated by a desire to reverse the fragmentation of modern U.S. history and to encourage synthetic perspectives on social movements and the state, on gender, race, and labor, and on intellectual history and popular culture.

DESERT DREAMS

Mexican Arizona and the Politics of Educational Equality

Laura K. Muñoz

PENN

UNIVERSITY OF PENNSYLVANIA PRESS

PHILADELPHIA

Published by
University of Pennsylvania Press
Philadelphia, Pennsylvania 19104-4112
www.pennpress.org

Printed in the United States of America on acid-free paper
10 9 8 7 6 5 4 3 2 1

Hardcover ISBN: 978-1-5128-2511-4
eBook ISBN: 978-1-5128-2512-1

A catalogue record for this book is available
from the Library of Congress.

For Natasha

CONTENTS

Introduction

onrado Santiago "Jimmy" Carreón believed "education was the key"
to improving the lives of *Arizonenses*, or Mexican American Arizonans.[1] Across the state and across generations, they valued Carreón
as an advocate. In 1938, *Tucsonenses*, or Tucson Mexicans, elected him to
the 14th Arizona State Legislature. When he moved to the state capital in
1940, Arizonenses along the Rio Salado (Salt River) elected him to the 15th
legislature, making him the first bilingual, Mexican American politician ever
elected from Phoenix and the first elected by both towns.[2] In November 1941,
Carreón led a well-publicized statewide effort to stop the public school segregation of children born to parents of Mexican or Latin American heritage.
He resolved to end the discrimination ["acabar con la discriminación"] at
the fiftieth golden jubilee convention of the Arizona Education Association
(AEA) held in Phoenix. The city's Spanish-language weekly, *El Mensajero*,
reported Carreón's appeal for an investigation of the unequal treatment these
children received in certain districts.[3] He anticipated an annual report and
recommendations from the AEA executive committee to the Arizona State
Board of Education to correct these wrongs. Given the looming possibility
that the United States might enter World War II, Carreón laced the resolution
with the language of inter-American solidarity—a political idea and federal
policy that promoted mutual support among the United States and Latin
American nations. He hoped Anglo Arizonans might extend such tolerance
to their compatriots of Latin American descent.[4] Two hundred teachers at the
AEA delegates' assembly agreed and unanimously endorsed the resolution.

A few weeks later, Carreón attended the third annual Mexican Youth
Conference (MYC) at Arizona State Teachers College (ASTC) at Tempe.[5] The
conference theme, "The Transmission of Education in a Democracy," fit per-
fectly with Carreón's antidiscrimination resolution and the growing anxieties

of the global war. His ideas invigorated the future teachers and young leaders, who came from across Arizona, California, and New Mexico, to discuss a range of civil rights issues affecting Mexican Americans. Like Carreón, who was thirty-one years old and close to them in age, the college students had experienced degrees of social and school segregation because of their heritage and Spanish-language fluency. Carreón's advocacy aligned with the MYC's aims and with the goals of Los Conquistadores (the Conquerors), who formed the very first university-recognized Mexican American student club in Arizona. Created by siblings Rosalío "Ross" F. Muñoz and Rebecca F. Muñoz Gutiérrez, Los Conquis (as they affectionately referred to themselves) strove to expand high school and college attendance among Mexican American children.[6] They considered Carreón among their allies as they built international, intergenerational, interracial, and interfaith alliances to improve the educational conditions of Mexican American youth in the Southwest. The MYC conference speakers reflected this agenda and included Jane H. Rider, Arizona director of the New Deal's National Youth Administration; Gonzales Morelos, the Mexican Consul General in Phoenix; ASTC president Dr. Grady Gammage; and representatives from the Mexican Youth Movement of the Young Men's Christian Association (YMCA) in Southern California.[7]

On December 7, 1941, the second day of the MYC conference began shortly before the Japanese bombed Pearl Harbor at 10:55 a.m. Arizona time. The attack stunned the participants and instantly dissipated its civil rights focus. Within days and months, most of Los Conquis's leadership—those at the ASTC as well as alumni employed as teachers—left the college and their jobs. In May 1942, Rebecca Muñoz married her sweetheart Felix J. Gutiérrez, quit her teaching job at Mesa, and relocated to Los Angeles with her husband.[8] By September 1942, Ross Muñoz had resigned three jobs—his teaching post at St. John's, a new teaching appointment at Tucson for the next academic year, and a summer social work job in Maricopa County. His schoolteacher-wife María del Socorro and their toddler Ricardo moved to her parents' home in Tucson, then the U.S. Navy sent Ross orders to join its censorship division at Bisbee.[9] Carreón's resolution also faded from the AEA's agenda as school officials turned to the immediacy of war preparedness.[10] He focused his attention on the direct concerns of his legislative district. The uncertainty of war meant that any possible social change or educational uplift was postponed. School segregation remained in place for all Arizona schoolchildren for more than another decade.

Carreón's and Los Conquis's aspirations to change the educational status quo were not new ideas. They tapped an esprit de corps long held by older generations of Arizonenses who had trumpeted similar calls for educational access. During the late nineteenth century, Mexican American families invested politically and financially in founding a statewide public education system. Anglo and Mexican American leaders forged alliances, such as the partnership between territorial governor Anson P. K. Safford and Tucson merchant Estevan Ochoa that resulted in the Safford-Ochoa Act, which created Arizona's public schools in 1871. Mexican American assemblymen, including Ochoa, held ranking seats on the territorial legislature's Committee on Education and helped secure the new law. In nine legislative assemblies between 1871 and 1891, at least one Mexican American representative served on the education committee. In their hometowns, Arizonenses subsidized public education, too. In 1875, Ochoa donated the land for Tucson's Congress Street School and then at no cost to Pima County hired his freighters to drive the lumber into town in order to build it. This legacy of Mexican American political and financial support for public education through interethnic alliances and personal investment had been overshadowed by the anti-Mexican sentiments and systemic discrimination that permeated Arizona society by the time Carreón and Los Conquis had come of age.[11]

Education as Citizenship

Desert Dreams maps the literacy and schooling that link Ochoa in 1871 Tucson to Los Conquis and Carreón in 1941 Tempe in order to offer a new origin story about Arizonenses, the making of Arizona, and the declaration of a national Mexican American political consciousness. Arizonenses intellectualized a politics of education—rooted in theory, history, and practice—to demand constitutional rights for themselves and their children. Understanding the fundamental nature of education and its critical power to advance individuals and communities, they chose schooling as the centerpiece of their political initiatives for civil rights in the aftermath of U.S. conquest, from Reconstruction and through the post–World War II era. Arizonenses insisted on their right to obtain public education and on the opportunity to benefit from it because they recognized how educational access provided the necessary foundation to challenge their disenfranchisement in other arenas, such as labor, voting rights, and language rights.

Arizonenses not only incorporated themselves into the citizenry of the territory and state but also sustained a politics of education in order to undergird a much larger platform for Mexican American civil rights across the border-lands. Arizonense leadership—who benefited from access to education and worked to sustain it for rising generations—collaborated through organiza-tions such as the Alianza Hispano-Americana and the Liga Protectora Latina (LPL) at the turn of the twentieth century, as well as new organizations such as the Latin American Club and Los Conquistadores at mid-twentieth century. These organizations funded civil rights actions such as *Romo v. Laird* (1925), the first lawsuit filed by Arizonense parents to demand access to desegregated education, and they built political, economic, educational, and social networks within a constellation of communities across Arizona and the Southwest bor-derlands. Relying on a range of sources, including public school records, uni-versity and government archives, court cases, Spanish-language newspapers, and family histories, this book narrates how this Arizonense politics of edu-cation emerged and the kinds of action that students, parents, educators, and leaders engaged in to bring Arizonense achievement into the historical record. Since the days of the common school movement, citizenship has been consid-ered the foremost function of public education; yet, at the same time, Anglo Americans cast ethnic Mexicans outside the bounds of full American citizen-ship.[12] Weaving together macro views of the development of public schools and micro histories of Arizonenses and their communities, this book delin-eates how they negotiated the complexities of a changing borderland society bound by Indigenous, Mexican, and Anglo worlds and colonized three times over, by Spain, Mexico, and the United States, in order to secure their rights as Americans.

This book argues that Arizonenses consciously designed local, personal philosophies and politics of education with the intent to improve their chil-dren's lives and futures in the United States. The parents' ideas were ordinary and based on desires of progress associated with cosmopolitanism, modern-ism, and the rise of the nation-state, such as the myth of the American Dream. Ochoa's sponsorship of school legislation falls within this purview, as do the countless petitions drafted by parents to create new school districts across the state so that their children would have access to nearby local schools.[13] In other instances, Arizonense educational politics were calculated attempts to outmaneuver and combat the classic discrimination and xenophobia gener-ated from the fallout of the Mexican-American War (1848) and the uneasy race relations that ensued among Anglos and Mexicans in the century that followed. Carreón's school segregation challenge and Los Conquis's youth conferences were definitive examples of this sort of contestation and, as other scholars have shown, reflective of ways in which educational demands were critical to the formation of Mexican American identities in similar places such as Texas and Colorado during the early twentieth century.[14]

This book investigates how Arizonenses confronted anti-Mexican educational politics that led to the rise of Americanization and school segregation in the twentieth century. Discrimination marked Arizonense schooling experiences as detailed in lawsuits such as *Romo v. Laird* (1925) and *Garcia v. Arizona* (1937). Tempeneños (Tempe Mexicans) filed *Romo*, the first school desegregation lawsuit in the state, against the town of Tempe and the Tempe Normal School, known today as Arizona State University, to challenge the creation of a separate "Mexican school" for Mexican American children. The *Garcia* case disputes embezzlement claims made against Amelia Hunt García, a county school superintendent and state board of education member who was, in the 1930s, the highest ranking Mexican American elected official in Arizona. These cases also exemplify this book's third objective: to introduce a nascent civil rights project by parents, teachers, and lawyers to preserve educational equality for Mexican Americans in the decades before World War II and to further the national civil rights movements of the twentieth century. Arizonenses developed their own educational pathways and cultivated a small but recognizable professional class, including teachers, lawyers, and politicians, who worked to uphold and sustain their citizenship claims.

Civic Integration and Civil Rights

This Arizonense history hinges on two central themes: civic integration and civil rights. *Civic integration*, a term introduced here, names the collective practices of political, economic, and social action that Arizonenses took to sustain their belonging in the region after U.S. conquest.[15] Arizonenses who remained on the U.S. side of the border after the 1848 Mexican-American War and the 1853 Gadsden Purchase, as well as those who entered the region in the decades that followed, did so with the intent of supporting the nation, just as they had done under the Spanish and Mexican flags. Unwilling to abandon the territory to its original Native American nations or to newly arrived Anglos, Arizonenses continued to assert their settler prerogatives and generational land claims.[16] They embraced the American state and used its laws to build communities and schools to solidify their presence. Arizonenses, such as Ochoa and Tucsonense Mariano G. Samaniego, had lived, worked, traveled, and attended school in the U.S.-Mexico borderlands. Samaniego, for example, was born in Bavispe, Sonora, in 1844; was naturalized in La Mesilla, New Mexico, after 1853; and graduated in 1862 from Saint Louis University in Missouri. When he moved his family to Tucson in 1869, he entered territorial politics as a legislator and served on the first Board of Regents for the University of Arizona.[17] By the time of his death in 1907, he had been elected to more public offices at the local, county, and territorial levels than any other Arizonense.[18] Both Ochoa and Samaniego practiced civic integration and strove to reproduce this vision of an educated society based on their experience and movement across these borderlands. Generations of Arizonenses from the border to the Gila River and to the northernmost reaches of the territory embraced this politic into the twentieth century.

Ochoa, Samaniego, and Arizonense communities also contended with an Anglo antagonism toward Mexican-heritage people that increasingly diminished their broad civil rights, economic opportunities, and educational access. These challenges took many forms, from the massive influx of Anglo settlers who overran the territory and passed new laws to disenfranchise ethnic Mexicans, to the corporate and technological investment in industries such as agriculture, mining, and railroads that changed the political, economic, and social structures of their society. For example, Ochoa, who once worked as a Wells Fargo express agent, is famously known for both his economic ascent as a freighter before 1880 and his penniless demise after the completion of the transcontinental railroad in 1881.[19] While Samaniego was elected four times to the territorial legislature, he was often the only Arizonense representative in the entire state. By 1894, he and his compadres formed the Alianza Hispano-Americana, a mutualista, or mutual aid society, to preserve what little public stature they had sustained and to unite against Anglo domination. Arizonenses organized several statewide mutualistas, but the Alianza's binational male membership made it by far the largest Mexican-heritage organization in the American Southwest with over 17,000 members in 1939.[20]

Like opposite sides of a door, civic integration and civil rights were hinged by this anti-Mexican tension or "framework of hostility" ever present in Anglo Arizona.[21] As Arizonenses engaged their new American citizenship, most Anglos pushed back with discrimination, banning the Spanish language, paying "Mexican wages," and squeezing Arizonenses out of higher education.[22] "Always the peon laborer and never the potential citizen" is how one historian depicted the Anglo opinion of the Mexican.[23] In the public schools, teachers called it a "Mexican Problem" that needed solving through Americanization and workforce training.[24] The Mexican Problem, it turns out, was actually a turn of phrase among Anglo-American intellectuals of the era who questioned what to do with unassimilated, Spanish-speaking Mexicans, especially immigrants and their children.[25] Like Puerto Ricans and other "colonial citizens" across the American empire, Anglos perceived ethnic Mexicans as a conquered people who were tied to the land, destined to labor, and never the student.[26] The Mexican Problem, thus, became both evidence and rationale for required educational policies designed to "de-Mexicanize" ethnic children and to transform them into suitable, English-speaking laborers.[27] Arizonenses, however, took refuge in their right as citizens of Arizona, in their own educated understanding of the past, and in the anticipation of possible futures.

Arizonense Identity and the Origins of Literacy

Most Arizonenses claimed a history rooted in the region and identified with its transnational, transborder heritage. This book refers to the ethnic Mexican people of Arizona as *Arizonenses* because they described themselves on occasion as "miembros de nuestro pueblo Arizonense," or as the nation/people of Arizona.[28] Over the last two centuries, Arizonenses have called themselves many names, such as Spanish or Españoles, Mexicanos or Mexican Americans, Hispanos or Hispanic, as well as *hermanas y hermanos* (brothers and sisters). They even described themselves as teacher-turned-lawyer Rafael "Ralph" Carlos Estrada once did, "as members of the largest white and Christian minority not only of Arizona but of the United States."[29] Within American society, Arizonenses belong to a group described by historian Katherine Benton-Cohen as "perhaps the quintessential 'inbetween' people" who have never "fit" within conceptions of national belonging.[30] Congress delayed Arizona's admission to the Union as the forty-eighth state until 1912 and regarded the territory alongside New Mexico as "overseas colonies" mostly due to their Mexican settlement.[31] While Mexicans *de adentro y de afuera* described themselves as mestizos and their people as the ultimate representation of *mestizaje*, or progeny born of Spanish European and Indigenous mixing, the in-betweenness of Arizonenses was amplified by migration from across the borderlands and also because Spain, Mexico, and the United States carved the place into existence from Indigenous lands. Hewn from parts of California, New Mexico, and the Mexican state of Sonora, many disparate groups from northern Hispanos to Sonoran Tucsonenses found themselves bound together in this place called Arizona. Their reference to themselves as Arizonenses encapsulates these differences and accounts for the community sensibility that they cultivated and for the cultural citizenship they prioritized alongside national belonging.

The earliest people of Mexican heritage in Arizona came to the region under the auspices of the Spanish viceroyalty in the sixteenth century.[32] The famed Álvar Núñez Cabeza de Vaca and Fray Marcos de Niza briefly surveyed the region in 1536 and 1539, respectively. Francisco Vázquez de Coronado performed the most extensive survey several years later and, to him, we attribute the beginning of Spanish settlement in the region known as the Pimería Alta, which the Spanish named after the Akimel O'odham, whom they called the Pima Indians. This expanse of land ran from the Gila River north of Tucson, down through the southern desert to Hermosillo, Sonora. From its western border where the mouth of the Colorado River meets the Gulf of California, it spreads east across the desert and northernmost mountain ranges of Sierra Madre Occidental to the San Pedro River. Despite this massive region, actual Spanish settlement in the area remained sparse for the next three centuries. Efforts to build presidios and missions were tenuous at best. The movement of Spaniards, Mexicans, and others, such as European Jesuit and Franciscan priests sent into the region, varied in conjunction with diplomatic relations between the Spanish—later, Mexican—governments and the nearly two dozen Indian Nations, especially the Hopi and Diné (Navajo) in the north and the Tohono O'odham (Papago), Akimel O'odham, Pascua Yaqui, and various Apache in the South, who contained European encroachment.

Small Spanish-speaking communities, which became civil centers in the 1770s, emerged near the southern presidio of Tubac and its later replacement, St. Augustine, now called Tucson. These communities are notable because they were the first sustained Mexican settlements, populated by immigrants moving northward out of the Sonoran valleys. In 1789, for example, Toribio de Otero became the first Spaniard to request and to receive an Arizona land grant from the Spanish Crown. In 1813, Tubac elected its first justice of the peace, whose primary record-keeping job demanded literacy in order to note the activities of the local civil government. Anglo-Americans entering Arizona en route to California, even the 1849ers compelled by the Gold Rush, took little interest in the small towns and described the region as harsh and brittle. By the mid-1800s, the Spanish Mexican settlements amounted to less than 1,000 people in the southernmost reaches of Arizona along the present-day U.S.-Mexico border. In Northern Arizona, the first Spanish Mexican settlers would not arrive from New Mexico until the 1860s.[33]

In the earliest Arizona towns, only the elite were literate. The military leaders appointed by the Spanish and Mexican governments documented civil activities, such as the marriages, births, deaths, and land transactions, of the residents. Historians have not uncovered any sustained evidence of state-sponsored schools before 1848. The earliest histories, such as the 1906 work of Mormon pioneer Joseph Fish, attribute the founding of Arizona's schools to U.S. territorial legislation of the 1860s-1870s; however, as early as 1807 Toribio de Otero was identified as a schoolteacher in the town of Arizpe near Tubac when he filed a government complaint for stolen lands.[34] When Mexico won its independence from Spain in 1810, the military officials intentionally burned the Spanish presidial records, and the evidence of Otero's teaching post amounts to a small manuscript remnant, as well as family lore. As a result, it appears that people who claimed Arizona were not necessarily educated there in formal government or church-sponsored schools but in the larger cities from which they originated or migrated. Appointed military officers, for example, came to Arizona from central Mexico and had served in a range of civil and military posts in Alta California, New Mexico, and Sonora before being sent to manage the garrisons at Tubac or Tucson.[35] These men were educated precisely because they joined either religious orders or the military, which elevated their social and economic status and subsequently afforded them the opportunity to educate their sons as well. Poor men, wives, and daughters from all social ranks may have been denied literacy. Few Mexican women appeared to be formally educated before American occupation. For example, Encarnación Comadurán, whose father commanded the Tucson presidio, signed her name with an "X" in a deposition recorded by the Arizona territorial surveyor.[36] Nonetheless, Mexico claimed education as part of the national project in its 1833 and 1836 congresses and passed laws to establish primary schools and normal schools (teacher training schools). While the national government did not provide funding, it encouraged local efforts, particularly class-based and religious ventures, to establish systems to tutor and to train children in various subjects and occupations.[37] Thus, while many Arizonenses continued to sign official documents with their "X" marks, the ideas of literacy and schooling grew in value and in practice throughout the nineteenth century under both Mexican and American flags.

Arizonense Educational Politics

As the forty-eighth U.S. state, Arizona formally joined the union on February 14, 1912. The state borders shifted significantly between the Mexican-American War in 1848 and its territorial status in 1863. Congress officially created Arizona by dividing New Mexico Territory in half; its western side becoming Arizona Territory. Ten years earlier, the Gadsden Purchase ceded the northern portion of the Mexican state of Sonora to the United States, moving the border south of the Gila River to incorporate Tucson and Yuma and allowing for a transcontinental railroad.[38] In this U.S. territorial period from 1863 to 1912, Arizonenses incorporated educational institutions, served as board members, taught classes, and sent their children off to schools and universities. Within one year of President Abraham Lincoln's 1863 visit to the territory, Anglo Americans and Mexican Americans formalized public education and introduced English-language instruction in the towns of La Paz, Mohave, Prescott, and Tucson.[39] In every hamlet or town with a sizable Spanish-speaking population, parents sought out schools to enroll their children. When no school existed, parents sponsored home schools, or they drove by wagon or walked their children miles to the nearest one. Some parents petitioned the state to build new schools. And if parents had the means, when their children were old enough or advanced enough, they sent them to high schools, junior colleges, state normal schools, and universities. Some parents even sent their children across or out of state to attend private institutions.[40]

Arizonense educational politics were intimately tied to the post-treaty, economic recovery of the Mexican-heritage people living and working in the United States. Education—especially a solid bilingual, bicultural educational foundation—offered their children a potential gateway to financial security, political citizenship, and social mobility. In their study of paid wage labor, scholars Luis F. B. Plascencia and Gloria H. Cuádraz describe how Arizonense parents "hoped their children could benefit from education, pursue less arduous occupations, and achieve what their generation struggled to reach."[41] Optimistic about the promise of education, parents made hard decisions about when to begin and end their children's schooling. Should they send older children to work to augment the family income, or should they sacrifice the extra money in the short run so that their children could continue school beyond the eighth grade and expand their future earning potential?

The families' economic conditions, alongside the territory's inconsistent settlement patterns, resulted often in uneven educational outcomes that were

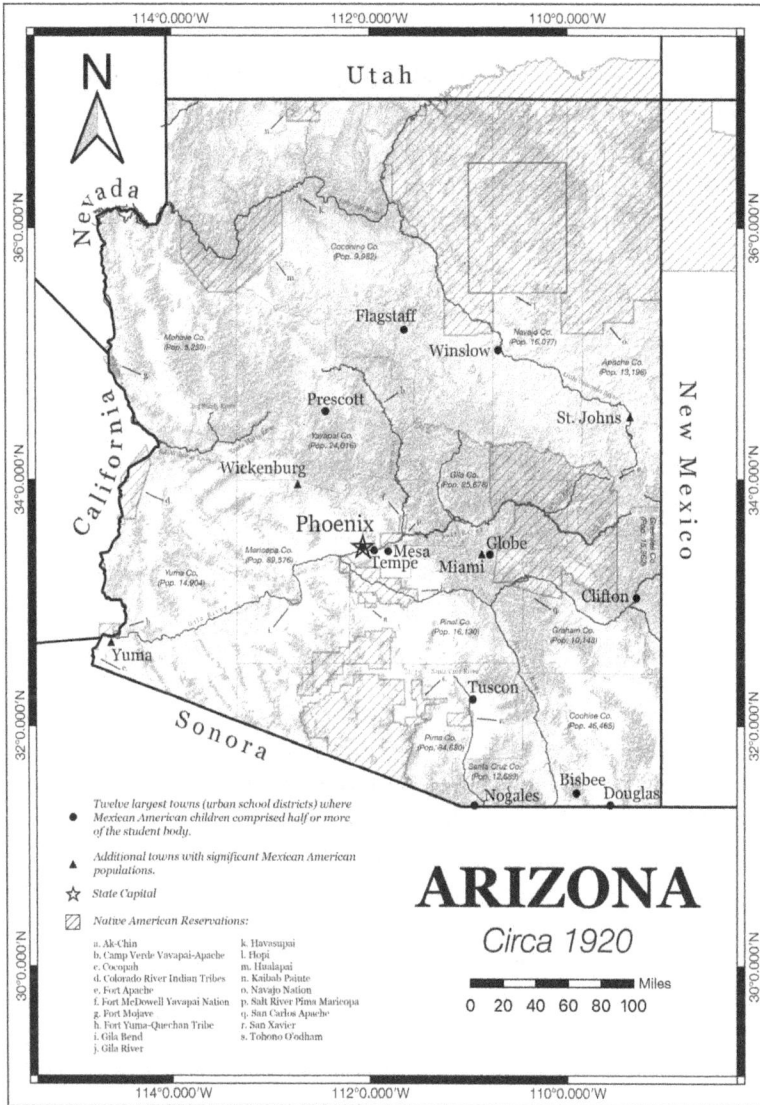

Figure 1. Arizona, circa 1920. Map by Patrick T. Hoehne Cartography. American Indian Reservation data from the University of Arizona Institutional Repository (https://uair.library.arizona.edu/item/292543/browse-data). County population figures from *Fourteenth Census of the United States: State Compendium, Arizona.* U.S. Census Bureau, Washington, D.C., Government Printing Office, 1924. Enrollment information from *Educational Conditions in Arizona* (Report of a Survey by the United States Bureau of Education). U.S. Department of the Interior, Washington, D.C., Government Printing Office, 1918 [Bulletin, 1917, No. 44]. All other county, state, and water data from the U.S. Census Bureau (www.census.gov /geographies/mapping-files/time-series/geo/tiger-line-file.html).

further exacerbated by educational segregation and the exclusion of Mexican Americans from good schooling *before and after* statehood. In a study by sociologist Hannibal G. Duncan, Tempe merchant Antonio A. Celaya recalled how he came to the United States as "a mere babe in arms" in the 1860s but was not able to secure a solid education "as schools, even in the United States, were not very plentiful at the time."[42] His parents managed to send him to school only for six years and he later vowed to fully educate his seven children, three of whom completed high school and normal school. In her memoir of growing up in Tucson, historian Lydia R. Otero tells us that her mother, Cruz "Chita" Robles who was American born in 1913 to American-born parents, "left school after the seventh grade at age twelve to work at menial jobs to help support her family."[43] In the mining town of Miami, Arizona, Ross Muñoz's immigrant parents, the Reverend Esaú P. Muñoz and Febronia Florián Muñoz, made the painstaking decision, as did many ranch families across Arizona, to board him at the Linda Patterson Institute, a Methodist preparatory school in El Paso, Texas—over 300 miles away—so that he could enter high school in 1927.[44] Ross worked part-time and split the cost of his schooling with his parents. Later, they transferred him to Phoenix Union High School (PUHS), where he lived with compadres until the whole family relocated to join him. Eventually, he and all of his siblings graduated from PUHS and then enrolled at local colleges. Across generations from the 1860s to the 1930s, Arizonenses experienced the American promise of education as fleeting, elusive, and exclusionary.

Arizonense educational politics also signaled the critically important activities of placemaking and citizenship. The legacies of conquest challenged Arizonenses to find cooperative ways to engage citizenship and they turned to education as a form of racial uplift and a potential salve for the growing inequities they encountered in post-Reconstruction America. In the act of building schools, just as in the act of homesteading, Arizonenses asserted their own settler claim to the region, to the land, and to their citizenship. They thought of themselves as both frontier people—as Northern Mexicans (Norteños) and American Westerners—as well as "treaty citizens" who survived American conquest and as cosmopolitan members of a new nation-state.[45] This meant that they understood the function and rule of the state—in this case, the Arizona Territory—and applied its laws, as often as possible to serve their advantage (e.g., Ochoa's school legislation) and to build their version of the ideal civilized society. Conversely, they also used their remote locale in the borderlands and their distance from federal (and often state) authorities to shape their own vision of Arizona. This ability to maneuver within a shifting borderland society allowed them to cultivate and sustain the ethos of civic integration. This Arizonense mentalité empowered them to preserve their cultural heritage and simultaneously assert a new national identity, one flexible enough to hold dual allegiances and to thwart the limitations Anglos placed on them. As Anglo Americans overtook the territory, especially in new towns like Phoenix, many (not all) envisioned a complete transformation of the region from a desolate military outpost to a modern, Progressive, and democratic society led by an educated, non-Mexican middle class, but sustained by Mexican American and Yaqui (Yoéme) labor.[46] Anglo Americans spurned Arizonense demands for better schooling and incorporation into the body politic, but civic integration provided them a psychological and social buffer, first to tolerate and then to challenge Anglo-American privilege and racism.

Civic integration also depended on the willingness of Arizonenses to uphold American laws and to practice American citizenship in order not only to weave themselves into the fabric of the new social order but also to use as a strategy to create space to sustain ethnic cultural values and to improve their prior economic, social, and political capital. Some scholars describe this interaction between citizens and their nation as cultural citizenship, or the ways that people express their relationship or sense of belonging to the nation.[47] Civic integration is a form of cultural citizenship, as much as it is a form of cultural coalescence. Historian Vicki L. Ruiz explains that Mexican Americans are constantly in the process of creating "permeable *cultures*" and they do so by drawing from and combining elements of both Mexican and American traditions.[48] Arizonenses thus deployed civic integration, specifically using the public civil and legal traditions of American society and government in order to inaugurate their citizenship and solidify their place in Arizona society.[49]

Schools became the principal venue for civic integration. Historian Katherine Benton-Cohen found that once Anglo Americans assumed political and economic control over the region, the schoolhouse became the last public institution where Arizona Mexicans maintained any sort of political authority.[50] This is most clearly seen in their determination to maintain Spanish language in the public schools in the nineteenth century and in their continued efforts to sustain bilingualism within their families after 1883 when the Arizona legislature imposed an English-only curriculum.[51] Language politics figured significantly in the late nineteenth-century pedagogy of Arizonense parents who strove to retain Spanish, of Arizonense teachers who struggled to create bilingual curriculums, and of Anglo Arizonans who strove to eradicate the Spanish language across the territory. Arizonenses also fashioned civic integration as a compromise in the wake of Anglo-American settlement and subsequent Anglo-American denigration of the role and place of Mexican Americans within this new society. Arizonenses accepted, although sometimes begrudgingly, the responsibility of "learning" the English language and American customs and laws. This so-called learning aided their participation in territorial and state building, as well as in their relationships with new Anglo-American neighbors, who migrated to the region not only from the American East and South but from across the world.

Deploying civic integration in educational matters allowed Arizonenses to strategize around Mexican racialization and the new forms of racial caste and racism that emerged in the American West. By racial caste, I refer to the ways that "Juan Crow"—the version of Jim Crow segregation that Anglo Americans extended to ethnic Mexicans in the American Southwest—emerged to shape distinct "white Arizona" and "Mexican Arizona" societies.[52] Legal scholars such as Michelle Alexander and Laura Gómez explain how racial caste emerged in nineteenth- and twentieth-century America in popular language, laws, and customs to stigmatize people perceived as nonwhite into subordinate social, political, and legal positions.[53] As Arizonenses lost political and economic control, Anglo Americans circumscribed their lives with new rules about citizenship. The 1927 obituary of Don Luis Chávez of Apache County plainly commented on the ways that Juan Crow stripped Arizonenses of full civic participation. "When the educational clause was placed on our law books, Mr. Chavez was disenfranchised along with many other Spanish people, although educated in Spanish he could not read or write English. He felt the disenfranchisement very keenly, as he had been one of the political leaders before this happened and also a heavy taxpayer."[54] In preparation for its statehood application and 1910 constitutional convention, the Arizona Legislature passed a literacy law over Governor Joseph Kibbey's two vetoes to require all male voters to read and write in the English language.[55] For Arizonense men, this law cemented their degraded political power as evidenced in the last seventeen years of Don Chávez's life. The literacy law completed a process of subordination begun decades earlier, in 1863, when the first disenfranchisement law limited the vote to "White men and white Mexican men," and, subsequently, in 1883, when the legislature decided "all schools must be taught in the English language," a legislative move thought to be copied from California law and reaffirmed in 1885 and 1887.[56] The territorial legislature also passed laws barring "male citizens" who did not "understand the English language" from serving on juries.[57] Historian Rosina Lozano explains that the Arizona territorial legislature expressed extreme ambivalence over language issues, passing laws that prevented voters from choosing electoral candidates "who cannot read and write in the English language" but then allowing translation assistance to voters who could not read the English-only ballots.[58]

The Arizonense experience of Juan Crow and the Arizonenses' awareness of racialization informed their educational activism. Historian Natalia Molina explains that the ways people think and act toward each other are coded by "racial scripts," meaning that they use race as a marker to determine how to treat people, especially people who differ from their racial or ethnic group.[59] The racial scripts mark the ways that humans categorize themselves and others over time and in various settings in order to sustain privilege in mainstream society. These scripts always denote a continuum of power relations between and among racial groups.[60] This means that Arizonenses, like Don Luis Chávez, contemplated their positionalities as "legally white" and as "treaty citizens" within Arizona society and in relation to Indigenous people, immigrant Asians, migrant blacks, and white settlers. Amid these complicated and changing race relations, Arizonenses acted to achieve and to sustain for themselves the best possible status—culturally, economically, politically, and socially.

Arizonenses had to figure out how to maneuver around racial scripts in order to secure a reasonable education for their children, but this was often difficult to do as white Arizonans constantly reinscribed the Mexican Problem. From the advent of Arizona's public schools in 1871 and well beyond 1900, Anglo-American teachers, administrators, and parents employed this racial script to establish separate curricula, programs, classrooms, and whole schools for Mexican children. Despite the efforts of Arizonenses to maintain authority over their children's education, by the mid-1920s, segregated, vocational education for Mexican children was status quo across the state. A well-known school superintendent once asked readers of the *Arizona Teacher and Home Journal*, "Does it pay to educate a Mexican?" He concluded, yes, because Americanization made it possible for the Mexican child to enter the labor force and to become the best possible helpmate to future Anglo-American employers.[61] This was the ingrained attitude that Carreón and Los Conquis attempted to unroot on the eve of World War II.

Mexican American parents and students who embraced education as a tool (or defensive weapon) to combat prejudice, colonization, and Juan Crow strategized to overcome these racial scripts and emerging racialized pedagogies. They carefully monitored access to education, especially as Anglo Americans mandated changes such as language-based and race-based school segregation, which the Arizona legislature authorized after statehood. In 1925, for example, Mrs. Manuel R. Peralta (Juana Estrada), the wife of a rancher who also worked as a packer at the Hayden Flour Mill, wrote in English two lengthy letters from her Tempe home to Governor George W. P. Hunt, asking him to intercede with the legislature to stop Mexican school segregation. "Could you tell them how things are here in the schools, how our children are separated from the American children, as if they were Negroes. They may do it with them, they have been slaves, but we have not been anybody's slaves," Peralta insisted. Using racial scripts to elevate her white citizenship status, she distanced herself further and further from African Americans and from her own racialization in this Juan Crow regime. After a terse exchange of letters, Peralta realized that the governor would not help "the despised Mexicans" (her words) and conceded in frustration over the ways that racial logic had narrowed her life and her children's lives.[62] Governor Hunt chastised her "bitter tone" and wrote that he had no authority in legislative matters.

Still, parents like Peralta and Esaú and Febronia Muñoz, often asserted the value of education as liberatory regardless of the psychological or financial penalties they or their children might incur in state institutions and precisely because education at any level could have such lasting and positive ramifications for the children's futures. These factors also alleviated the duress of potential criminal charges for truancy or delinquency that parents (and children) could face if they did not send their children to school despite the segregation and unequal school laws. Mrs. Peralta subsequently sent her sons to the segregated Eighth Street School even though the "boys were real sore" and her "ideas and faith . . . received a terrible shock."[63] Esaú and Febronia Muñoz also sent their seven children to segregated schools in various towns across the state. Although they moved often because of Esaú's religious appointments as a pastor with the Methodist Episcopal Church, South, they negotiated a series of concessions with each child's education because they, too, "had worked their way through higher educational levels and wanted their children to have opportunities for service which such educational preparation would make possible."[64]

Educational and Civil Rights Genealogies

Desert Dreams places Arizonense children and their families at the center of this narrative. One of its goals is to showcase as many people and communities as possible in order to bring to the forefront how often Arizonenses participated in public education between 1870 and 1940.[65] One significant finding of this broad sweep over time, place, and people, is that Arizonense school experiences varied greatly. There is no single Arizonense educational experience and no single Arizonense history of education because of the diverse demographics, distinct settlement patterns, and different economies that emerged across its varied terrain. As a result, the following chapters reflect this drama and diversity of experience. For example, the children of Rebecca Muñoz Gutiérrez donated their mother's college scrapbooks to the Chicano Research Collection at the Arizona State University Libraries shortly after her death in March 2000.[66] This collection, in particular, demonstrates how generations of one Mexican American family pursued education. Rebecca's college-educated parents, Esaú and Febronia Muñoz, worked for the Methodist Episcopal Church, South, to establish Mexican congregations across the Southwest. The family migrated on Armistice Day 1918 from Torreón, Coahuila, to West Texas, where they opened a church and a Spanish-language day school because no "Mexican school" existed for the children of the migrant laborers, whom they served in the towns of Marfa, Marathon, Sanderson, and Alpine. Esaú and Febronia Muñoz ran the day school for several years, until their church reassigned them to Arizona congregations in Tempe (1924–1926), Miami (1926–1928), Sonora-Ray (1928–1930), and Phoenix (1930). They also lived briefly in Flagstaff and Prescott. Each Arizona town had its own method of Mexican school segregation and each Muñoz child experienced segregation and integration differently.

The extended Muñoz family, along with the descendants of the García and Romo families, shared with me their private collections and their parents' unpublished manuscripts to assist in this recovery. The Muñoz descendants also allowed me to sift through unprocessed family records at the Chicano Studies Research Center at the University of California, Los Angeles.[67] While occurrences like these between a historian and living descendants of subjects are rare, they do reflect how these families value, anticipate, and desire to document the historical record. Community-based research methodologies, such as the "vernacular history making" of these Arizonense families, further demonstrate their continued commitment to an Arizonense philosophy of education: the idea that education, particularly continuing education, enhances not only individual potential but also group success.[68] In practice, Arizonenses, then and now, seek to educate every child for as long as possible at any school with whatever means might be available.

By constructing family genealogies of students and by crossmatching them in scrapbooks, yearbooks, teacher directories, teacher certificate registers, university records, and public school records, as well as birth, death, and marriage notices, this book offers a significant historical construction of the Arizonense lives and career trajectories of women educators. This book takes a first look at cohorts of U.S.-educated, Mexican American teachers and "normal school" women. Normal schools specialized in teacher training, and the Tempe Normal School, founded in part by Arizonense families, became the central training ground for Mexican American public school teachers. This history traces their professional evolution from teacher certification exams to normal school diplomas to bachelor's and master's degrees earned between 1885 and 1940. The educational experiences of these Mexican American daughters demonstrates that the Arizonense educational vision not only included women but also depended critically on their labor as they became primarily responsible for educating children of their own heritage in Arizona's segregated Mexican schools before and after statehood.

Bringing together the histories of education, the Arizona borderlands, and Mexican Americans and simultaneously unlacing connections between various historical figures invested in educational progress across the Southwest, *Desert Dreams* also offers the potential to help scholars from numerous disciplines uncover how Mexican American civil rights may have evolved over many decades, across multiple generations, and across the Southwest prior to the notable political efforts of the Mexican American and Chicano Movement generations.[69] This narrative explains how Arizonenses highlighted education as a decisive action issue that linked groups concerned with exercising Mexican American citizenship across a wide swath of time from the Reconstruction era to the Truman years. This long view, combined with a careful reading of archival details, allows us to think both broadly and deeply about major changes in U.S. history from the territorial period to the Progressive Era, into the Great Depression, and beyond World War II. For example, teachers María Urias and Ross F. Muñoz are the parents of Rosalío Urias Muñoz who was the co-chair of the Chicano Moratorium Against the Vietnam War. Ross F. Muñoz also is the oldest brother and brother-in-law of Mexican American Movement leaders Rebecca Muñoz Gutiérrez and her husband Félix J. Gutiérrez. As noted earlier in this introduction and by several Chicana and Chicano historians, Rebecca and her brother Ross founded Los Conquistadores, a politically minded student organization at the Arizona State Teachers College in Tempe in the 1930s.[70] Initially, the Muñoz siblings chose a club name that reflected their dual cultural allegiances as Mexican Americans, but college officials asked them to deflect their racial identity.[71] Instead, and in order to get college approval for the new organization, they selected as the club's namesake the Spanish historical figure of the Conquistador, a symbol of the fantasy heritage popularized by Anglos in the early twentieth century. Los Conquis, however, did not exist in a vacuum and they were very well acquainted with the fledgling professional class of Mexican American women and men residing in Central Arizona. Los Conquis often engaged college recruitment programs across Arizonense communities with letters of support from the Latin American Club, a statewide political and business association that promoted voting rights and whom Anglo-American political leaders heavily courted. Los Conquis also relied on the religious Protestant and Catholic networks of their youth to educate Mexican American teenagers and their parents about college possibilities.

By focusing on these relationship circles of Mexican American students, families, teachers, professionals, and business owners interlaced by degrees of separation or social networks, *Desert Dreams* unfolds seemingly disparate connections among Arizonenses concerned about education and civil rights, and within the social-movement sectors of U.S. history.[72] Woven together, the connections imply a much larger framework of latent social protest and transnational consciousness, quite similar to models of action conceptualized by Latina feminist historians as "circuits of knowledge resulting in generative connections."[73] For example, teacher Amelia Hunt, a young woman of Anglo and Hispano heritage (and a distant relation to Governor Hunt), married another young Arizonense teacher, Monico García, in 1902 in St. Johns, Apache County. Monico's younger brother Gregorio is known as the first and only Mexican American attorney to work in Phoenix, Arizona, before 1930.[74] He built a thriving practice and often represented Spanish-speaking clients. By the late 1930s, Gregorio mentored Ralph Estrada, who grew up in Tempe, and together they cofounded the Latin American Club in Phoenix. Ralph's older brothers and father also helped found two chapters of mutual aid associations—the Alianza Hispano-Americana and the Liga Protectora Latina. These associations are partly responsible for organizing agitation against Mexican school segregation that led to the 1925 *Romo* desegregation case in Tempe. When Gregorio's brother and sister-in-law—Monico and Amelia—were ousted from their teaching positions in St. Johns in 1935, Ross Muñoz, María Urias, and several of Los Conquis replaced them and continued teaching their Spanish-speaking students. In the meantime, Estrada and García served as legal counsel and as presidents of the national Alianza, where they began to strategize a long-term civil rights agenda that resulted in Estrada's 1951 victory in *Gonzales v. Sheely*, the federal case that led to the demise of Mexican school segregation in Arizona. These multigenerational networks—even as tenuous as they appear—suggest that Mexican Americans across Arizona and over generations nurtured a clear political consciousness about the importance and role of education in shaping Mexican American progress. These networks reveal the essence of civic integration and a decidedly Arizonense politics of education.

Desert Dreams provides a historical space and moment for Arizona Mexicans by accounting for their history of educational access from their perspective. The history of Mexican American education in Arizona is built along two broad axes: combating racial scripts and stereotypes, while simultaneously volleying for the uplift, not only of individual children but of whole communities. Through civic integration, Mexican American parents and students maneuvered themselves into literacy and into educated worlds, where they could begin to assert their rightful citizenship in Arizona and in American society. The title of this book, *Desert Dreams*, echoes this sentiment, referring to Arizona as both place and aspiration. The Sonoran Desert, its mountainous horizons, and its expansive mesas fill the senses with possibilities. The land represents to Arizonenses, newcomers and old-timers alike, the hope and desire they have infused into their children's lives. Mexicans came to Arizona with dreams in hand, and, even when they failed, the aspiration resonated across generations. Arizonenses, once thought to be outside the scope of the state's educational history, were in fact integral to the success of its public schools.

CHAPTER 1

Civic Integration in the Territorial Schools

Manuela Sánchez de Sotelo owned 160 acres of desert in Tempe, Arizona, before she ever set foot in the town in 1872. Her husband, Tiburcio Sotelo Quintana, along with their two sons, José and Feliciano, had claimed land on the banks of the Salt River a few years earlier. In search of work, they had migrated first from Tubac, the original locale of the historic Spanish presidio, then to Tucson, and finally northward to Tempe, where they labored to build the Salt River Valley canal system that would open the desert floor to irrigated farming and electricity. In 1870, before Manuela's arrival, the Sotelo men helped construct two important ditches: first, the San Francisco Canal, commonly called the "Mexican Ditch," that brought water to the Mexican families living near the Tempe Butte and, then, the Kirkland-McKinney Ditch (on 8th Street near S. McClintock Drive) that became the central line of the Tempe Irrigating Canal Company and part of the future Salt River Project, which currently provides water and energy to the Valley of the Sun. For a hundred days of labor, each worker earned a water right of way, or share, valued at $200 to access the canal. In 1871, the Sotelo men had earned the family two water rights, critical to converting the arid sands into grasslands to feed their cattle and to nourish the orchards and crop fields that sustained their large extended family. Manuela did not have much time to converse with Tiburcio or her sons about their labors, nor did she have time to reminisce with them about their hopes and dreams for the ranch. Shortly after her arrival, all three men succumbed to the perils of nineteenth-century desert life.[1]

Manuela Sotelo and her family represent the typical aspiration and action of the many Mexican American settlers in Arizona's frontier society. Dubbed the "Mexican mother of Tempe" by historian Christine Marin, Sotelo also may well be the "mother of Arizona State University."[2] Manuela was the first

Figure 2. Manuela Sánchez Sotelo, the "Mexican mother of Tempe" and the "mother of Arizona State University," n.d. Donated by Esther Carrillo Canchola. Courtesy of the Chicano/a Research Collection, MP SPC 349, Arizona State University Library.

woman settler to bring her family to Tempe and she single-handedly welcomed newcomers, such as Charles T. Hayden, who is considered the town's founder, by offering him a place to stay and plant cuttings to begin improving his homesteads.[3] According to her descendants Esther Carrillo Canchola and Nell Ryder, Manuela was among a group of Mexican and Anglo settlers responsible for fundraising and purchasing land in 1885 for the Territorial Normal School at Tempe (referred to as the Normal School and now known as Arizona State University, ASU) and that Manuela, herself, specifically donated property.[4] Canchola's and Ryder's telling of Manuela's critical contributions represents what historian Monica Muñoz Martinez calls "vernacular-history making"; that is, memory shaped and preserved within a community's oral tradition that challenges conventional narratives.[5] The official history of ASU and its University Archives do not include any specific reference to Sotelo's land donation, but Canchola carefully triangulates family lore and a variety of sources, including conspicuously missing land-acquisition records that correlate to "the possible years when Manuela would have donated land."[6]

The family even remembers that the university later honored Manuela in a special recognition ceremony for her generosity. Manuela's reputation as a landowner, whose original 160-acre homestead sat along the edge of the ASU campus at University Drive and Rural Road, is remembered today by the neighborhood's place name as the Sotelo Addition.

Like Manuela and her husband Tiburcio, women and men of Mexican heritage had entered the territory during the Spanish and Mexican occupation, and they were present at the creation of its schools. The Arizonense movement within the region remained continuous even as the 1848 Treaty of Guadalupe Hidalgo and the 1854 Treaty of La Mesilla changed its boundaries and designated it a U.S. territorial possession.[7] By the 1870s, Mexicans from across the northern Mexican states and the U.S. southwestern states regularly migrated to Arizona with the prospect of building new lives and with an ambition to work as homesteaders and miners, especially in the cattle and copper industries.[8] These migrants helped to renew old towns, such as Tucson, and to build new ones, such as Phoenix, which would grow into the territory's future capital.[9] From farms to small towns across the valley, "the Mexican people made this town," said civic leader Joe Torres, who shined shoes on Phoenix streets as a boy and served in the U.S. Army at the close of World War II.[10] Like Torres and his parents, who migrated from Mexico to the Morenci mines, most Arizonenses brought with them a vision common to many in the region to improve the condition of their lives as well as the lives of their children. They imagined for themselves independent livelihoods, aspired to wealth and knowledge, and hoped to extend such possibilities to their children and grandchildren.

Mexican American families used the public schools as one way to cultivate their lives in Arizona in the late nineteenth and early twentieth centuries. Mexican American parents not only established schools but were intricately involved in the full spectrum of the educational project. Their democratic citizenship is evinced through lobbying and sending signed petitions to the county school superintendents and through exercising their suffrage to vote and to elect themselves as school board trustees and clerks. The infrastructural needs of a new educational enterprise were the result of Arizonense dedication to public schools. Mexican American landholders donated, leased, and maintained their property for public schools. Parents were involved in the physical creation of the schools, wielding hammer and nails to build walls, and taking apart old buildings for lumber. Financially elite school boosters, such as Estevan Ochoa, donated the labor of his freighters to haul timber from the mountains. The civic participation in this founding stage of the public schools generated a place for their children to learn and thrive, a space for the young Mexican American women and men of the Normal School to use their professional teaching skills, and employment for ordinary adults in such positions as custodians and groundskeepers. This was no easy task as it was tangled with the politics of race, language, and citizenship, but it is an important departure that distinguishes Arizonenses from Mexican Americans in other parts of the Southwest where they had significantly less influence in the creation and administration of public schools. The schoolhouse and the school board election became, as historian Vicki L. Ruiz conceptualizes, venues for claiming space and negotiating place in Arizona society.[11] Individual aspiration and initiative—such as the small task of enrolling a child in school or the larger undertakings of creating schools and school districts—invested Mexican Americans in communities and, simultaneously, cast their claim to the region.

Arizonenses engaged schooling as a public policy issue. Historians have revealed how schooling drove local politics in places like Pima (Tucson) and Cochise (San Pedro River Valley) Counties, but this chapter demonstrates how school building was an Arizonense priority not only near the border but also across the territory from its establishment.[12] The state's cultural geography suggests that pre-twentieth-century Arizonenses developed five different types of communities across the state: Heritage Pueblos, such as Tubac and Tucson; Borderline Towns, such as Douglas and Nogales; Mining Enclaves, such as Miami and Globe; Emergent Salt River Valley Cities, such as Phoenix and Tempe; and Mountain Plateau Settlements, such as Concho and St. Johns. In each of these communities, different types of capital shaped the economic push and pull of the Mexican American movement across the territory. Despite their physical location within the region or their generational identifications as *fronterizos*, Hispanos, Norteños, Californios, or Sonorenses, they and their children also claimed a Spanish-speaking, Arizonense identity. This chapter thus strategically redirects the historical gaze both to document and to incorporate the Arizonense educational project as a territory-wide endeavor from the Mexican border to the Grand Canyon. School building emerged as a central function of Arizonense community development from Yuma to Tucson, and much farther north, in towns such as Tempe, Wickenburg, and St. Johns, than is typically accounted for in Arizona history. Although the Mountain Plateau Settlements and the Emergent Salt River Valley Cities were smaller in number when compared to the Borderline Towns, each developed recognizable settlements with its own patterns of labor, migration, and politics.[13]

In every community, these Arizonenses centered their placemaking and their sense of belonging on the educational ambitions they had set for their children and the schoolwork they pursued for them. With a firm commitment to egalitarianism and a clear grasp of territorial law, they began this project by gathering the electorate and fulfilling the procedural requirements to found schools. The First Territorial Legislature granted voting rights to "every white male citizen of the United States, and every white male [treaty] citizen of Mexico" who chose to naturalize and, in 1883, extended limited voting rights in school elections to women, stating "that no person shall be denied the right to vote at any school district election, or to hold any school district office on account of sex," thereby legitimizing participatory democracy for any adult person of Spanish-speaking heritage.[14]

Building Schools and Communities

By 1872, with eight daughters and her last surviving son in tow, Manuela Sotelo quickly organized a new life for her large extended family on the banks of the Salt River. Over the next two decades, she parceled the 160-acre homestead among her children and relatives and secured the precious water rights she had inherited from her husband. Because of his foresight and her sharp management, she became one of the few women in the Salt River Valley to hold shares in the Tempe Irrigating Canal Company. This safeguarded her family's ability to develop the ranch land, enabled her to file a homestead claim, and generated enough income to be able to purchase more property in eastern Maricopa County. As Manuela's local reputation and wealth grew, so did public interest in her daughters. In the frontier era of Arizona where men outnumbered women, the Sotelo ladies were thought to be among the first families and first group of non-Indian women to reside in Tempe.[15] Anglo-American Winchester Miller, who was the *zanjero* (water distribution engineer) at the canal company, soon asked for permission to marry twenty-year-old María. The family jokes that María's older brothers knew Miller and before they died they had gambled her away in a card game.[16] But María's granddaughter Marie Zander remembers that María actually had several suitors who offered marriage proposals. Because of her family's prior friendship with Miller, she eventually chose him.[17] Miller owned land adjacent to that of the Sotelo family and subsequently "filed the plat" for the extended Sotelo families living on the Sotelo Addition.[18] With their combined ranching spreads, the blended Sotelo-Miller clan, as they came to be known, soon encompassed large sections of northeastern Tempe.

As landowners and parents of ten school-aged children, María Sotelo and Winchester Miller became heavily invested in Tempe school politics. In 1874, the town established a small school district, Tempe School District No. 3 (the third founded in the state) and Winchester won election to the school board of trustees. The school board included other Anglo-American men like Miller who had married into Mexican families and the student population included the interethnic children from these "sanctioned marriages."[19] For example, a Canadian named James T. Priest (also a zanjero) married schoolteacher and businesswoman Mariana Gonzales, whose father Mariano also fled Sonora and resettled first in Tucson, then in Tempe.[20] The Priests had eight children, six of whom attended Tempe schools. Dr. Walter Wilson Jones, a physician, married Alcaria Montoya, also a Sonoran, and they raised their seven children on a ranch just west of Tempe.[21] The men—Jones, Priest, and Miller—all served on school boards in the Tempe vicinity and all of their children attended the public schools together. The twenty-five children of the Sotelo-Miller, Gonzales-Priest, and Montoya-Jones families carried Anglo surnames in the public realm, but they also were Mexican in language and culture. They formed a nucleus of the generation of Arizonenses whose familial political and economic capital during the incipient stages of the public schools would use education as a tool of mobility. Until territorial funds were sufficient to create public high schools in the mid-1890s, the Mexican elite relied on private secular and parochial schools, near and far, for their youths' secondary schooling. The Normal School also offered high school level courses to close the gap between admission requirements and the absence of publicly funded high schools. The acquisition of secondary schooling then permitted ascendance to the next step on the educational ladder to collegiate institutions.

By 1885, Maricopa County residents sounded the call for higher education and convinced the 13th Territorial Legislature to build a normal school at Tempe.[22] To resolve a political squabble about the location of the territorial capital, the legislature negotiated a deal to keep it at Prescott by authorizing the establishment of a university at Tucson and a normal school in the Salt River Valley. The Normal School opened in 1886 as the first institution of higher education. As a state-funded, teacher-training institute, the Normal School became responsible for preparing young women and men to manage the state's public schools, which, by 1900, would number over three hundred.

The Sotelo-Miller and Gonzales-Priest families were among the twenty families who contributed cash for the $500 land purchase.[23]

Between 1892 and 1906, six of the ten Sotelo-Miller children matriculated at the Normal School.[24] Notably, their daughters Anna Manuela and Clara María completed high school and two years of college coursework, earning teaching diplomas in 1897. Anna's diploma outlined her credentials and coursework in thirty-one subjects, including the history of education.[25] Territorial school laws required applicants who wanted to teach in the public schools to show proof of their education either by passing a certification exam (offered by the county) or by graduating from a U.S. university, college, or normal school. After 1893, normal school graduates, such as the Sotelo-Millers, were awarded first-grade territorial certificates, valid for four years, to teach in any territorial school.[26] With their teaching certificates in hand, both young women quickly entered the workforce. Anna, who was also known as "Manuela," taught at Flagstaff for three years, while Clara stayed closer to home, teaching at Buckeye and Tempe. Clara's daughter, Marie Zander, later enrolled at the Normal School in the 1920s. For generations, they and other young Normal School alumni of Arizonense heritage became responsible for educating youth across the state.

Even though the Sotelo-Miller family actively participated in building schools, as did other families, most teachers and political leaders commonly believed that Arizonense educational participation was nonexistent. The general and popular attitude held by Anglo Americans who entered the region after 1848 was that Arizonenses cared little, if at all, about schooling their children. In 1870, the U.S. Commissioner of Education reported that "Arizona has never had any school system worth mentioning."[27] In his annual address the following year, the territorial governor Anson P. K. Safford lamented, "The mortifying fact has to be admitted that we have not a public school in the Territory."[28] Even the earliest Arizona school historians, such as Samuel Pressly McCrea who wrote the state's first school history in 1902, overlooked the Sotelo-Miller family and other well-known Arizonense teachers, such as Amelia Hunt and Normal School alumni Aurelia Borquez and Mariano Aguirre, who was a treasurer of the Alianza Hispano-Americana and the youngest brother-in-law of Mariano Samaniego.[29] The daughter of Nuevamexicana Juanita Rubi, Amelia Hunt began teaching in the mountain-plateau schools of Apache County in 1891 after passing the territorial teacher's examination, while Aurelia Borquez, who was born in Tucson to Spanish-descent parents from Sonora, began her teaching career at the border town of Nogales in 1893 after completing two years at the Normal School. Aguirre and Borquez were the first Spanish-surnamed students at the Normal School, in 1889 and 1892, respectively. Like McCrea, later school historians such as Felix O. Bishop who taught in the Phoenix schools attributed the lack of early territorial public schools to non-compulsory attendance laws, the U.S. Civil War, Arizona's small population, and the "large percentage of Mexican and Indian habitants."[30]

Kingman's *Mohave County Miner* reported that this general presumption about Mexican educational disinterest stemmed from the class politics of elite Arizonenses who had always discouraged the "tractable" working classes from literacy, especially in the English language, as a way of maintaining their influence over them and inciting "their natural prejudice against the 'gringo.'" "They [the Mexican leaders] know that education begets reasoning—reasoning begets independence—the more enlightened they [the Mexican population] become the weaker the hold of their leaders."[31] All along Beale's Wagon Road (U.S. Route 66), from Gallup, New Mexico, in the east to Kingman, Arizona, on its western edge, newspapers reprinted the news article attributed to an anonymous "old-timer" who spoke initially to the *St. Johns Herald*. Ironically, Arizona capitalists—whether Anglo or Mexican—had a general disdain for the working classes, so it is unsurprising that the English-language press would lampoon the Mexican elite over such ignorance.[32] The reading habits of the Arizonenses, however, clearly contradicted the ridicule. The Heritage Pueblo of Tucson supported a substantial Spanish-language press that included twelve different publications between 1877 and 1899, as well as *El Fronterizo* (1878–1908, 1922–1930) and *El Tucsonense* (1915–1957), which had some of the largest weekly press runs in the borderland region comparable to Albuquerque, Los Angeles, and San Antonio.[33] Editor Pedro G. de la Lama, who owned several Phoenix newspapers, boasted that he expected at least five thousand subscribers (roughly 4 percent of the state's population) when he opened a new Spanish-language daily in Tucson in December 1903.[34] Clearly, subscriptions from both the Mexican elite and the working poor sustained these Spanish-language dailies.

Anglo opinion of Mexican American schooling in this territorial period denies the archival record. From references to literate military officers in the Sonoran presidios to children's memories of admired teachers who rented rooms in their family homes, Mexican American reminiscences suggest a clear engagement with literacy and learning.[35] Drawing from broad works on Arizona history, oral histories, popular magazines such as the long-running serial the *Arizona Teacher and Home Journal*, and territorial school archives, the historical record confirms that Arizonense parents, in addition to work and family responsibilities, kept quite busy attending to their children's educational needs. These concerns were often community-wide, such as the effort to build a new school at mountain-plateau settlement on the northern Little Colorado River in 1890. Twenty-one fathers working on a new irrigation project in a "Mexican Settlement" outside St. Johns signed a general petition requesting a new school district for their fifty-one children.[36] The families had moved to the northeastern plateau specifically to work and homestead, but the nearest school was several miles upstream. The children spent hours each day on foot or on horseback hiking to and from school; it was a cumbersome trek and even more difficult in the winter snow. The Apache County school superintendent granted their petition and opened the new school district that fall. Their request was characteristic of Arizona school founding just like those in the San Pedro Valley, west of Tucson in Cochise County. Historian Katherine Benton-Cohen details how Mexican American parents there opened three schools: the old Tres Alamos School (1881), the Soza's ranch school (1900), and the Cascabel's Apodaca School (1908).

These Arizonense school-building initiatives were rooted in a clear sense of place and belonging that many, like Tiburcio Sotelo, possessed and espoused. While Anglo-Americans perceived them as transients, laborers, and immigrants, the Arizonenses characterized themselves differently. They nurtured a borderlands *conocimiento*, a spirit of cultural and historical mindfulness of their heritage and settlement.[37] Like the Californios, Hispanos, and Tejanos, they worked to secure their language and cultural identity.[38] This self-awareness combined with an understanding of their antecedents' purpose on the land centered the Arizonense mindset and fortified their community action. The Sotelos' great-great-granddaughter Esther Carrillo Canchola surmised that Tiburcio probably thought little of the U.S. acquisition of Arizona. He moved freely across the "imaginery [sic] boundary." "The Tubac Sotelos had already lived under four different flags and one more probably made very little difference at that time. Tubac would always be home no matter what flag."[39]

Tiburcio Sotelo Quintana had lived in Arizona before it became Arizona Territory in 1863. Like the many "treaty citizens" who remained after the Mexican-American War and the Gadsden Purchase, Tiburcio always knew and considered this place his home.[40] His father, Lieutenant Ygnacio Sotelo Olivas, had served from 1813 to 1814 as commanding officer of the Spanish forces at the Tubac presidio, roughly forty miles south of the Tucson pueblo.[41] Born in 1757 at La Ciénaga de los Olivos, Chihuahua, México, Lieutenant

Sotelo joined the Spanish Royal Army at twenty-one years of age in 1778 along with his older brothers. A career soldier and Indian fighter at Santa Fe, Lieutenant Sotelo transferred to Tubac in 1810. He brought from Chihuahua his wife Ysabel and four children, including the infant Tiburcio. They joined other military families, including the Sánchez family whose daughter Manuela later married Tiburcio. The colonial project at Tubac proved very difficult. Lieutenant Sotelo, along with an infant son, died in 1816 as a result of a small-pox epidemic.[42] The generosity of the surviving families who labored together at the presidio sustained his wife and remaining children despite continued contests over the land among the Apache, Seri, and Mexicans.

Like many treaty families, the Sotelos moved often within the bounds of the Pimería Alta. The local conflict between the Mexican settlers and the Apaches, the unfolding civil war in Mexico, and the ensuing Mexican-American War forced the Sotelos to abandon Tubac in 1848 as did many of their neighbors.[43] Tiburcio and Manuela retreated 150 miles south and for seventeen years raised their oldest children in Pitiquito, Sonora. Tiburcio traveled regularly to southern Arizona to visit his landholdings and family. In 1864, he returned permanently with his sons, José and Feliciano, to prevent them from being drafted into the Mexican Army, and within two years Manuela and the remaining children joined them in Tubac.[44] Just as the family reunited, Tiburcio lost his claim to his father's land grant because the records at Tubac were demolished, which scholar Anita Huizar-Hernández attributed to American political control.[45] Because he was unable to convince the U.S. government of his inheritance rights, Tiburcio and his older sons were forced to join the mass migration of Arizonenses and Sonorenses moving north to work. In 1867, they went first to Tucson, but it was inundated with economic refugees, so they kept trekking until they laid claim to land near the Salt River.[46] The Sotelo ranch was only a short walk to the base of the Tempe Butte where other Sonorense settler families established a town called San Pablo, which the incoming Anglos called "Mexican Town."[47] These *barrios*, or neighborhoods, had nicknames that marked Arizonense presence, such as the Sotelo Addition, La Cremería (Creamery Road), and Mickey Mouse, a neighborhood nickname for the homes below the butte because it looked like a *ratonería*, or mouse's den.[48]

While the Sotelos and many Arizonense parents perceived schooling as a typical settlement activity, lack of financing hampered their earliest efforts to build a public school system in the emergent Salt River Valley cities. In 1864, the First Territorial Legislature's Joint Committee on Education recommended instead a "donation" for towns where "the number of children warrant the establishment of schools." Chairman Gilbert W. Hopkins first recommended that Padre Messaya at the Catholic Mission of San Xavier del Bac (outside the Tucson pueblo) receive $250.00 given that he has, "at great trouble and expense to himself, educated all children free of charge. His pupils are Mexican and Papago [Tohono O'odham, and] he has been sadly impeded in his efforts by want of suitable school books."[49] For the towns of Prescott, Mohave, and La Paz, the committee offered $250, but it included a proviso that locals match the funds or the money would be "null and void."[50] Tucson was treated as a unique entity. Although a larger sum of $500 was offered, the education committee used a carrot-and-stick strategy to limit the power of the Arizonense population through linguistic imposition. The legislature promised Tucson $500 *only* if "the English language formed a part of the instruction" for the two hundred children eligible for attendance. But none of these donations ever came to pass in 1864, nor in any year until the Safford-Ochoa Act was passed in 1871, because locals never raised enough funds to sustain the schools beyond a few months.

The lack of funding, however, did not deter the Arizonense parents who continued to pursue school-building initiatives across the territory. The Tucsonense elite, for example, led by Estevan Ochoa promoted public education for boys of all classes and supported the opening of a Tucson public school in 1867. The first class of "55 Mexican boys" began in January 1868 and ran for six months under the tutelage of Augustus Brichta, who was not a trained teacher but an alumnus of St. Louis University. Even though the public school subsequently closed for a number of years before reopening, Arizonenses pursued a range of educational activities reflected in both advocacy and school enrollments. In 1870, a well-known group of Tucsonense businessmen lobbied Governor Richard McCormick, who also served as congressional representative, for a territorial public school system.[51] This helped encourage the passage of the Safford-Ochoa Act the following year and, subsequently, when Safford became the new territorial governor he reported to the U.S. Commissioner of Education how "a large proportion of the children were Mexicans by birth . . . [and] quick and eager to learn."[52] By 1873, Governor Safford reported that 343 (20 percent) of the 1,660 non-Indian children in the territory attended public school, including 140 in Pima County (Tucson) alone.[53]

Tucson's Spanish-language press also printed a number of advertisements for private day and night schools offered by entrepreneurial educators in the 1870s and 1880s. These included classes for children and adults taught

by Miss Cruz R. Parra, Miss Donaciana J. Parra, Juan "J. M." Silva, Manuel
Uruchurtu, and M. Vasavilbaso.[54] For example, the Parra sisters who were
trained as teachers in Magdalena, Sonora, opened a small private school in
1881 for ten students in Tucson.[55] Their father, José, also a teacher, resided
with them. From 1879 to 1882, the Chilean-born Juan Silva and his Mexican
wife Francisca opened a school in Tucson called La Escuela Moderna. They
offered courses in math; English and Spanish languages; and the histories
of the world, Mexico, and the United States; as well as "good manners and
urbanity."[56] Mr. Silva also taught evening classes, including French, English,
and Spanish grammar, plus arithmetic and bookkeeping. His wife and teenage daughter helped supervise more than forty students, particularly those
who boarded with them for the $200 ten-month session that ran from Sep-
tember to June. The school closed in 1882 only because of Mr. Silva's untimely
death.[57] By 1880, eight public and private Tucson schools enrolled more than
800 students at the behest of Arizonense parents. The public school enrolled
230 students, the private Catholic schools counted 520 students, and two
independent private schools registered another 54.[58] Evidently, the uneven
state funding mechanism for the development of educational provisions
during the first two decades did not dissuade parents.

Across the territory as migrant populations from the eastern United
States and northern Mexico grew, Arizonenses and Anglos organized public
schools in accordance with shifting territorial laws. In 1868, communities
were authorized to organize new districts if they had at least twenty children between the ages of four and twenty-one.[59] In the emergent Salt River
Valley city of Phoenix, for example, children of Anglo and Mexican heritage attended the first public school together in 1871, which was held in the
territorial courthouse.[60] By 1879, the law shifted to allow for the formation
of a new school district when "five heads of families petitioned the County
Superintendent." It changed again in 1895 (and remained so into statehood)
to allow new districts only when the parents of at least ten children petitioned and the nearest schoolhouse was at least two miles away, or if a large
school district with at least 250 "School-Census children" might be divided
into two districts and the tax revenue split."[61] The territorial superintendent
of education reported that parents founded 187 public school districts by
1890, and at statehood in 1912 the number had surged to 366, reflecting
the steady increase of Anglo settlers. In 1870, the Phoenix population was
nearly 50 percent "Mexico-born," but three decades later that figure dropped
to less than 25 percent, mirroring trends in southwestern cities along the

transcontinental corridors.[62] With 5,544 residents in 1900, Phoenix was now an Anglo-majority city.

Despite this sharp population shift, Arizonense parents organized schools regularly and demonstrated their value in and commitment to public education. In Wickenburg, a small town on the Hassayampa River north of Phoenix, teacher Dora Quesada remembers that her great-great-grandfather, Ramón C. Valencia, whom she lovingly called "Pa Ramón," helped organize Wickenburg School District No. 9. She described the small city, which at the time was solely located in Maricopa County, as being evenly populated between Anglos and Arizonenses. "About half of the population was like me . . . born in the U.S. of Mexican descent or newer immigrants from Mexico."[63] Pa Ramón was born down south in Yuma in the Gadsden Purchase era. He owned one of the last Mexican cattle ranches near Wickenburg, where Dora's father, uncles, and cousins on all sides worked under the family brands—the WE and the BAR T.[64] At night, after the roundup and dinner, the family read "aloud by the light of a kerosene lamp" from all sorts of "books, novels, newspapers or periodicals which were printed in Spanish."[65] This literary tradition was generations old. She recalled how Pa Ramón had served on the first school board of trustees for Vulture City (gold mine) in 1880, and other Spanish-surnamed men such as A. García and William Moreno followed him in 1881.[66] Pa Ramón and his in-law Teodoro Ocampo voted in 1894 to create the Wickenburg School District No. 9; about ten years later, they voted to build the Wickenburg Public Library.[67] When Vulture City closed down after the mine ceased operation, Pa Ramón transported the "salvaged lumber" from the old schoolhouse to build the new one in Wickenburg. School trustees allocated fifty dollars for the cost of relocating the school.[68] Pa Ramón made sure that his children and grandchildren attended the public school taught in English as well as a private "Saturday Spanish school," or escuelita.[69] The family hired tutors who came from Phoenix for two dollars a session to teach "Spanish language and culture." Dora's mom Francisca and her cousin José attended the Wickenburg public school called the "Little Red Schoolhouse," known today as the García School and listed on the National Register of Historic Places.[70] In 1895, school trustee Don Ygnacio García Sr. and an unidentified woman known as "Mrs. Verdugo" donated the acreage for the schoolhouse.[71] Dora Quesada and her four siblings—Alicia, Josefina, Bernard, and Eugene—attended the school through the 1930s.

These acts of school building continued actively into the early twentieth century. For example, Dolores Urias Wright, remembered as "Tia Lolita" by her schoolteacher niece María Urias, is the matriarch who founded a new community called "Wrightstown" with her husband Fred in 1912. At that time, Wrightstown was a small rural enclave east of Tucson; it was eventually absorbed into the city and is remembered only by one street name, Wright-stown Road. A fourth-generation Tucsonense, Dolores was born in 1886. Her mother, María Juana Gallego, descended from a presidial family and married Antonio Urias, a Sonoran who is credited with opening Tucson's first jewelry store. Dolores and Fred married in 1905 after meeting on the job at a local department store. They claimed a 640-acre homestead north of Tucson along the old "cow path" and convinced their neighbors to join them in founding a new post office and town center. The Wrights "took a petition for the road and also for the public school to the other homesteaders in the area and donated three acres for the [brick school] building."[72] In fact, the Wrights built the school twice: an adobe in 1912 that a storm soon destroyed and a brick build-ing in 1914. Wrightstown Elementary operated as a Tucson public school for ninety-six years until its closing in 2010.

Other families tell similar stories of cooperative school building. Living in the Rincon Mountains east of Tucson, Ramona Benítez Franco remembers how her father Angel Benítez gathered the community to build a new school around 1900. Initially, Ramona attended a home school led by the English-speaking Señorita Carmen Téllez, who taught the classes at the family ranch. "No one wanted to go out there to teach because it was so far from town. Then my father began to insist that there be a [public] school . . . and he went around collecting signatures, and finally a school was built. It was about a mile from our house, and we would go to school in a horse-drawn buggy."[73] Like Mexican Settlement fathers four hundred miles north on the Little Colorado River, Pa Ramón Valencia in Wickenburg, and the Wrights of Wrightstown, Mr. Benítez asserted his children's educational right to attend a proper school-house near their ranch. He also exercised his citizenship rights as a voter and election judge for Rincon Precinct No. 20.[74] The schoolhouse served as the polling place, too.

Arizonenses embraced this provincial educational mission despite the complicated social and cultural confrontations that emerged in their efforts to promote literacy and sustain educational access. In 1887, for example, the Catholic priest in Yuma judged parents quite harshly, denying them sacra-ments—confession, in particular, which also meant no communion, confir-mations, or baptisms—for sending their children to the public school.[75] In Tucson, Mexican-heritage parents supported bilingual schooling by enrolling their children in significant numbers in both public and private Catholic schools.[76] The Spanish-language press particularly endorsed the private, bilingual schools and regularly chided the public schools for "de-Mexicanizing" their children.[77] The original 1864 territorial school law coerced the Tucson schools to offer "partial English-language instruction" in exchange for funding; by 1883, it required English-only instruction in every school in the territory.[78] The territorial and state legislatures reiterated this in 1885, in 1901, in the 1910 state constitution, and in the 1913 revised statutes, which said, "All schools must be taught in the English language."[79]

The legislature's continued proclamations over the English language suggests that Arizonense families refused to disregard their mother tongue. One historian described the elite's position as a "combination of selective assimilation and determined cultural preservation."[80] For example, Pedro García de la Lama publicly asserted bilingual literacies. A Spaniard and Mexican Army officer who attended the Jesuit College at Cádiz and the Heroic Naval College at Vera Cruz, de la Lama came to Arizona in 1886.[81] He took a teaching position in Solomonville before moving to Phoenix in 1893, where he owned several successful Spanish-language newspapers. In 1914, he was a founder of the Liga Protectora Latina (LPL), a mutual aid society organized to serve the political, fraternal, and educational needs of Spanish speakers from any nationality living in Arizona.[82] Other parents, especially those who were literate, also homeschooled their children, including their daughters. Young María Antonia Parra who was born in 1883 near Wickenburg learned to read and write in Spanish, English, and Latin because her father taught her.[83] Carlos Parra escaped the priesthood and the monastery at Guadalajara, Jalisco (over a thousand miles south of Phoenix). He set up a small home school at the Vulture Mine for his daughter and neighboring children, probably his *hijados* (godchildren). When his wife died, he sent María Antonia to live with her aunts in Tucson and she attended the St. Augustine Cathedral School until she was sixteen. In Patricia Preciado Martin's superb oral history of Mexican Americans, Carlotta Parra Rodríguez Sotomayor recalled her mother María Antonia's passion for reading. "She had a lot of books that she read, and she passed on her love of reading to us." She treasured her books, especially "a book of poems and stories by Henry Wadsworth Longfellow. She used to keep it in a trunk wrapped in cloth."[84] For three generations, the Parra family preserved their appreciation for languages and literatures, demonstrating the cultural value of multilingual, written, and oral traditions within Arizonense society.

Negotiating Culture, Language, and Assimilation

The Parra family's intellectual desires, alongside those of de la Lama and the LPL, reflect longer and broader traditions of education, citizenship, and social organization of the Spanish-speaking settlements in the American Southwest.[85] For example, early settler schools were designed as part of the Spanish colonial project for children of the elite. The Spanish state particularly emphasized its commitment to educate its criollo (American-born Spanish citizen) population, as well as its goal to Christianize the Indigenous populations. The Spanish colonial schools specifically safeguarded "culture transfer" and emphasized "preservation of Spanish language, culture, and religion," while the missions intentionally subtracted language and culture from Native American children who were then taught Spanish language and customs by the priests.[86] Ironically, Arizonense youths and their parents would experience this same cultural subtraction under U.S. colonialism. This forced Arizonense families in the nineteenth century to cling tightly to nonformal education traditions rooted in the home, such as private tutoring in Spanish language, literature, and culture to ensure that their children and grandchildren remained bilingual and bicultural. This signaled a serious commitment to the political and social worlds of the Arizonenses whose families moved freely and sustained international (cross-border) and interterritorial family and business relations.[87]

Connecting Arizonenses to Norteño society is critically important because the Mexican migrants residing in New Mexico (later, Arizona) Territory came from Sonora, California, New Mexico, and other northern Mexican and southwestern U.S. states.[88] Some Arizonenses, like Rosalío "Ross" F. Muñoz and his parents, hailed from as far as the Gulf states of Tamaulipas and Texas. This meant that most Arizonenses, like the Sonoran-born Manuela Sotelo, were already attuned to patterns of migration and immigration, the state processes of claiming space, and the personal processes of forming identity. Many possessed a notion of citizenship and of belonging to a nation-state that included "civil, political and social rights" and that depended on the acquisition of economic (land) and social (family) resources.[89] In the Spanish borderlands, a frontier ethos emerged and this meant that people continuously negotiated relationships with the land, with each other, and with the various governments (Indigenous nations, Spain, Mexico, and the United States) that claimed control of the region.[90] As a result, some consider the Arizonenses a "border people," "fronterizos" (frontier people), or simply individualists who asserted citizenship rights and a sense of equality rooted in hard work, independence, and gendered notions of bravery and honor.[91] They were people who acted on their own and created a new world as they transplanted old values into this place called Arizona. Often, they ignored the state being so far from the grips of its official authority in Mexico City, Albuquerque, or Washington, D.C. Other times, they harnessed the power of the state to their advantage in order to insert themselves into this place.

As fronterizos, Arizonenses embraced public education as a site of political and cultural representation. Without forfeiting individualism or ethnic identity, they worked to integrate themselves into the civil body of the state that laid claim to the region. In the process of establishing authority over their children's education in the name of the state—by petitioning, building, and supervising community schools—they also asserted their sense of identity and purpose into the region. For example, Don Sabino Otero, a great-grandson of Toribio de Otero, is credited with establishing the first U.S. public school in the Arizona Territory at Tubac.[92] Sabino, who was born in 1846, attended school in Santa Fe until the age of 19, where the only Catholic school in the region existed at the time. His interest in the public good—he also supported an orphanage and the church parish—likely stemmed from his family's vast cattle wealth and his great-grandfather's legacy as a schoolteacher under Spanish rule. Toribio, as mentioned earlier, may have operated the first Mexican state-funded school at the Tubac presidio generations earlier.[93] In northern communities, Arizonense parents also actively engaged school authority. For example, in the town of San Cosme, also known as Walnut Grove, school trustees Marcos Baca and Francisco Saís posted bilingual announcements for the school board elections. "Para abisar atodas las que tengan derecho Comisionados de escu[ela] sebotaran el dia 25th de June [sic] y seabriran La Elec[ción] de la mañana deste Mes. Elecion [sic] sera tenida es de escuela."[94] The town fathers completed the legal task of posting election notices—in English and Spanish— in the same way that they conducted most of their territorial business and their daily lives in both languages through the nineteenth century.

This seemingly incongruous action reveals how Arizonenses embraced the American state while simultaneously preserving their sense of a Mexican cultural identity. For the Arizonenses this was not a discontinuity, even when Anglo-Americans clearly and often pointed to this paradox. In the Arizonense worldview, it was possible to be both an American citizen and a cultural Mexican within Arizona society. It had to be an option—otherwise, how could one unify his or her sense of self in a world of ever-changing polities. This is exactly the kind of acculturation that many Anglo-American men experienced when they married into Arizonense families, and exactly how the Tucsonense Estevan Ochoa crafted his own image and his legacy when he helped authorize the territorial public schools in 1870. Thomas Sheridan's assessment of the Tucsonenses, for example, reflects such civic integration. "Mexicans in Tucson became merchants, politicians, artists, and intellectuals, transforming an isolated Sonoran outpost into an oasis of middle-class Mexican society in the United States."[95]

Now, Arizonenses were not particularly imaginative in their relationship to the state. They were not revolutionaries attempting to create a new utopian society or to preserve an old one. They were average colonials engaged in their daily lives and accustomed to negotiating a state apparatus to achieve personal goals. The national shifts from Spain to Mexico to the United States mattered less to them because the state's power did not necessarily change their vested interest in Arizona or education, whereas it might have in other realms, such as land or water rights, which were bitterly challenged well into the twentieth century and remembered in oral history to this day. Even when the state interceded in homestead disputes, parents remained focused on education. Luis Acuña Gastellum recalled how his siblings "commute[d] for three hours" on horseback each day in the early 1920s to reach the school in Tubac, the same school his mother had attended in the 1880s, after the U.S. government evicted his family from their 1886 homestead as part of the Baca Float No. 3 land dispute negotiated by Congress and the courts.[96] His parents relocated to a small cottage they owned near Reventon, five miles north of Tubac and outside the Baca family's claim. Young Luis rode the "school buggy" as did his cousins and children from eleven families, including the "Gómezes, Aldays, Gortarezes, Olivases, Oteros, Sierras, Valdezes, Megarízes, Gutíerrezes, Madrils and Castros."[97] All the children secured their horses in the stables owned by Raymundo Rojas. After school, Luis waited "with [his] godmother, Nina Luisa Rojas, who lived across from the school, until [his] older brothers and sisters got out of class." In fact, Luisa whom they affectionately called "Nina" (short for *madrina*, or godmother) was also known as Luisa Rojas de Yoas. She was born at Tubac in 1893 and died there in 1989.[98] She lived in the house her father Raymundo built across from the Tubac presidio and its schoolhouse. Upon completing grade school, Luisa worked as the school caretaker for thirty years.

In each period of state control and regardless of the national flag, Arizonenses learned the law, rules, and bureaucracy necessary to serve the educational needs of their children. What mattered to them was sustaining Mexican culture, identity, and the Spanish language, and preserving them in tandem with other personal aspirations amid the pressure of Americanization.[99] Cultural legacy is what makes civic integration such an important strategy for Arizonenses in the early territorial period. Parents cooperated with the government to build schools because it served their interest and their children's interests. The 1879 territorial school law allowed parents to form their own districts when "five heads of families petition[ed] the County Superintendent."[100] Between 1871 and 1890, Maricopa County parents opened thirty-five districts with thirty-seven primary schools and thirteen grammar schools, with 1,756 enrolled and nearly one thousand in daily attendance.[101] In these three decades, for example, Spanish-surnamed parents, as well as Anglos married to known Arizonense women, served as trustees in many of these school districts. For the record, some of these parents included Ramon Corrella, Jesus Noriega, and Ramon Valencia at Washington No. 6; Winchester Miller at Tempe No. 3; B. B. Castro and Ignacio García at Wickenburg No. 9; Elijio Amabisca, Pedro Amabisca, and Ramon García at Aqua Caliente, No. 12; J. T. Priest at Tempe Double Butte No. 20; Mrs. Luz Redondo Balsz, David Balsz, Ramon Valencia, and A. Trujillo, at Balsz No. 31; José Carillo, Damacio Encinas, Valente Loroña, Francisco Meza, Ramon Perez, Ramon Pacheco, José Sotelo, and Pedro Sotelo at Hancock No. 36; José J. Badilla (who was Costa Rican) at Madison No. 38; and Frank Valenzuela at Fowler No. 45.[102]

In several instances, the families—the Balsz family, for example—named school districts after themselves. German immigrant David Balsz and his California-born wife, María Luz "Lucy" Redondo de Balsz, founded Balsz School District No. 31 in 1888 for their nine children and, in all likelihood, the sixteen children of his brother Frederick whose last wife was Soledad Bracamonte.[103] According to the local newspaper, "Mrs. David Balsz held classes for eleven children," including six of her own.[104] Others remember her oldest daughter, María "Mary" Piedad Balsz, as the schoolteacher. At the age of seventeen, Mary had been celebrated in 1894 as the "first graduate" of the Sacred Heart Academy, which had opened two years earlier. Anglo and Arizonense parishioners of St. Mary's Catholic Church, which was founded in 1870 at the urging of Trinidad Escalante Swilling (considered the "Mother of Phoenix"), fundraised to bring the Irish order of nuns to the city after they closed their school at Florence.[105] While the academy enrolled fifty-two girls in its opening week, the public schools across Maricopa County had already operated for more than twenty years also at the behest of parents such as Redondo de Balsz and Escalante Swilling.[106]

In March 1894, the Balsz trustees garnered considerable attention from the *Arizona Republic* for their outspoken position on bilingual education. The elected trustees Pedro Sotelo, Francisco Mesa, and Ramon Pacheco recommended, to the ex officio county superintendent of education and probate judge T. C. Jordan, that teacher Richard Stuart be retained for the next school year. Stuart possessed Spanish fluency and the students made significant progress, more "in the past five months . . . than in the five preceding terms." Most of the children at Balsz school were native Spanish-speakers, and few spoke any English. Based on the trustees' report, the newspaper detailed the matter extensively: "Previous teachers have been unable to speak or understand Spanish so that there were absolutely no means of communication between the teachers and a large body of pupils. The latter might as well have been deaf and the former dumb so far as their relations to each other were concerned. The result of this state of affairs has been that the pupils quit attending school and if the teacher earned his salary at all it was by the daily loneliness he was subjected to."[107] Tongue-in-cheek humor aside, the newspaper editors encouraged education officials to consider how this situation affected many of the territorial schools.

This interest in the perspective of Arizonense fathers, however, did not extend to Mrs. Lucy Redondo de Balsz. Later that year, the *Arizona Republic* ran a front-page story mocking her for inserting herself in the school district matters. "The high pitched and excited voice of a woman rang through the court house corridors yesterday afternoon, penetrating chambers and offices, arousing half a dozen officials and clerks from misty dreams."[108] Political disputes left the district without elected trustees and Redondo de Balsz filed a complaint with Judge Jordan. The newspaper described the Balsz district as the "most thoroughly torn and tattered" in the county, which contradicted the depiction cast four months earlier. Judge Jordan appointed Redondo de Balsz as a new school trustee and its clerk, responsible for reporting the district's official business to the county.[109] She served as a trustee until 1897, when her family relocated to Yuma. Like her fellow Arizonenses, Redondo de Balsz did not expect to abandon her investment in the school, her cultural identity, or her intellect for the sake of her children's education. Whether trustees retained Stuart as a teacher is unknown, but it is clear that parents preferred an educational curriculum that included both Spanish by custom and English by law.

Like the Balsz family, Arizonense parents in the Colorado Plateau worked to sustain their influence or direct control of six of Apache County's twenty-two districts. Between 1880 and 1920, more than 300 Spanish-surnamed

Figure 3. Amelia Hunt García, circa 1890. A scanned photocopy in the author's possession. Courtesy of Charlotte Walker, James Hunt García Jr., and the García family descendants.

women and men from seventy-five families served as school petitioners, trustees, election judges, election inspectors, clerks, teachers, principals, and custodians.[110] Like their contemporaries, they paid careful attention to the territorial educational policy. They knew they had the right to maintain public schools as long as they met minimum attendance requirements, maintained a taxpayer base, and enforced school law. They sought and hired bilingual teachers, such as Amelia Hunt, who came from an Anglo-Hispano family and grew up in the region (she was born on the family ranch near Joseph City).[111] In 1889, Hunt completed grammar school at the Prescott academy operated by the Sisters of St. Joseph where she earned awards for merit, then she advanced to the public high school, earning her diploma.[112] She completed high school work at St. Johns Academy (a Mormon school) and Prescott High School. At the age of fifteen, she passed the qualifying exams for a First Grade Teaching Certificate and garnered immediate employment in schools that catered to Spanish-speaking families. She held private tutoring positions (which the territory allowed), such as her first job for Lena Rubi and her husband Don Lorenzo Hubbell, who was a well-known Navajo trader and politician.[113]

Hunt managed one-room schools, such as Las Tueces, and taught at the district schools of St. Johns No. 1, Concho No. 6, and Malapais No. 13. At the 1899 county teacher's institute, which she chaired, she shared the podium with district attorney Alfred Ruiz Sr., a Californio educated in San Francisco. While he spoke on the revised compulsory attendance laws, she presented a paper on "Teaching English to Spanish-Speaking Children."[114] That same evening, the group hosted a debate on the topic, proclaiming: "In View of Our Extended Territory Inhabited by Spanish-Speaking People, *Resolved*, That Spanish Should be Taught in the Public Schools."

Hunt's discussion on the pedagogy of bilingual education must have brought her into larger conversations with other teachers who specialized in this work. Although there is no direct evidence from this era, we can surmise that such exchanges took place at teacher institutes, on the job, and, if not in person, then across newswires. For instance, Monico García also taught Spanish-speaking children with Hunt at St. Johns No.1; in 1910, he was elected county probate judge and school superintendent. No doubt, he relied on Hunt's influence and expertise as they had married in 1902. Other teachers also may have held similar appointments, such as fellow Apache County teachers Mrs. Lucy Gonzales and Raymundo Angel; Cochise County teacher J. M. R. Acedo, as well as Petra C. Ochoa, Margarita Corra, Teofilo Aros, and Carlos Tully in Pima County; and in Graham County, Pedro Michelena (who once served as an interpreter for Teresa Urrea, La Santa de Cabora).[115] Reporting on a school celebration of George Washington's birthday, the *St. Johns Herald* applauded Hunt's proficiency at the primary school where she taught "all" of the Mexican-heritage children. "She is not only teaching them the English language and giving them all ordinary school instruction, but is also . . . giving them practical instruction in patriotism that is highly beneficial to the rising generation."[116] While Hunt's teaching appeared effortless, it was difficult work that many attempted to replicate. At the Normal School, Anglo-American faculty began experimenting at the turn of the twentieth century with new methods for teaching English to Mexican children at their "practice school," where the college students taught for the first time in preparation for their graduation. Professor Margaret Graham Hood and college student Ethel Orme of Phoenix began a "special class formed among the Mexican children . . . to see if they cannot evolve a better method for teaching the Mexican children English."[117] Hood and Orme even enlisted a teacher from the Tucson Indian School with whom they compared notes on teaching "Mexicans and Indians."

Figure 4. Monico García. A scanned photocopy of Monico García included with his biography in *Who's Who in Arizona* (1913), comp. Jo Conners.

Ironically, Hunt had been doing this work for nearly ten years before Hood and Orme's experiment at Tempe and she was not the only Arizonense teacher engaged in bilingual education. In 1898, when Manuela Sotelo's granddaughters Anna and Clara Miller graduated from the Normal School, they too entered the public service as teachers. Clara Miller first agreed to take charge of a new parochial school built by the Mexican American parishioners at Our Lady of Mount Carmel Catholic Church.[118] The new school opening coincided with criticism of the secular schools for their failure to serve the Spanish-speaking children. According to the priest, Father Severin Westhoff, "The public schools were unable to get more than half of the Mexican children to attend and that the parents sooner or later took the half that did not attend out because they could not keep up with the other children on account of not understanding the English language, that being a drawback to the others, and of no benefit to themselves."[119] Like Hunt, Clara Miller was bilingual and designed the new parochial school specifically to teach twenty Mexican and Yaqui children to speak English in addition to the standard territorial curriculum so that when or if they transferred to a public school they would transition easily. At year's end, Miller hosted a closing ceremony that included student performances, a speech by Samuel Brown who was an Alianza leader (later, the only Arizonense mayor of Tempe), a picnic dinner, and even school photographs. She resigned her post to join the faculty at the Tempe public school, passing the helm to Clara Priest, whom she knew from the Normal School and who also possessed a bilingual, Anglo-Hispano heritage.[120] In December 1900, Miller and Priest attended the joint teacher institute held at Tempe with classmate Petra C. Ochoa, another bilingual teacher who taught at the Tohono O'odham Indian School at Topawa and Tres Alamos in Cochise County.[121] A naturalized immigrant from Mexico, Ochoa also graduated from the Normal School in 1897. According to family oral history, she taught at the Tohono O'odham Nation Reservation in Topawa "because she couldn't get a job [anywhere else] because of racism."[122] At Tucson, through the 1910s no known Arizonense or Spanish-surnamed teacher appeared on the teacher roster after Ignacio Bonillas (1874) or Carlos Tully (1891–1894, 1896).[123] Instead, they actively recruited bilingual Anglo-American women, such as Elizabeth "Lizzie" Borton, a New Yorker who as a child migrated to Tucson with her family. Borton opened a new ward school in Barrio Libre (Free Town) in 1899.[124] "Miss Borton speaks Spanish fluently and for this reason she was chosen to take charge of this school," which served "the poorer children who had never attended the public schools before."[125] Petra Ochoa returned to her hometown of Tres Alamos, where she taught until she married Tiburcio Diaz in 1901.

Borquez, Hunt, Miller, Priest, and Ochoa were among the earliest known Arizonense women teachers in nineteenth-century schools, but their assigned duties to teach English to Mexican and Indigenous children fulfilled an agenda forced on them as a result of American colonization. Borquez rejected this agenda and resigned her post at Nogales to accept a position in her parents' hometown of Hermosillo, Sonora, where she taught English as a foreign language in a girls' school.[126] She later opened a very successful private language school in Los Angeles, where she published a series of books on teaching English and Spanish, including the *Elementary Spanish Reader*, which the state of California adopted for its public schools and the New York Public Library promoted as a "new book" in its collection.[127] Between 1914 and 1917, Borquez offered a Spanish course for the suffragist-sponsored, Ebell Women's Club in

Los Angeles. Like Carlos Tully a generation earlier who spent his career as a teacher and translator in Tucson, their vocation became increasingly racialized and invested with communal responsibility because of rising Anglo-American anxieties over "Mexican Americanization," a play on words introduced here to describe the never-ending emphasis whites placed on the English-language acquisition and assimilation of Mexican-heritage children.

Language Anxieties, Cultural Tolerance

Anglo Americans pushed for Americanization as soon as they entered the territory. They distinguished between two classes of Arizonenses—the "better Mexican families" who supported this education movement and the "ignorant and bigoted" majority."[128] While the Mexican elite may have held similar views about the working class, this early distinction between the two groups arose from the ambiguous racial and class identities of Mexican-heritage people. The U.S. government considered them treaty citizens and, by extension, "white by law," but in daily life they also were subject to distinctions of appearance and language.[129] These racial scripts factored heavily in the school success and failure of Mexican American children, and they lent credence to what Anglo Americans called the Mexican Problem as early as 1870. Historian and Tucson school superintendent Samuel Pressly McCrea described the pupils as "seemingly hopeless" given the "large foreign element, mainly Mexican."[130]

McCrea noted that as early as 1864, during Arizona's First Territorial Legislature, Arizonense and Anglo-American politicians attempted to formalize public education and English-language instruction in the towns of La Paz, Mohave, Prescott, and Tucson.[131] However, the territorial legislature required that each town provide a matching appropriation levied through taxes to support the creation of these local schools, but no town did between 1864 and 1870. Then, in 1871, Governor Anson P. K. Safford and Tucson representative Estevan Ochoa persuaded the majority of the legislature to create a public school system. Ochoa proposed the law and won its passage, but the legislature refused to allocate the funding. Instead, local communities subsidized the schools themselves. When county tax revenues proved insufficient, wealthy citizens paid in kind or by donation to build the schools and support the teachers. In Tucson, Ochoa donated the land, the building supplies, and the labor to build the Congress Street School after the county depleted its coffers. Historian Thomas Sheridan insists no one did more than Ochoa to establish the Tucson public schools.[132] This expectation of patronage extended across the territory, as families, Mexican and Anglo alike, built local schools often with no government compensation. This was the case, too, with the private, religious schools. While Ochoa underwrote the public school, his business partner, Pinckney Randolph Tully sponsored a parochial school at the urging of his first Mexican Catholic wife, María Trinidad Conklin, an Hispana from Santa Fe.[133] In Phoenix and Tempe, Catholic families helped fundraise for public, secular, and private religious institutions as well.

Throughout the territorial period (1864–1912), the few Mexican American assemblymen elected to the bicameral legislature, including Ochoa who served in the fifth and sixth sessions, managed to secure ranking seats on the territorial legislature's Committee on Education and voted to pass new school laws. In nine legislative assemblies from 1871 to 1891, at least one Mexican American representative served on the education committee.[134] Nasianceno Gonzales, for example, who served in the twentieth and twenty-second territorial legislatures as well as the first state assembly in 1912, possessed a "lively interest in public education, being especially anxious that Spanish speaking children of his [Apache] county and State received all the advantages of good schools."[135] He also advocated for free textbooks, proposing House Bill No. 36, one of three such proposed laws in the first state session.

This legacy, however, was not necessarily apparent to Anglo-Americans such as McCrea, who entered the territory in earnest after the completion of the intercontinental Southern Pacific Railroad in 1880. Anglo-Americans generally held very negative opinions about Mexican Americans, let alone their educational values or their ability to benefit from schooling.[136] McCrea's perspective is especially troubling, though some might say informed, because he graduated from the University of Arizona (and, later, Stanford University) and served as Tucson school superintendent from 1896 to 1898. He knew and worked with educated members of the Arizonense elite. The only Tucsonense to serve as superintendent of schools, Charles "Carlos" H. Tully held the post from 1891 to 1894 and again briefly in 1896 prior to McCrea.[137] Among the earliest teachers in the territory, husband and wife Louis Cameron "L. C." Hughes and Josephine Brawley Hughes also had a close friendship with Tully.[138] Together, Hughes and Tully founded the *Arizona Daily Star* in 1877. Given Tully's background as an educated man of Anglo-Mexican parentage, Hughes must have separated him from the rest of the Tucsonense population, which he described as "a country bordering on the confines of a semicivilized nation, and where the population is largely made up of a class of people who are strangers to the real elements of civilization."[139] As the Pima County ex officio school superintendent (and later territorial governor), Hughes viewed public education as "enlightenment of the masses." His ideas echoed popular tracks of egalitarianism and the common school crusader's political construction of republican education that emphasized citizenship.[140] This buoyed him as he coped "out here in the border lands of civilization."[141]

Superintendent Hughes's mission focused on assimilating Mexican American youth by teaching English and arithmetic as the core curriculum at six Tucson schools. In 1865, the first session of the Arizona Territorial Legislature passed a law requiring English lessons in the Tucson schools. But Hughes pushed for full-time daily instruction, as opposed to bilingual education. In 1872, he reported success "beyond expectation."[142] The Mexican American children in nearly every school "can read and write the language remarkably well and many speak the same quite intelligently."[143] In 1874, teachers John Spring and seventeen-year-old Ignacio Bonillas continued the trend as all of their pupils over the age of eight could read, write, and complete basic arithmetic in English.[144] A Sonorense by birth, Bonillas studied under Spring and found a mentor in Governor Anson P. K. Safford who helped him enroll at Massachusetts Institute of Technology.[145] Bonilla's success, alongside that of his former classmates, only reaffirmed the need for an explicit English-only language policy for all public schools, which the territorial legislature formalized in 1883.[146]

This emphasis on English-language acquisition succeeded in Arizona schools partly because elite Arizonenses endorsed the curriculum as a negotiation point in the new Anglo-American political and social order.[147] The Mexican American merchants and ranchers were well-versed in how bilingualism led to success in their business ventures, and they shared this notion with some Anglo newcomers, such as former territorial governor Richard C. McCormick Jr. who advocated "as a matter of justice" for bilingualism in the courts given that the Arizonenses controlled "much of the business of the Territory, and is identified with nearly every pursuit."[148] The Arizonenses also bowed to English-language instruction in the public schools because they supported Spanish-language instruction in the private schools.[149] As a result, they encouraged English acquisition as a second language, a move often critiqued as "anti-Mexican" by Mexican nationalists but also as a practical preservation strategy. Scholars such as Elise DuBord and Rosina Lozano offer several rationales to explain why Arizonense parents cultivated dual cultures and languages (or, in the case of intermarriages, triple cultures and languages). For instance, as a political compromise, Arizonense legislators endorsed public schooling in exchange for the continued use of Spanish in official government procedures, such as bilingual court proceedings, elections, and the publication of territorial laws.[150] The legislature regularly appropriated funding for the Spanish translation and printing of the governor's annual message and for some laws, such as the 1875 compulsory education act.[151] Arizonense translators and printers, such as Tully, won these contracts.[152] This shrewd bargain over English-language instruction gave them a chance to assert and sustain dwindling Mexican American political power. They fought, instead, to preserve Arizonense electoral participation across the territory because they had other venues for educating their children in Spanish.

Mexican Americans particularly valued European Catholic school orders for their multilingualism. After school funding from the first territorial legislature failed to materialize in 1864, Arizonense mothers pushed for private Catholic education as an alternative for their children. That same year, for instance, the Tully's sent young Carlos, who was then about twelve years old, to the Colegio de San Miguel (St. Michael's High School) in Santa Fe, New Mexico, to complete high school.[153] Organized by the Christian Brothers, this Catholic day and boarding school has operated since 1859 and it became one of the leading Catholic boys high schools in the Southwest. While missionary priests at San Xavier del Bac had unsuccessfully operated a school for Mexican and Tohono O'odham youth in the 1860s, the Arizonense mothers hoped to establish a permanent school for girls and boys of diverse economic and cultural backgrounds within the Tucson vicinity. Elite Arizonenses such as Inez García, wife of the former Tucson mayor William S. Oury, and Josefa Fernández, wife of merchant Juan Fernández, recruited the Sisters of St. Joseph of Carondelet, a French Catholic order of nuns from St. Louis in 1870.[154] With philanthropic support from the Tully family, the nuns opened St. Mary's Hospital and four schools: a girls academy, a parochial school, a ranch school, and a novitiate that operated as a "kind of Normal School for the preparation of Novices for teaching and for religious life."[155] A Catholic school for boys called St. Augustine's also opened in 1874. Between 1878 and 1881, the Tucson parochial schools enrolled twice the number of students as the public schools and offered the same curriculum.[156] In 1885, the Sisters of

St. Joseph also opened a second academy in the pine-forest mountain town of Prescott, then the territorial capital.

Arizonense parents across the territory perceived English-language acquisition and multilingualism as economic opportunities. Bilingualism, if not multilingualism, secured their socioeconomic and political foothold within this border culture.[157] While the Spanish language remained "the universal medium of communication" in the 1870s, according to historian Karl Jacoby, Arizonenses also learned a range of indigenous languages and dialects from Apache to Tohono O'odham, as well as English. Many became multilingual as entrepreneurs when they entered transnational trade routes that connected the Midwest and the southern United States with markets across northern Mexico to California.[158] In January 1880, *El Fronterizo* noted the cosmopolitan nature of Tucson's socioeconomic landscape and the linguistic facility of its residents who conducted their businesses and daily lives in thirteen different languages, including "Spanish, English, French, German, Italian, Hungarian, Russian, Chinese, Papago, Pima, Yaqui, Mayan, and Apache."[159] Ramón Cervero Valencia, a.k.a. Pa Ramón, of Wickenburg emphasized the importance of these multilingual, multicultural competencies among his "greatest accomplishments." His granddaughter, Dora Quesada remembered, albeit nostalgically, how "he appreciated and nurtured the friendship of Native Americans who would trade at his stores. He trusted them and they passed the word along so that later when [he] would travel the routes to Maricopa on mining business, he was never harmed or robbed." He said he was called "The One of the White Hair." In period photos, his thick, bright hair and mustache seem to glow against his dark complexion.[160]

In the late nineteenth century, the nature of relations among Anglos and Arizonenses often determined Mexican American school attendance.[161] Civic integration only succeeded in communities where the two groups tolerated each other. In contrast to Tucson, where hundreds of Mexican-heritage children attended schools, white Phoenicians expressed outright hostility toward Mexican American residents who in turn argued that "[the] Mexican people made this town."[162] They labored to construct its buildings and to operate its farms and ranches, and they endorsed its politicians. Overlooking this cooperation, in 1872, Maricopa County School superintendent J. T. Alsap detailed a potential Mexican attack on the city and thanked Governor Safford for his decision to ready military forces.[163] The next year, a lynch mob assassinated two Mexican men charged with robbery.[164] This vigilantism spurred some Arizonenses to leave Phoenix, and it convinced most parents to keep their children safe at home.[165] The 1874 school census for Maricopa County revealed that only 5, or 2.5 percent of the 199 Spanish-surnamed children in Phoenix School Districts No. 1 and No. 2 attended any school.[166] In contrast, 59 of 145 (40.6 percent) of Anglo-American children were reported attending school.[167] The five Arizonense children in regular attendance included merchant Jesús Otero's three daughters and the two children of Trinidad Escalante and John W. (Jack) Swilling, the founder of Phoenix and the Swilling Irrigation and Canal Company.[168] Swilling told the census taker that they had three children—a son and two daughters; two attended public school and one was literate.[169] A Gadsden Purchase treaty citizen, Otero later owned a partial claim on the Monte Cristo silver mine in northern Maricopa County, and he was the brother of future New Mexico governor Miguel Otero and uncle of teacher-suffragist Nina Otero-Warren.[170] Otero's youngest daughter, Bessie, later graduated from the Sacred Heart Academy in 1894, a few years after Mary Piedad Balsz.[171] Otero's sons also attended Santa Clara College near San José, California. The Swilling and Otero children were the only verifiable, Mexican-heritage youth who attended the Phoenix public schools at their founding. The political and financial power their fathers wielded protected them from the racial conflict of the town, particularly in the early absence of private or parochial schools.

In other Arizona communities, civic integration succeeded as evidenced by growing school attendance. As in Tucson, these schools emphasized English acquisition and served as initial sites of American socialization. In the border town of Yuma (also known as Arizona City), Mexican wives attended with their small children from the school's founding in 1872.[172] On the banks of the Colorado River at Ehrenberg (on the California border), teacher Mary Elizabeth Post also opened a new school with fifteen Spanish-speaking children.[173] Since she did not speak Spanish, trustee Joseph Goldwater (Senator Barry Goldwater's great-uncle) interpreted on occasion.

Similarly, in the mountains roughly one hundred miles north of Phoenix, principal Moses H. Sherman, a native New Yorker and future territorial school superintendent, supervised the Prescott Graded School that contained three integrated classrooms in a custom-built, two-story building with 163 students, ages six to twenty-one, in primary, intermediate, and high school classes.[174] From 1877 to 1889, the town of Prescott served as Arizona's capital city and during Governor John C. Frémont's appointment (1878-1882) his wife Jessie Benton Frémont gave history lectures. She described the children as "jolly, bright-eyed, red-cheeked, clear-voiced little men and women, Americans, English, German, Mexicans, and mixed—admirably taught and trained."[175] Although she considered Arizona "*outside* the world" (her emphasis), she shared stories and souvenirs of European travel with the children as "many, coming overland from our border country, had never seen a great city, or the ocean."[176]

The memories of Anglo teachers, such as Jessie Benton Frémont, working with Arizonense children in late nineteenth-century Arizona Territory require a close textual analysis. For example, Mrs. Ada Jones (formerly Ada Ekey) came with her parents to Nogales as a young girl and attended the new public schools in the 1880s.[177] After passing the territorial teacher's exam in Tucson and teaching in several Santa Cruz County schools, Jones garnered a permanent post in Nogales in 1893, the same year Aurelia Borquez joined the faculty. Echoing language characteristic of urban school reformers confronted with truant immigrant children, Ada Jones recalled that the Nogales trustees, "decided to enforce the school law and compell [*sic*] all of the Mexican children living on the Arizona side of the line to attend school. There seemed to be so many roving the streets."[178] Once the town officers instructed parents to send their children to school, Mexican children were seated in "six or seven school rooms" across the town, including Jones's class at Marshes' Opera House.[179] Jones asserts that the "true founding" of the Nogales schools could thus be attributed to the enrollment of Mexican children.[180]

The Anglo instructors in Nogales congratulated themselves on their success with their new charges, stating, "Despite a lack of supplies and furnishings, we [teachers] succeeded fairly well in getting them interested to study and learn English, there are many on the streets here today who were pupils in our school then and they have made good citizens."[181] Jones was particularly proud that her students included siblings Jesús and Abelardo L. Rodríguez, who later became interim president of Mexico from 1932 to 1934.[182]

Teaching Mexican children in Nogales did not deter Jones from taking an assignment requiring considerable walking distance (for which she received an extra monthly sum). In 1895, she taught in a school described as possessing a "small adobe room, dirt floor and dirt roof."[183] Unfortunately, Jones did not provide the name of the school; it may have been one of Nogales's first segregated Mexican schools. She wrote, "During the next year or two the pupils were segregated and were classified [graded] and we had three well filled rooms." Jones notes that she taught in an addition that had been built onto the segregated school and "about the third day after school opened some 84 small children had registered in my room alone."[184] Jones's experiences in Nogales occurred during a time in Arizona when the Mexican population was increasingly marginalized. The school attendance of Mexican-heritage children in Arizona's territorial decades can be illustrative of parents' interest in civic integration. However, as the social, economic, and political conditions for Mexicans became increasingly harsh in the territory, the coerced attendance of Nogales Mexican children in a crowded, physically inferior, and segregated facility with English monolingual teachers reflected how schools were increasingly dismissive of Arizonense parents' interest in a substantive education.

Arizonenses, in places north and south of the Gila River, built communities and schools where their families and children could thrive. As laborers, homesteaders, and entrepreneurs, their emphasis on civic integration as a form of social activism and their focus on education for cultural preservation startled most Anglo-Americans who perceived Arizonense culture and the Spanish language as vestiges of older, un-American political eras. Even though Arizonenses negotiated public education and embraced the spirit of school laws, the tensions that emerged in the territorial era over the future of Mexican American children came to reflect both the generalized fear of Mexico and Mexicans and the growing national desire to Americanize them.

Given the high stakes of Anglo-American occupation and the growing subordination Arizonenses encountered at the turn of the twentieth century, Arizonenses recognized their dwindling political authority and leverage.[185] In cities like Phoenix, the "near majority" Mexican-heritage population that existed in 1870 found itself outnumbered three to one by Anglo Americans at the century's end.[186] The economic conditions mirrored the population shift; by 1900, only thirty Mexican American families owned farms compared to 1,180 farms owned by Anglos who now controlled the "largest employment sector in the county's economy."[187] As this critical economic scenario unfolded across the territory, it pushed Arizonenses deeper into the working class and led to the expansion of support networks, such as the Alianza, which by 1899 had one thousand members in twelve cities.[188] Paradoxically, this poor state of affairs compelled Arizonenses to hold tight to the educational ambitions they had set for their children. Parents scrambled to preserve local control of schools, pushed for dual-language instruction, and promoted high school and college education for those who qualified and could afford to attend.[189]

The dilemma, however, was that the majority of their children spoke Spanish. While this remained a critical cultural priority for parents vested in civic integration, Anglo-American teachers and administrators had little interest in preparing these youth academically and sent most of them on the path toward work preparedness. With the growing realization that they might be indefinitely subordinated in the laboring classes, Arizonenses responded by cultivating a small, educated elite who might fulfill their desert dreams.

CHAPTER 2

Adelante to High School and Beyond

Tiempo hace que yo, joven ignorante
Vine a esté colegio, lugar ideal,
Llena de ambiciones seguí delante
De moral y ciencia ví un fanal.

Time reveals that I, naïve youth
Came to this college, the ideal place,
Full of ambitions, I forged ahead
Toward the beacon of scientific and moral truth.

—Ida Celaya, "El Adios de una Senior"

The Urquides family huddled in their modest living room to have a talk with Mary Balch, a teacher and counselor from Tucson High School.[1] Balch had noticed that María, the youngest daughter of the eight Urquides children, had potential to go to college. When María was a sophomore, Balch pulled the teenage basketball star aside (she was named to the All-State Basketball Squad in 1924) and asked her what she planned to do after high school. María expected to continue clerking at Steinfeld's department store, but her teacher had other plans. "You will be an elementary school teacher," María remembered her saying. A bit stunned, María thought about the suggestion and then, within a few weeks the two began a daily regimen of early morning and after-school tutoring for college preparatory courses in algebra, geometry, music, and drama. Just before her high school graduation in 1926, María asked for her father's audience. Balch came to their home to help María secure permission to attend the Normal School, now called the Arizona State Teachers College (ASTC) at Tempe—114 miles from home.[2]

Figure 5. María Legarra Urquides, senior portrait from the 1928 yearbook, *The Sahuaro*, Tempe State Teachers College. Courtesy of the University Archives, Arizona State University Library.

María's brother Fernando adamantly rejected her idea and insisted that his baby sister stay home. "At that time tradition stipulated that 'nice' Mexican girls did not go away to school. 'This is why my brother was so against it,'" María explained.[3] Years later, she incisively described the scene: "My older brother pitched a fit, my mother cried. But I went." Despite Fernando and her mother Mariana's anguish, María had already convinced her father Hilario, who had never attended school.[4] Although hesitant about sending his single and unescorted daughter so far from home, Hilario considered what it might mean for her to be the first person in the family to attend college. A founding member of the Alianza Hispano-Americana, he understood and supported the value of public education. He had always encouraged her in school and he gave permission with one caveat. "You may go, but if you do, you will have to earn at least half of your keep and you will have to stay from September through May without coming home for the holidays, unless you earn it."[5] Two years later, with her family sitting in the bleachers, María Luisa Legarra

Urquides accepted the Governor's Golden Medal for academic achievement and graduated as the 1928 ASTC valedictorian.

Urquides represents a small group of Arizonense youth who attended a range of secondary and postsecondary institutions such as high schools, normal schools, and college in the late territorial and early statehood periods (1890–1930) of Arizona. This portrait of their experience is based on personal narratives, yearbooks, recollections, and academic records. Territorial and state legislative records, local newspapers, and the Arizona Department of Education and superintendent of public instruction sources provide a key contextual backdrop of shifting state educational priorities. Despite Juan Crow school segregation and Mexican Americanization at the lower levels that came to predominate public education in this era, Arizonense parents encouraged their children's educational aspirations and relied on the wisdom of family *dichos* (idioms), such as "la educación abre puertas" (education opens doors) in order to influence their children's persistence and achievement.[6] In addition, no de facto or de jure school segregation for Mexican American youth occurred at the secondary and postsecondary levels in Arizona public schools. Although explanations for integrated high schools are absent in the written record, the few ethnic Mexican children reaching that level most likely discouraged the justification and expense of duplicating institutions.

Arizonense students who enrolled at high schools, normal schools, colleges, and universities were considered "white by law," an extension of their "treaty citizen" rights incorporated in the Arizona Territorial Constitution, although scholar Laura Gómez has emphasized that Mexican Americans were rarely treated as white; rather, they were treated as "off-white."[7] The tenets of white supremacy in Arizona rendered the financing and extent of education for Mexican Americans to be viewed as utilitarian and brief. Through segregation and Americanization, most Arizonense youth were tracked into vocational programs and aged out or were pushed out of formal public education into the workforce. High schooling was scarcely necessary to train subservient workers in agricultural, mining, service, and household labor sectors. As a result, the resilient few who persisted to high school experienced negative reactions from all sectors. These Arizonense youth likely encountered microaggressions, hostility, and violence from peers.[8] Teachers, counselors, and administrators often failed to support their collegiate ambitions and, instead, attempted to dampen high expectations. Mexican American students thus succeeded against the odds by carefully maneuvering through English-only and predominantly white high school and collegiate spaces. Sociologist Ruth Tuck described the schooling conditions these youth encountered as "extra-legal discrimination." "Rather than having the job of battering down a wall, the Mexican-American finds himself entangled in a spider web, whose outlines are difficult to see but whose clinging, silken strands hold tight."[9] These "Fortunate Few," or "Chosen Few," somehow eclipsed this discrimination and graduated from high school and colleges in the late nineteenth and early twentieth centuries.[10] Because these students have been overlooked in the literature, we know very little about the factors that led this small, talented cohort to excel academically. Contextualizing their school success allows for a closer examination of these select students and for a reconceptualization of Mexican American scholastic performance.[11]

The statistical data on the actual numbers of Mexican American youth attending high school in the Juan Crow era is elusive. Government-sponsored educational studies did not include data on their high school attendance or graduation. The earliest estimates of this group's educational attainment focus on primary school completion. During the World War I era, the U.S. Bureau of Education and the Arizona State Board of Education estimated that ethnic Mexican children constituted half of the elementary enrollment in Arizona's twelve largest towns, but that only 17 percent of these "Mexican pupils" remained in school through the eighth grade, compared to 56 percent for the "total population."[12] This small percentage (17 percent) suggests that few ethnic Mexican children advanced to high school compared to those they left behind. School authorities often pathologized these youth as incapable of learning and described the difficulty of teaching them as the central issue in most of their schools. Officials linked school failure to the "Foreign Born Problem," which "in Arizona is typically a Mexican problem, and more so than any state in the union."[13] School officials concluded that they had very little "holding power" with this population. "Mexican pupils thin out rapidly, very few remaining in the fifth and sixth grades."[14] Fifty percent dropped out by the fifth grade and 83 percent dropped out by the eighth grade. Of those who attended school, the state estimated that 28 percent were enrolled in the first grade and that 73 percent of all Mexican pupils (compared to 42 percent for the total school population) were overage, or slow for their grade level or, worse, "mentally defective."[15] In many school districts, the mandatory "pre-primary" programs for "non-English speaking children" (which was often used as code for "Mexican") further delayed promotion to the second grade and often resulted in a three-year lag as the child completed three years of first grade (from 1C to 1B to 1A) in an Americanization curriculum known informally as the "1C" program.[16] These conditions help us understand in part why Mexican American children were frequently older, undereducated, and often ineligible to enter high school as they aged out of compulsory attendance requirements before reaching the eighth grade. The few Mexican American students who successfully completed the eighth grade received the standard "certificate of promotion" that all eighth-grade students earned and that served as an endorsement for high school admission.[17]

Given the lack of governmental evidence on Mexican American student performance, school officials consistently assessed these students, not in comparison to their Anglo peers but in comparison to African American youth in segregated schools in the American South.[18] The 1925 study reported statistics for "all pupils" or "Mexican pupils," but never "white" or "Anglo pupils," and then "approximated" Mexican American student performance to African American students in Virginia and Kentucky. These sorts of statistical comparisons and the racialized context Mexican American students experienced suggests that academic achievement signaled survivance and a strong determination to embrace the civic integration negotiated by prior generations.[19]

The racialized pathways that Arizonense teenagers encountered in academic institutions also generated alternate visions of "Mexicanness," or what it meant to be Mexican American. María Urquides recalled how Mary Balch's unexpected mentoring resulted in María taking rigorous new academic courses often reserved for her advanced white peers. Socially, however, she felt isolated and "in between" the races.[20] "In my junior and senior years, when I was into music, I began to notice that although I was friends with Anglo girls within school, I was never asked to go to their homes for parties," María remembered. In parallel, "The Mexican-Americans decided I was being a *gringacita* [Anglicized]."[21] Mexican American students often observed each others' engagement across race and class, so María was presumably ostracized for associating with Anglos, for taking college preparatory classes with them, and for acting "white" to be like them. María's awareness of how racialization affected her schooling experiences points to the liminal or third spaces that Arizonenses negotiated and claimed as they pursued the American promise of equal educational opportunity.[22]

Arizonense student achievement, including estimates of attendance and individual experiences, presented here is based on yearbook assessments from high schools and colleges. For example, even though ethnic Mexicans constituted one-third of the total territorial population in 1900 (approximately 40,977 of 122,931), estimates drawn from the ASTC yearbook counts of Spanish-surnamed students suggests that only about 150 students, roughly 2 percent, may have hailed from Arizonense families in its first fifty years (1885–1936).[23] The ASTC offered several types of degrees, including the high school diploma (called "academic curriculum"), a two-year college diploma or normal school degree (called "professional curriculum"), and baccalaureate degrees in education. At least 72 (roughly 48 percent) of the 150 Spanish-surnamed students who attended the college during this period earned the two-year diploma, qualifying them to teach in Arizona public schools. In addition, fifteen of these Spanish-surnamed students completed the bachelor's degree after 1925.[24]

In the late nineteenth and early twentieth centuries, the scarce presence of Arizonense students in high schools and colleges cast them as exceptional students, accentuated their ethnicity and socioeconomic status, and differentiated them from their Anglo peers. Some Arizonense students expressed ambivalence about these complicated race relations, while others emphasized their ethnic heritage and retooled civic integration into an incipient race consciousness. This shift toward a racialized identity emerged from the students' self-awareness. Indigenous studies scholar Eve Tuck explains that this turn toward critical consciousness is a signal of the "complex personhood" these youth developed as they came of age and into their own sense of "human agency, complicity, and resistance" to the systems of public education.[25] For example, when William Martinez graduated from Globe High School in 1916, he was the only Mexican American in a class of fourteen. His peers dubbed him "Mex," but William, who lettered in track and debate, defended himself with typical teenage bravado: "Greater men than I have lived, but I doubt it."[26] Similarly, when student Ida Celaya published her Spanish-language poem "El Adios de Una Senior" in the 1917 Normal School yearbook, *The Sahuaro*, her classmates noted her mood or "reaction" as synonymous with "El Club Hispánico." Known for her friendliness, the dark-haired poet established herself as the president of the Spanish Club and described her purpose at TNS as "forging ahead" (*"seguí delante"*). These students' journeys reveal how Arizonenses transformed educational ambitions from desert dreams into bonafide realities.

High School Origins in the Arizona Territory

Native American scholars and historians of education have documented how the public school infrastructure in the American Southwest emerged from territorial land grabs and state formation in the twentieth century.[27] The more familiar narrative of the development of the common school in the nineteenth century of the East Coast and Midwest centered not only on community building but also on the emerging divisive issues of controlling the factors of industrialization, urbanization, and immigration. Arizona was no exception, admitted as a state with New Mexico in 1912. The territorial legislature authorized the creation of public schools through the eighth grade in 1871 with the passage of the Safford-Ochoa Act.[28] More than a dozen years later, in 1885, the territorial legislature agreed to open and finance public institutions of higher education. However, high schools were the missing link in the developing landscape of public education in Arizona.

Prior to the 1895 high school act, public school systems adopted a variety of ad hoc strategies to extend schooling for advanced students.[29] The public schools of Tucson offered secondary coursework as early as 1880, as did other public schools, including Prescott, where Amelia Hunt earned her diploma. The 1887 public school laws charged local school trustees to adopt textbooks "as they may deem best" for "high school studies."[30] Larger towns provided a "high school course," as it was described by the acting governor of Arizona to the U.S. Secretary of the Interior.[31] Some private religious schools, such as St. Johns Stake Academy (Mormon) and the Tucson Catholic schools, also offered high school work.[32] The twenty-five high school pupils reported in Tombstone Public Schools in 1893 also represented some of these early high schoolers.[33] Superintendent J. M. Wollam of Phoenix spearheaded high schooling in the territory's largest district. In 1893 and 1894, Wollam organized new courses of study and a library; he also convinced the board of trustees to move the high school from the Opera House, which he called a "death trap," into the new public "Central School Building."[34] In the early 1890s, secondary coursework expanded to a full four years. Seniors took courses ranging from zoology, geometry, civil government, and Caesar to learning practical skills such as shorthand and "type-writing."[35] Prior to the passage of the territory-wide high school act, Phoenix held bond elections for building a high school.[36] Overall, at the cusp of the formal passage of the high school act, the territorial superintendent of education reported that there were only 188 high school students in 1893 and only 258 in 1894 across the territory.[37]

The top tier of public institutions, the Territorial Normal School and the University of Arizona, also attempted to close the gap between the small number of university-level-ready students and the lack of public high schooling when they opened in 1885. At Tempe, students who had completed grammar school, or the eighth grade, could begin a "full four-year high school course" and then continue into the "two-year professional course" that would prepare them for teaching in the public schools.[38] Tempe offered the high school preparatory course through the 1920s.[39] The University of Arizona also provided a one-year preparatory course for students who had not completed high school. The course, as they described it, was not intended to replace a "common-school education, but simply ... prepare students for taking up the technical work in the schools [colleges] now organized in the university."[40]

The struggles that progressive educators and civic boosters in the Arizona Territory faced to establish high schooling mirrored some of the issues educational historians have recounted in studies of individual or citywide initiatives in the Northeast and Midwest. Most historians agree that Boston English Classical School, established in 1821, was the first public high school in the United States.[41] Historians closely examined a pre-Civil War controversy in which citizens voted to close a high school in Beverly, Massachusetts, using petitioners' occupations and addresses to analyze their motivations.[42] During the economic and social strains of American society in the immediate pre- and post-Civil War years, the expense and necessity of high schooling was still tenuous.[43] However, by the late 1880s and early 1890s, high schools had become institutions where middle-class parents believed their children could secure upward mobility, and boosters viewed them as vital to attract enterprising residents. No longer dubious, high schools became permanent components of public school systems and faced few detractors.

The Arizona Territory also experienced both proponents and detractors of high schooling in the foundational years. Phoenix, for example, faced an injunction against its newly approved union high school tax levy in 1895. Nathaniel "Captain" Sharp employed the law firm of Cox & Wills to enjoin the county board of supervisors from taxing citizens for the union high school, alleging that proper voting procedures were not carried out.[44] When the case rose to the Territorial Supreme Court in Case 514, *Sharp v. Board of Supervisors of Maricopa County (AZ)*, the justices affirmed that the county acted properly and taxes could be levied in all twelve districts encompassing Phoenix Union High School (PUHS).[45] Whereas debates on secondary schooling in other regions largely revolved around social class, immigrant integration, and accusations of elitism, the central question in the territory's high school development pertained to the issue of whether high schools should operate within a single district, or consolidate to serve two or more elementary districts.[46] The 1895 high school act allowed single school districts with at least two thousand residents to establish a high school, or adjoining school districts with a combined population of two thousand to form a "union" high school. Some counties also operated consolidated high schools for rural school districts. Regardless of its district form, the call for any new high school required a petition by at least one hundred voters, followed by a local election to approve a tax levy to fund it. The city of Phoenix voted in April 1895 to open the Phoenix Union High School District No. 1, which enrolled white students from the city and eleven rural districts across the Salt River Valley into one downtown high school.[47] Considered the first official territorial high school, PUHS had four male teachers and graduated its first senior class of two students in May 1896, even though Tucson schools had done so in 1893 under the direction of Professor Charles H. Tully, the well-known Tucsonense educator.[48] Tucson offered a three-year high school course as early as 1880, but it operated inconsistently given personnel changes and the opening of the University of Arizona's preparatory department in 1885. Tucson High School marked its formal opening with a class of forty-five in fall 1906.[49]

By statehood in 1912, Arizona taxpayers had opened seventeen high schools with 1,824 students; by 1920, thirty-eight high schools existed with nearly 5,500 students.[50] PUHS was by far the largest with more than 1,300 students, followed by Tucson High School with over five hundred. In 1930, with 4,400 students registered in day courses (and another 4,000 in its night school), PUHS claimed to be "the largest high school in the inland Southwest" and "west of the Mississippi."[51] That year, Arizona operated forty-one high schools, each organized according to local needs, including county high schools that reflected the small size and diversity of the towns they served. Some high schools offered coursework from seventh to twelfth grades; others admitted students at the ninth grade and offered evening classes for adults. An hour north of Phoenix, the Wickenburg High School, for example, held its first high school graduation commencement in 1927 for a class of five seniors—Ivy Letha Deming, Arthur García, Marcela Andrea Ocampo, Lucile Pauline Rogers, and Cassie Ethel Walker.[52]

As territorial Arizona crafted its educational infrastructure, Mexican American youth whose families could afford to send them to school considered a range of secondary and postsecondary opportunities. In small towns and rural counties where high schools had yet to emerge, some youth continued in "high school studies." In the larger, urban centers, such as Phoenix, they attended newly built territorial high schools. In Tempe and Tucson, they enrolled in preparatory courses that led to college programs. Because the territorial high schools and higher education institutions grew simultaneously in the last decades of the nineteenth century, the first cohorts of Arizonense high schoolers and collegians also attended and graduated from these institutions concurrently. The next sections of this chapter consider these students' experiences through the 1920s as they pursued high school and collegiate opportunities.

Finding the Right Path to High School and College

Before Arizona's secular and private religious high schools officially organized in the 1880s and 1890s, elite and middle-class Arizonense parents sought options for their sons to attend secondary schools across the Southwest. Many of these parents hailed from among the professional, immigrant classes or from families that had sustained some capital after the U.S. conquest. The Tucsonenses preferred to send their sons to Catholic colleges, such as St. Michael's in Santa Fe or St. Vincent's in Los Angeles, since many had familial connections in those places or had attended the schools themselves, such as Carlos Tully, who graduated from St. Michael's in 1869. At these college preparatory schools, boys completed the high school diploma and college coursework. Tucson merchant Rosario Breña's younger brother Ramón Rafael attended St. Vincent's College, which advertised its classical, commercial, scientific, and engineering degrees in the *Arizona Daily Star*.[53] He graduated with a commercial business degree in 1896 and returned to Tucson, where he owned a brokerage firm.[54] Yuma merchant José M. Molina took his oldest son Ignacio who was fourteen on a tour of "potential colleges" in Santa Clara, San Mateo, and Stockton, California, before deciding on Stockton (probably the University of the Pacific).[55] Ignacio remained at the college for at least two years, before returning in 1896 to work as a salesman in his father's general store. Sonoran Evarista Cañedo, the widow of William Cartwright Barney also of Yuma, sent her son James Mitchell Barney to school in California when his father died. His paternal grandfather enrolled him in private schools and, later, Stanford University (with future president Herbert Hoover). Barney graduated in 1901 before returning to Phoenix.[56]

Arizonense parents required their daughters to remain close to home, however, or under the close supervision that Catholic convent schools and, later, the normal schools provided. The convent schools, such as Sacred Heart Academy in Phoenix, operated more like finishing schools, offering courses in needlework, music, and languages, but, in some cases, girls, like Amelia Hunt who attended the Prescott Academy operated by the Sisters of St. Joseph, learned the foundational skills that prepared them to enter high school and pass teacher certification exams. Amelia Hunt later sent her eldest daughter, Adela García, to "the convent school at Prescott," too.[57] The appeal of the Catholic academies and colleges stemmed from their cultural familiarity as Mexican and Mexican American families historically patronized them and the religious orders "actively recruited" their daughters as students and novices.[58] In 1877, Sister Clara of the Blessed Sacrament (Gabriella Martínez Otero), a descendant of a prominent land-grant family from Tubac, entered the first class of novitiates with three other Mexican American women at the Tucson convent of the Sisters of St. Joseph of Carondelet.[59] Sister Clara trained as a teacher and worked at St. Joseph's Academy and other convent schools. TNS graduate Petra Ochoa Diaz's three oldest daughters—Josefina, Hortencia, and Amelia—joined the teaching order of the Sisters of the Immaculate Heart of Mary. Known as Sisters Josephine, Gertrude, and Regina, respectively, they were distant paternal cousins of Sister Clara.[60] The Catholic orders also provided gendered instruction in secondary and higher education as in the case of the northern California colleges: Santa Clara College for men and Notre Dame College for women. At these colleges, one-quarter to one-half of the students hailed from "Spanish" families. Historian Victoria-María MacDonald attributes these higher enrollments to "the Catholic Church [which] represented a smooth continuity and accommodation with Spanish language and religion." This trend also paralleled educational patterns in Latin America from the colonial period through the twentieth century where privileged daughters often attended private, Catholic colleges, and poor daughters received basic schooling through charitable Catholic societies.

Given that the Catholic orders had barely established themselves in the Arizona Territory and emerged simultaneously with government-sponsored public schools, the Normal School became a popular destination for Arizonense daughters from its founding in 1885. While it was coeducational, as a teacher-training institute it attracted far more young women than men. It offered several courses of study, ranging from four years of high school to two years of professional teacher training. Its appeal may also have stemmed from the presence of Tempe's well-established Arizonense community whose roots extended to the 1870s. Not only had the Tempeneños developed the irrigable lands of the East Valley, but they also established a Catholic church called Our Lady of Mount Carmel across the street from the college and maintained some political clout in the town leadership. In 1898, "Mexican voters" elected Samuel Brown (of Anglo-Mexican heritage) to the town council and, in 1902, as mayor.[61] That same year, the Alianza Hispano-Americana voted for Brown to succeed Mariano Samaniego as its *suprema*, or supreme president, a post he held until 1927.[62] Brown had organized the Alianza's Tempe Lodge No. 5 in 1897.[63] As the leading official of the largest Mexican mutual aid society and insurance company, with membership across Arizona, the Southwest, and northern Mexico, Brown's reputation extended across the borderlands. Arizonense parents wondering about the safety of their daughters in a coed college town only had to look to Brown whose daughter Frances attended the Normal School, which in 1901 changed its name to the Tempe Normal School (TNS).[64]

As public institutions of higher education, U.S. normal schools were notable for democratizing access to high school and college, especially for women; the middle and working classes; immigrants; and racial, ethnic, and religious minorities, including African Americans, Latinos, Jews, and Catholics. Historians typically describe normal schools as institutions that provided education and professionalization to "the masses and not the classes," similar to modern-day junior or community colleges.[65] Despite their locale or their status as gendered or segregated institutions, normal schools in the Progressive Era "opened a form of higher education to those types of students who would struggle for access to mainstream higher-education institutions for decades to come."[66] The presence of normal schools, especially for women, contrasted significantly with the private liberal arts colleges and public university campuses reserved for elite, Anglo-Saxon Protestant men.

Among Mexican American women in the Southwest, educational opportunity was meted out against a gendered, sociopolitical context. Female minority students at majority-white normal schools "remained outside the mainstream of campus life" even though they shared similar working- and middle-class backgrounds.[67] The TNS was a typical example of the turn-of-the-twentieth-century normal school from its "Old Main Building" to its gendered literary societies. According to historian Christine Ogren, few

Mexican American daughters who were considered "non-black, minority students" attended normal schools in this era.[68] Cecil E. Evans, president of Southwest Texas State Normal School in San Marcos (where President Lyndon Baines Johnson attended from 1927 through 1930) attributed the low enrollment of Mexican American students to failure at the primary and secondary levels. "Very few Mexican students ever get high enough in the grades to reach us."[69] Indeed, as noted previously, few Arizonenses possessed the eighth-grade certificate required for TNS matriculation compared to white students. Nevertheless, a small group of Mexican American women and men would later integrate themselves and their interests into the curricular and extracurricular character of the institution as it grew in the early decades of the twentieth century.

Besides the TNS and the limited territorial high schools, Arizonense youth also considered professional training options, such as normal schools in other states and business colleges that offered secretarial and administrative training. In remote towns and counties, such as Apache County, which was equidistant from the major centers of Phoenix and Albuquerque, youth such as Monico García and his younger brother Gregorio applied to such programs. When Monico was elected to *Who's Who in Arizona*, he described his education as a combination of the public schools and the normal course.[70] He completed "advanced" courses in the county public schools (St. Johns did not have a high school yet) and passed the teacher certification exam in 1897.[71] He taught briefly in Apache County rural schools before applying to the National Normal University in Ohio in 1899.[72] The *St. Johns Herald* reported Monico's departure and return from "the famous N.N.U. [National Normal University] at Lebanon O."[73] In the spring of 1900, Monico wrote to the newspaper about his progress. "It appears to me more plainly every day [*sic*] that if any person wishes to spend his days on the hills of fame or in the valleys of success adjacent, he must educate himself. It seems to me that nothing else can be so necessary to me as an education, and so I am determined to struggle on though an easier life may be within reach."[74] Decades later, after he served as a county school superintendent and while his own children completed college, he finished the bachelor's degree at the Northern Arizona State Teachers College (Flagstaff).[75] His brother, Gregorio, who was sixteen years younger, finished high school and took a secretarial course at Lamson Business College in Phoenix, which allowed him to work as a court reporter and study law. He passed the Arizona Bar Examination in 1919.[76]

The Arizonense High School Experience

Access to territorial high schools was complicated not only by locale and distance but also by the status quo of Jim Crow and Juan Crow race relations. Qualified Mexican American youth—that is, those who had completed eight years of schooling—were eligible to attend and enroll in Arizona's white high schools, unlike black youth who were segregated by both territorial and then state law. At Tempe and Phoenix high schools, the first Spanish-surnamed students began to appear on class rosters in the 1910s. Mariano Martínez graduated from Tempe Union High School in 1911, followed by Ophelia Celaya the next year.[77] At PUHS, the freshman "class roll" of 1911 included four Spanish-surnamed students: Albert Córdova, Sara Martínez, Rafaleta Ochoa, and Fernando Rodríguez.[78] While these Arizonense youth joined their white classmates, black youth attended segregated schools such as the Phoenix Colored High School, which was held in the PUHS basement and later moved to a small cottage on the campus grounds. In 1926, voters approved a bond to build a new building for the Phoenix Colored High School (later, Carver High School), which operated from 1926 to 1954 and enrolled black students from across Maricopa County. Many Indigenous high school students, whose education fell under the purview of the Bureau of Indian Affairs, attended the nearby Phoenix Indian School. When Tempe incorporated its union high school district in 1908, it enrolled mostly white students, a few Indigenous students from the nearby Gila River and Yaqui communities, and Mexican American students, including Eugenia Sosa, whose father worked as the high school custodian, and Ralph Estrada, who, like Ophelia Celaya, was the child of a merchant family.

For Arizonense students and parents, deciphering the racial scripts and codes of public education could be a dizzying process, not to mention learning the campus, district, and state regulations. Consider the school pathway of Elizabeth Muñoz, one of the daughters of immigrant Methodist missionaries, whose family moved regularly around the state during the 1920s and 1930s. Elizabeth attended "mixed Anglo and Mexican schools" outside Miami, Arizona, where Mexicans and Anglos sat on opposite sides of the same classroom. She enrolled at strictly segregated "all-Mexican" schools in the towns of Tempe and Sonora-Ray. And she integrated an "all-Anglo" sixth-grade class at Adams (Grace Court) School in Phoenix, where Mexican children who spoke "enough English" were allowed to attend.[79] After successfully passing the eighth grade and earning the primary school certificate as did her

Figure 6. Rebecca, Lucinda, and Elizabeth Muñoz with their father, Reverend Esaú Pérez Muñoz, July 1932. Courtesy of Rebecca Muñoz Gutiérrez Photographs, MP SPC 323, Arizona State University Library.

older siblings, Elizabeth advanced to PUHS. At Phoenix Union, the seven Muñoz siblings—including Rosalío, Lucinda, Rebecca, Elizabeth, Josephine, Solomon, and Abel—decoded yet another set of rules as they adjusted from segregation to integration. Their parents took an active role in their course selection to circumvent counselors who tracked the children into vocational classes "such as shorthand, typing, bookkeeping, and other secretarial classes."[80] Elizabeth's oldest sister Rebecca recalled that they were allowed to take the "[college prep] classes so long as they continued with the Mexican track of classes, so that they would have something they could fall back on in case they failed the college prep classes."[81] Decades later, Rebecca reflected on how her siblings utilized the dual tracks "to their advantage" by working their way through college with those business skills.

The Muñoz siblings graduated from Phoenix Union in the early 1930s, but scholars, then and now, have struggled to determine how many Mexican American high school students graduated before World War II. Arizona school districts and colleges rarely collected or published data that measured the educational progress of Mexican American youth; state and federal data sources also omitted them. This study, for instance, relies on counts of "Spanish surnames" in yearbooks and accessible student data drawn from public sources. Historians Victoria-María MacDonald and Alice Cook explain that the U.S. decennial census and the National Center for Education Statistics (NCES) did not count Mexican Americans and other Latina or Latino groups until the 1970s and 1980s because they were considered "legally white."[82] The one time that the U.S. Census Bureau accounted for "Mexicans," specifically in 1930, it omitted questions on education. MacDonald and Cook, more importantly, ascertained that these omissions confirmed a second national trend—that *before* 1950, Mexican American youth were effectively excluded from high school participation. Among adults over the age of twenty-five, white girls graduated from high school at nearly three times the rate of Mexican American girls (24.6 percent vs. 9.8 percent), while white boys graduated at nearly two times the rate of Mexican American boys (19.3 percent vs. 10.3 percent).[83] MacDonald and Cook argue that such low graduation rates signaled a "cumulative effect of high school exclusion" for Mexican American youth in the generations prior to the Servicemen's Readjustment Act of 1944 (the G.I. Bill) and the national civil rights movements.

The absence of conclusive national and state data from the first half of the twentieth century reflects deeper perceptions of the educational era. First, western educators generally perceived Mexican American academic achievement as nonexistent because they also believed that Mexican Americans as a group were intellectually incapable of school success. This perception resulted in school policies and programs aimed at Americanization and workforce preparation, which contemporary scholars describe as subtractive schooling where the intent is to strip children of their ethnic heritage.[84] Second, the lack of data also resulted from the disregard of Mexican Americans as a class of people, as well as the inconclusive ways that social scientists categorized Mexican-descent populations in major governmental data sets that regularly tracked individual educational attainment as well as citizenship. In this era of immigration restriction, which resulted in the 1924 Johnson-Reed Act (the quota act) and the formation of the U.S. Border Patrol, educational studies tended to fuse Mexican Americans with Mexican immigrants. For example, in the 1925 Arizona school survey, Charles Ralph Tupper presumed that every Mexican-heritage person was an immigrant. He generally conflated the "Mexican Problem" with the "Foreign Born Problem" given that the majority of Arizona's foreign-born population also claimed Mexican heritage. "The problem of the foreign born element in Arizona is typically a Mexican problem, and more so than in any state in the union. It is concerned with a group of immigrants more recent than any group in any state; it is the problem of a group coming from a country classed as three-fourths illiterate, a country harassed by revolution, unrest and lawlessness. In magnitude, and in degree of difficulty, Arizona has one of the most serious foreign-born problems existing in the state."[85] Tupper focused on the school attendance patterns of children in the "foreign born" category because Arizona possessed the largest proportion of foreign born children in the nation, ahead of Texas and New Mexico. These children comprised roughly 15 percent of Arizona's total school population, age five to fourteen. Tupper concluded that even though Arizona had "a larger proportion of foreign-born children than are found in any state . . . [, it also] gets a smaller percentage into school than any state."[86] Only 61.3 percent of them had ever attended school—the worst ratio of school attendance among foreign-born children in the nation.

Tupper knew his assessments of Mexican-heritage children were based on incomplete data. He graduated from Stanford University where he taught courses on survey methods and was mentored by Dr. Lewis Terman, the renowned educational psychologist known for intelligence testing and eugenics. Tupper would have recognized the dilemmas that stemmed from the haphazard records collected by school districts, which did not detail student demographics. The data also suffered from the flaws in classification of U.S. Mexicans as legally white and from local officials' perceptions of students' racial identities, such as a teacher's judgment about whether a child might be Mexican. As a member of the Arizona State Board of Education, Tupper spent two years studying the state's existing records alongside sources such as the U.S. Census in order to complete the 1925 survey. In this process, he stitched together piecemeal data to clarify who exactly might comprise the category he defined as the "Mexican pupil" and he whittled a statistical profile of the Arizona Mexican from various census categories.[87] "Spanish-American people constitute 76 percent of the foreign-born, 65 percent of the total foreign stock, 31 percent of the white population, and 27 percent of the total [Arizona state] population." From this aggregation, he determined the one-in-six ratio of Mexican American high school eligibility. Tupper's "Mexican pupil" possessed a wide range of origins and very low academic achievement. Or, as he described: "In general, the type of Mexican child taken into the Arizona schools tends to be backward in rate of mental development, lags a year or two behind other pupils, shows a heavy failure percentage, and an early elimination from school."[88]

Since Tupper, few education scholars have attempted to quantify the high school patterns of Mexican American youth in the five southwestern states before 1950. In a study focusing on interwar years, MacDonald concluded that Mexican Americans did not experience the upward mobility that high school provided to other youth. She describes a "fractured pipeline" that cut off Mexican Americans from high school.[89] Building on the work of Sylvia Martínez who assessed similar patterns from 1940 through 1980, MacDonald extrapolated the median years of schooling for Spanish-surnamed males who were born between 1906 and 1924 to build a general estimate of the overall education of the Mexican American population.[90] Educational attainment "ranged from a low of 5.6 years [Texas] to a high of 10.4 years [California]."[91] In Arizona, Spanish-surnamed students averaged 6.0 years of schooling— two years less than Tupper's estimate in the 1925 state survey. In MacDonald's words, "The overwhelming proportion of these youth before 1954 were blocked, discouraged, or pushed out through extralegal means."[92]

By turning to the experiences of the "Fortunate Few," such as children from the Barney, Grijalva, Muñoz, and Rosas families who are introduced here, we can distill a portrait of Mexican American high school students in the early decades of the twentieth century. Their experiences can help us understand the significance and outcomes of high school graduation for this small minority. These Arizonense youth came from varied Mexican-heritage and mixed-status families. The Barney and Grijalva children were American born; the Rosas children were Mexican born. The older Muñoz children were born in Mexico, while the younger children were born in the United States. The naturalization status of all the children also varied; some were not U.S. citizens and others became U.S. citizens upon their parents' naturalization, which was the case for the younger Muñoz children.[93]

Arizonenses harnessed the fluidity of race, economics, and social class to engage their "legally white" status and to ensure their children's educational access. Economic and social class factored critically in all four families and often determined the ways that Anglo Americans perceived their racial identities. James Mitchell Barney Sr. and his wife Jesús "Jessie" Zazueta offer one example. As a Stanford man of Anglo-Mexican heritage, James Sr. easily found employment as a government surveyor when he returned to Arizona, and he gained notoriety as the "unofficial state historian" for a regular newspaper column that he wrote about the region's early settlement. In the early 1900s, the Maricopa County school marshal registered the four Barney children—Ernestine, Walter, James Jr., and William—as "white" and "native born" to "native born parents." This judgment, which if taken literally could be considered erroneous, demonstrates how social class "whitened" Arizonenses. The census taker made assumptions likely based on Barney Sr.'s reputation because his wife Jessie was an immigrant. She was born in Mexico, naturalized in 1888, spoke Spanish as a natal language, and reported her parents as French and Spanish.[94] All four Barney children attended PUHS in the 1920s. By the time James Jr. and Walter Barney began their freshman year together in 1920, they joined more than a dozen fellow Arizonenses.[95]

Similarly, their distant neighbors Higinio "John" García Grijalva and his wife Elisa Alvarez came quite early to the territory as naturalized citizens, but their economic success elevated their racial status. John was born in the early 1860s in Altar, Sonora, and entered Yuma in 1870. Elisa was born at Hermosillo in 1871, was naturalized in 1878, and had lived in Phoenix since 1882. By 1910, the couple owned a significant farm and ranching spread in central Phoenix at 12th Street and Henshaw, just south of the Southern Pacific Railroad. The census enumerators listed the Grijalva family, including their five children—Carmen, Carlos, Marie, Ernesto, and Raoul—as "white" and as "Mexican." Marie and her younger brother, Raoul, attended Phoenix Union together in 1911.[96] Marie disappeared from the yearbook the next year, but Raoul graduated from Phoenix Union in 1916 and from Lamson Business College in 1917. He eventually joined the Magma Mine Co. in Superior as paymaster, one of the rare Mexican-heritage men to work "above ground" in the company's central office for decades. To Mexican miners, such as Ramón R. Denogean who began working at the smelters in 1929, Grijalva's role as paymaster "mean[t] a lot. He was a big office guy."[97]

Phoenix Union enrolled roughly one hundred students in 1895 and by 1935 its senior class alone had more than seven hundred students, including Lucinda and Rebecca Muñoz.[98] With its claim as the largest high school in the Southwest, its shallow numbers of Mexican American students give us a sense of the obstacles Arizonense students faced as they confronted racism and classism, but it also showed the opportunities that educational privilege extended. Few Spanish-surnamed students appear in the extant yearbooks from the high school's opening, but among those who did, their presence is clearly discerned as they often became exemplars of Americanization as well as race representatives. The 1935 Phoenix Union yearbook featured a romanticized Mexican art theme partly in tribute, the editors wrote, to "the number of students of Mexican extraction."[99] Their school popularity and their engagement in extracurricular activities signaled toward levels of economic and social class privilege hard won by their parents. Yet it appears that they also used their bicultural and bilingual assets to cultivate their own identities within student politics and as they entered their postsecondary lives.

The Rosas brothers—Alejandro "Alex," Felizardo "Felix," and Oscar—were among the earliest Mexican American students at Phoenix Union in the 1910s.[100] Originally from Hermosillo, Sonora, they deployed their educational advantage to embark on glamorous lives. Their desires stemmed, in part, from the tireless ethic of their parents who worked as candymakers at Donofrio's Candy Store on Washington Street in downtown Phoenix.[101] Although the boys and their sisters Amanda and Matilde often worked at Donofrio's, too, the boys used their high school diplomas to acquire clerkships and worked as professional stenographers most of their lives. Upon graduation in 1914, the oldest son, Alex, hired on as a stenographer for the Walter Hill Company, a grocery wholesaler, but his true ambition was entertainment. His younger brother, Oscar, remained at Phoenix Union through 1916 and by then their brother Felix had secured a desirable secretarial job with the silent movie star Romaine Fielding, who fronted the southwest branch of the Lubin Film Company.[102] Alex, however, possessed the gift of song, a baritone voice worthy of an opera career, and the dashing good looks of a leading man.[103] By the 1920s, he had traveled to Italy to study under the renowned baritone Mario Sammarco and subsequently debuted the part of Figaro in an Italian production of *The Barber of Seville*. Rosas later became a well-known singer and radio personality across North America as he was often broadcast on NBC as a lead singer of Mexico City's Orquesta Típica.

Arizonense youth in towns north and south of Phoenix also aspired to the promise of education and the exhilaration of extracurricular student activities and socialization. In northern Arizona, Navajo County, brothers Juan and George I. Sánchez enrolled at Winslow High School (WHS) as juniors in 1922.[104] Having transferred from the high school in the nearby town of Jerome, the brothers seamlessly matriculated at WHS with unfaltering academic and extracurricular participation. WHS became the second of three high schools the brothers attended in Arizona and New Mexico, while their father worked off and on at the United Verde copper mine in Jerome. Their father, who was politically active and a registered voter, was also a union member and likely involved in the strikes that led to the Jerome Deportation of 1917 (which occurred two days before the infamous Bisbee Deportation).[105] Despite their short time at WHS, the Sánchez brothers left a clear imprint. Elected to the staff of the WHS student yearbook, *The Sandstorm*, George carefully documented their activities. They participated in the band, orchestra, drama, and the newly formed Spanish Club called "El Pasatiempo." They earned excellent grades, which landed them on the Honor Roll. George, who was known as "Isadore" (his second name being "Isidoro"), earned honors in five of the seven grade reports that year, outshining his older brother who earned honors only once. George also showed his early inclination for discourse, as an actor in school plays and as a member of the WHS debate team that participated in the Arizona Debating League and "inter-school debates."[106] At a Parent Teacher Association (PTA) meeting, George argued the affirmative in a debate that addressed the immigration question: "Resolved, that further legislation to restrict immigration into the United States would be injurious to the industrial development of the country."[107] Imagine the conversations that George and his labor union father must have enjoyed over this topic!

Juan and George were two of only ten Spanish-surnamed WHS students, who made up less than 10 percent of the student body (10 out of 117), even though Mexican American children may have comprised more than 50 percent of the district's total student body.[108] The ten students included senior Louis Sandoval; juniors Isadore Sánchez, Juan Sánchez, and Archie Garduño; sophomores Lewis Chacón, Soledad Cabrera, Vicente Gallegos, and Alice Gallegos; and ninth-graders Ella Garduño and Christina Ortega. George Kimura, a Japanese American student and the only Asian American student, was also a sophomore. The yearbook staff noted how the high school's Spanish-language activities, such as their club El Pasatiempo and the production of the Spanish play *Zaragueta* by Miguel Ramos Carrión and Vital Aza, fostered a larger engagement with the town's Mexican American residents. According to the yearbook writers, "*Zaragueta*, the first Spanish play given by the High School proved very successful in that it was of great help to the Spanish students and also afforded a pleasant evening for the Spanish speaking people." Juan Sánchez, Lewis Chacón, and Vicente Gallegos joined the cast, with Vicente playing the lead role of Zaragueta, "a Madrid money-lender." Both Vicente and Juan served as elected officers of the Spanish Club. Their teacher Mary King, who directed the play and sponsored the club, advocated for the practical and "commercial value of Spanish," emphasizing how the WHS Spanish curriculum provided "insight to the customs and the characteristics of the people, in an attempt to bring about a more sympathetic understanding between English speaker and Spanish speaking people."[109] This open appeal to the local Arizonense community may have been the influence of the high school principal Grady Gammage, who, throughout his career as a schoolman, came to be a recognized advocate of Mexican American students, teachers, and their larger communities.[110]

Mexican American girls also made their presence known as talented students in the state's high schools. During their freshman year at Jerome High School, the Sánchez brothers surely must have known Cuca Tisnado, class of 1924. Though she only participated in the Glee Club her freshman year, she gradually joined a range of student clubs, including drama, orchestra, and athletics. Her steely eyed, senior portrait with wavy bobbed hair reflected determination and she must have been resolute in her opinions because the yearbook staff described her as defiant.[111] In the "Class Prophecy," she imagined herself as a gainfully employed teacher and living independently in a shared apartment with her best friend Johanna Svob, who hoped to work as the school secretary. Cuca graduated with a teaching degree from Northern Arizona State Teachers College in 1926.[112] Cuca's younger sister, Aurora Tisnado followed in her footsteps in 1929.[113] In Tucson, another future teacher, the young María del Socorro Terrazas Urias completed the eighth grade at Safford School in May 1928. She came from a long line of Tucsonenses who traced their heritage to the old presidio's Spanish founding and to which her parents harnessed their children's successful schooling.[114] Her father Antonio G. Urias, a member of the Woodworkers of the World, traveled across Northern Mexico as a sales representative for Steinfeld's department store. Her homemaker mother, Ignacia Terrazas, raised their ten children whom she named for her favorite literary characters. She also subscribed to four newspapers.[115] Like many teenage girls, María took her autograph book to school to collect memories and best wishes from her closest companions during the last days of spring. Her teacher, Miss Faith G. Richardson, contributed a positive entry, recounting how María was the third of her sisters to pass the eighth grade and to have completed "Food and Clothing work" with her at Safford. "I have become greatly attached to each of you and am sure your mother may be justly proud of her girls," Miss Richardson wrote. "I shall miss you as I have missed the others and shall follow you through your H.S. [high school] work with much interest."[116] Teacher after teacher raved about the Urias children. "To teach an Urias is always a pleasant piece of work. I have taught many and loved them all." Young María also received praise. "I shall miss your diligent work in my writing class," wrote Miss Madaline Spain. And Miss Balch (perhaps the same teacher who helped María Urquides), called María Urias: "one of my very best students." In the fall of 1928, María Urias entered Tucson High School following in the footsteps of her older siblings and cousins. She graduated with a bachelor's degree from the College of Education at the University of Arizona in 1937.[117]

By the 1920s, the threads of race, ethnicity, class, assimilation, and educational opportunity fused in the long-term enrollment patterns of Mexican
American youth in the public high schools. Understanding this, their parents
actively negotiated interpersonal relationships and social dynamics within
their local communities to ensure their children's access to secondary education. María Urquides' s older cousins, Evangeline and Genevieve Romo, grew
up in the twin cities of Ray and Sonora, Arizona.[118] Their father secured a lucra-
tive management position at the Ray Consolidated Copper Company that built
the two towns for its workers.[119] In Ray, "a sprinkling of Mexican Americans
with highly paid positions lived" with the whites while the Mexican miners
lived in a separate enclave called "Sonora."[120] Children from the two communities attended the Ray District No. 3, but they attended two different segregated primary schools through the eighth grade. By residing in Ray, the Romo's
guaranteed that their daughters would attend the "American" school, securing
their automatic promotion to the Ray High School. Sonora did not have a high
school and the district bused the few children who completed the eighth grade
there to Ray. From 1924 to 1928, Ruby Estrada (née López) remembered rid-
ing the bus from Sonora to Ray to attend high school with her three sisters.
She recalled that roughly "5 or 6, not more than 10" children completed the
eighth grade each year at the Sonora School, despite student body enrollments
that exceeded several hundred. Estrada and her siblings completed school
because their father owned a hardware and furniture store in Sonora, unlike
the majority of his customers who were miners. "My father was a businessman.
He had more money. He made more money. There was a big difference."[121]

The first decades of the twentieth century proved critical for Mexican
American school success. Doubly impacted by the Mexican Revolution and
World War I, these youth were encouraged to attend high school precisely to
preserve and to improve their personal, familial, and communal outcomes.
At the border, Douglas City Schools superintendent R. E. Somers noticed the
growing trend of Mexican American pupils passing eighth grade and attending high school. "We account for this fact in the increasing friendly attitude
on the part of the American pupils in the grammar and high schools [e.g.,
less race conflict]; greater interest in going to school due to more athletics and
play organization; and due to an awakened interest on the part of the Mexican parent in the education of their children."[122] Schools became friendlier,
more welcoming places and perhaps more engaging places for these youth
and their parents. Or it may be that Mr. Somers detected for the first time
in his community the Arizonense desire for education. He pointed to the

Figure 7. "Students in front of Sonora School, Ray School District, No. 3," 1920. The Ray Consolidated Copper Company built two towns for its miners in the mountains of Pinal County along with two segregated primary schools operated by Ray District No. 3. The Sonora School served as its "Mexican School." From the collection of the History and Archives Division, Arizona State Library, Archives and Public Records.

exemplary success of "five Mexican boys" who graduated high school and found employment at the local bank, as well as two Mexican American teachers—the sisters Concepción and Rose Faras—"who graduated from the local high and Arizona Normal schools" and taught in the Pirtleville School.[123] The academic and professional trajectory of the Faras sisters, Cuca and Aurora Tisnado, María Urias, and María Urquides and her cousins Evangeline and Genevieve Romo—from high school to college to professional teaching careers—became status quo for the most educated Arizonenses.

Arizonenses at the Tempe Normal School, a.k.a. the Arizona State Teachers College

By the time Frances Brown enrolled at the Tempe Normal School in 1904, a number of Arizonense heritage daughters and sons had graduated from the institution. In its first year, in 1886, the TNS enrolled thirty-three students and by 1936 it had awarded 3,522 diplomas, which was the last year it issued the two-year, teaching diploma.[124] Registrar's records and oral history corroborate Arizonense attendance at the TNS soon after its opening.[125] By 1896, Mexican American and Spanish-surnamed students, particularly young women, enrolled at the college nearly every year, completing high school degrees, two-year college diplomas, and baccalaureate degrees in education. As previously mentioned, a yearbook count suggests that about 150 Spanish-surnamed students attended the TNS through 1936 and about half earned the two-year diploma, qualifying them to teach in Arizona public schools.[126]

The TNS student body grew quickly at the turn of the twentieth century and its popularity as an educational institution stemmed from its academic leadership. In 1891, two TNS professors supervised 30 students; by 1900, six professors taught 131 students.[127] With the recruitment of a new president, Arthur John Matthews in 1900, the TNS aligned its academic programs with those offered by California normal schools at Chico, Los Angeles, San Diego, and San Jose, gaining accreditation from the California State Board of Education in 1902 and authorizing TNS alumni to teach in its grammar schools.[128] This dual certification for Arizona and California public schools increased attendance to 194 students in the school year 1903–1904 and 224 students in 1904–1905.[129] Between 1897 and 1915, Arizonense students, especially young women, became a recognizable presence on campus. These early TNS students included Anna Casanega, Nellie Casanega, Dora De Leon, Antonia Diaz, Concepción Faras, Rosa Jaime, Henry López, Eliza Loroña, Carmela Martinez, Concepción M. Mazón, Manuel Salvador Mazón, Anna Manuela Miller, Clara Miller, Rose Miller, Sallie Miller, Petra Ochoa, Marina Priest, Lourdes Priest, and Cresencio "Chris" Sigala.[130]

While the backgrounds of these Arizonense students remain fairly obscure, their social and economic standing probably mirrored that of Frances Brown and the early Tempeneños, such as the Jones, Miller, and Priest children who also attended. For example, Chris Sigala, who was born in 1874 in Sonora and came to Tempe as a child, enrolled in the 1890s, where he was lauded for his athleticism as a football and baseball player. He played right guard for the offensive line of the TNS Bulldogs (as they were then known) and his team won the first Thanksgiving Day championship for the coveted 1899 Territorial Cup against its rival the University of Arizona.[131] Sigala's stepfather, Miguel Oviedo, worked for the Hayden Flour Mill and saved enough money to purchase rental property in the San Pablo barrio. This suggests that the college's proximity, as well as the social and financial capital of some Mexican American families made higher education an obtainable option.

Some Arizonense students attended the TNS either with or in succession of one or more family members. This was the case for Chris Sigala, too, whose younger half sister Rose Oviedo attended in 1917.[132] The presence of students with shared surnames, such as the Mazóns and the Casanegas, suggested that these parents and extended families could afford to send multiple children to high school and college. For example, sisters Anna and Nellie Casanega first attended the TNS Training School, a laboratory grammar school operated by the college, before enrolling in the Normal school's high school program. The girls boarded at the school or in a private home, as their parents resided in the southern Arizona town of Calabasas, near Nogales.[133] Their immigrant parents, Thomas Casanega, who was Austrian, and Julia (neé Parra), who came from Jalisco, owned a ranch where they raised cattle and farmed commercial staples, such as cabbage and watermelon.[134] When their daughters graduated, they returned home, and Anna taught school.

The class standing of these families mattered because paying for college was costly, given the combined expenses of tuition, books, housing, and personal items, such as clothing, transportation, and supplies among other necessities. In its first year of operation, the TNS provided room and board through local families for $5-$6 per week ($20-$24 month).[135] By 1913-1914, the college charged a minimum of $16.75 *paid in advance* for board and shared dormitory quarters.[136] While many students, especially those from Maricopa County, lived at home or boarded near campus, the parents of Concepción and Manuel Mazón paid a minimum of $190 for tuition, room, and board for both their children to attend the TNS for one semester.[137] Concepción Mazón even paid fifteen dollars for one semester of tuition in lieu of signing a teaching promise that would have waived her fees.[138] In comparison, laborers such as Mexican miners earned two dollars a day for a ten-hour shift.[139] The TNS paid similar wages to day laborers such as Ramon Samora who earned $1.50 per day for odd jobs, such as moving furniture into buildings.[140] Work-study students earned similar wages. In 1906-1907, Rosa Jaime earned twelve dollars a month for assisting in the campus dining room or washing clothes.[141] Certainly, the parents of Rosa Jaime and other working students must have scrimped and saved to help pay their children's school fees.

Although most of these Arizonense youth benefited greatly from their family's financial security, questions of race affected their experiences and

constantly shifted their public identities. While school records offer no commentary on their racial backgrounds, this silence may suggest their Americanized or middle-class standing, as well as the state's ambiguous acceptance
of their whiteness. The state of Arizona never barred Mexican Americans
from attending its land-grant colleges and universities, yet racialized perceptions associated with ethnic heritage or acculturation of some Mexican American students can be gleaned from public documents. For instance, Mexican
American daughters who married white men secured a degree of white
privilege, if not inclusive white American identities, as well as non-Spanish
surnames for themselves and their children. After graduating in 1907, Rosa
Paula Jaime, for example, became "Mrs. Fred Dick," a fact noted on the Register of Non-Degree Graduates and the name that she used professionally and
publicly.[142] Eliza Loroña, who graduated in 1911, married Andrew J. O'Connor, a U.S. Customs Inspector from Redwood City, California, who was sta-
tioned in Nogales, Arizona.[143] Birth certificates for children born to Lourdes
Priest Martin in 1913 and Marina Priest Wellington in 1921 and 1925 note
their "race" or "color" as "American" and "white." Lourdes's husband George
worked as a "converter foreman" in Clifton, while Marina's husband worked
as an electrician in Glendale and then as Tempe's city manager.

Perhaps the most compelling evidence of the Americanization of these
Arizonense alumni stems from newspaper clippings. Marriages and deaths
relating to the young women highlighted the social pages of local newspapers. In 1906, a 5-inch column on the "Marriage of a Popular Tempe Girl"
recounted the union of Miss Sallie Miller, daughter of Winchester Miller and
María Sotelo. "She [Sallie] graduated from the Normal with the class of 1904,
and is a young lady highly regarded by a large circle of friends." Sallie married Mr. Paul Seitz, a New Yorker, employed by the Wells Fargo Company in
Nogales, Arizona.[144] Unfortunately, a few years after the wedding, the tragic
murder of Sallie's sister's husband generated bold, front-page headlines: "Phoenix Man Killed in North." Anna Manuela Miller, class of 1897, received notice
that an allegedly drunk sheepherder named Alejandro Gallegos shot her husband Louis Dozier Yaeger over a dispute involving their herds in the mountains
north of Prescott.[145] Originally from St. Louis, Yaeger and his extended family
owned a sheep-raising business. The reporter noted that a nearby saloon-
keeper whisked Gallegos into custody to avoid a lynching, while the young
widow and her three sons awaited Yaeger's body in Phoenix.[146]

The social standing of these Americanized daughters contrasted sharply
with others in their cohort who married Mexican men. Among daughters

of mixed Anglo-Mexican heritage, marriage to Mexican men lessened their social capital as more whites moved into the area.[147] When thirty-six-year-old, Kathryn "Kate" Gómez (neé Jones) gave birth to her sixth child, Ralph Frank Gómez, on September 4, 1909, the attending physician marked the mother's "race" as "Half breed, Mexican and American."[148] In 1911, when Kate had Inez, her seventh child, the same doctor called the mother "Mex."[149] This racialization reflected the eugenic beliefs of public health providers in the American West who mongrelized Mexican Americans as "half Southern European and half Amerindian" regardless of personal histories or individual accomplishments.[150] Kate's husband, rancher Jesús Gómez, migrated from Sonora and managed portions of his father-in-law's original homesteads in addition to his own twenty-three acres in Tempe. His status as a landowner, however, failed to recompense his Mexican lineage or diminish negative perceptions of his *mestizo* family despite his deceased father-in-law's reputation as the first medical doctor in the Arizona Territory. These racist attitudes, however, did not deter the family's educational aspirations as their daughters Inez and Mary later enrolled at the college.[151]

The questions of race, language, and education were ever present among Arizonenses, and debates over Spanish-language education did not escape the TNS, either. One question often raised to the territorial superintendent of public instruction was whether the TNS curriculum should include basic Spanish-language training for future teachers.[152] In September 1906, the TNS hired Gracia Lilian Fernández as its first Spanish professor.[153] Fernández came to the college with solid experience and academic credentials. Before moving to Arizona, she earned a bachelor's degree from the University of Maine (her home state) and taught in Cuba, Puerto Rico, and the Philippines.[154] On December 8, 1900, she passed the Arizona state teacher's examination with 1st Grade marks, the highest certificate offered, and taught for two years at the El Tule School in Apache County.[155] Since she renewed her teaching certificate in 1904, she probably continued teaching in Apache County until she joined the TNS faculty in the fall of 1907. In a joint appointment as librarian and Spanish professor, Fernández offered elementary and advanced Spanish as an elective within the professional teacher-training curriculum.[156] In 1908–1909, the TNS paid her a nine-month salary of $1,150 (approximately $128/month). She taught at the college for five years, through the spring of 1912.

Fernández's presence significantly influenced the TNS and its student body. She recontextualized the presence of Mexican American students at the college and the purpose of Spanish-language instruction into "race work."[157]

According to Fernández, the Spanish course served three student needs: "first, [for] those intending to teach in the Southwest where many descendants of the early Mexican settlers live; second, [for] those who may identify with the industrial development of Spanish-America where there is a constant demand for Spanish-speaking Americans with the necessary technical qualifications; third, [for] those students who wish to gain college entrance credit in modern languages."[158] Her professorial appointment slightly predates but parallels the goals of the Spanish American Normal School at El Rito, New Mexico, opened in 1909 to train Hispana women to teach Spanish-speaking students.[159] Although Fernández's purpose involved training mostly white students, her role as a "bridge person" legitimized Spanish as a course of study, which, alongside Latin, was the only other foreign language offered. She also provided students with a Hispanic role model. While she gave white students a sense of how Spanish might contribute to nation-building and Americanization work, she reaffirmed for Arizonense students the value of their Spanish-language skills and encouraged them to use bilingualism to improve themselves and their communities. Students such as Eliza Loroña who hailed from Tempe enrolled in the course.[160]

Like African American women in the South, ethnic-immigrant women in the Northeast, Chinese women in California, and *hermanitas* in New Mexico, Fernández used her vocation not only to educate white students about their culture but to exemplify how Mexican Americans could become "New Women" or "Best Women" who could combine personal fulfillment, educational achievement, and race pride to benefit themselves and their communities.[161] Fernández's teaching philosophy mirrored that of her New Mexican contemporaries Adelina "Nina" Otero-Warren and George I. Sánchez, who advocated education "to both preserve *Nuevo-Mexicanos*' traditions and uplift them economically."[162] Using the language of progressivism, Fernández explained in the 1908-1909 course catalog the advantage students would gain from learning Spanish. "A practical knowledge of Spanish has become a recognized factor in modern education, owing to its growing importance, in our colonial and international relations."[163] By 1910, Fernández's explanation took on a sophistication and self-assurance as she contextualized her work in the imperialist project.

> Spanish is the language of eighty millions of people, the greater part of whom now have active business relations with the United States. These relations are increasing rapidly through the acquisition of the Philippines and Puerto Rico, the steady investment of American

capital in Mexico, the constructing of the Panama canal, and, chiefly, on account of the trade possibilities North Americans have seen in the great rich territory of South America. In truth, the best business opportunities of the day are offered to Spanish-speaking Americans with the necessary technical qualifications to identify themselves with the industrial development of Spanish America.[164]

Her central teaching goal, as she explained, became "to have students think in Spanish as a living language." To this aim, she introduced students to the Spanish-language press and arranged for "correspondence . . . with some secondary schools in Mexico."[165] Fernández broadened her students' worldview beyond the parochialism of Americanization by sharing her perspective of American imperialism and globalization.

Fernández's groundbreaking work at the TNS generated long-term effects for incoming Mexican American students who now found the standard Spanish elective as one avenue for achieving academic distinction among their classmates. Although Fernández left TNS in 1912–1913, her replacement Edith Salmans continued the work with enthusiasm, creating opportunities for students to publish Spanish writings in the yearbook, to organize clubs, and to host plays and cross-cultural festivities.[166] In 1913, for example, Concepción "Chonita" Faras, who would go on to teach at the Mexican School at Pirtleville, published an essay in the TNS yearbook titled "Sueños de España."[167] Through a fictional dream adventure, she chronicled her yearlong Spanish studies, imagining herself in the home of three kings, not those from the Bible but the Spanish dramatists Pedro Calderón de la Barca, Félix Lope de Vega y Carpio, and Benito Pérez Galdós. After a gallant voyage abroad, Faras awoke to find herself at school and proclaimed, "Oh! Mis líricos sueños en ocaso! / Y tu mi infancia que ya no existes, / Cuantos recuerdos me dejas de tu paso." (Oh! My idealistic dreams in these my last years / And you my youth that no longer exists / How many memories you leave me on your passing.) Her sentimental yearning for the end of her school days mirrored the English contributions of her fellow classmates, but the presence of her Spanish text suggests the growing importance of Spanish as an elective at TNS and the growing presence of Mexican American students. Her essay cataloged the Spanish class's activities, which included an annual spring "musical and literary program entirely in the Spanish language."[168]

By 1917, the Spanish-language students formalized their annual spring reviews by officially organizing a new student association called "El Club

Hispánico" sponsored by Professor Edith Salmans. With twenty-three members, including Rose Buzan, Ida Isabel Celaya, Clotilde Colmenero, and
Aurora Morales, the club introduced interested students to "Spanish language and customs" and held regular meetings in Spanish given the caveat
that "we learn to do by doing." To showcase their scholarship, the club featured a poem by Ida Celaya, elected secretary-treasurer, on its yearbook
page. In "El Adios de Una Senior," she described how as an ignorant youth
full of ambition she had arrived at this ideal college that became her lan-
tern.[169] The Spanish students continued hosting regular literary programs,
including a "Christmas program with the Piñata" and a spring review "when
a number of Spanish people contributed to the pleasure of the evening." This
latter development suggests that the students envisioned the club as a portal
for cultural exchange between themselves and the regional Mexican American community.

By introducing Spanish curricula and contextualizing its regional utility,
Professors Fernández and Salmans integrated the TNS into the larger normal
school movements of the United States and Latin America. A 1909 graduate
of Ohio Wesleyan University, Salmans taught and held principalships at the
Preparatory School at Guanajuato, Mexico, and the Normal School at Puebla,
Mexico, before joining TNS in 1912. Both professors' backgrounds and
movements throughout the Americas mirrored older patterns of educational
development and exchange between Latin American and U.S. educators.[170]

Mexican American Student Life

By 1917, as a result of the recognition of the Spanish Club and their rising numbers, Mexican American women became a recognizable minority
at the TNS. From 1917 to 1920, three to four Arizonense women earned
diplomas each year, including both Rose Mary Faras, Concepción's younger
sister, and Ida Celaya, the Spanish Club poet, in 1917. Mexican American
women's attendance and graduation outpaced their male counterparts, which
was common among Anglo students, too.[171] For example, after Chris Sigala's football victories in 1899, the TNS yearbooks jump to 1914 before the
next Spanish-surnamed male student is noted. In the mid-1910s, a trickle
of Spanish-surnamed men, such as George Murillo, Louis Barrera, Henry
Armenta, and Chris Celaya, appear in the annuals.[172] In 1923, Tempeneño Ralph
Estrada graduated with Benton James, the first African American student and

graduate of the TNS.[173] Comparatively, African American women began enrolling with the class of 1928.[174]

In terms of retention, Mexican American women had more success completing the two-year professional course. By 1936, Mexican American women had earned sixty (83 percent) of seventy-two verified teaching diplomas and nine (60 percent) of the fifteen baccalaureate degrees compared to Mexican American men, who earned twelve (17 percent) teaching diplomas and six (40 percent) baccalaureate degrees.[175] Although no specific evidence within TNS records accounts for these trends, these local patterns mirrored national patterns of higher female enrollments at normal schools given the feminization of teaching and the wider range of professional opportunities open to middle-class men of the era.[176] For example, during World War I, Louis Barrera withdrew from the college to enlist in the U.S. Navy.[177] The TNS alumni association also reported that many white male graduates left teaching to pursue careers in law, banking, business, mining, ranching, agriculture, and the U.S. Civil Service.[178] Ralph Estrada followed this course as well, leaving teaching to practice law.[179] Conversely, women's limited career opportunities, the social sanctity of the teaching occupation, and the long-term financial investment in a daughter's education further propelled many of these young Mexican American women to complete the degree.

For these early alumni, the implementation of Spanish-language courses and the founding of El Club Hispánico created a foundation for Mexican American student life on the TNS campus. While El Club Hispánico limited its membership to twenty-five students per year including whites, over the course of the 1920s and early 1930s the club became a gathering place for Mexican American students. Dozens of Spanish-surnamed students claimed membership in El Club Hispánico or its successors Los Hidalgos del Desierto and Los Conquistadores.[180] Like other U.S. normal schools, the TNS boasted an elaborate network of extracurricular societies such as the Clionian Society, a literary society that Miss Salmans sponsored prior to the Spanish Club.[181] According to historian Christine Ogren, these societies proved critical to socializing normal school students into "'a higher degree of culture' through prestigious knowledge and social refinement, or elements of cultural capital."[182] The societies also supported private "library collections and reading rooms, which provided additional resources for class and society work, as well as general exposure to literary culture."[183] Unfortunately, Spanish-surnamed students rarely appeared on the membership rosters of these literary groups even through the 1920s.[184] For example, in 1915, Miss Salmans directed the

Clionian Society in "a study of Old Mexico, its history, art, literature, and people," yet not a single Spanish-surnamed student had been initiated into the society. However, with the formation of El Club Hispánico the presence of Spanish-surnamed students became noticeably consistent.

As a public forum for Mexican American students and sympathetic Spanish-speaking white students, El Club Hispánico provided a focal point for students to reaffirm their bicultural, bilingual knowledge and to integrate themselves into the college's social networks. As one of their mottos explained "Si es cierto Somos joviales/ alegres y sociales/ somos Los Hidalgos del Desierto."[185] Their emphasis on a positive collective identity and their self-referent as "hidalgos," or "nobility," aligned them with the middle-class standing that college enrollment secured for them, as well as an elitism they could attribute to their "Spanish" past. According to the class of 1934, they strove to "incorporate the ideals of honor, nobility, courage, love, warmth, color, and charm as exemplified in Cervantes's immortal *Don Quijote*."[186]

From 1917 to 1936, the club asserted its social status by annually sponsoring a yearbook page featuring a group portrait, membership lists, and rosters of elected officers.[187] Prior to 1917, only one Mexican American student, Concepción Faras, had gained any personal recognition in the yearbook and that was for a 1913 Spanish essay. After 1917, however, graduating club members listed their affiliation next to their senior portraits. Spanish Club membership saved senior Ida Celaya from the lowbrow humor of the 1917 yearbook staff that marked students' social identities under the category "Reaction" to suggest their campus reputation. If you had not established a campus identity or did not belong to any student association, the staff labeled you as "obscure" or "none perceptible," as were Rose Mary Faras and Rose Oviedo.[188] For other students, the membership tagline served as an indicator of their transition to the college or as a badge of pride. James Barney Jr. transferred to the TNS from Phoenix Junior College, after graduating from PUHS. Barney joined only two student groups his first year: the men's-only Letterman's Club and the Spanish Club.[189] When he earned his B.A. in 1928, he held seven memberships, in six athletic groups and the Spanish Club. Similarly, his classmate María Urquides boasted nine memberships. Next to her senior photo in the yearbook, she listed all of her affiliations, starting with the Spanish Club.[190]

Nearly a dozen Arizonense students served as club officers and Mexican American women held more leadership positions within the Spanish Club than in any other TNS student association. Three women—Aurora Morales (1917), Clotilde Fraide (1924), and Amelia Fraide (1925)—served as presidents. The Fraide sisters joined the club together in 1924 and graduated together in 1925. In back-to-back senior portraits featuring bobbed haircuts and high collars (including Clotilde's in fur), they noted the "Spanish Club" and the "Spanish Society" as their primary memberships.[191] Three more women—Teresa Palicio (1927), Elena Mendoza (1930), and Ida Ojeda (1934)—held vice presidencies, as did Richard Curiel (1923) who also served as secretary-treasurer and whose younger sister Blanche joined the club, too. Palicio and María Urquides both worked as the club's publicity chairwomen in 1927 and 1928, respectively, while Marion Figueroa assumed the secretarial post in 1930. This early leadership hinted toward an independent, feminist outlook and broader notions of women's competence.[192] This leadership also exemplified how these modern Mexican American women restyled gendered notions of community leadership from the barrio or ranch to the white university campus.

The Spanish Club, in fact, symbolized a microcosm of the emerging Mexican American community that these educated "new women" and "new men" espoused as part of the civic integration mission of their parents who attempted to sustain or to achieve solid American identities for themselves and their children. Through this process, the Spanish Club membership replicated patterns of class privilege and leveraged social capital to promote and to preserve the members' reputations as individuals and as a group on campus and within state politics. Like their fellow alumni of the 1890s, Mexican American students on the TNS campus in the 1920s and 1930s hailed from among the most financially secure Mexican American families and often entered the college with their siblings and cousins, who in turn joined the same organizations. Ida Celaya, for example, was the daughter of Antonio A. Celaya, a Tempe merchant who also served as the president of the Liga Protectora Latina, a statewide mutualista whose Tempe chapter was founded in 1915 by Ralph Estrada's older brother, Pedro.[193] Ida's first cousin María Celaya Escalante entered the TNS in 1919. Cousins Genevieve Romo and María Urquides, whose Tucsonsense father was a founding member of both the Alianza and the Club Demócrato Hispano-Americano, held simultaneous Spanish Club memberships, as did the Fraides and the Curiels.[194] Mary and Inez Jones Gómez also held memberships. According to the 1929 yearbook entry, the club held a campus-wide "fiesta in which we gave the faculty and students a glimpse of the beautiful, old Spanish customs, dances and songs."[195] For themselves, they hosted "Spanish suppers," "Spanish bridge parties," and "a banquet at La Casa Vieja," a prominent local restaurant, in addition to "informal dances and parties on our meeting nights."[196] These posh events predated the 1929 stock-market crash, but even in the midst of the Great Depression and repatriations that affected most Mexican American communities across the Southwest, the club hosted a "reception given at South Hall, honoring [college president and former Winslow High School principal] Dr. and Mrs. Grady Gammage, Señor E. C. Cota, the Mexican Consul at Phoenix, and his charming wife."[197] Clearly, these youth envisioned themselves as members of an elite leadership stratum.

By 1920, Arizonense students also pursued additional extracurricular activities alongside or in lieu of the Spanish Club. They joined the Young Women's Christian Association (YWCA), the Catholic Newman Club, the Hiking Club, the Pasteur Scientific Society, and the Inter-Racial Club, which brought together African American, Anglo American, and Mexican American students. They also participated in the annual college follies, numerous theatrical and musical productions, and orchestral and choral clubs, as well as the military cadets. For example, in 1927, Caroline Lupe Contreras helped found the Froebel Club.[198] Named for the German educator Friedrich Wilhelm August Froebel, the founder of the kindergarten movement, Froebel Club members specialized in early childhood education. In 1929, Contreras assumed the vice presidency of the club and completed her first degree, a "Special Kindergarten-Primary Diploma." Before she completed the B.A. in 1931, Contreras's resumé read like that of an All-American college woman. For her athleticism, she earned a Letterman sweater and coaches named her to four "all-star" teams—for women's volleyball, baseball, archery, and speedball (a field game that blended elements of basketball and soccer). One of the few Arizonenses to join a literary society, she also served as vice president of Phi Beta Epsilon.

Contreras represented the iconic student-athlete and her record exemplified one of the most significant avenues for Mexican American entrance into the TNS and into higher education generally.[199] Alongside memberships in the Spanish Club, Mexican American athletes at the TNS earned impressive individual reputations and campus popularity. They participated on the official college athletic teams, including football, baseball, basketball, volleyball, soccer, speedball, and track and field. For example, athletes Ralph "Wheto" Estrada (1920-1923), James "Google" Barney (1924-1928), and Carlos "Teammate" Jimenez (1930-1934) charmed the TNS student body with their athletic prowess and gained fanatic acclaim as heralded sportsmen. All three men lettered in multiple sports, proved vital to the Bulldogs' victories in individual and regional competition, and were elected to the exclusive all-male Letterman's Club. An athletic star at Tempe High School, Estrada brought his homegrown talent and victory to the TNS football, basketball, and baseball teams. In 1923, *The Sahuaro* yearbook dedicated a full page to "Captain Estrada," featuring the graduating senior in a full-body photograph.[200] Outside of academics and sports, Estrada joined only one student organization, Los Hidalgos del Desierto.

Perhaps Estrada's personal success paved the way for Barney and Jimenez, who followed him nearly in succession. Within a year of Estrada's departure, Barney arrived from Phoenix College, and he played football, basketball, and baseball.[201] He also joined the Spanish Club. In 1925, the TNS became a four-year college and Barney earned both the teaching diploma and the baccalaureate. He earned his way through school as "Coach Barney," managing and training the basketball second team. Known for his charisma, his classmates described him as a "good man" and "the fellow who kept the team full of fighting spirit." Within a year of Barney's graduation, TNS recruited "leather-lunged" Carlos Jimenez, a track-and-field star from Mesa.[202] Like Barney, Jimenez also became a student-worker, coaching a cross-country team of long-distance runners in his senior year and earning the baccalaureate in 1933. He served as president of Los Hidalgos del Desierto, but his classmates remembered him as "the boy who can run all day and then hike to Mesa at nights." The description suggests that he continued to live at home with parents or family members who did not own a vehicle. Many TNS students, especially those from within Maricopa County, commuted to school.[203]

Despite the publicity surrounding the athletic careers of these three men and the expanding extracurricular participation of many Mexican American or Spanish-surnamed students, questions of race, gender, and inequality also shaped their experiences. Aside from the "Spanish beauty" Della Eckardt whose photo appeared among the class favorites in 1923, no other Arizonense student gained the attention of the TNS student body or faculty in the way that Captain Estrada or Coaches Barney and Jimenez had.[204] Several Mexican American women, such as María Urquides and Caroline Contreras, lettered in as many sports and participated in more academic associations than their male counterparts but received little public or collegiate accolade for their achievements. Gender and racial prejudice also loomed large in the white, middle-class expectations of women's propriety that girded the academic curriculum. For example, Urquides recalled that Vera Chase, the critic teacher who nominated her for the Governor's medal and who was an expert on teaching the immigrant child, also voiced two concerns about her future in the classroom: "First, you have such a resonant voice that I'm afraid you might scare your students. Second, I don't know what you can do with your hair, but it never looks combed."[205] In all her yearbook photos, Urquides pulled her long hair into a bun at the nape of her neck. She wore the same style most of her professional life.

Acculturation and discrimination also penetrated students' lives in more complicated ways that stemmed from the insidious nature of institutionalized racism and the anti-Mexican prejudice prevalent in Arizona society. This subordination affected Mexican American students at the TNS. In a spoof of campus societies, the 1924 yearbook staff described the "Spanish Club" as "a bunch of Rudies and Vasalinesses banded together under a high-falutin' name. You can tell the male members by their side-burns, and the lady members by their 'tango fling.'"[206] Surely, Mexican American students saw past the casual jibe to the ethnic slur of "greasy Mexicans" using Vaseline hair tonic to slick their hair. Or worse, they may have internalized the white perception that Mexican Americans could only become, at best, cartoon versions of the Italian American silent-film star Rudy Valentino, known for his slicked hair and typecast roles as the "heavy" or "Latin lover." These kinds of microaggressions continued in yearbook banter about a new fraternity called "Tappa Kegs" sponsored by adviser "Señor Don Juan Morales."[207] No doubt, this pun intended to evoke the stereotype of the "drunken Mexican."

In contrast, other perceptions of Mexican people as "poor" or "laborers" (which many were) also affected Arizonense students. One group of civic-minded, white dormitory women collected recycled Christmas gifts and raised money to donate to the "needy Eighth Street children" who attended the segregated Mexican American training school operated by the college.[208] In oral histories, María Urquides expressed considerable awareness and concern about the racial climate on the campus. She recalled her first work-study assignment, "cleaning toilets," as her first bout with discrimination.[209] Having "clerked" in a department store while in high school, she had hoped to work as a "desk girl." Urquides's expectation was not unreasonable, as many students worked on campus to pay for tuition. The college employed students in the dormitories, in the dining halls, and in department offices. Yet college staff assigned students of color, especially African American women, "nothing but housecleaning." With the help of Professor Sally Hayden, Urquides instead found work as a "singer" at La Casa Vieja, a Mexican restaurant (later, a steakhouse), owned by Hayden's family. Still typecast, Urquides, nonetheless, honored her father's compromise, working her way through college until she graduated.

Race affected both women's and men's experiences on the TNS campus. African American students, for example, could not live on campus and usually commuted from Phoenix.[210] Prior to 1938, African American students participated in very few extracurricular associations. In 1928, for example, four of five African American seniors participated in the only club open to them: the Inter-Racial Club.[211] Urquides and a handful of white students joined them. While Mexican American students did not suffer these extreme forms of discrimination, ethnicity factored into all "setbacks" that they perceived. As a friend of Urquides's recalled, "I do not think that María allowed obstacles to frustrate her objectives. There may have been times that she was angry and resentful for not being chosen for something because she was a woman and a minority, but she never viewed the setback as a reason to slip into mediocrity. Rather, she saw it as a challenge."[212] This comment definitely negates the depth of the discrimination that may have occurred. Shortly after Urquides's graduation, her father died. College friends who came to express their sympathy were surprised to learn of the Urquides family's "Spanish" heritage. One friend even admonished her for not claiming her European heritage. "Why didn't you tell us you were Spanish and not Mexican? It would have made things easier." In her retirement, Urquides laughed off the remark as she shared it in an oral history. "I guess if I had told them that, I would have gotten a job doing something besides cleaning toilets!"[213]

Several white professors and white high school teachers who became mentors to Urquides and her cohort helped offset these kinds of challenges by helping them focus on their college goals and the promise of becoming educators. These teacher allies took an interest in these high-achieving Arizonenses and encouraged their higher educational pursuits, believing that they could go on to "teach their people." One of these critically important role models was ASTC Spanish Professor Irma Wilson, who assumed the sponsorship of the Spanish Club in 1923 and suggested its name change to Los Hidalgos del Desierto.[214] Wilson influenced the club and its mostly Mexican American members to study the culture and history of Mexico (not only of Spain), supported the members' social activities, invited them to her home for discussions about her travels, and often helped them pay for school supplies.[215] As the Mexican American students' ethnic consciousness developed through the 1920s and 1930s, Professor Wilson agreed to sponsor both Los Hidalgos del Desierto and their new political action club, Los Conquistadores, which continued to exist through the 1950s.

As each class of Mexican American students graduated from high school and college, they reiterated in yearbook farewells their original and continued aspirations to become educators and to fulfill the promise of civic integration. In the 1913 class prophecy, Chonita Faras indulged her originality and surprised her classmates by announcing her "big catch:" "I caught the position of Spanish teacher in the Douglas High School. I took a special course in it after my graduation at the Normal, having finished studying it in the University of Arizona."[216] In 1919, Rachel Orduño and Felicitas Colmenero decided to forgo Arizona for "teaching in Hawaii."[217] And just as Mary Balch had imagined for María Urquides, in the fall of 1928 Urquides actually returned to Tucson to assume her very first teaching assignment at Davis Elementary in the heart of Tucson's Westside Barrio Anita. These young educators soon discovered, however, that their personal aspirations would be challenged yet another time by the limitations of a society and public school systems that continued to promote Americanization and segregation as a pedagogical necessity for Mexican American students and teachers alike. As exemplars of Americanization, Arizonense teachers found themselves pigeonholed into assimilating children of their own heritage and virtually locked into elementary education.

Although civic integration provided an opportune strategy for Arizonenses to assert their visions of self and community, Anglo Arizonans held fast to the legacies of manifest destiny and Americanization. As citizens of the last of the forty-eight states admitted to the union, Anglo Arizonans strove to disconnect the state's reputation from a Mexican past and to promote its American future. To education leaders, this meant that they needed to double down on their efforts to Americanize every student who entered their public schools and to build a requisite infrastructure—from buildings to curriculums to personnel—geared to solving what they called Arizona's Mexican Problem.

CHAPTER 3

Mexican Americanization

On New Year's Eve 1917, Miss Evan Skinner replied to a letter from John C. Monahan, a rural school specialist at the U.S. Department of the Interior, Bureau of Education.[1] Monahan wanted a photograph and description of Skinner's experience teaching a one-room "Mexican school" near Congress Junction, Arizona, a mining town at the nexus of the Congress Consolidated Mining Company and the Santa Fe, Phoenix, and Prescott Railroad seventy miles north of Phoenix.[2] Unable to secure a photo because "no one around here has a camera," Skinner detailed for Monahan that Mexican American parents had founded the school and their Spanish-speaking children excelled in her classroom. She concluded that they were "intelligent and seem quite free from the usual Mexican vices of dirt, disease, and laziness. They seem to really enjoy coming to school. And that is unusual for Mexicans."[3]

Monahan and his research team explained Skinner's sentiments and those of her teacher colleagues in the 1918 report, *Educational Conditions in Arizona*. Based on seven months of fieldwork and a survey of more than 1,700 teachers, administrators, elected officials, and "prominent citizens," the Bureau of Education characterized Mexican American schoolchildren in Arizona as illiterate, overage, and unable to speak English. Statistics pointed to a high rate of school failure and a low rate of attendance due "chiefly to the presence of the large Mexican population, native and foreign-born."[4] The investigators estimated that at least 50 percent of Arizona's schools wrestled with a Mexican Problem and, as a result, needed to change their teaching and recruitment efforts to convince these children and their parents to participate in the educational system.[5]

Instead of acknowledging the high rates of Mexican American student attendance and engagement documented by teachers like Skinner, the investigators described Arizona's Mexican Problem as a broad class of genetic, pathological, and cultural deficits that physically and permanently afflicted the ethno-racial Mexican child. These inadequacies could not be cured, but they potentially could be rehabilitated.[6] Teachers described Mexican children as slow, unhygienic, and animalistic, such as young Ramón "whom the teachers in private dubbed 'Pig Brother.' He is like a pig in both looks and actions."[7] Teachers perceived that with "time, hard work and courage" they could teach these children "how to live [because] the textbook alone will never do this."[8] In their dedication, teachers believed they could transform ethnic Mexicans into English-speaking, hardworking Americans.

Arizona educators conceptualized Mexican American schooling through policies such as Americanization, and both Anglo Americans and Arizonenses responded to these initiatives. Philosophically, most Arizonans regardless of their racial background understood the idea of Americanization as the process of teaching the "language, customs, manners, laws, and ideals of America" to foreign-born and to U.S.-born ethnic groups.[9] Arizona's early schools established from the 1870s focused only on English-language acquisition, which Arizonenses generally supported. But after 1900 Anglo-American administrators developed a variety of school regulations and curricular programs, such as manual training and domestic science, that prepared Mexican-heritage children to enter a racialized, economic hierarchy of workers.[10] Educators also combined Americanization with segregation by using race, biology, language, and culture as markers for separate schooling, which Arizonenses challenged and endured well into the twentieth century.[11]

Mexican Americanization initially preoccupied Arizona teachers because these Mexican American youth constituted the population majority. Bureau officials reported that ethnic Mexican children comprised 50 percent of enrollments in twelve major cities and that roughly half of the state's 451 school districts had the "problem of teaching the English language to Mexicans."[12] The 1915-1916 school census figures for the twelve cities, which included only three border towns, showed a total enrollment of 49,051 children, half of whom were Mexican.[13] These towns included Bisbee, Clifton, Douglas, Flagstaff, Globe, Mesa, Nogales, Phoenix, Prescott, Tempe, Tucson, and Winslow. In fact, ethnic Mexican children had constituted this school majority since at least 1870.[14] This emphasis on a "Mexican majority" seemed incongruous with poor attendance rates, but the looming Mexican Problem overshadowed this paradox and pressed teachers to develop school reforms for Spanish-speaking children.

Arizona teachers prioritized Mexican Americanization in order to link their work to larger plans to whiten Arizona's national reputation. Americanization combined common school goals with Progressive Era ideals of nation building and civic responsibility. In 1910, Arizona had the lowest school attendance rate (53 percent) but also one of the highest population growth rates (sixth, at 22.5 percent) in the nation. Eighty percent of Arizonans hailed from outside the territory, reflecting Anglo-American westward expansion as well as Mexican labor recruitment in agricultural and mining industries. Arizona's 1912 statehood and the Bureau's 1918 report intensified Americanization efforts as national and international politics heightened regional anti-Mexican attitudes. The Mexican Revolution and Pancho Villa's skirmishes on the border, the U.S. entry into World War I and the impact of the Zimmermann Telegram on U.S-Mexico relations, and continuing labor conflicts within the mining and agriculture industries all generated a preoccupation with Mexicans and their integration into American society. This preoccupation, in hindsight, appears to have never faded given contemporary state politics. Nonetheless, as Arizona became the last of the forty-eight continental states to join the Union, teachers realized—then and now—that any attempt to improve the state's reputation entwined the destiny of its Mexican schoolchildren.[15]

Mexican Americanization also attracted educators because it connected their mission directly to the state's economy. When combined with vocational education, Americanization offered teachers and boosters the potential to sustain economic development and Mexican American labor-force participation. The evolution of Arizona's commercial industries (in copper, iron, silver, oil, agriculture, and railroads) replicated patterns of American capital investment heavily dependent on working-class labor in the American West, but this capital also needed workers with basic job skills.[16] If these youth characteristically failed or dropped out of school as a result of the "usual Mexican vices" that Miss Skinner described, then educators were determined to target these children—at all ages for the brief period they enrolled—through work-based curricula. Arizona's need for trained labor combined with teacher perceptions influenced the emergent school policies.[17]

Finally, teachers linked Mexican Americanization to racial segregation. Like other southwestern states, Arizona practiced de facto (social custom) segregation toward Mexican Americans.[18] However, because ethnic Mexican children constituted the school-aged majority, de facto segregation saturated public schools from the Grand Canyon to the U.S.-Mexico border. Arizona's

1913 school code authorized de facto segregation, allowing districts to separate children for pedagogical reasons.[19] Legal de facto segregation thus facil-
itated Americanization, which in turn became the blueprint for sustaining
labor-force preparation and participation. By establishing Mexican Americanization as a key public education reform, the Bureau investigators and
schoolteachers positioned themselves as essential actors in the state's progress. Skinner's letter reflected this value.

Debates over Mexican American Schooling

In 1900, a shift from assimilation to segregation developed in the public schools as Anglo Americans became increasingly preoccupied with the
growth of ethnic Mexican communities. The Mexican immigrant population
in Arizona doubled to nearly thirty thousand between 1900 and 1910.[20] By the
1905-1906 academic year, the Arizona school census estimated that 30,230
children between the ages of six and twenty-one were eligible for enrollment.[21] Of these, 17,689 were "native born" to "native parents," including
Anglo-American and some Mexican American children. Another 9,616 were
"native born" to one or two "foreign parents." And 2,925 were "foreign born."
White Arizonans used terms such as "foreign-born" or "non-American" as
code for "Mexican" or "Mexican descent" because Mexican laborers predominated over Asian and European immigrant workers in its industries.[22]

Segregation as an administrative practice also gained strength among
school leaders as social, economic, and political segregation between Mexicans and whites was consolidated at the local level. The ethnic Arizonense
elite lost its financial base and its political clout in the midst of increased Mexican immigration, as well as continued migration of Anglo Americans and
European immigrants who entered the region in ever greater numbers and
secured settler colonial claims. As both class and racial privilege reversed,
Anglo-American self-perceptions also shifted toward a white American nativism.[23] These boundaries of whiteness grew into settlement patterns and neighborhood schools. In Tucson, Arizonense residents pressed deeper into barrios
south of the original presidio.[24] In "copper towns," such as Clifton-Morenci
and Globe-Miami, ethnic European enclaves morphed into whiteness and
segregated themselves from "Mexican camps."[25] In Phoenix, the summer
monsoons accentuated discriminatory housing patterns as the cresting Salt
River flooded Arizonense families out of their South Phoenix homes. Anglo

Americans had moved northward, leaving the bottom lands to workers at the "railroads, factories, warehouses, and stockyards along the riverbanks."[26] Their children and grandchildren attended "Mexican schools," such as Grant School, "where Mexican pupils are taught Americanization."[27]

Teachers and superintendents developed school responses, such as segregation (or work-training programs as we will see later), within the strained context of Anglo-Mexican relations. Educators possessed the flexibility to do this because the territorial school regulations did not provide any specific guidance. In fact, the state did not have a unified curriculum until superintendent of public instruction Robert Lindley Long wrote and implemented a general "course of study" in 1887.[28] These regulations did not differentiate a separate curriculum for non-English speakers, nor did Long's 1899 revision.[29] Prior to this, some school districts hired city superintendents who wrote courses of study, or teachers independently created lessons or surreptitiously followed the "uniform textbooks" adopted in 1881 (although territorial "Instructions to Teachers" criticized this latter method). As a result of such lax policy, county superintendents, school trustees, and teachers possessed incredible latitude to resolve the Mexican Problem as they best determined.

During Superintendent Long's last tenure, from 1906 through 1909, the territory began calculating "nationality" in school census records.[30] Long did not explain the demographic shift, but we can attribute his emphasis on assessment to the growing preoccupation with the increasing immigrant population. The census form differentiated "native-born" and "foreign-born" children. "Native-born" implied "Euro-American" or "European descent" regardless of immigration status. "Foreign-born" implied "Mexican" and included Chinese and Japanese children regardless of citizenship. American Indian children were not counted, given the perception of federal control over Indian education and boarding schools, such as the Phoenix Indian School.[31] Over the next three decades, the state sharpened the race-based attendance calculations, tallying the "Net Enrollment of Colored and Foreign Pupils" into seven "race" categories: "Mexican, Negro, Japanese, Chinese, Indian, Porto [sic] Rican and Filipino."[32]

County superintendents quarreled over how to educate children of different races and ethnicities. Should Mexican children have access to education? Should that education be bilingual or integrated? The answers developed locally. The 1879 Arizona school law authorized "communities having ten census children residing within two miles of a schoolhouse to organize a school district."[33] By 1913, this distance doubled to four miles. So for every two to four square miles, public school scenarios varied and often were "magnets for conflict."[34] Where animosity or difference emerged, families organized their own public schools, just as the Arizonense parents did at Congress Junction. This legal flexibility explains why Arizona's 223 school districts in 1883 grew to "427 rural and 24 city districts" by 1917, and why multiple scenarios for educating Mexican youth emerged throughout the region and across the decades from territory to statehood.[35] For example, in 1907–1908, northern Arizona superintendents Alfred Ruiz of Apache County and Robert C. "Bob" Smith of Navajo County voiced opposing resolutions to the Mexican Problem. Their opinions fell in sync with two management styles of Progressive Era educators. Ruiz, who had ties to California and New Mexico, was a "social progressive" and he advocated a child-centered approach to learning, where Spanish language and culture should not be subtracted. Smith imagined his role as an "administrative progressive," who adopted a paternal style and promoted school efficiency.[36] Although they resided only 45 miles apart, Smith in Snowflake (a Mormon colony named for church leaders, Erastus Snow and William J. Flake) and Ruiz in St. Johns, they represented two conflicting racial, religious, and historical trajectories that emerged in Arizona settlement.

Bob Smith grew up with the privileges of a white westerner. His father served as president of the Snowflake Stake of the Church of Jesus Christ of Latter-day Saints.[37] After completing high school at the Mormon-owned Snowflake Academy, Smith attended a Salt Lake City business college. He returned in 1900 to a bookkeeping position in Holbrook for the Arizona Cooperative Mercantile Institution.[38] In 1905, at the age of thirty, Smith was elected by the town to the joint county post of probate judge and school superintendent. He later founded the town newspaper, the *Snowflake Herald*. According to Smith, integrating Mexican and American children in "mixed schools" proved to be the "greatest obstacle" of the Navajo County schools. "I most earnestly favor the maintenance of separate schools for the white children and the Mexican where there is a sufficient number of each to warrant such a separation. At Winslow a separate school for the Mexican children was maintained this year, which resulted in a benefit to the pupils of both schools and an increased attendance."[39] His perspective reflected a generational animosity between white Mormons and Mexican Catholics who had competed for land—often quite violently—on the Little Colorado River plateau since 1870.[40]

A generation older, Ruiz established mercantile stores in St. Johns and Concho in the 1890s. He and his wife Rufina (a.k.a. Ruth S.) occasionally appeared in the *St. Johns Herald* gossip column. "If Alfred's appearance denotes the condition of business, it must be very prosperous." In fact, the newspaper editors often noted Ruiz's dress as a signal of his personal wealth and style. Along with his department store, Ruiz actively pursued a legal career, serving as court clerk, district attorney, and probate judge and school superintendent of Apache County. In 1910, he returned to Gallup, New Mexico, as the prosecuting county attorney, where he regularly filed cases, some of which he argued at the New Mexico Supreme Court.[41] In contrast to Smith, Ruiz advocated bilingual education for both teachers and students: "I would respectfully suggest that the Board of Education require a course in Spanish to be provided in our Normal Schools for the purpose of supplying teachers of the Spanish speaking districts. I find from personal observation that where the teachers understand Spanish, the children have made rapid progress; while on the other hand, where the teachers did not understand the language, no good results have been obtained. Therefore, it would be wise to have a course in Spanish taught in our Normals, as such teachers would be in great demand in both Arizona and New Mexico."[42]

The predominance of Spanish-speaking families in Apache County created an opportunity for successful bicultural, bilingual, assimilation-based programs. In St. Johns School District No, 1, El Tule School District No. 5, and Concho School District No. 6, children achieved continued success because teachers in these districts not only "understood both languages" but also possessed fluency and literacy in both languages.[43] These teachers included Gracia L. Fernández in St. Johns, and Mrs. Amelia Hunt García and Abel Ortega in Concho.[44] The Tempe Normal School (TNS) pursued Ruiz's suggestion, hiring Fernández who had graduated in 1897 from the University of Maine to teach Spanish at the college.[45]

Ruiz carefully negotiated Spanish-language advocacy in the light of racial prejudice and older Mexican American educational debates familiar to the state superintendent and the board of education. In his report, Ruiz tactfully stressed his points with legal phrases such as "respectfully suggest." He praised successful teachers who had been "educated here in Arizona, and have done as well, or better than strangers for the reason that they are well acquainted with pupils, patrons and general conditions."[46]

Ruiz's emphasis on the local context echoed the frustrations of his predecessor (and perhaps mentor) John T. Hogue, who had advocated bilingual education since 1899.[47] In his 1905 annual report, he attributed the school failure of Mexican children and a 23 percent increase in truancy from the previous year to "the lack of knowledge of the Spanish language on the part of English speaking teachers, and their inability to interest or explain to their pupils," as well as to "the absolute failure upon the part of county officials to enforce the law in regard to compulsory education in Spanish speaking districts."[48] The next year, Hogue repeated nearly verbatim the same complaint. He pointed to the Concho schools, where in 1905 a bilingual teacher managed an average daily attendance of seventy students (95 percent), but in 1906 a monolingual teacher barely retained fifty-two students (70 percent).[49] As a result, in 1907, the Concho trustees hired principal Amelia Hunt García, a highly regarded teacher who possessed both Mexican and American heritage. She later became a well-known advocate for bilingual education, the Apache County school superintendent, and a member of the Arizona State Board Education.

Meanwhile, in Navajo County, Superintendent Smith expanded Mexican segregation efforts to two more school districts. He called for an amendment to allow school boards to segregate "mixed populations" and "to enforce the compulsory attendance law upon the complaint of any school patron."[50] He argued that segregation increased attendance rates and appeased white parental protest in three central, highland communities, particularly in Holbrook.

We have one Mexican school at Silver Creek, where the advancement of pupils is very slow, owing to the fact that the English language has to be learned before the course of study can be taken up properly, and still a very much worse state of affairs at Holbrook, where about forty per cent of the children are Mexicans and necessarily have to attend a mixed school with the American children, which is a great mistake, since there is a very strong prejudice between the two races which is continually inflamed by the parents, particularly the Americans who object in no compromising terms to the association of their children with the Mexicans, and since the beneficial results and advancement of such schools are poor, which can readily be seen from the enrollment and attendance of the Holbrook school, which is fifty and twenty-nine respectively; while at Winslow a much better state of affairs exists with the Mexican children who constitute about twenty per cent of the school and are separated from the Americans in a branch school to themselves and are taught by a lady, Mrs. Mary Weinert, who has a fair knowledge of the Spanish language in whose praise I cannot speak too highly for the good work done.[51]

While Ruiz and Smith both garnered community support, Smith's comments reveal how segregation emerged as a "community concern" of local whites who perceived their citizenship differently from the Arizonense residents. Relying on a racialized discourse, the Anglo Americans in Navajo County cast ethnic Mexicans outside the realm of whiteness, of citizenship, and of Americanness.[52] This allowed Smith to create the segregated schools. Smith's supporters further bolstered this discourse by emphasizing the low attendance of the Mexican students instead of the language barriers or prejudice, both of which may have deterred enrollment and attendance. While teachers like Mrs. Weinert may have acted as bridge persons who encouraged the academic progress of the Winslow Mexican children, after ten years, her school still wrestled with "the problem of . . . adding sufficient space to completely segregate the Spanish children."[53]

This racialized school segregation marks a drastic shift from the late nineteenth century trends toward assimilative education for Mexican children. While Mormons and Arizonenses had experienced a half century of conflict in Northern Arizona, school segregation on the basis of race and as explicit school policy only became evident after the turn of the twentieth century. These policies and the public perception necessary to enforce them brought Anglo-American Arizonan attitudes on par with the rest of the Southwest, where Mexicans were seen as part of the "'colored' or 'partly colored' races," as unskilled wage laborers, and as noncitizens.[54]

Correlating Industrialized, Segregated Education with Restricted Citizenship

Most school leaders valued some form of Mexican education that could simultaneously benefit the students and the state economically. Superintendent Smith's discourse incorporated this "beneficial" motive and accomplished de facto segregation "administratively" to satisfy local desires.[55] The shift from assimilation to a segregated, industrialized Americanization curricula satisfied the requirements of racialization, capitalist enterprise, and a rising nationalism. Teachers concerned about Arizona's future embraced this solution to the Mexican Problem because it paralleled the state's emergent economic hierarchy.

In mining communities in the Arizona-Sonora zone, evolving divisions based on class, race, and national allegiance separated Anglo Americans from

Arizonenses. For example, the families of Anglo-American mine owners, managers, and laborers, including recent immigrants from across Europe, lived apart from the Arizonenses, recent Mexican immigrants, and Native American laborers who worked at the same facilities.[56] This stratification and subordination extended from the mine pits into the towns where an ethnic, "economic pecking order" ranked Anglo-American railroad, mine, and cattle barons over middle-class white and Arizonense merchants, farmers, and ranchers who predominated over the remaining laborers.[57] Among the workers, race aligned whites into the higher-paid, skilled jobs despite the predominance of Mexican American laborers who sustained the railroad, agriculture, and mining industries throughout the Southwest. By 1911, the U.S. Immigration Commission had determined that "sixty percent of Arizona's smelter workers were Mexican, half of whom had been in the United States less than five years," and that "the percentage of Mexicans working on farms and ranches was undoubtedly higher."[58] According to the 1918 U.S. Bureau of Education survey, nearly a quarter of the state's male population worked in mining industries.[59]

This socioeconomic realignment guaranteed that state politics and labor concerns would center on race conflict as Anglo-American owners and unionists continually suppressed the "Mexican wage" and, by consequence, the political power and social interests of the Arizonense communities.[60] In the mines, the Mexican wage averaged $1.75–$2.00 per day through the 1910s, while the Anglo pay scale rose from $3–$4 per day by 1910 for the same work.[61] This coercive inequity incited the largest mine strikes, often Mexican led, in Arizona history before and after World War I.[62] Through the use of mutual aid associations, Mexican miners at Clifton-Morenci organized a walkout in 1903 to protest the dual wage system and the passage of Arizona legislation that limited underground work to eight hours per day. At the behest of white union men, this legislation purposely targeted companies hiring Mexican workers who agreed in desperation to overcome lesser pay to work ten-to-twelve-hour days. Although the 1903 strike failed in part due to police pressure, the walkout exposed an unforeseen unity among Mexican and other immigrant labor against Anglo-American unionists and management.[63] It also deepened the distinction between the two groups "toward an Anglo-Mexican binary."[64]

Historians Linda Gordon and Katherine Benton-Cohen illustrate how this economic hierarchy infused the social organization of Arizona towns, grafting race and class together across the spectrum of life's activities, including education. From Morenci's boom circa 1900 through the 1950s, the central highland town owned by Phelps Dodge was "strictly segregated" into two sites: Stargo for the Anglos and Newtown, also known as "Tortilla Flats," for the Mexicans. Strikingly, in these company-built living quarters the "American families" could choose between two model homes, either "a three-room semi-detached house" or "a four-room detached house" with indoor plumbing for the bathroom and kitchen, while all of the "non-detached Mexican homes . . . consisted of two rooms . . . with no bathroom or indoor plumbing."[65] Children from Clifton-Morenci also attended "four elementary schools, segregated both internally and between schools: North Clifton, mixed but with separate classes for Mexicans and Anglos; South Clifton, all Anglo; and two Chase Creek schools, one Anglo and one Mexican."[66] For fear of integration, attempts to merge the Chase Creek schools because of low attendance at the Mexican school failed in 1905. This social bifurcation replicated itself across the state, as in the former twin towns of Ray and Sonora, built in south-central Arizona in 1909. The Ray Consolidated Copper Company opened the two towns exactly one mile apart to separate its Anglo-American and Mexican American laborers, and the two towns remained segregated until they were swallowed by the open-pit mine in 1957. For more than four decades, the two groups lived separately and educated their children separately even though they worked for one enterprise and sent their children to one school district. A team of thirty teachers and two principals taught Mexican American children at the "Sonora School" and Anglo-American children at the "Ray School."[67]

These examples reveal how labor and race unified to shape the boundaries of citizenship and the limits of education for Mexican children in Arizona. The inequalities of the workplace mirrored the inequalities built into the civil and political structures of Arizona society.[68] Especially after the 1903 Clifton-Morenci strike, the unrelenting racism sustained an Anglo-American definition of citizenship that excluded Arizonenses.[69] This general sentiment became exceptionally clear in November 1906 when Arizonans voted against joint statehood with New Mexico precisely because of its Hispanic-majority population.[70] Over the next decade, white unionists and their supporters continued to barrage Mexicans with a battery of anti-immigrant initiatives. In 1909, despite a gubernatorial veto, the territorial legislature passed a literacy law to impede Mexican American voters.[71] At the 1910 state Constitutional Convention, white labor leaders proposed three anti-Mexican labor initiatives, winning restrictions against Mexican labor in public projects.[72] In 1914, voters passed the notorious "80 percent law" (endorsed by the Arizona State Federation of Labor and opposed by copper companies and railroads) to limit foreign labor to 20 percent of an employer's workforce.[73] The U.S. Supreme Court invalidated the law in favor of San Francisco's U.S. District Court ruling that it violated the Fourteenth Amendment. Arizonenses responded by organizing political protests and labor boycotts through their mutual aid associations, such as the Alianza Hispano-Americana and the Liga Protectora Latina,[74] which since 1894 had expressed consistent dismay over the unceasing discrimination toward the Arizonense population.

Still, in the minds of Anglo Arizonans, "Mexican" was equated with "laborer," and "the labor [Mexicans] performed came to define the limits of their potential as workers and as citizens."[75] Conversely, their limited potential restricted their educational opportunity. By the end of 1916, after assessing 427 rural school districts and 24 city school districts, the U.S. Bureau of Education scientists clearly saw how this sociological pattern affected school organization and the education of Mexican children.[76] "In practically all cities in Arizona and in [rural] graded schools large enough to make the adjustments, the non-English-speaking children are segregated for the first two, three, or four grades."[77] The Bureau supported this practice as "a step in the right direction, particularly for those over age" and recommended a revised course of study featuring "English, practical problems in arithmetic and prevocational work" for the primary grades. This administrative solution also highlights how Progressive educators classified de facto Mexican segregation as a "child-oriented" teaching solution to the Mexican Problem as opposed to the racialized de jure segregation applied to African Americans by Arizona state law and to Native American children under federal jurisdiction.

In private, at least two U.S. Bureau of Education scientists recognized a correlation between segregated Mexican schools and restricted citizenship. They also understood its powder-keg potential. Rural education specialist Katherine M. Cook, a former state superintendent of Colorado who surveyed Yuma County in southern Arizona, and the school administration specialist Walter S. Deffenbaugh, also a former city superintendent from Pennsylvania's western mining region, attempted to quantify Arizona's Mexican segregation.[78] In a letter, Deffenbaugh wrote to Cook: "I do not have any data showing the number of years the Mexican children are kept separate from the American children. I have been wondering whether my comment on this point should stand. The segregation is presumably not for racial reasons, tho [sic] it is no doubt in reality for this reason. It will no doubt be well to question this for Dr. Claxton's [the commissioner's] attention."[79] Deffenbaugh's "comment" may have been a reference to his week-long stay in the Clifton-Morenci schools.[80] Unfortunately, the report explained that Arizona school districts did not maintain cumulative data on student progress by age or racial group, so researchers could not calculate the number of years children in specific communities attended any school, let alone a segregated Mexican school or class.[81] The published survey results, thus, contained no square data on Mexican segregation even though the Mexican Problem loomed large in school census figures. Calculations on the number of overage children in the lower grades (that is, children too old for their grade level) revealed that Mexican children constituted one-half of the total enrollments in the majority of twelve city school districts, including Bisbee, Clifton, Douglas, Flagstaff, Globe, Mesa, Nogales, Phoenix, Prescott, Tempe, Tucson, and Winslow.[82] In all of these towns, Mexican children attended segregated schools or classes.

Truants, Platoons, and Mexican Segregation Styles

Arizona's social order combined with Progressive educational trends highly influenced school leaders' perceptions of the Mexican Problem before and after the U.S. Bureau of Education's 1916 field study. Educators believed that the slow academic progress and truancy of Mexican American children prevented schools from fulfilling their missions.[83] In official state reports and the *Arizona Teacher and Home Journal* (*ATHJ*), educators testified to the endemic Mexican Problem from the kindergartner who could not speak English to the overage immigrant child with no formal schooling.[84] Resolved to combat these problems, teachers used segregation, vocational education, and other homegrown solutions to suit local needs. At the core, however, academic policies turned on social efficiency.[85] Regardless of philosophical or political allegiances, Progressive educators accepted a fundamental belief in "differentiated schooling" where experts designed education to suit the child's perceived needs and future life course.[86] This conviction spurred the Arizona School Officials Association, led by university men and superintendents, to sound the call for the Bureau's survey.[87]

Helen Roberts, a TNS professor and later principal of its "Mexican training school," explained the mission of teaching the non-English-speaking child as character modification. The teacher must reshape the child's personality, behavior, and actions. Roberts delineated the Mexican child's initial failures to three areas: "the course of study, civic problems, and the moral problems."[88] By this, she meant teaching English comprehension, speaking, reading, and

Figure 8. "Pedro Hop." Reading class being taught outdoors, Rural Training School, Tempe State Teachers College, Tempe, Arizona, circa 1926. Courtesy of the University Archives Photograph Collection, Arizona State University Library.

writing; teaching work skills such as gardening and sewing, which would generate productive citizenship; and teaching the "cardinal school virtues" of regular attendance, punctuality, personal cleanliness, and parental support. These would successfully guide the child and the teacher in "the making of a true American citizen."

Roberts's philosophy and interpretation proved typical among her colleagues, including Nona Rodee who directed Tucson's Americanization program and Superintendent R. E. Somers of the Douglas city schools at the U.S.-Mexico border. Rodee believed English acquisition to be the most critical element of Americanization.[89] The "Rodee Method" emphasized the oral skills of the English language, such as pronunciation through imitation, "ear-training" (to hear new sounds correctly), and "visible speech" (vocalization). This curriculum was taught at all grade levels in the "Mexican schools of Tucson" and all primary schools in Pima County, with the goal of transforming these "foreign-speaking children" into "more loyal and better citizens."[90] Superintendent Somers sensed that Anglo Americans perceived "Mexican indifference" toward education, which he attributed to the popular saying "Does it pay to educate a Mexican?"[91] Facing rising criticism from the business sector, Somers implemented "Mexican work" programs for children to correct failures employers had observed in adult Mexican laborers. For example, Anglo-American women complained, "Why don't you teach these girls to do the fundamentals of housework well? They cannot cook, they do not clean well, and they are not dependable." From 1913 to 1923, the Seventh Street School and the Pirtleville School targeted what they determined to be seven major Mexican problems: hygiene, racial antagonism, truancy, English acquisition, poverty, parental participation, and attrition/retention.

Harmonizing Mexican American student needs to the school curriculum occurred gradually in the public schools between 1900 and 1930, and it was always in tandem with highly complicated, cross-cultural, cross-class negotiations. For example, educators in different cities wove industrial education into the core curriculum for Mexican-heritage children as a response to truancy and child labor. As early as 1904, state superintendent Long proposed industrial education for "habitual truants," largely classified as "foreign children." He argued for stronger compulsory attendance laws for children under fourteen so that administrators could apprehend "regular truants" who could then be shipped off to industrial schools, where, conveniently, they would be put to work for the state. Long's recommendation coincided with territorial expenditures for trial industrial schools in Prescott and Phoenix.[92] By 1906, superintendents regularly attributed truancy and attrition increases to foreign children.[93] By 1910, photographs showed Mexican students picking cotton in the fields surrounding the Territorial Industrial School at Benson.[94]

The superintendents conveniently blamed industry for luring foreign children away from school and illiterate immigrant parents for depending on child wages. In Cochise County (Bisbee and Douglas) and Graham County (Clifton, Morenci, and Metcalf), superintendents reported child labor practices to the state board of education. They asked "that mining companies and other employers of child labor . . . be respectfully requested not to employ children of compulsory school age during the school term, unless the child be excused by the Board of Trustees of the School."[95] In 1907, Graham County superintendent A. R. Lynch plainly excused the 1,557 children missing from his classrooms. "This is accounted for by the large increase in Mexican population in Morenci and Metcalf."[96] In Morenci, many Mexican children worked in the mill, as "mothers' helpers," or as "ore sorters" in the mines.[97] Further, they entered the workforce by default as the Morenci "Mexican school" only provided instruction through the third grade.

When school administrators expressed concern about Mexican truancy, such complaints often hinged on ambivalence. Mexican absences had the potential to ruin efficiency as school financing continued to depend on the average daily attendance and territorial law required school officials to apprehend truants. Yet the labor truants performed for lower wages in menial, manual jobs also served the greater financial interests of local employers and of families they helped support. In Douglas, Somers identified truancy as "a hard problem to solve," estimating that most Mexican children left school by age sixteen.[98] The U.S. Bureau of Education added that statewide most Mexican students had not advanced beyond the third grade and few beyond the fifth grade.[99] The boys entered the "transient labor class, if they work[ed] at all"; the girls became "domestics or clerks."[100]

In this "Mexican as laborer" context, both Roberts and Somers adjusted their school curricula to include "special vocational work" in the "social settlement" style.[101] After conducting a home visit to an impoverished Mexican family, Roberts concluded that her Tempe school had overemphasized teaching English to the detriment of providing practical skills. She concluded, as did the Bureau of Education survey, that the few years Mexican children spent in school amounted to superficial impressions.[102] To better prepare these future workers, she "organized a sewing class for the first and second grade girls" and "a class in agriculture for the boys." Moreover, she "urged" the forty boys to plant gardens at their homes, which she visited. Roberts's success led to curriculum changes at the TNS and, in 1922, she began training teachers "to handle the Mexican population."[103] In 1925, when the normal school contracted rights to operate Tempe's Eighth Street School for Mexican children as a teacher-training facility, Roberts became the principal, a post she held for several decades.

In Douglas, Somers also authorized principal Grace Gainsley to reorganize the Pirtleville School curriculum. She was determined "to teach the Mexican how to live and to become someday a good law-abiding citizen. To do this he must be taught cleanliness, loyalty, obedience and to speak English."[104] Her task proved monumental with 430 Mexican children, but during home visits she "kindly demand[ed]" parental cooperation.[105] Her faculty, which included TNS alumnae and well-known Mexican American teacher Concepción Faras, urged parents to assume responsibility for their children's absences, tardiness, and hygiene. The school board pressured Mexican parents to raise money and provide labor to build a school bathhouse. Gainsley also organized a cobbling course for fifty boys, as well as a series of courses in "simple cooking,"

Figure 9. Mexican American children from the segregated Eighth Street School and Professor Helen Roberts (center) visit the fountain in front of the Old Main building, Tempe State Teachers College, Tempe, Arizona, n.d. Courtesy of the University Archives Photograph Collection, Arizona State University Library.

"darning and mending," and light sewing, such as "making aprons, underwear, and simple dresses."[106] Gainsley's curriculum soon spread to other Douglas schools. At the Fifteenth Street School, Mexican girls learned "things that will make it possible for them to be efficient domestic help, when they go into American homes to work."[107]

Despite these vocational programs and home visits, improving Mexican attendance and tardiness still proved problematic.[108] Mexican children missed school for a variety of reasons. Migratory labor patterns forced many families to move with crop seasons. During school hours, able-bodied youth regularly picked cotton, fruits, and vegetables in the fields. Some left to visit dying relatives or to return to homes on both sides of the border. In Casa Grande, on the southeastern edge of Maricopa County, several students boycotted school after the trustee's wife scolded them for drinking water from her hydrant.[109]

In Douglas, some Mexican children avoided school fearing racial confrontations with "American" students. Superintendent Somers reported that the
Mexican children "were not welcome in the classroom or on the playground
and gang fights on the way home from school were frequent and often of
serious nature."[110] Alleviating Anglo-American intolerance, he said, "helped
to improve Mexican attendance but after all the good truant officer is still the
important factor in regularity."[111]

In 1922, the Arizona legislature officially amended the compulsory attendance law, granting attendance officers "the powers of deputy sheriffs"; however, truant officers and self-appointed citizens had rounded up youth for
several decades.[112] In one rural school, "the appointment of a truant officer
brought in twelve new Mexican children."[113] In another school, the teacher
tasked "overgrown" Mexican boys to ferret out missing students.[114] In Tempe,
truant officers J. M. Piersol and Cresencio "Chris" Sigala, who came from a
locally prominent Tempeneño family, arrested parents on misdemeanor
charges for "failure to send children to school."[115] From March 1920 to January
1922, the Criminal Court of the Tempe Justice of the Peace arraigned seven
fathers for the continued absence of one or more children. Porfirio Miranda,
Luis Ledesma, Feberano Martínez, Orculano Ledesma, Juan Estrada, Jesus
López, and Porfirio Romo—all pleaded guilty and waived trials for immediate verdicts. The presiding judges found each guilty but suspended their sentences, which ranged from ten to thirty dollars or ten to thirty days in jail,
with the caveat that their children would stay in school. Fine or imprisonment
would become mandatory if they faced a second charge. The fear of Arizona
justice must have struck Porfirio Romo, a laborer who received the harshest
sentence of 30 days in jail or approximately one-half to one month's income.[116]
His child "reported to school" before the court even heard the complaint!

Policing parents and children unified educators and community leaders
as their attempts to control Mexican populations quite often mirrored one
another. Bisbee provides a dynamic example for understanding how the con-
fluence of public and educator attitudes toward "non-Americans" and the
influence of an emerging corporate capitalism prejudiced public policy. In
January 1915, an *ATHJ* contributor proudly characterized Bisbee as a "white
man's city" with sundown laws, as well as a "democratic school system" that
supported local needs. The writer praised the school superintendent C. F. Philbrook, a suburban Chicagoan: "To hear him talk you would conclude he has
been a mining capitalist all his life."[117] Such renderings proved all too telling
of the privilege white Arizonans expected and cast within their communities

in the name of Americanism. They also helped explain the racial and class conflict that undergirded the town's 1917 Industrial Workers of the World (IWW) mining strikes and emergent school segregation.

Superintendent Philbrook's vision of the Bisbee public schools reaffirmed the "white versus other" binary of the mines and the larger imperial agenda of the Americanization movement.[118] In February 1917, one month after the release of the Bureau's survey and four months prior to the infamous IWW deportation, Philbrook announced a modern makeover for the Bisbee schools, featuring the recommended "six-six plan" or "six-three-three plan" (six years of elementary and six years split between junior and senior high schools), new buildings, and a new vocational training program—the Gary plan—for Mexican children.[119] The Gary plan, or platoon system, originated in the public schools of Gary, Indiana, created in 1906 by the United States Steel Corporation.[120] The brainchild of Superintendent William A. Wirt, the Gary plan featured a split-schedule for student "platoons" that maximized use of the school facility while socializing the child to the world of work. The platoon system gained national popularity in the 1910s through the 1920s when the New York City schools adopted the curriculum and the U.S. Bureau of Education began promoting it. According to historians Ronald Cohen and Raymond Mohl, "The Gary schools epitomized the two separate and contradictory goals of progressive education—the drive toward efficiency, economy, and scientific management on the one hand, and the urge to provide a natural and enriched schooling in which children learned by doing, on the other."[121]

Superintendent Philbrook, who served on the Bureau's survey steering committee, advocated the Gary plan as ideal for the learning needs of Bisbee's 400 Mexican students.[122] The Bureau had determined that 34 percent of Bisbee students were overage for their grade level.[123] Children in the first, second, and third grades ranged in age from five to sixteen years.[124] While Bisbee compared favorably to other large districts, this trend based on "age-grade data" affected the entire state where the percentages of overage children in the twelve city districts ranged from 29 percent at Clifton (a mining town) to 34 percent in Phoenix (the state capitol) to 65 percent at Nogales (on the borderline). Bureau scientists correlated overageness, mental slowness, "repeaters," and "dropouts" to Mexicans "who enter school at an advanced age" and leave early, as soon as they reach the compulsory age of sixteen.[125] This meant that for the brief time that Mexican children entered school they did not receive the minimum education necessary for "intelligent citizenship."[126] The Bureau recommended "special classes" for the older children, especially those over fifteen regardless of their ethnic background. The aggregate data strongly indicated an immediate need "to take steps to lower the high rate of retardation among American as well as Mexican children."[127] While Mexican children often received blame for this trend, the Bureau argued that they did not "account for all of it." In fact, the Bureau proposed that the state adopt remedies that would decrease failure, increase promotion, and prepare "all children, American and foreign" with the "kind of work that will be most helpful to them as a preparation for efficient living."[128] Superintendent Philbrook heard this message, but given the racialized politics of his border town he took the suggestion as a solution to the Mexican Problem.

With an emphasis on social and economic preparation, he argued that the Gary plan would enable Bisbee teachers to effectively instruct Mexican children in English and job skills through the elementary grades. In 1919, Philbrook publicized his vision of Bisbee's platoon system to *ATHJ* readers:

> The new Mexican school will be ready for occupation within ninety days. This building will contain ten classrooms, five of which will be for industrial education. The industrial course, which will take half of the time the pupils will spend at school, has the purpose of teaching English. Teaching children English by the way of making them work together in manual [*sic*] training, is recognized as one of the most practical methods. The school classes will be regulated under the platoon system, which places half of the students in the five industrial classrooms, while the other half are attending to their three R's in the regular classes. This makes full use of the capacity of the building, leaving no rooms vacant during school hours.[129]

Philbrook's plan repeated nearly word for word the prescription to the Mexican Problem that the U.S. Bureau of Education had proposed in 1917. "Approximately, half time should be devoted to regular classroom work, half to hand work."[130] In fall 1920, Bisbee celebrated the Franklin School's grand opening with a town parade eerily reminiscent of the IWW deportation three years earlier. Teachers marched four hundred Mexican children across town to their new segregated school.[131] Now Philbrook and his teachers confidently asserted that even the least-educated Mexican children "would be much better equipped to take their places among the wage earners of the community" as opposed to those who had studied "abstract work only indirectly related to the work of the world."[132]

IQs and Tracking the Mexican Child

The Bisbee school district's implementation of a segregated, work-based Americanization curriculum reflected trends apparent in other Arizona schools. Segregation in small classes or in entire schools proved to be the most efficient method for instructing so-called problem children and fit within modern social science remedies that called for "differentiated" instruction. According to historian Gilbert González, "Traditionally, [Mexican] segregation was meant to instruct the child in proper methods of behavior, meaning learning to think and [to] act like the mythical model American."[133] But with the advent of intelligence quotient (IQ) testing in the 1910s, racial segregation merged neatly with educational segregation theories based on group performance. School experts argued that the "group IQ test" would allow administrators "to segregate students by ability, to aid in vocational guidance, to detect unusually able or retarded students, and to diagnose learning problems."[134]

Arizona teachers of the "foreign-speaking element" credited segregation in the primary grades for aiding them in administering discipline, structuring lesson plans, and building student confidence.[135] Despite concerns that segregation was "undemocratic" or lessened the children's incentive to speak English, teachers advocated separation and retention for Spanish-speakers to enhance the "slower process" of English acquisition.[136] Separation also prevented non-English speakers from hindering the progress of white American youth, a key argument for grouping children. TNS professor Helen Roberts advocated grade retention as a necessary policy for the non-English-speaking child. Advancing the Mexican child prematurely prevented the student from failing later or dropping out altogether.[137]

The U.S. Bureau of Education survey seconded Roberts's philosophy, recommending "differentiated" courses, textbooks, and methods that emphasized English, arithmetic, and prevocational work for the "non-English-speaking" child.[138] The survey suggested "grouping" as a potential solution, leaving the responsibility for "organization and classroom practice" to each local school until a new state course of study could be written.[139] Throughout the 1920s, state educators "grouped," or "tracked," Mexican students with gusto, implementing local solutions as quickly as they could organize them. For example, Miami School superintendent Charles R. Tupper recruited his mentor, renowned IQ expert Lewis Terman of Stanford University to conduct group intelligence tests on 1,500 students, half of "Mexican nationality."[140] Terman sent his research assistant Miss Mildred Thompson to Miami to conduct two assessments: the Binet Intelligence Test on first graders and selected students, and the National Intelligence Test on all children in the second through eighth grades.[141] Educational psychologists advocated that grouping, particularly in the primary grades, would lessen failure rates and improve promotion rates.[142] Instead of failing children at the end of a term or stalling the exceptionally bright child, the IQ test results would allow Miami administrators to place children of the same intellect or with the same deficits in class groups where they could proceed at a level pace through the grades in a timely manner. In fact, Professor Terman recommended nothing less than segregation and work-based training for Mexican children whom he described categorically as "dull" and eugenically unsuited for reproduction.[143]

The IQ test results, of course, confirmed Tupper's belief in segregated, industrial Americanization for Mexican children. Ninety percent of Miami's Mexican children already attended a separate school. But their IQ test results seemingly validated this need and helped explain why Miami's "Mexican enrollment lagged consistently behind corresponding classes in other schools." Armed with Tupper's IQ data and Progressive rationales, the school board designed a new $125,000 vocational Bullion Plaza School for the Mexican children.[144] Tupper explained their position: "When it is recalled that the children of the Mexican laborers in the mines of the district almost invariably drop out after the sixth year to take up unskilled manual labor or to set up home of their own, it will be readily appreciated that the schools owe it to these children to provide them with definite training in this direction in place of condemning them to failure, discouragement, and early elimination by confining their school training to the traditional course of study looking toward high school entrance and graduation."[145] Tupper's conclusions matched standard interpretations. The Mexican children's poor IQ revealed that Miami policies toward Mexican children had been correct all along—"there was practically no real retardation."[146] This meant, according to Tyack's interpretation, that the "children were actually performing at their mental level (that is, the fault lay not in the teachers but in the genes of the children)."[147] By assessing "mental level" or "naturally ordained intelligence," Tupper—following Terman's social-engineering lessons—prepared Miami's Mexican youth for their rightful role in the corporate economic order.[148] With success at Miami, Tupper toured other Arizona schools "to observe methods and means of providing practical industrial and homemaking training for Mexican classes."[149] Teachers at the Bullion Plaza School followed Tupper's plan until 1951 when desegregation finally arrived in Miami.

Similar reforms continued to appear across Arizona throughout the 1920s. Aside from designated segregated "Mexican rooms" or "Mexican grades," the most popular tracking programs for these children included the "1C-1B-1A" immersion system and "Opportunity Rooms" for problem kids. The Tucson Public Schools implemented both methods for instructing more than six hundred non-English-speaking children who entered the schools annually.[150] In 1923, these children identified themselves as "Yaqui or Papago Indian," "Chinese," and "for the most part . . . Spanish-speaking."[151] Significantly, one hundred of these youth possessed Spanish literacy. Nonetheless, the majority entered the immersion system, where they spent three years on average in the first grade. The 1C-1B-1A curriculum divided students into three sections based on presumed intellectual ability and English proficiency.[152] Students started with 1C before advancing to 1B, then to 1A. Finally, at about the age of eight or nine, the children advanced to second grade if they could speak English. María Urquides, who "went along with the program" as a young teacher in 1928, explained it as an immersion course that could last from months to years.[153] That year in Tucson, Urquides witnessed the program where she taught at Davis School, but it was also standard curriculum at Drachman, Mansfield, Menlo Park, Ochoa, and Pascua schools. Nine teachers, mostly Anglo American and one Arizonense—Amelia Maldonado, who graduated from the University of Arizona—managed the program and their credentials included degrees from state teachers colleges and universities across the nation, such as California, Kansas, Tennessee, and New York.[154] Phoenix also reported 1C-1B-1A programs at Grant, Washington, Lincoln, and Douglas primary schools. TNS alumna Rose Oviedo taught 1C at Douglas.[155] Theoretically, the protracted curriculum permitted Spanish-speaking and Mexican American youth an extended opportunity to achieve English mastery so that they could compete successfully when or if they were integrated with the American children. Tucson schools designed 1C as "the first step" of Americanization and used the system through 1965.[156]

"Opportunity Rooms" and "Opportunity Schools" also appeared in towns with significant immigrant populations. Sometimes they were called "ungraded Mexican rooms."[157] In Hayden, southeast of Phoenix, teacher Lillian Ruth Higgins explained the Opportunity Room as a place where the most disadvantaged children learned reading, writing, math, and citizenship.[158] A Missourian trained at Rutgers University's School for Feeble-Minded Children, Higgins described her classroom as the last resort for "the sub-normal and retarded children," but it was also for older immigrant children who might advance quickly with language training.[159] Still, she made little distinction between the two groups when she described her Mexican American pupils: Pig Brother Ramón who "loves dirt, has a large head and a shock of hair that is nearly always standing on end" and his sister "Juana, a big fat, mature Mexican girl fifteen years of age who has an intelligence quotient of about eight years."[160]

Pig Brother Ramón symbolized the stereotypical, twentieth-century Mexican American student. Across Arizona, teachers regaled others with stories of their success at civilizing these youth while administrators prided themselves on these achievements. Theories of civilization and economic progress undergirded the state's public school policy from its inception and, by the early twentieth century, these policies matured into Juan Crow segregation that differentiated schooling for "American" and "Mexican" children. Educators distilled the purpose of Mexican Americanization to teaching "a common language, a common standard of living, [and] a common ideal of citizenship."[161]

Mexican Americanization, however, was fundamentally flawed and undemocratic. Arizonense youth might learn the "standards" and "ideals," but the promise of American equality was never intended for them. The theoretical and technological advancements of the Progressive Era resulted in segregated curriculums justified and supported by intelligence testing and tracking programs. These tools helped teachers transform Pig Brother's generation into a new class of Mexican American workers. But some Arizonense parents remained unconvinced that labor would be their children's only trajectory into adulthood and they braced themselves to challenge systematic segregation by taking the issue out of the classroom and into the courtroom.

CHAPTER 4

Los Tempeneños Sue for a Fair Deal

On September 23, 1925, Adolpho "Bebé" Romo and his wife Joaquina Jones sued the Tempe, Arizona, School District No. 3 (TD3) for segregating their four children at the Eighth Street School, the so-called "Mexican Training School."[1] On October 5, Judge Joseph S. Jenckes of the Maricopa County Superior Court ruled in their favor. Eight days later, on October 13, their children Antonio (age 15), Henry (age 14), Alice (age 9), and Charles (age 7) took their seats in the Tenth Street School, joining their classmates "on the same terms and conditions . . . as children of the white race."[2] By the end of the school year, 34 percent of the students—105 of 308 children—at the Tenth Street School claimed Mexican American heritage.[3]

Adolpho Romo v. William E. Laird et al. (no. 21617, Sup. Ct. Ariz. 1925), an unpublished case filed in the Maricopa County Superior Court, is the first known Mexican American school desegregation case filed in Arizona and among the earliest argued in a U.S. court. *Romo* is a watershed moment because it documents how Arizonenses laid claim to their American citizenship in mass action through the U.S. courts. In *Romo*, they pursued a public, political, and legal battle to prove they belonged in Arizona and belonged there "on the same terms and conditions" as white Americans. The case reveals their individual and communal commitments to self-determination and self-identification as U.S. citizens and Mexican Americans. It highlights how Arizonense investment in civic integration catalyzed an emergent civil rights consciousness and the Arizonenses' challenge of this racialized social order.

Romo fits within a regional framework of Juan Crow contests over educational equality in the early twentieth century. Across the southwest, in cases including *Maestas v. Shone* (Colorado, 1914), *Del Rio ISD v. Salvatierra* (Texas, 1930), *Alvarez v. Lemon Grove* (California, 1931), and *Mendez v. Westminster* (California, 1947), Mexican Americans protested second-class citizenship in public schooling.[4] I argue that *Romo*'s standing in this pantheon of landmark school-desegregation cases significantly alters Mexican American civil rights chronology, not only as an early twentieth-century challenge to segregation and educational inequity but also in its cultural geography as both Arizona and Arizonenses have been categorized historically as a place and a people with no civil rights history. *Romo* predates by twenty-six years the Arizona federal case of *Gonzales v. Sheely* (1951) that disputed the race-based separation of Mexican children in Tolleson, a rural community in western Maricopa County.[5] *Gonzales* was the second federal case to affirm the unconstitutionality of racialized school segregation as a violation of equal protection prior to *Brown v. Board of Education* (1954).[6] The *Gonzales* decision relied on the more famous *Mendez* precedent, in which Mexican and Puerto Rican parents successfully challenged the arbitrary racial separation of their children in Orange County, California, public schools.[7] Two decades before, in *Romo*, Mexican American parents in Tempe sought similar remedies and began testing comparable legal arguments. Together, the two Arizonense cases of *Romo* and *Gonzales* frame the early litigation era of Mexican American civil rights in education.

Romo clearly confirms an Arizona history of Mexican American educational segregation. The nature of Juan Crow as a de facto social construction that is fluid, dynamic, and chimerical has made it difficult to locate concrete, historical evidence of intentional Mexican American segregation. Yet, as in other southwestern states, Arizonans justified Juan Crow as a form of segregation necessary for pedagogical or language rationales, such as teaching the immigrant-heritage child how to speak English, and also as a racial logic that mirrored the "separate but equal" standard of *Plessy v. Ferguson* (1896) and "color of law" validations of later desegregation cases. The TD3 carefully defined the purpose of the Eighth Street School as "restricted and limited to the accommodation of 'Spanish-American' and 'Mexican-American' children."[8] No evidence suggests that students of any other nationality, racial, or ethnic background attended the Eighth Street School. From its initial opening in 1915, the TD3 publicly announced in the local newspaper that the Tenth Street School was intended only for "English speaking children," while "all others should attend . . . at the Eighth street building."[9] The Maricopa County Superior Court permitted this linguistic and racialized segregation of Mexican-origin students in the public schools, so long as districts upheld the *Plessy* standard of "separate but equal."[10] Arizona educators understood the *Plessy* standard quite well, as it was the basis for the 1912 Arizona Supreme

Court verdict of *Dameron v. Bayless*, which confirmed "separate but equal" accommodations for African American children in Phoenix and statewide.

In casting the history of *Romo*, I examine the lawsuit from three perspectives drawn from court records, school board minutes, and oral history. Each perspective—the Mexican parents, the school administrators, and the court—unearths different interpretations of "belonging" in Tempe, a small town on the banks of the Salt River. The administrators—college and school district trustees—implemented the segregation policy in response to local whites' preferences for racial separation and to help the Tempe State Teachers College grow its teacher-training facilities. The Romo family embodied the Mexican American community at large, including its heritage of mutual assistance, blended families, and borderlands settlement. Judge Joseph S. Jenckes, the son-in-law of the former territorial governor Joseph H. Kibbey, represented the American legal system and ultimately determined how race, citizenship, and belonging would be handled in this western town.

The *Romo* case began officially on September 23, 1925, when Adolpho Romo's attorneys submitted a Complaint for Writ of Mandamus, demanding that Judge Jenckes issue a ruling to stop the Tempe school district from segregating Mexican American children. Courts issue writs of mandamus, or mandatory orders, when no other legal remedy exists to compel government officials—in this case, public school district administrators—to fulfill their duties. Although the judge ruled within twelve days of the complaint, the immediate events surrounding the case lasted three months, from September 14 to November 9, 1925. Consuming one-third of the school year, *Romo* signaled an important legal challenge to the community's understanding and practice of race and citizenship.

White Tempe

In spring 1925, the president of the Tempe Normal School (TNS), Dr. Arthur John Matthews, achieved a monumental coup. He convinced the Arizona State Legislature to convert the normal school into a four-year teachers college, changing it from a junior college into a baccalaureate institution. Students who had graduated from TNS after its 1887 founding earned two-year diplomas and teacher certificates that allowed them to work in Arizona and neighboring states, including California.[11] Matthews's new college now had the authority to issue a four-year bachelor's degree in education, reflecting a broader national trend of longer and more rigorous preparation in teacher education.[12] In celebration of TNS's new status as Tempe State Teachers College, Matthews hosted a town party, closing the college and its three elementary training schools for an official holiday.[13]

As part of the college expansion, however, Matthews needed to acquire additional training school classrooms to prepare the growing undergraduate student body, which now numbered nearly seven hundred and served students from across Arizona and the western states.[14] Historically, the TNS had engaged in cooperative agreements with two local school districts to operate county-funded schools with "student teachers."[15] Matthews hired certified veteran teachers or professors who specialized in teacher training to work as "critic teachers," overseeing the college students at both the Rohrig School, a rural district less than a mile east of the college, and TD3's "Rural School" several miles south. In addition, the TNS also operated its own independent "training school" on campus. The TNS retained controlling legal jurisdiction over all three training schools in cooperation with each school district.[16]

As early as October 1924, Matthews began negotiations with TD3 to take over its largest elementary school, the Eighth Street School, a three-story building with more than five hundred students and nearly adjacent to the college, at the corner of Eighth Street (University Avenue) and Mill Avenue.[17] The TNS board agreed that if they could not secure an arrangement with the TD3 trustees, then the TNS would pursue "proper legislation" to garner training schools "through the adjacent school districts."[18] To avoid state interference, the TD3 trustees shared the TNS proposal at a town meeting and allowed voters to help determine the issue in a special referendum during the fall school board election. Tempe voters passed the measure "369 for and 198 against," allowing the "use of the Eighth Street School Building for normal training purposes."[19] The following spring, President Matthews and the TD3 trustees finalized a Memorandum of Agreement. The TD3 relinquished the Eighth Street School and its full operation, including the students, to the college. The trustees even added the proviso that the Eighth Street School "shall be restricted and limited to the accommodation of Spanish-American or Mexican American children."[20]

According to TD3 trustee Isabel Waterhouse, this arrangement followed the "established segregation plan of the past several years."[21] TD3 had segregated the Eighth Street School in 1915, when it built a new Tenth Street School for the "American" children.[22] TD3 superintendent G. W. Persons reported that the district worked to ensure "conditions . . . as nearly equal as

Figure 10. The Eighth Street School, Tempe, Arizona, 1946. From 1925 to 1945, the Tempe School District No. 3 allowed the Arizona State Teachers College to operate this segregated "Mexican school" as a teacher-training facility so that the college students could learn how to work efficiently on "Mexican education problems." Courtesy of the University Archives Photograph Collection, Arizona State University Library.

it is possible to make them" in the two schools.[23] Teacher Ruby Olive Haigler Wood, who understood Tempe's race politics from her own ethnically mixed extended family, ascribed the early segregation to Tempe's Americanization efforts.[24] "A special feature of the Tempe Public School is the method of handling Mexican children. There are many of them in the town, and they form a difficult problem for the educator. In the Tempe Schools these pupils are put by themselves, under one or more teachers, according to the size of the class. The teachers give them special attention, study their character and peculiarities, and endeavor to make school attractive for them. This plan has been found to work better than where races are taught together."[25]

When Haigler Wood graduated from the TNS in 1914, progressive educators such as Dr. Matthews, who was a two-time president of the Arizona State

Teachers Association and a vice president of the National Education Association, valued school segregation as a solution to the "Mexican Problem," which they defined as the dilemma of teaching monolingual, Spanish-speaking children, including recent Mexican immigrants who were often overage for their grade level and who had never or had rarely attended school in the past.[26] These immigrant Mexican and Mexican American children comprised the majority of the state's school population in twelve of its largest towns, including Tempe.[27] Many educators across the state thus advocated Americanizing these children as quickly as possible to avoid what some immigration opponents called "a new racial problem" akin to that of Southern blacks.[28]

In 1918, three hundred Arizona teachers participated in a U.S. Bureau of Education survey to assess the dilemma of how to improve public schools and the teaching of its Mexican-majority school population.[29] Arizona teachers from across the state, along with a select group of five hundred civic leaders, quite boldly shared their assessment of the public schools and their critique of Mexican-heritage students. For example, the Clifton superintendent implemented special "ungraded rooms" for overage children to avoid placing Spanish-speaking teenagers in first-grade classrooms with six-year-olds. This technique allowed the "retarded" children to learn English and advance through the curriculum independently "with dignity."[30] Educators resolved wherever possible to implement Americanization curriculums that emphasized traditional academic "classroom work," such as reading, writing, and speaking English, as well as vocational "hand work" in the domestic and agricultural sciences to prepare Mexican children to enter the workforce.[31]

The Tempe Normal School and its training schools specialized in preparing future teachers to educate Spanish-speaking children.[32] In 1906, the TNS hired Spanish professor Gracia L. Fernández at the suggestion of Arizonense leaders who promoted the need for qualified bilingual teachers to the state superintendent of education.[33] Fernández explained in the 1907–1908 TNS course bulletin that one goal of the foreign-language requirement was "to equip our graduates for better work as teachers."[34] A former Arizona public school teacher and a graduate of the University of Maine, the American-born Fernández taught her native Spanish at TNS until 1912. Her successors continued to develop the Spanish-language program, which became the hallmark of the foreign-language department through the 1920s and included courses for beginners as well as courses in advanced composition and literature.[35] TNS encouraged student teachers to learn basic Spanish so that they could teach English to Spanish-speaking children. As the TNS training schools enrolled growing numbers of Spanish-speaking youth, the college shifted its curriculum to meet the demands of this Americanization work taught in segregated classrooms across the state and now at the segregated Eighth Street School.[36]

TNS professor and Eighth Street School principal Helen Roberts argued that segregated, protracted curriculums benefited the non-English-speaking child. Most children of Mexican descent, regardless of their language abilities, spent three years at minimum in the first grade as part of English-immersion programs, such as the 1C-1B-1A curriculum taught in Phoenix and Tucson.[37] Writing to the *Arizona Teacher and Home Journal* in 1918, Roberts explained this pedagogical philosophy: "The only reason I can see for segregation is that it is a slower process, until the non-English speaking children have their vocabulary established. I firmly believe that we should not allow the non-English speaking child to enter the third grade until he is on equal footing with the English speaking child. I have followed up not [*sic*] a few cases where he was put on while still lacking in understanding of English, and I find he gets into deep water and can't wade thru [*sic*], becomes disgusted and drops out of school."[38]

Roberts helps us understand why Mexican American children attending elementary schools often were retained and overage for their grade levels. For example, the Romos' teenage sons, Antonio who was 15 and Henry who was 14, were still attending the Eighth Street School in 1925.[39] Progressive American educators insisted that segregation served the Mexican child's best educational interests and, as a result, Juan Crow "Mexican schools" became the gold standard despite the patterns of underachievement, school failure, and educational inequity that segregation generated.[40] Within the first three decades of the twentieth century, a "Mexican school" existed in nearly every community across the Salt River Valley.[41]

From 1915, when TD3 designated the Eighth Street School for Mexican children, through the Great Depression and into the 1940s, white Arizonans—regardless of whether they were educators—held consistent assumptions about the type of schooling proper for a population that, in their opinion, was outside the civic polity. The TNS professors and alumni, including Haigler Wood, Roberts, and President Matthews, alongside New Deal home demonstration agents, believed that children of Mexican heritage could not be true Americans. Their lack of English skills and their "character and peculiarities" rendered them outsiders and their schooling needed to be adjusted to help them to prepare for a limited future. For example, Arizona officials communicating with the Works Progress Administration (WPA) administrators in

Washington, D.C., described how county 4-H Clubs "enriched the lives of girls of Mexican parentage" in Maricopa County.[42] "Often it has the means whereby these girls have learned to fit into the general pattern of living in their particular localities. Parents have been induced to adopt better standards of feeding the family, of clothing the members and of housing the group for greater comfort as a direct result of the activities of these girls."[43] In Gilbert, only fifteen miles east of Tempe, teacher Wayne McFrederick recalled that even though their Mexican school "might have been discriminated against a little bit," the 4-H programming supplemented the children's learning experiences. "We had a huge 4-H garden plot for the boys. For several years, we won many ribbons at the 4-H Fair in Tempe. I remember Alfred Sotomayor winning five blue ribbons one time."[44] The youngest son of a farm laborer, Sotomayor eventually made it to Gilbert High School, where he continued to win "shop awards."[45] When he graduated in 1941, he was twenty years old and the only Spanish-surnamed student in a senior class of eighteen.[46]

Coupled with Americanization and vocational curricula, school segregation reinforced the outsider status of all Mexicans within Tempe and across the state. When TNS president Matthews first proposed adopting the Eighth Street School as a new training school, the boards of trustees at both the college and the school district worked methodically to sustain segregation. The TD3 tapped Superintendent Persons to clarify the legality of continuing Mexican American segregation, even though the school district would no longer control the elementary school. A career educator, Persons knew quite well that in 1925 no Arizona law authorized Mexican American school segregation. Nonetheless he wrote to the county deputy attorney Gene Samuel Cunningham, explained the proposed agreement, and asked very pointedly, "Can the trustees compel these Mexican children to attend the Eighth Street School after it is a training school should they not desire to do so?"[47]

In Cunningham's interpretation, segregation at the new "Mexican Training School" would be illegal.[48] Cunningham, who had practiced Arizona law since 1912 and in the employ of the county attorney's office since 1916, determined the legal issue was not a matter of race but, rather, one of technicalities in the statutory law.[49] The school district garnered its authority from public school laws, specifically the 1913 Arizona Revised Statutes. If the trustees relinquished control of the Eighth Street School to the college, then the school would no longer be a part of the public school system and therefore no longer subject to the protections and privileges of the civil code. This forfeiture would prevent the TD3 trustees from legally enforcing Mexican attendance at the Eighth Street School. The revised statutes required trustees to maintain schools "as far as practicable with equal rights and privileges; provided that the board of trustees of any district may make segregation of groups of pupils as they may deem advisable."[50] But with the new Memorandum of Agreement, the pupils would cease to be under their control. More important, Cunningham concluded that "such manipulations" could be enforced only by state legislation to revise the education laws and, as a result, was "not within the purview of the Board of Education governing the Normal School, nor the Board of Trustees governing the district school.[51] Further, state law did not address the question of segregation within higher education.[52] The TNS, like other southwestern normal schools and universities, integrated the few qualified Mexican American college students who managed to enter their ranks.[53]

To Deputy Cunningham, the TD3's legal questions about continuing Mexican American school segregation would not have raised his initial concern because segregation between Anglo Americans and Arizonenses was commonplace. School boards often wrote to county and state attorneys about the parameters of school law, including their authority over race-based segregation. George W. Harber, an assistant attorney general and Cunningham's colleague, had answered a similar question ten years earlier for a Mrs. Luther Stover of Williams, Arizona, who asked "whether or not Mexican children can legally be segregated from the white children in the public schools."[54] Harber offered Stover a short but precise interpretation of the rule on record—per subdivision II, paragraph 2733, of the Revised Statutes of Arizona, 1913: "Our law empowers the trustees to segregate children of the African race, but does not empower them to segregate children of the Mexican race unless, of course, children of the Mexican race might also be of African descent, by being intermingled with African blood through birth."[55]

Harber's assessment revealed that Mexican children could not be segregated under Jim Crow laws affecting African Americans. Because Mexicans were legally white, the laws did not apply to them. In the town of Williams, then, as in 1925 Tempe, this sort of Mexican race-based segregation would have been illegal.[56]

Taken together, Cunningham's and Harber's legal interpretations pinpoint how the establishment of the new "Mexican Training School" skirted through the 1913 Arizona Revised Statutes. The state legislature authorized school districts to separate students "as deemed necessary."[57] The state legislature also allowed normal schools to establish laboratory training schools in contract with local school districts. The statute did not address segregation within public institutions of higher education or in the maintenance of training schools.[58] No law specifically prevented the new arrangement between the TNS and the TD3.

Recognizing this legal loophole and despite the attorney general's opinion, the TNS and TD3 trustees moved forward with their decision to transfer the Eighth Street School and its Mexican American students to the college. Part of their rationale extended from the broad control granted to normal schools to operate training schools as public schools in cooperation with local school districts. Under statute 4515, training schools became "a part of the public school system and . . . [were] governed by laws and regulations relating to the public schools."[59] Further, statute 4518 authorized trustees to "prescribe from time to time, such rules and regulations as they may deem proper, governing the admission and attendance at such training schools."[60] Thus, given this combined authority and the successful school referendum, both school boards voted unanimously to support the memorandum naming the Eighth Street School as a "normal training school" effective July 1 and to continue the de facto educational segregation.[61] On April 10, 1925, both parties signed the agreement. The college acquired full responsibility for conducting the new "Mexican Training School," including its administration, budget, faculty and staff employment, and the "admission and entrance of pupils."[62]

Los Tempeneños

Tempeneño memory of *Romo* is one of vernacular history-making.[63] Mexican American families in the town of Tempe, known originally as San Pablo, kept alive the history of the lawsuit, retelling its significance over generations. The story keepers, such as Irene Gómez Hormell, recalled that her Tio Bebé sued the college on behalf of all the Mexican children in Tempe.[64] She described him as very community minded and willing to challenge the inequity or, as she described him, "¡el unico que quiso pelear!" (The only one who would fight!).[65] Known as the "matriarch of San Pablo's history," Hormell is Bebé's grandniece, the granddaughter of Quina's sister Kate Jones Gómez. Hormell is also a member of Los Amigos de Tempe, a group of Tempeneño descendants who gather annually to remember their former neighborhoods, some demolished through eminent domain to make room for ASU dormitories. In 1992, Los Amigos agreed to share their private archives and family memories with the Tempe Historical Museum's "Barrios Oral History Project"; it was the first time the town had officially invited the Tempeneños to participate in its projects.[66] Hormell expressed great pride in her uncle for stepping forward as the plaintiff and representing the community because she also remembered the fear "of speaking up" that forced many Tempeneños to submit to Anglo authority.

Like the claimants in *Mendez* and *Gonzales*, Bebé Romo pursued the legal challenge on behalf of his children, but also with community endorsement. The TNS trustees described the case as "being filed in Court by the Mexican people whose representatives were Adolpho Romo and others."[67] Hormell added that Romo became the spokesman because he was light skinned and had a better chance of winning than a dark-skinned person. She said, "That's the way it was!" Romo's portrait, displayed in a Soto-Gómez family album at the museum where Hormell has actively worked to record and acknowledge Tempe's Mexican history, reveals a man with black hair, deep dark-blue eyes, and a fair complexion.[68]

The memory of Romo's complexion points to the enduring racialization that Tempe's Mexican community navigated. Although his physical appearance may have factored into the community's decision to advance him as the petitioner, the Romo family clearly possessed the classic genealogical heritage of Mexican Americans. According to family lore, Romo was a "Spanish immigrant" who came to Arizona as a *ranchero*, or cowboy, who had worked on several homesteads in Phoenix as a young man.[69] His wife Joaquina Jones, called Quina, was the daughter of Alcaria Montaño from Altar, Sonora, Mexico, and Dr. Walter Wilson Jones, a Virginian considered the first white physician (a tubercular specialist) in Arizona Territory.[70] In 1878, Jones settled his family along the Salt River west of Tempe. He hired Romo to work on his ranch. Quina was the youngest of four sisters who married into both Mexican and white families, including the Currys, Franks, Turners, Villanuevas, and Romos, many of whom continue to live in the Salt River Valley today.[71]

Despite this mixed ethnic heritage, the Romos identified themselves as "Spanish-Mexican."[72] This point is important given the racialized historical context of Mexican Americans in Tempe. As in many Arizona towns, segregation came to Tempe late, after 1900, when its labor-segmented economy developed across race and class lines.[73] Between 1850 and 1900, Anglo Americans and Arizonenses initially collaborated in the development and building of the Salt River Valley towns. Historians Jaime R. Águila and F. Arturo Rosales described this mutual reliance as "a fragile symbiosis . . . in which the two groups cooperated at different levels of the economic and

Figure 11. Joaquina Jones
Romo, circa 1877.

societal structures."[74] As Anglo American settlement overtook the Valley and
as white Southerners established themselves in towns like Tempe, the Mexican American enclaves worked to preserve their socio-economic standing as
well as their Spanish and Mexican Arizona heritage. Most Anglos lived west
and south of Tempe's "N" mountain, a double butte (recognized today as
Sun Devil Stadium) that centered the town at the edge of the Salt River. Most
Spanish-Mexican descendants of the 1880s lived east of the butte in a neighborhood they called "San Pablo," and which some Anglos dubbed "Chihuahua" or "Mexican Town."[75] As early territorial settlers, these Tempeneños
often distinguished themselves from the *recién llegados* (recently arrived) or
México Lindo immigrants who planned to return to "beautiful Mexico."[76]

The Romos did not live in San Pablo, but, like other Tempeneños, they
joined the effort to challenge the steady growth of Juan Crow practices. In
1897, Mexican American middle-class and working-class men, including
Adolpho Romo, who became a butcher, helped found the Tempe Lodge
No. 5 of the Alianza Hispano-Americana (hereafter Alianza). This mutual

Figure 12. Adolpho Romo
(seated) with his brother
Miguel, n.d. Adolpho Romo
and his wife Joaquina (neé
Jones) were plaintiffs in
the school desegregation
case *Romo v. Laird* (1925).
Courtesy of Irene Gómez
Hormell.

aid society, or mutualista, unified the Mexican American community by providing funeral insurance, social activities, and public defense through limited
political activities, such as the formation of Tempe's volunteer fire department
Hose Company No. 1 that served the Mexican neighborhoods.[77] In 1914,
many of these same men helped organize a chapter of the Liga Protectora
Latina (also called the Latin Protective League, or LPL). With 115 members,
the LPL publicized in the *Tempe Daily News* its activist platform "solely for
the betterment of the condition of the Spanish-American citizens."[78]

The LPL possessed radical labor roots, having been established in Phoenix by Spanish-language newspaper owner Pedro G. de la Lama in response
to "civil rights violations and labor abuse."[79] The LPL, for example, opposed
the Arizona Legislature's 1915 Kinney-Claypool Bill intended to ban "non-
English-speaking men from employment in hazardous occupations, an
obvious threat to Mexicans who spoke only Spanish."[80] Significantly, the bill
conflated "non-citizen" with anyone of Mexican descent who did not speak

English. The LPL, with a combined state membership of more than 1,500, rallied the "Mexican and Latin races" to challenge such open hostility and racism.[81] With its largest membership hailing from Maricopa County, the LPL held its annual convention in East Tempe in 1915. The English-language press took note of the "Big Spanish Rally" with five hundred in attendance and, in particular, their interest in the public schools.[82] The LPL formed a subcommittee to inspect local schools and "lend what aid they can towards the betterment of the Mexican conditions in the schools."[83] Given that the Tempeneño lodge hosted the meeting, they likely discussed the recent segregation of the Eighth Street School, which opened for the first time that September as the town's designated Mexican school.

The Romos' son Antonio turned six years old that fall, just as the Tempe school district initiated de facto school segregation.[84] According to the *Arizona Republic*, the TD3 trustees built a new school called the Tenth Street Grammar School that opened in fall 1915 and restricted its enrollment to "English speaking children."[85] The district required "all others," including Antonio and the rest of the Mexican American children in the district, to continue at the Eighth Street School. Although the newspaper reported that "reclassification may be made at any time during the year as best interests of the children seem to require," the Arizonense parents interpreted this new arrangement as racial segregation based on language ability. The Tempeneño lodge followed through on its promise and formed a special education committee to investigate this new policy, while the statewide organization contemplated legislation for bilingual education.[86] The Tempe newspaper reported that "the Mexican population is very worked up over what it claims is the 'segregation' of the Mexican children attending the public school."[87] But white Tempeans insisted that the "arrangement [was] better for both the Mexican children and the American children."[88]

The *Tempe Daily News* never followed up on the actions that the LPL or the Mexican American parents pursued in 1915 and the historical record remained dormant about any sort of racial segregation until the Romos filed their surprise lawsuit in 1925. The ten-year delay may have resulted from the TD3's acquiescence to "reclassify" a few Mexican American children. The 1917 class of eighth-grade graduates from the Tenth Street School included thirty-seven students—six of whom descended from Arizonenses parents. For example, Manuela Sotelo's granddaughter Marie Zander, the Romos' first cousin Floyd Jones Gómez Jr., and the future teacher-attorney Rafael Estrada, whose father was a well-known and controversial businessman in the Salt

River Valley, participated in the 1917 graduation ceremonies.[89] The delay also may have been connected to other pressing political priorities, such as the LPL's 1915 protest of mass executions of Mexicans at the Florence state prison and its national labor complaints against the Estrada family and Arizona Cotton Growers Association (headquartered in Tempe) for abuse and abandonment of Mexican farm workers during World War I and the 1920s cotton bust.[90] Across the state, Mexican immigrant and Mexican American labor union activists also absorbed heavy blows that resulted in mass firings and expulsions from their hometowns, such as the 1917 Bisbee Deportation, where more than one thousand members of the Industrial Workers of the World were arrested, forced by gunpoint onto trains, and dumped in the desert at Columbus, New Mexico. These issues and internal organizational conflict led to the LPL's demise in the 1920s. Still, the Romos and the Tempeneños must have contemplated the school desegregation lawsuit for ten years.

The Legal Challenge

Like any proud parent on the first day of a new school year, Aldopho Romo eagerly escorted his four youngest children—Antonio, Henry, Alice, and Charles—to the Tenth Street School on the morning of September 14, 1925. But when he presented the children, Superintendent G. W. Persons declined to admit them. Persons informed Romo that he had inadvertently come to the wrong school and directed him to the Eighth Street School, a few blocks north, dedicated to the teaching of "Spanish-American and Mexican-American children."[91] Persons explained the new agreement between the school district and the college, but Romo refused to leave and demanded that his children be admitted to the Tempe public schools, not the college's training school. Still Persons turned him away "under orders and by virtue of the directions and commands of the Board of Trustees," and "directed [the Romo children to] report to the authorities of the Normal Training School of the Tempe State Teachers College."[92] Romo took his children home and, between that moment and filing the writ, Adolpho and Quina contemplated their options.

Although the historical record is sketchy here, we can surmise that the Romos strategized carefully and probably with input from the Tempeneño community because they were not alone in their political action. Shortly after the referendum passed, Juana Estrada Peralta petitioned Arizona governor George W. P. Hunt to plead their case to the state legislature in session in

Phoenix.[93] A naturalized citizen, her decision to reach out to him reflected immense courage and boldness. But as a registered voter and Democrat, she also had a reputation for being politically and socially engaged.[94] Even though she learned to read and write English as a second language, she wrote to him anyway. Her gesture reflected the confidence that many Arizonenses held in Hunt because of his support of Mexican immigrant and Mexican American miners who challenged the dual-wage system during strikes between 1913 and 1917 at Ajo, Clifton, Globe, Morenci, Ray, and, significantly, Bisbee.[95]

Over the course of four letters exchanged between the two, Peralta urgently pressed her opposition to segregation and pushed the governor to expose the events unfolding in Tempe given the fate of her four children who were "real sore when they were separated." She highlighted her constitutional rights "not as a Mexican mother, but as an American citizen," placing her allegiance as an American over her ethnicity and gender. With political incisiveness and references to President Theodore Roosevelt's "square deal and fair play" slogans, Peralta wrote, "Don't you think we have a right to ask for a fair deal? . . . I wish I could speak to you or some other person who could help us and tell you our side of the story. It's all right for the Normal to become a college, but why should it be over the anguished pride and trampled feelings of the Mexican residents of this town?"

As she analyzed the unfolding segregation, Peralta exposed a spectrum of racial dynamics and racism at play among Anglos and Arizonenses toward African Americans. Asking the governor to relay her concerns to the state legislators, she wrote, "Could you tell them how our children are separated from the American children, as if they were negroes? They may do it with them, they have been slaves, but we have not been anybody's slaves."[96] These anti-black sentiments reflected the Jim Crowism that white Southerners had brought to Arizona, as well as the deep history of slavery in both Mexico and the United States. The Alianza even banned "people of Chinese and African descent" from its membership.[97]

White Southerners who migrated to the Salt River Valley in the early twentieth century also brought their visions of white supremacy to Maricopa County, which by the 1920s had four Klans of the Ku Klux Klan, including the Butte Klan No. 3 of Tempe.[98] Democratic governor Hunt, in whom Peralta had invested so much faith, had a reputation for being pro-Klan, protecting the Klan from legislative attacks in exchange for political support.[99] These anti-black sentiments also stemmed from the whiteness claims that many Mexican Americans made for equal treatment under the law.[100] Further, Peralta's internalized cultural biases emerged in her description of the children, as she referred to the white children as "American," her own American-born children as "Mexican," but then separated both groups from "negroes." As Peralta distanced herself from African Americans, the architects of white supremacy and those seeking its privilege had erected Juan Crow in her own backyard.[101]

Governor Hunt did nothing to assist the Tempeneños. He explained to Peralta that he had no real authority over the state board of education, nor any power to write state laws. Frustrated by his inaction, she chastised him: "You could have at least given me advice on what to do. But in a way I don't blame you. I think that if you could help us, you would not do it. Everything would crash around you if you did just because you helped the despised Mexicans." Governor Hunt resented her "bitter tone" and insisted that he could only enforce laws, not make them. Peralta had unnerved him, but his dismissal did not deter the Tempeneño challenge to the anti-Mexican hate and the institutionalized racism they were now confronting.

This stalemate pushed the Mexican American community, and especially the Romos, to conceptualize a plan of action that would take them on a course from inquiry to nonviolent direct action, and on to court. First and foremost, they understood that they would have to act within the law. For example, the Romos knew their children would be subject to the state's compulsory attendance laws. The Romos could have refused to send the children to school, although the truant officer Cresencio "Chris" Sigala would have advised against absenteeism. Constable Sigala, like the Romos, came from a long-time Tempeneño family and had joined the mutualista. He monitored attendance at five area schools, including Scottsdale, Eighth Street, Tenth Street, and Kyrene, and he regularly cited Mexican American parents, bringing them into criminal court for failing to send their children to school.[102] Quina and Adolpho Romo also could have considered sending their children to the private school at St. Mary's Catholic Church or moving their children into a nearby district. But St. Mary's had a history of separating its white and Mexican parishioners, as well as its schoolchildren.[103] The neighboring schools at Scottsdale and Rohrig also practiced segregation or had been co-opted into the college's training school system. By default, the Romos enrolled their children at the Eighth Street School while they sought legal assistance.

Instead of turning to the Mexican Consulate as many Mexican American plaintiffs and Mexico Lindo immigrants often did as they negotiated inequities in the United States, the Romos hired two private attorneys, Edward Bray Goodwin and Harold Jennings Janson.[104] Goodwin possessed liberal notions of race in sync with older, pioneer attitudes of "Anglo-Mexican integration" and cooperation.[105] The Goodwin brothers had arrived in Tempe in the 1880s and, with the help of Mexican and Indian laborers, had dug six miles of canal called "the Goodwin and Kyrene ditch," which opened a new section of the southeast valley to irrigated farming and ranching.[106] Edward Goodwin graduated from the TNS, then studied law in Denver and passed the Colorado bar exam in 1895. He opened a law practice in Tempe on Mill Avenue, next door to his brothers' downtown grocery.[107] In 1908, he gained notoriety for successfully representing the Salt River Pima-Maricopa Indian community in a claim against Colonel J. B. Price, who squatted on land along the reservation's southwest border near Tempe (marked today by Price Road or State Loop 101).[108] By 1925, Goodwin lived in South Phoenix, where he was elected county representative to Arizona's sixth (1923) and seventh (1925) legislatures.[109] With a home "south of Washington and west of Central Avenue," the Democrat represented a diverse constituency in the town's "colored section."[110] Goodwin and Janson filed Romo's Complaint for Writ of Mandamus on September 23, 1925, and it was reported the next morning in the *Arizona Republic*.[111] The complaint included Romo's signed affidavit and his allegations of racial segregation in the Tempe schools. The lawyers argued that the Romos' four children possessed the right to attend the schools without "race or descent" as a factor in their admission. As citizens and taxpayers of "Spanish-Mexican descent," the parents specifically contested the agreement on two points: the Eighth Street School's enrollment restriction to "Spanish-American or Mexican-American children" and their instruction by noncertified, apprentice teachers. According to the writ, "Mexican-American and Spanish-American children . . . between the ages of six and twenty-one . . . who are qualified and entitled to enter into, and be admitted to the public schools . . . on account of their race or descent without regard to their age, advancement or convenience, are segregated, excluded and compelled to attend the 'Eighth Street School,' which . . . is taught exclusively by student teachers of the Normal Training School."[112]

The Romos' two-pronged argument opposing unequal race-based education and its delivery by noncredentialed teachers forced the Maricopa County Superior Court to consider the question of "separate but equal" as it applied to Mexican Americans. Unlike other plaintiffs in Mexican American school desegregation history, the Romos challenged teacher qualifications and school district jurisdiction in court.[113] The Romos claimed that, as a result of the TNS agreement, their children received substandard instruction by student teachers.[114] They further asserted that the TD3 now admitted "only white children alone." They requested the judge to issue an order "as justice may require" demanding that the school district admit their children to the Tenth Street School "to which they have a right of admission."[115]

Judge Jenckes recognized the public importance of the *Romo* complaint as no legal remedy or case law addressed the question of Mexican schools. He did not deny it, which was within his purview, and allowed it to proceed through the Maricopa County Superior Court. He issued an order for an Alternative Writ of Mandamus and a summons calling on the TD3 to respond to the complaint in court within two days or to admit the Romo children as they "now admit children of the white race."[116] Maricopa County attorney Arthur T. LaPrade and deputy county attorney Gene Cunningham, acting as defense counsel for the TD3 trustees, met the short, two-day deadline. On Saturday, September 26, they filed a demurrer to quash the complaint, arguing that the plaintiff had no legal grounds, since the writ did not give any supporting evidence entitling the Romo children admittance to the Tenth Street School, nor did it offer any evidence that they had been denied admission. LaPrade and Cunningham further notified the court that the school district would not answer the writ unless the judge ordered it to do so.

That same day, Judge Jenckes and deputy clerk N. C. Moore swiftly composed an amended alternative writ, changing the order to show that superintendent Persons "did refuse and still refuses to admit said [Romo] children to the public schools of said Tempe School District No. 3 on the same terms and conditions as children of the white race."[117] Jenckes then ordered Cunningham and the school board to answer the amended writ within four days. On Tuesday, September 29, Cunningham returned an answer to the plaintiffs and the court, denying allegations that the trustees had refused admittance to the Romo children.[118]

According to the TD3 board of trustees, all children who lived in the district possessed the same right to attend the public schools, and all children who had presented themselves to the superintendent had been admitted, including the Romos, who were now attending the Eighth Street School. The board confirmed that they had organized two elementary schools, commonly known as the Eighth Street School and the Tenth Street School, which together comprised the "Tempe public schools." More important, they insisted that they did not segregate Mexican children "except as is necessary, proper and expedient for the education of such children of such extraction and descent."[119] Pedagogical pragmatism, the board had determined, required that the Mexican children could be "most expeditiously and advantageously educated by persons employed as teachers who are able to speak and understand the Spanish or Mexican language."[120] The board and the superintendent intentionally "placed" these students in classes with teachers who claimed Spanish fluency and, for "convenience and advantage," those classes were located in the Eighth Street School.

The defendants followed the "separate but equal" logic without directly invoking *Plessy*. The trustees and superintendent asserted that students at both schools followed the "same relative course of education and the same assignments and the same methods of instruction together with the same surroundings, advantages and equipment."[121] They claimed that the administration hired teachers of equal ability for both schools and ensured that all children "in like grades in all school houses receive like education in like surroundings."[122] Therefore, the defendants reasonably denied that they had "ever failed and refused to admit" the Romo children to the Tempe public schools.[123]

The Judgment

On October 5, 1925, Judge Jenckes issued his Findings of Fact and Judgment. The verdict resulted in two outcomes that allowed both sides to reaffirm their notions of belonging in Tempe. Judge Jenckes agreed that the TNS and TD3 had exercised "sound discretion" in separating the Mexican children as provided by school law. But the TNS and TD3 also failed to meet the *Plessy* standard because they did not provide true "separate but equal" conditions at the Eighth Street School. In the Findings of Fact, Judge Jenckes emphasized that the key failure was that undergraduate student teachers taught the Mexican American children at the Eighth Street School, while state-certified teachers taught the white children at the Tenth Street School.[124] Correcting this situation—by hiring an equally certified teaching force for both schools—would be essential to a lawful solution that met the *Plessy* standard. Otherwise, "to compel [Mexican American children] to attend schools taught by so-called student teachers" was illegal.

Throughout the week and into the weekend of October 10 and 11, the TD3 and TNS boards of trustees held a series of meetings to devise a legal remedy to continue Mexican segregation "on race lines." They proposed two solutions, which they called Plan A and Plan B, and appointed TNS president Matthews, TD3 superintendent Persons, and TD3 board chairman William E. Laird to present the plans to county attorney Cunningham. In Plan A, the TNS would hire two additional certified "critic" teachers, for a total of six (one per grade) to oversee the student teachers at the Eighth Street School. The critic teachers would be the "official" teachers of record, while the student teachers observed and presented lessons.[125] In Plan B, the TNS would continue its practices as usual "for the Mexican children whose parents do not object" and also would hire two additional certified teachers to work with the Mexican children whose parents do "object to the Training School System."[126] Cunningham did not care for Plan B, since it intimated a "double system in the building." Nonetheless, he conferred with Judge Jenckes, who determined that both options would be legal only if critic teachers taught the classes and the Mexican children and the American children had "similar advantages." The next day, October 12, the TNS board implemented Plan A, but limited the student teachers to observation.

To support the *Romo* judgment and the subsequent modifications of the teaching plans at the Mexican Training School, Judge Jenckes relied on the 1912 Arizona Supreme Court verdict in *Dameron v. Bayless*, regarding African American school segregation in Phoenix.[127] In this case, the Arizona Supreme Court affirmed that the 1909 Territorial Legislature had authorized racial segregation in public schools by allowing the districts "when they deem it advisable . . . [to] segregate pupils of the African from pupils of the White races."[128] The Arizona Supreme Court cited the U.S. Supreme Court holding in *Plessy* and the federal district court rulings in school-segregation cases involving Chinese children in San Francisco in *Wong Him v. Callahan* (California, 1902) and "colored children" in Washington Township, Ohio, in *United States v. Buntin*.[129] In *Dameron*, parent Samuel F. Bayless had challenged the *Plessy* "separate but equal" test by arguing that his children, who walked across busy railroad tracks to attend the Phoenix Madison Street School designated for "African pupils," did not have safe and equal access to school compared to white students who did not have to cross the tracks to get to school.[130] The Arizona Supreme Court denied the Bayless appeal, deciding that it is only "after children arrive at the school building that it be as good a building and as well-equipped and furnished and presided over by *as efficient a corps of teachers* as schools provided by children of other races."[131] Judge Jenckes held that this qualification for equally "efficient" teachers in both white and black schools applied to *Romo*. To further emphasize his interpretation, he quoted directly from *Bayless*, stating that "the language employed by our [Arizona] Supreme Court . . . is equally applicable to the [Mexican] situation presented here."[132]

On the basis of this one inequality, Judge Jenckes granted the Romos a "permanent peremptory writ of mandamus." In the judgment, he commanded the trustees to admit "upon pain and peril" the Romo children to the Tenth Street School "on the same terms and conditions to the public schools . . . as children of other nationalities are now admitted."[133] The Tempeneños took advantage of this opening and interpreted the judgment as halting *all* segregation because in the Findings of Fact the judge described the segregation as having applied to the Romo children "as well as all other Spanish-American and Mexican-American children."[134] The Tempeneños expected Superintendent Persons to admit the Romo children and, by default, all Mexican American children who presented themselves for school registration on October 12, 1925.

Now Tempeneño community action truly emerged, as the Arizonense parents and children descended on the Tenth Street School to gain admission. According to the school board minutes, "Several Mexican parents and children presented themselves . . . claiming it was their right to have their children enrolled and instructed at said school."[135] But just as events had unfolded one month prior, Superintendent Persons again obstinately refused to admit the Romo children or any others.[136] Regardless of the court's ruling, Persons explained, the TD3 board of trustees had reconfirmed that no Mexican child would attend the Tenth Street School.[137] This time, however, the Romos and the other Mexican parents refused to leave the campus. "The children was [*sic*] taken into one of the classrooms and seated comfortably—while the parents present were being conferred with in the office."[138]

Unable to disperse the parents, Persons finally called the TD3 trustees. Chairman William Laird dashed out of his Mill Avenue soda fountain at the Laird & Dines Drugstore, which he co-owned with his father and pharmacist brothers, and intercepted secretary Isabel Waterhouse.[139] Together they joined Persons at the Tenth Street School and tried to intimidate the Mexican parents, who still refused to budge. The impasse between the parents and the school board members mirrored the town's larger sociopolitical divide. Many of the Arizonense parents held memberships in the Alianza and the La Liga Protectora Latina, which had publicly challenged the school segregation ten years earlier. The school board trustees, William Laird and Hugh Laird (who later became Tempe mayor) were known members of the Butte Klan No. 3.[140] This moment encapsulated Arizona race relations and neither side would yield. At a loss, the trustees called county school superintendent A. L. Jones, missing board member J. H. Daniel, and deputy county attorney Cunningham, who agreed to negotiate the standoff at 2 p.m. that day.

Cunningham was a mediator at heart. When Judge Jenckes had issued the verdict on October 5, Cunningham had tried to convince the TD3 trustees to be mindful of the lawsuit's implications. He warned them to let the "just and sound opinion" stand, and he closed the case. He did not anticipate any "legal advantage" in pursuing an Arizona Supreme Court appeal, which he felt would only result in "hardship." In a letter to Superintendent Persons, Cunningham argued, "I am against further litigation in the matter, as I am fearful of the ultimate results . . . in creating a condition of race animosity in your community, which might, under certain circumstances, become prevalent over a much greater territory."[141] What kind of "race animosity" did Cunningham mean? Had he anticipated or been warned of a community protest? Is this why he agreed to mediate the standoff with the parents?

When Cunningham arrived at the school, the Tempeneños stood resolute. Waterhouse recorded in her minutes that Cunningham "tried in vain" for several hours to convince the parents to acquiesce to the revised segregation remedies approved by Judge Jenckes. Plan A offered a "peaceable" solution and equal accommodation, but the Tempeneños refused to accept any standard less than full integration, which the writ promised and which they viewed as a victory and as a civil right. Because the parents remained steadfast, Cunningham managed instead to sway the TD3 trustees, who conceded that evening and now agreed to admit all of the Mexican children. "They [the Mexican parents could] send their children Tuesday morning to Tenth St. School and if they belonged in grades One to Six—Mr. Persons would enroll them and provide them with slips starting their grade and to report there."[142] Secretary Waterhouse recorded that only a few children arrived for classes the next morning. But her records also indicated that by the end of the academic year, 34 percent—105 of 308 children—of the Tenth Street School's enrollment claimed Mexican American heritage.[143] Clearly, Cunningham had avoided a "race war," and the Tempeneños asserted their right to belong "on the same terms and conditions" as white Americans.[144]

Mexican Racialization

While Judge Jenckes's split ruling fell in line with the era's case law, it also revealed the careful parameters of Arizona's race politics and the common knowledge of Mexican racialization. In fact, Judge Jenckes's findings were congruent with the "racial prerequisite cases" of the late nineteenth and early twentieth centuries. Critical race theorist and legal scholar Ian Haney López has determined that holdings in the racial prerequisite cases relied on legal precedent and, if none existed, two kinds of rationales: scientific evidence and common knowledge.[145] These cases determined the racial classifications of groups of people in the United States, including Mexican Americans. In 1897, a Texas court declared, "Mexicans are White," based on legal precedent established in the 1848 Treaty of Guadalupe Hidalgo, which ended the Mexican-American War.[146] In all of these cases, "whiteness" was the measure of naturalized citizenship. Haney López tells us that effectively until 1952 "being a 'white person' was a condition for acquiring citizenship."[147]

Judge Jenckes used both legal precedent and common knowledge of race in the *Romo* ruling. He knew what the law said and how people in Arizona practiced race relations. Although he was new to the superior court, having been appointed to the bench in early 1925, Jenckes had practiced Arizona law since 1912.[148] He clearly understood and applied, in his decision, the Jim Crow laws applicable to African Americans as well as the educational rules outlined in the 1913 civil code of Arizona's Revised Statutes. In the Findings of Fact, Judge Jenckes's reference to *Dameron* carried with it a clear knowledge of the law, as well as a very personal and localized history that emerged directly from Maricopa County race politics.[149] In 1909, the Arizona territorial legislature overrode the veto of Governor Joseph H. Kibbey who opposed the new Jim Crow school laws that allowed for the segregation of African American and white children. Governor Kibbey was Jenckes's father-in-law.

A Quaker who studied at Earlham College and under the tutelage of his lawyer father, Kibbey came to Arizona in 1888 as a practicing attorney and he developed a reputation for pursuing cases of import to him, such as segregation. During his career, he served in nearly every legal capacity within the territory, including as an associate justice of the Arizona Territorial Supreme Court (1889-1893) and attorney general before President Theodore Roosevelt appointed him territorial governor (1905-1909). After stepping down as governor, Kibbey reopened his law practice just as the Phoenix school board voted to segregate its black students in accordance with the revised civil code.[150] Kibbey chose to represent the Bayless family.

In the midst of *Dameron*, territorial legislators, led by Tempe representative and education committee chair Dr. Benjamin B. Moeur (a physician, future governor, and later a Klan member), hoped to incorporate Jim Crow school laws into the new draft of the proposed state constitution.[151] At Dr. Moeur's request, TNS president Arthur Matthews drafted the constitutional language for school segregation, as well as new civil codes for the public schools. These were intended to replace the territorial laws, but the legislature perceived too many complications in adding school segregation to the proposed state constitution because it might require local communities to create new schools for other "non-whites," especially Asian Americans.[152] Instead, the legislators retained the 1909 territorial law on African American school segregation and, later, after statehood and after the *Dameron* decision, they revised the education section of the 1913 civil code to allow school boards to segregate "any group of pupils they deem advisable."[153] This change expanded school segregation to every conceivable group of students, including Mexican Americans, who could be racialized and separated for a variety of pedagogical reasons.

In 1912, the same year the Union admitted Arizona as the forty-eighth state, the Arizona Supreme Court published *Dameron* honoring *Plessy* and its "separate but equal" holding. At that moment, *Dameron* had no particular bearing in Tempe other than the fact that some of Tempe's elected and appointed officials, namely Moeur and Matthews, advocated racial segregation. Known by reputation "as a 'sundown' town," few African Americans lived there.[154] Between 1900 and 1930, Tempe's African American population grew from three (all men) to thirteen, compared to a total population of 4,464 in the town proper and its rural districts.[155] The 1910 school census counted only "one colored child," and one historian noted that African American children were "conspicuously absent from the census count[s]" in the 1920s and 1930s.[156] In 1926, the Tempe school board voted to pay to bus the unnamed children of one black family to the segregated Washington School in Mesa, rather than enroll them. When the TNS began admitting African American college students in the 1920s, these young women and men were barred from the dormitories and from teaching in its training schools.[157] They commuted to Tempe or boarded with Mrs. Theodore (Maggie) Thomas, a.k.a. "Mother Thomas," one of the few black women who owned property in Tempe.[158] The black TNS students completed their practice teaching requirements at the Phoenix "colored schools," an arrangement also negotiated by the college.

Dameron, however, did provide a precedent for the kind of educational segregation that Moeur and Matthews had hoped to craft for the entire state. *Dameron*, combined with the flexibility of the 1913 civil code, allowed white Tempeans to justify the legal segregation of Mexican-immigrant and Mexican American children in 1914 and again in 1925. Understanding the relationship between these race-relations patterns within Tempe and their correlation to state and federal Jim Crow precedents, Judge Jenckes recognized that Arizona

law accommodated the dual legal (white) and social (non-white) constructions of a "Mexican American race."[159] As legal scholar Laura E. Gómez, so
eloquently explains, this *"legal* construction of Mexicans as racially 'white'
alongside the *social* construction of Mexicans as non-white and racially inferior" was the central paradox of Mexican American racial identity.[160]

Equally significant, the consultations and legal documents exchanged
among Judge Jenckes, deputy attorney Cunningham, and the plaintiff's attorneys Goodwin and Janson also reflected the shifting social constructions of the
Romo children's racialization. Judge Jenckes never specifically addressed the
race of the Mexican American children, nor did he reference legal precedents
related to their racialization. However, he did accept common knowledge and
relied on Goodwin's and Janson's descriptions from the original complaint.
They described Romo as a "resident citizen and taxpayer ... of Spanish-
Mexican descent." They also quoted the college's memorandum describing
the Eighth Street School segregation as limited to "Spanish-American and
Mexican-American children."[161] The memorandum, however, contained two
odd clauses, one asking "for a more particular definition of the term 'Spanish-
American and Mexican-American'" and another clarifying that "Spanish-
American or Mexican-American 'student teachers'" would be exempt from
the segregation. The TNS had a long history of Mexican American alumni
and financial support dating to its founding.[162] Between 1924 and 1936, more
than seventy-five Mexican American college students attended TNS.[163] So
it appears that the TNS trustees understood how the common knowledge
of Mexican racialization might complicate notions of ethnicity and class, as
well as the personal and practical negotiations of deciding who belonged in
these imaginary communities. But Judge Jenckes never expressly defined the
terms *Spanish American* and *Mexican American,* nor did he address the issue
of the protected Mexican American student teachers. Instead, in the order and
request for an alternative writ, he "command[ed]" the TD3 to enroll the Romo
children "as they now admit children of the white race."[164] Did this mean that
Judge Jenckes considered the Romos to be white? Or did he think they were
non-whites who warranted equality under the law?

Deputy Cunningham expressed serious concern that Judge Jenckes considered Mexican Americans to be white. Cunningham observed in a letter to
the TD3 trustees that the judge "pointedly uses the words 'Caucasian Race'"
when referring to the Mexican American students.[165] These references, he
explained, occurred *in dicta* (as an aside in conversations among the judge
and the attorneys) and their insinuation seriously decreased the defense's

plea for race-based exclusions, which could have been arguable in an Arizona Supreme Court appeal. "The phraseology," Cunningham opined, "used both in the agreement between the District and the Normal School and that used by the plaintiff in his application for a writ and the alternative writ, I feel have been most unfortunate."[166]

We can interpret the dilemma Cunningham observed by drawing on legal analysis of the post-1930 Mexican American educational desegregation cases. After 1930, Mexican American lawyers shifted legal strategy away from arguments for "equal protection under the law" toward arguments for "due process" as guaranteed under the Fourteenth Amendment.[167] This specifically changed the nature of the legal conflict from racial "difference" to "whiteness." Mexican Americans objected to educational segregation because it denied them "the privileges of their 'whiteness' under Jim Crow."[168] Perhaps this was the strategy that the Romo attorneys pursued as well?

Goodwin and Janson carefully attempted to shape the Romos' racial identity to emphasize race-based segregation without exempting them from white privilege. In the initial complaint, the attorneys argued that the "Spanish-Mexican" children possessed "a right of admission without excluding them on account of their race or descent" to the school district "to which white children alone are admitted."[169] In their draft of the order for the alternative writ, which the judge adopted verbatim, the attorneys also called on the TD3 to enroll the Romo children "as they now admit children of the white race." These statements, however, suggest ambiguity. The Romos may or may not be white. To clarify white lineage, then, in the amended alternative writ, the plaintiff's attorneys shifted the Romos' description to "children of Spanish-American and Mexican-American *extraction*."[170] In the answer, the defense attorneys adopted these notions of "extraction and descent" but now qualified the segregation as a matter of the "Spanish or Mexican language," not race. This pushed Judge Jenckes to adopt and insert an amended terminology of "children of other nationalities." The Romos, now presumably of the white race, had to be admitted to the public schools "on the same terms and conditions . . . as children of other nationalities are now admitted."[171]

Goodwin and Janson, however, were still not satisfied with the court's description of the Romos or the possibility of continued school segregation based on language rationales. The day after the verdict, Harold Janson sent a sharp note to Superintendent Persons reminding him to enroll the Romo children at the Tenth Street School or face contempt charges. "In other words," he wrote, "no discrimination can be made in the matter."[172] On October 30, several weeks later, Goodwin and Janson also filed motions to amend the Findings of Fact and the Judgment. Judge Jenckes agreed to add an eleventh finding that specifically described the Mexican American racial segregation, and to change the "conclusions of law" to omit the *Dameron* case and civil code references. The eleventh finding stated that the TD3 historically "segregate[d] the children of Mexican-American and Spanish-American descent on the basis of blood, descent and nationality," including the Romos, who now attended "a segregated and separate school."[173] The revised judgment now forbade the TD3 from discriminating on the basis of genealogy.

To emphasize the matter of due process, the new conclusion also downplayed civil code exceptions allowing "separation" and black/brown comparisons of Jim/Juan Crow. Reducing a one-page conclusion to two sentences, Judge Jenckes removed the "separate but equal" analysis of *Dameron* that shaped his original judgment. Instead, he emphasized legislative authority, not local authority, over school segregation. He criticized the TD3 for failing to hire equally qualified teachers; he also chastised them for "exceed[ing] their authority" by creating the segregated Mexican school. "It is true," he wrote, "the Legislature has the authority to confer such power upon school boards, but in my opinion, the Legislature has not exercised or attempted to exercise any such authority in this State, except as to children of African descent."[174] This new conclusion echoed Maricopa County's original position, which Deputy Cunningham had relayed to Superintendent Persons in February 1925, that school segregation remained a legislative issue. By sharpening the judge's findings and conclusion, Goodwin and Janson, in agreement with Cunningham, attempted to tighten spaces in the law that allowed for the coexistence of dual legal and social constructions of a Mexican American race. They brought the Romos' racial identity into closer alignment with the guarantees of due process that accorded white privilege.

This rewriting of the Romos' racial identity highlights not only how Arizona law structured whiteness but also how it structured citizenship. Whether Tempeans viewed the Romos as white or non-white, legal loopholes subjected them to "Mexican segregation" and disenfranchised them in ways similar to African Americans, but on the basis of perceived citizenship. Even as Goodwin and Janson argued to close the gap on local control in public schools to stop race-based segregation, they failed to deal with the issue of "nation," which was so often tied to children of immigrant heritage. Despite the fact that the Romo children were native-born U.S. citizens, common knowledge of their ethnicity marked them as aliens and diminished their right to belong.

This is significant because the federal Immigration Act of 1924 (the Johnson-Reed Act, known for its "quota system") designated nationality according to country of birth; in this instance, however, "common knowledge" and local Arizona practices superseded national law.[175] The Romos' Mexican heritage, not their American births, determined their identity. The modified judgment hinted at this complexity as the lawyers bound "blood, descent and nationality" into the final definition of the Romos' racial status. This mixed racial legacy justified continued segregation at the Eighth Street School for "immigrant" children in need of Americanization. The later *Mendez* and *Gonzales* courts confronted similar patterns of racialized citizenship.[176]

Failed Justice

Romo resulted in a travesty of justice for the Tempeneños. In the realm of daily life, the Romos and many more Arizonenses gained admission for their children to the Tenth Street School, but in the legal infrastructures of education and politics, Juan Crow was not outlawed. In the spectrum of belonging, yes, the Romo children and their extended kin, including Adolpho Romo's grandniece Irene Gómez Hormell and granddaughter Lillie Parra-Moraga, achieved a level of educational equality and racial parity as several generations of Romo family members attended the Tenth Street School. "Once my grandfather fought the case, people had the choice," recalled Parra-Moraga.[177] During the 1925–1926 school year, Mexican American parents enrolled 108 of their children at the Tenth Street School, changing the school demographics by 34 percent.[178] The *Arizona Republic* reported that the school district hired two new teachers at the Tenth Street School to assist with the increased enrollment of "Mexican children being added to the already crowded rooms."[179] The town of Tempe had intended to have one "Mexican school," but, in the eyes of white parents, they now had two. Infuriated, Superintendent Persons resigned his post at the end of the school year. A mysterious fire, which the *Tempe Daily News* later attributed to Persons's anger, destroyed the district's administrative offices and most of the school records, except for Secretary Waterhouse's minute book, with her extra notes on the *Romo* case, which she kept safely at home.[180]

In an effort to meet the "separate but equal" legal standard for a "Mexican Training School," and with Judge Jenckes's permission, the college began hiring certified teachers for the Eighth Street School, which still had

an enrollment of 420 Mexican American students.[181] TNS president Matthews assessed the Romo complaint as a surmountable, "unforeseen cir-
cumstance."[182] The Mexican Americanization work offered at the segregated
Eighth Street School continued as planned. By spring's end, the college newspaper touted that the Mexican American children received an education that
was a "privilege superior to that of many schools peopled by the wealthiest."[183]
That summer, on June 15, 1926, Matthews renewed the TD3 memorandum
to oversee the Eighth Street School, except this time the trustees deleted any
specific references to "Mexicans" or "segregation."[184] Matthews retired from
the TNS presidency in 1930 and remained an esteemed professor emeritus
until his death in 1942. The segregated Eighth Street School operated under
the college's authority through 1945.[185]

The legal institutionalization of Juan Crow forced the Tempeneños to
decide whether they should continue to confront school segregation on a
daily basis. In spring 1926, TD3 trustees noted that twenty-two Mexican children left the Tenth Street School, decreasing the school's total enrollment of
Mexicans by 24 percent, from 108 to 82.[186] Hormell recalled family stories
that Tempeneños who challenged discrimination feared retaliation, perhaps
from the local Klan.[187] As a result, many parents sacrificed integrated education for economic welfare, and they capitulated to the public pressure to
return to the old social order. They simply did not have the economic and
psychological resources to transgress the racial codes, or to cope with the
fact that, as Pedro de la Lama at the time told anthropologist Manuel Gamio,
"pocas veces le hacen justicia al mexicano" (Mexicans rarely get American
justice).[188] After *Romo*, some Tempeneños retreated or left the state, including one of Hormell's aunts who moved to California. "She had that hate for
Arizona, because she felt like she was a person and she wanted to be treated
as one."[189] For those who couldn't leave, they defiantly reclaimed the school:
"Well, we don't need their damned [Tenth Street] school; we'll go to our own,
the Eighth Street School."[190]

Across Arizona, the near win or failed justice in *Romo* reestablished Anglo-
American authority. The push for Juan Crow Mexican schools grew across
the state, not only as a way to maintain the social boundaries between Mexicans and Anglos but also as a remedy for the state's economic decline in
the decade of the Great Depression. The New Deal's promise of employment
for the working poor in programs such as the Works Progress Administration brought funding for new public works, including segregated Mexican

schools. As a visual and public representation of the civil inequality between Mexicans and Anglos, these schools, their student bodies, and their Mexican American teachers symbolized the restored social order and an expectation that Arizonenses would learn their place and stay there.

Juan Crow's growth, nonetheless, did not deter Arizonenses who had resolutely endorsed civic integration as a way to negotiate the legacy of conquest. The small elite who had emerged over the generations continued to navigate the race and class politics that they encountered in public life and within their professions. The Arizonense press urged its readers to remain steadfast and to hold onto their dignity regardless of the dimming economy and the rising anti-Mexican sentiment. Arizonense teachers and parents united to advocate for their children and collaborated to pursue new pathways to sustain their communities. The youth themselves, as student-now-teacher Ida Celaya once wrote, "seguí delante," kept going forward.

CHAPTER 5

Teacher Advocates, Juan Crow Realities

> We are indeed fortunate in living in an era in which the
> world is still sensitive to the movements of a people, but
> even more fortunate are we when we consider that we
> are at the threshold of a new era for the betterment of
> our people.
> —Rebecca Florián Muñoz, *The Mexican Voice* (1939)

The twin goals of Americanization and segregation shaped the educational futures and employment trajectories of Arizonense children at the onset of the Great Depression. Mexican American children comprised nearly 35 percent of the state's elementary school students, but by the eighth grade they dropped out of school at a 93 percent "rate of elimination" (in the parlance of the era).[1] During the 1930-1931 school year, the Tucson school district reported that for one hundred Mexican American children in the first grade, only seven remained in the eighth grade. The low holding power of the elementary schools matched the statewide data for Mexican American high schoolers who comprised less than 8 percent of all high school students. Because the U.S. Census Bureau intentionally counted "Mexicans" in the 1930 Census, the state of Arizona relied on this new data to measure its progress with Mexican American student retention. The high school attendance rates jumped in 1935-1936 to 11 percent; 2,158 Mexican Americans enrolled in grades nine through twelve compared to a statewide total of 18,859 high schoolers. This figure was quite low, however, given the overall total of 29,021 Mexican American children enrolled at all grade levels.[2] Education officials noticed this trend and attributed it to the "selective character of the high school requirements," the Spanish language, and self-segregation.[3]

"Probably the great majority of these foreign pupils speak their native language at home. They also tend to segregate themselves socially. The problem of language and social segregation is evident in schools where foreign pupils attend in appreciable number, and is a challenge to the administrators of the state."[4] According to the state's analysis, this was not an educational problem, it was a Mexican Problem.

Cast continually as problematic, Arizonenses found their world constrained and divided. In nearly every aspect of social life, Anglos drew boundaries between themselves and Mexican Americans. The outcome of the *Romo* case created an opening for the continued growth of Juan Crow segregation or, as the Arizona State Teachers College described it, "training in Americanization and problems connected with teaching non-English speaking elementary children."[5] This separation extended from schools to neighborhoods to employment to public recreation. In August 1936, *El Fronterizo* ran a full front-page editorial challenging the *Arizona Republic* for hosting a segregated "day at the park" for the city's children. "¡Alerta Padres de Familia! Se Humilla a Nuestros Hijos," (Attention Parents with Families, Our Children Are Humiliated), the headline warned.[6] The *Arizona Republic* planned the festivities as a summer hurrah and divided the event by race: Monday for white children, Tuesday for black children, and Wednesday for Mexican American children. The editors, Pedro G. de la Lama and Luis H. Córdova asked parents to maintain their dignity and forgo the "music, soda, and sandwich." They wrote, in capital letters, "Mexicanos: No vendamos nuestra dignidad por una soda." ("Mexicans: We cannot sell our dignity for a soda.")

In the face of segregation and economic depression, Arizonenses maneuvered carefully, continuing their daily lives as ordinarily as possible, sending their children to school if they could afford it, and doing their best to sustain employment. In 1930 Phoenix, Mexican Americans comprised only 15 percent (approximately ten thousand) of the general population, but the majority worked in farm labor and in the domestic and service industries. Roughly "7,300 residents" lived in the city proper, while another "3,500 Mexican agricultural workers lived around the city in growers' camps, cheap auto courts, or 'squatters' camps' located near canals and dirt roads."[7] According to historian Jean Reynolds, most Spanish-surnamed women who worked in the decade did so in the service industry, especially the laundries—"Phoenix Laundry, Maricopa Laundry, Arizona Laundry and Bell Laundry"—that supported the tourist industry. In her oral history, Mary López García explained that in 1929 at the age of fourteen she dropped out of school. "I wanted to keep going but couldn't because my father didn't have any work. There was no WPA then, when the Depression started, there was nothing, no work, nothing (for men)."[8] Mexican American women and their daughters, who were paid much less on the dollar than men, picked up the economic burden with what little work they could find.

The young ASTC graduate María Urquides encountered this bleak scenario as the backdrop to her fledging career as a public school teacher assigned to Tucson's Davis Elementary, the largest school in the city in the heart of Barrio Anita. "I'm sure I got the job because I spoke Spanish," she recalled. "It was 1928, just before the Depression. The school was 98 percent Mexican, along with a few Indians, and two Anglo families."[9] Her students' families resembled that of sixteen-year-old Cruz "Chita" Robles, the oldest daughter of ten children who left school to work in 1929.[10] With an unemployed father, she abandoned her Hollywood dreams (she resembled Gloria Swanson). Chita and her younger sister Licha worked as live-in domestic servants. Their income, roughly $4-$7/week, helped support the family, which relied on everyone's contribution.[11] Urquides attempted to stave off her students' poverty by fundraising to support meals and after-school activities. She planted shade trees on barren campus grounds and fixed up her classroom—"painted a cool apple-green and filled with bright animal and nursery prints."[12] In 1932, she helped the Young Women's Christian Association (YWCA) organize "Club Adelante" for Mexican American parents.[13] Together, they convinced the city to let them use an abandoned property near the school, and they transformed it into Oury Park (now Oury Center). "We cleaned the bathrooms, cleared the fields, built a library and a baseball diamond."[14] She remembered visiting every single child's home in Barrio Anita. The economic problems they faced pushed her into social work and she volunteered every day after school for nine years at Catholic Social Services.

Like many Arizonense teachers of her generation, Urquides was not alone in the racialized experience of her vocation. Most primary school teachers, regardless of race or ethnicity, found themselves performing some level of social work for their students. For teachers of color, the difference was the paradox of race. Mexican American teachers' legally white status helped them negotiate their personal educational paths from the first day of school to the day of graduation to the first job offer. This perceived whiteness, however, did not protect them in the profession. Like African American teachers in the age of Jim Crow, Mexican American teachers in the age of Juan Crow found themselves locked into Mexican schools. Assigned for the most part to work with Mexican American children in the lower grades, they experienced very little upward mobility in the profession, save for an opportunity to teach high school Spanish as a foreign language. Gender and location made a difference. A few Mexican American male teachers rose to principalships of rural schools and taught upper grades. The politics of race, however, outstripped most Arizonense educators' hopes for advancement. Even the most successful of them, Amelia Hunt García who in 1928 became the first Mexican American on the State Board of Education and the highest ranking Mexican American politician in the state, suffered a political scandal so brutal that it prematurely ended her public career. The networks that Arizonense college students, teachers, and civic leaders developed helped them not only to sustain civic integration but also to buoy their efforts to move forward in the face of incredible hardship.

Mexican American Teachers

Juan Crow, the educational segregation of ethnic Mexican children, resembled Jim Crow in many ways. Arizona school districts divided children by "race" in "separate but equal" schools identified in newspaper headlines such as "Bullion Plaza for Mexicans Only," or by name such as the "Spanish School" at Scottsdale or the new "Mexican Grammar School" built "on the south side of Glendale, which will accommodate several hundred children of Mexican and Spanish-American parentage."[15] Districts, then, hired a few teachers of the same racial, ethnic, and linguistic heritage to work at these schools particularly in the lower grades, from pre-kindergarten to the third grade. Spanish-speaking teachers—Mexican and Anglo—were preferred for the lower grades for two reasons: These children often spoke no English and there was little expectation that they would advance beyond the fourth grade. In Phoenix, Reverend Esaú P. Muñoz and his wife Febronia Florián Muñoz sent their two youngest children who spoke only Spanish to Grant School, which was known for its Americanization work and only offered classes through the fourth grade.[16] Not a single Spanish-surnamed teacher worked there. Nine of the seventeen faculty (all white women) graduated from the ASTC, where they most likely trained "for efficient work in Mexican education problems" at the segregated Eighth Street School with Americanization specialist Professor Helen Roberts.[17]

Arizona's new Juan Crow structures emerged to expand Jim Crow segregation and to account for the in-betweenness of Mexican American racialization.

Technically, Mexican Americans were considered "white by law." This significant difference in the legal personhood of Mexican Americans versus African Americans meant that Mexican Americans could not be legally barred solely on the basis of race. Juan Crow, however, operated along *multiple nodes of perception*: race (the person's perceived racial identity), ethnicity (the person's cultural and linguistic heritage), nationality (the person's perceived, not actual, place of origin), and class (the person's economic position). If a person of Mexican heritage could be perceived as white, using a combination of these *nodes of perception*, then this person *might* be allowed to move within white society. Some Mexican Americans did, while many others did not. Jim Crow and Juan Crow operated simultaneously and in parallel to one another, but also to account for the *perceived* differences between African Americans and Mexican Americans in Arizona society. Some Mexican Americans promoted these differences to secure their whiteness.

School-district placement of Mexican American children offers us an immediate clue about how white Arizonans deployed Juan Crow rules and how Arizonenses maneuvered around them. The Muñoz daughters—Rebecca, Lucinda, Elizabeth, and Josephine—each attended a number of different schools throughout their childhood. By sixth grade, Elizabeth remembers that her family had settled in Phoenix and that she spoke "enough English" (her words) to be admitted as the only Mexican child in an all-Anglo class at Adams School.[18] Every morning, she walked her two younger siblings to Grant School, about twenty-seven blocks round-trip, before starting her day at Adams. The next year, 1931, her sister Josephine was double promoted, so she and Elizabeth attended seventh grade together. By 1932, they were the only two Mexicans in the "highest section" of eighth grade (8A). They sang in the glee club and made the honor roll. As members of the National Honor Society, Elizabeth and Josephine graduated from Phoenix Union High School (PUHS) in 1937. By her count, only fifteen Mexican Americans graduated in their senior class of eight hundred, including the co-valedictorian Bernard Carrascoso who was the 1939 valedictorian at Phoenix Junior College also.[19]

Similarly, Arizonense teachers negotiated these nodes of perception in the profession as they sought permanent, full-time employment. Unlike African American teachers who pursued promotion to administration and principalships within the few segregated Negro schools and even within schools operated by the Bureau of Indian Affairs, Mexican American teachers found themselves siloed in white-controlled districts where they were assigned to teach Spanish-speaking children at the pre-kindergarten, kindergarten, and lower primary grades.[20] Like their counterparts in New Mexico and Texas, Arizonense educators accepted these offers to teach English as a second language to monolingual Spanish-speaking and Mexican immigrant children because these were the only jobs available to them.[21] The teachers colleges at Tempe and Flagstaff, as well as the education department at the University of Arizona, operated "teacher placement bureaus" to locate jobs for their graduates. While many alumni found work, others publicly accused the bureaus of bias toward recent graduates and privately criticized them for enforcing Juan Crow and Jim Crow hiring practices.[22]

Garnering these limited teaching posts required shrewd diplomacy through hometown or familial connections. María Urquides downplayed her Tucson job offer, but her father Hilario was a longtime city employee and well known in county politics.[23] Sisters Concepción and Rose Mary Faras, 1913 and 1917 graduates from Tempe, acquired jobs in their hometown of Pirtleville, a Mexican enclave outside of Douglas where they shared a family home.[24] Similarly, sisters Alice, Evelyn, and Rose Buzan also lived and worked together for the Tucson schools in the 1920s.[25] Teachers Ida Celaya, María Escalante, and Sophia Sigala who hailed from well-known Tempe families worked at schools near their family homes. The Chandler Schools announced in the *Arizona Teacher and Home Journal* that they hired Ida Celaya "for the Spanish speaking children."[26] In 1930, Escalante taught the first grade at Scottsdale No. 48 located just across the Salt River (Rio Salado) that marked Tempe's northern edge. Sigala, whose father Chris was a county truant officer, assumed the "pre-primary" class at Tempe's Rural School No. 13, which operated as one of the ASTC training schools.[27] In 1937, Escalante transferred to the southeast district Gilbert No. 41 where she taught the "Pre-Primary Mexican" class until 1942.

Jobs at the smaller semi-urban districts offered consistent employment, and even smaller rural districts provided the most opportunity for advancement in this narrow career trajectory. In these out-of-the-way communities, teachers taught multiple grade levels, including the upper primary grades, and were hired simultaneously as principals. For example, at Concho School District No. 6, principal Rosalío "Ross" F. Muñoz, who had a master's degree, taught the seventh and eighth grades and supervised three faculty.[28] Less than a handful of Arizonense teachers, including women and men with decades of experience and advanced degrees, served as rural school principals before World War II. Nonetheless, rural districts such as Concho that were founded and controlled by Arizonense families, invested in hiring Arizonense teachers and principals from Amelia Hunt García in the 1890s to Muñoz and Eleazar Arvizu in the 1940s.[29]

Arizona's large, urban school districts rarely hired Mexican American teachers. In 1930, the largest district in the state, Phoenix No. 1, reported only one Spanish-surnamed educator among its 292 teachers at nineteen schools.[30] At Douglas School, which only offered grades one through four, TNS graduate Rose Oviedo taught the "1C" Americanization course. Oviedo was Sophia Sigala's aunt. In the decade prior, Oviedo taught at Washington School, also well known for its Americanization program. One other TNS graduate, Carmela Martínez taught "Americanization all grades" for one year in Phoenix during World War I, but after one year transferred to a smaller Maricopa County school district where she was assigned the first and second grades.[31] No Spanish-surnamed educators ever worked at PUHS before 1928, even though it employed well over one hundred faculty. Alice Castro, who completed a master's degree in child guidance at Stanford University, joined the staff as a PUHS counselor that year. The high school district initially hired her as an assistant to its research department where she offered public talks on intelligence testing and child development.[32] In Tucson, the employment scenario improved slightly as six of 158 primary school teachers had Spanish surnames.[33] Three of these teachers—Amelia Maldonado, Sabina Sandoval, and Lugarda Ortiz—taught first grade at three different schools. At Davis School, María Urquides taught "play" (physical education) and Beulah Rose Franco taught history and art. Rose Buzan worked as the district's "visiting teacher," providing social work services to students and families. Of forty-four teachers at Tucson High School, three had Spanish surnames, including Spanish teachers Ida Celaya (who transferred from Chandler) and Thelma Ochoa, as well as the bookkeeping instructor T. D. Romero. Tucson also operated three junior high schools with fifty-eight faculty, but none had Spanish surnames. Historian Thomas Sheridan found similar evidence of this slim hiring in his evaluation of the 1931–1932 academic year, when the district hired only eight Spanish-surnamed teachers out of 328 personnel.[34]

Arizonense teachers could analyze their employment conditions in a variety of ways, but the most transparent evidence appeared in the state's annual teacher directory. While the Arizona State Department of Education did not publicly disclose the racial background of its teacher workforce, the directory provided employment data on every public school teacher and school official, including names, addresses, credentials, and appointments. For example, the nine Mexican American teachers employed in Tucson in

1930 graduated from Tempe's ASTC, the University of Arizona, and New Mexico State Teachers College. For Ida Celaya, the shift in the notation of her alma mater from the Tempe Normal School (1917) to the University of Arizona (1926) signaled to her colleagues that she had completed the bachelor's degree.[35] She also completed the master's degree in 1933. Celaya's 1926 salary at Tucson was $127.50 monthly, a $16 drop from her previous salary at Chandler. In some academic years, such as 1926-1927, the state published salaries in the directory, so it would have been quite easy for teachers to compare their workload and compensation. For example, Rose Oviedo's last recorded salary was $195 monthly, which was the highest district salary paid to any experienced primary school teacher.[36] That same year, Amelia Hunt García earned $160 monthly as the Apache County superintendent and her husband Monico earned $175 monthly as principal of the Concho School.[37] In comparison, Pirtleville principal Concepción Faras earned $190 monthly, while Mrs. C. B. Caldwell, who directed the Phoenix Colored High School, earned $176.16 monthly. Principal O. W. Patterson at the Tucson High School earned $400 monthly. The PUHS superintendent E. W. Montgomery and the Tucson superintendent each earned $625 monthly, while Superintendent John D. Loper of Phoenix No. 1 earned $666.67 monthly!

The highest paid Arizonense teachers taught in the high schools or served as rural school principals. The shift from teaching Spanish speakers English to teaching English speakers Spanish became a classic strategy to break through the low ceiling of the primary school Americanization classroom. Ida Celaya made this leap quite early, leaving Maricopa County after a few years at Chandler. María Escalante did the same, transferring to the Gilbert High School as a Spanish teacher in 1943, although she had taught high school Spanish at Scottsdale in the past, too. The generation that followed them also used this strategy, crafting joint appointments in smaller districts where they served on the faculty of both the primary and high schools. Mary Gómez, a niece of the Romos, graduated from the ASTC in 1929. At Litchfield Park, the well-known labor enclave of the Southwest Cotton Company and subsidiary of the Goodyear Tire & Rubber Company in Southwest Phoenix, Gómez taught pre-primary, Spanish-monolingual children in the morning and then high school Spanish in the afternoon. The district listed her as faculty at both schools.[38]

The gender pay gap also factored into the salary scales, as male teachers earned more than female teachers regardless of experience. In 1923-1924, for example, as county school superintendent, Amelia Hunt García earned $150 monthly; yet Dan Romero earned $200 monthly for teaching bookkeeping

and commercial vocational courses at Tucson High School.[39] Some Arizonense women teachers almost gained par with Romero, such as Rose Oviedo
who earned $195 monthly in Phoenix.[40] The disparity is most glaring when
comparing entering salaries for Mexican American men. In 1923-1924,
Ralph Estrada earned $150 monthly for his first job, teaching upper elemen-
tary grades in Winslow, Arizona. Ida Celaya, however, earned $144 monthly
for teaching first grade even though she had five years' experience. That same
year, María Escalante earned only $166.66 per month for teaching Spanish at
Scottsdale High School.[41] Celaya, Escalante, and Estrada all hailed from merchant families in Tempe and each graduated from the normal school. While
teacher salaries varied across the state based on district pay scales, novice
male teachers still earned salaries equal to or higher than veteran female
teachers; this was the case among white women, too. Nonetheless, as a group,
Mexican American women pursued teaching because, compared to gendered
wage scales in other lines of work, this professional employment paid substantially better than agricultural, domestic, or industrial labor. In the 1930s,
Phoenix farmworkers earned $1.50-$2.50 a day, compared to the lowest paid
elementary schoolteacher who averaged $3.56 a day.[42] Teaching also offered
intrinsic benefits, such as clean work, less supervision, leadership opportunities, as well as community prestige as few women had the educational qualifications to engage professional work.[43] Historian Vicki L. Ruiz confirmed that
in 1930 only 15 percent of U.S. Mexican women held white-collar jobs and
barely 3 percent of these were among professional or technical occupations.
If we consider women's work by state, the figures narrow further. Historian
Sarah Deutsch reported that in 1930, "Only 5 percent of Colorado's gainfully
employed Chicanas worked as teachers, clerks, or in other professional and
managerial positions."[44] These trends improved at a very slow tick. By 1950,
white-collar work among Mexican-heritage women increased to 32 percent,
but the bulk of these women held clerical or sales positions and less than
5 percent worked as professionals.[45]

Mexican American women teachers who felt underutilized in the profession had few options for upward mobility.[46] The feminization of teaching
in the early twentieth century translated into an institutional structure that
created administrative advancement for men as principals, superintendents,
and district managers, leaving the classroom work with children to women.[47]
This structure provided white women educators with a pathway to stable and
reputable employment, an option that Mexican American women hoped to
pursue as well. But the combination of gender and race discrimination meant

that Mexican American women would find less opportunity in white districts where white women dominated the teaching force and white men controlled the administration. Instead, Arizonense teachers who were "white by law" but socially perceived to be people of color found themselves limited to teaching children of their own heritage in a variety of segregated spaces. Further, even though Arizonense women substantially outnumbered Arizonense men in the profession, the few men earned higher salaries and held more leadership positions than the women. They also had the option to leave teaching for other professional opportunities. After teaching stints in Arizona, New Mexico, and California, Ralph Estrada entered the University of Arizona law school in 1936 and passed the state bar exam in 1939.[48]

While confronting these life and work negotiations, Mexican American educators did perceive themselves, first and foremost, as teachers. They contemplated the paradox of Americanization and attempted to reconcile the aims of public education with the needs of their students. The sentiments of María Urquides may serve as one representation of how teachers resolved the dilemmas they encountered teaching Spanish-speaking children. Urquides claimed that much of her desire to improve education stemmed from her childhood memories of attending Mansfield School and Holladay School in Tucson in the 1910s. At the time, Tucson superintendent C. E. Rose described the schools as being, respectively, 60 percent "American" and 30 percent "foreign"; for example, "children of foreign blood, Mexican and Indian, who could not speak nor understand a word of English at the opening of the school year."[49] Urquides, herself, could not speak English when she entered the first grade. "I ALWAYS TRY to remember back to those days, and how I felt. That way, I can help children who today face the same experience."[50]

Like many of her Mexican American colleagues, Urquides attempted to bring this sort of sensitivity to her classroom at Tucson's Davis School, a segregated school where the student body was 99.9 percent Mexican American and Yaqui.[51] But bound by the Americanization curriculum, the English-only rules, and the 1C program, she found herself trapped by district policy. When she first began teaching, she mistakenly taught her class two songs in Spanish for a spring recital. "A supervising teacher came along, and said: 'Miss Urquides, what do you think you are doing?'" The supervisor forced her to translate the lyrics into English. To keep her job, Urquides complied and then learned to strike a balance by promoting pride in ethnicity and pride in America. Sidestepping the Spanish-language issue, she focused instead on improving the socioeconomic status of her pupils and often solicited clothes and food from local businesspeople on their behalf. She became a social worker "doing things like making sure a student's mother was getting care while she delivered her baby."[52]

On Saturday, February 6, 1932, teachers María Urquides, Ida Celeya, and Rose Buzan hosted the opening of a new Mexican Community Center near the Davis School in Barrio Anita.[53] As the link between the Mexican mothers of her Davis School students and the YWCA, Urquides helped bring the joint venture, known today as Oury Park, to fruition "for both Mexican and American women who have dreamed for years of having a center for the Mexican people."[54] The grand opening of the refurbished building drew more than one hundred women from across Tucson. Urquides welcomed everyone and Celaya gave a speech encouraging the Mexican mothers to embrace the center. "She said that the opening of the center was only the beginning—the rest depended on those for whom it was made ready, and it was for them to carry on the work of the center for the sake of the Mexican people."[55] Similar to Phoenix's Friendly House, which opened in the 1920s, the Mexican Community Center operated as a cross between a settlement house and an after-school center. For parents, it offered skill-based courses in "English, sewing, cooking, and child care," and the children's programs included a book club, a library, Boy Scouts, and YWCA Girls Reserves. Within a month, the Mexican mothers founded the Adelante Club and hosted a center open house, which was attended not only by local parents but also by members of the Tucson city council, representatives from the state vocational department, and the YWCA Girls Reserve Committee, of which Urquides was an active member. Within a year, the Adelante Club held regular meetings, parties, and events, such as a sewing circle, to help families repair clothing as the Great Depression took hold.[56]

Urquides's concern for public welfare may have stemmed from the poverty her own family encountered in Tucson. She remembered the kindness one teacher showed her as a child when her parents could not afford to buy her shoes. "The teacher was so nice and sensitive about it that one day she called attention to the students and said, 'I have seen María and she seems to be so comfortable without her shoes. Why don't we all do the same and take off our shoes.' I knew that she did it just to me make me feel good. I will never forget this as long as I live."[57] As a result, Urquides made continued efforts to improve her students' lives and the Davis School by adding fresh coats of paint to the building, planting trees for shade, and organizing a Parent Teacher Association (PTA) to pressure the administration for building upgrades. She sponsored the YWCA Girls Reserve chapter and helped fundraise so that they could attend summer camps, while her colleague, Richard Manzo organized the Boy Scout troop. Harnessing the resources of the school district and local civic organizations, Urquides and her fellow Arizonense teachers—Celaya, Buzan, Manzo, and Lugarda Ortiz—helped organize mothers' clubs at other schools as well. That same year, Carrillo School formed its club with eighty mothers at its founding meeting.[58] Ortiz, who married Manzo in 1932 and who both hailed from Tucsonense families, served as the treasurer of the Carrillo School mothers' club.[59] The Safford School PTA had organized an auxiliary "Spanish Mothers Study Club" the year prior. The Mexican Mothers Clubs were popular across the state, as segregated auxiliaries to the PTA, as district-funded welfare work, and as a genuine self-help organization that mirrored *comadrazgo*, or co-mothering, traditions within Mexican culture. The Scottsdale Mexican Mothers Club, for example, hosted a benefit Spanish supper in January 1933 to raise money for the "Mexican School" lunch program.[60]

After twenty years at Davis School, Urquides left her Mexican American students but not at her own request. The district superintendent intentionally transferred her to Sam Hughes Elementary, a predominantly white school, because "he felt she couldn't decide whether she wanted to be a social service worker or a teacher."[61] The contrast between her experiences at Davis and Hughes Schools soon influenced Urquides's future goals to reform public education in Arizona and, ultimately, in the United States.[62]

The Robin Hood of Apache County

On November 4, 1937, the front-page headlines of the *St. Johns Herald* announced the death of the beloved schoolteacher Amelia Hunt García. "The *Herald* force extends sympathy to relatives and friends of this very talented lady and friend of the poor."[63] The generosity of the newspaper editors belied the controversy surrounding Amelia's death in a Phoenix hospital under the guard of the state prison police. In 1936, the St. Johns County Superior Court convicted her of felony fraud for misappropriating school funds and sentenced her to the state penitentiary at Florence for thirteen months. The charges, her defense argued, stemmed from long-standing conflicts over race and power between Arizonenses and white Arizonans. Amelia said that "her prosecution was inspired by 'politics' and 'spite.'"[64] Both Catholics and Mormons had argued for decades over local control, each claiming that they had entered the White Mountains of Apache County first in the 1860s.[65] Amelia's conviction appeared to be the most recent political conflict among Arizonense Catholics and Anglo-Mormons vying for control of the county coffers in the midst of economic crisis. Judge Levi S. Udall launched the first volley "to clean the county's linen," issuing indictments for Amelia, her husband Monico, and a group of Concho school leaders in 1935.[66]

Like the Faras sisters in Pirtleville and Celaya and Urquides in Tucson, Amelia had dedicated her life's work to the people of Apache County.[67] As soon as she passed the territorial teacher's exam in 1891, the teenager easily found employment in St. Johns, as well as in the smaller Arizonense towns of Concho and El Tule where she often served intermittently as principal. She regularly participated in the county teacher institutes and became known for her pedagogical techniques for teaching English to Spanish-speaking children. In the summer of 1902, she married fellow teacher Monico García and they had four children. Motherhood only briefly interrupted her career, as she returned to the classroom often over the next two decades.[68] In 1909, the Arizona State Board of Education awarded her a Life Diploma, granting her tenure.[69] In 1923, voters elected her as the Apache County superintendent of education and she returned to her schoolwork full time. Apache County residents endorsed her leadership, reelecting her for thirteen years, until her forced resignation in 1935.[70]

A Republican, Amelia accepted a two-year appointment from 1928 to 1930 by Governor John C. Phillips to the Arizona State Board of Education where she demonstrated "a broad conception of the educational problems of the day and a ready familiarity with the most advanced educational methods."[71] At the time, the political post made her the highest ranking Mexican American government official in the state and the only Arizonense to have served on the board since its formation.[72] Besides Amelia, Concepción Faras appeared to be the only other Arizonense woman who worked as a school principal in the state before World War II.[73] Amelia and Monico also joined an elite group of Arizonenses, including Carlos Tully in the 1890s and Alfred Ruiz in the 1900s, ever elected as county superintendents.

As a couple, Amelia and Monico cultivated dual public, political personas. Monico was elected as the clerk of the county board of supervisors, followed by a stint as justice of the peace, then probate judge and school superintendent in 1910, and county treasurer in 1912.[74] Monico actually earned a living as a sheep rancher, like many of his extended family who homesteaded and ran herds in Apache and Maricopa Counties. He also relied on his teaching certification and university degree to augment his family's income. In 1934-1935, he was the principal of St. Johns District No. 1.[75] Because Monico's younger brother, Gregorio García lived and worked in Phoenix as an attorney, the families regularly spent time together. Amelia and Monico owned a private home in Phoenix, so as she settled into her public work as the county superintendent, she commuted between the two towns, reporting for board meetings and attending teacher institutes in Phoenix, then returning to St. Johns to host similar events for the teachers she supervised. Her reputation as a kind person and her growing political force in the county led many people to seek out her assistance. Her grandchildren remembered that "all kinds of people" came to her back porch asking for help. As Gregorio later told the Arizona Supreme Court in her defense, Amelia was "a woman of excellent character and beyond reproach, commonly known as 'the Robin Hood of Apache County' where no one in need left her home with an empty hand."[76]

Amelia's work seemed rather nondescript and followed the tried and true administrivia of an elected public school official of the era, until the spring of 1935 when an Apache County supervisor discovered a "shortage of county funds" and called in the state examiners to help uncover "irregularities."[77] The examiners discovered that a former special county auditor, Charles Weidler wrote fake warrants (checks) against the county treasury, stealing upwards of $150,000 (over $3.2 million in 2023 dollars).[78] The scheme, according to the county attorney, involved not only Weidler who had skipped town, but a group of county officials, including Amelia and Monico who were indicted on felony charges. As described in the court proceedings, the court accused Amelia of issuing and cashing fake warrants on school district accounts. When a school district contractor presented her with an invoice, she issued a warrant for payment, which the payee could take to the First National Bank of Holbrook for payment. Given the nature of rural life and distances people had to travel to town, Amelia often cashed these warrants herself. She kept a petty cash box in her office and would have the payee endorse the warrant to her in exchange for the cash. She then deposited the warrants directly into her personal bank account to reimburse herself. While this was not ideal, it was a common county practice. However, the state examiner raised questions about a series of warrants that he believed Amelia had intentionally embezzled, and with this evidence the Apache County grand jury indicted her on ten counts of forgery and one count of making a false claim.

Amelia immediately hired Gregorio, pleaded "not guilty," and paid a $10,000 bail (equivalent to approximately $217,500 in 2023), but the court proceedings quickly deteriorated into a comedy of errors.[79] The county attorney Dodd L. Greer was among those initially indicted, but the court soon cleared and reinstated him so that he could bring Amelia and the others to trial.[80] When Gregorio filed demurrers challenging the lack of sufficient allegations for both Amelia and Monico, the court released Monico from all four indictments but kept Amelia's eleven indictments intact, forcing the first of three trials to begin on July 30, 1935.[81] The first trial ended "abruptly" because the county seated a juror who had testified as a grand jury witness![82] The judge then dismissed one indictment for forgery and then Greer pursued a second trial for the remaining nine forgery indictments, plus another for a false claim. The second jury trial began on August 1 and lasted two days. Gregorio called on fifteen character witnesses, including Anglos and Arizonenses who "testified they had known Mrs. García for years as a law abiding citizen and that her character was good."[83] This jury deadlocked, the judge ruled it a mistrial, and the county attorney Greer called for a third trial the next day, August 5.[84] At this point, as Tucson's *Arizona Daily Star* proclaimed, "Mrs. García breaks under trial strain."[85] The case became a newswire sensation and newspapers across the region detailed the case with daily reports. "Mrs. Garcia became hysterical about noon, and when it was found she had a high fever she was taken to Phoenix by automobile."[86] Before she departed St. Johns, Gregorio, fearing for her health, submitted her letter of resignation effective September 1.[87] Amelia initially refused to give up her elected position as the county superintendent of schools, and only did so under duress because she could no longer tolerate the ongoing political and racial attack.

Before the case went to trial, Amelia's defense filed a motion to quash the indictment arguing that the Superior Court of Apache County had violated her Fourteenth Amendment rights to equal protection under the law.[88] The defense claimed that Amelia was not allowed to challenge the initial indictment or participate in the grand jury selection, which resulted in a jury that was *not* a panel of her peers. "Persons of the Spanish American race," the motion argued, were intentionally omitted from the grand jury roster. In Apache County, more than 1,700 eligible voters qualified to serve on jury panels, including 367 Spanish Americans. The county board of supervisors, however, only provided a list of 546 names for the grand jury selection. Of these 546 names, only 46 (8 percent) were Spanish-American voters. To clarify this egregious discrepancy, the defense pointed out the imbalance in the percentage of qualified voters drawn from each racial group. The board qualified 46 of 367 (12. 5 percent) registered Spanish-American voters, but also qualified 500 of 1,334 (37.4 percent) registered non-Spanish-American voters. The defense argued that this exclusion of "nearly all of the persons of the Spanish-American race" from the jury selection amounted to "gross discrimination."[89] Therefore, as a Spanish-American defendant, Amelia had "been denied and deprived of her constitutional right and . . . equal protection under the law."[90]

In light of Mexican American jurisprudence of the era, Amelia's Fourteenth Amendment claim of racial discrimination is probably one of the earliest argued on behalf of a Spanish-American woman defendant in a criminal case.[91] That both the attorney and the defendant identified as Arizonenses makes this claim even more important in terms of Arizona jurisprudence, because it highlights the scope and depth of anti-Mexican prejudice within Arizona society and its courts.[92] In the answer to the motion to quash the indictment, county attorney Greer denied any discrimination. He explained quite simply that the greatest factor in eliminating Spanish-American voters from the qualified jury roll was the lack of English-language fluency. By his count, there were less than "fifty Spanish-Americans left in Apache County who sufficiently understand the English language to serve as jurors."[93] Registered voters who did not speak or read the English language could request interpreters and translation, but this right did not extend to juries. According to Greer, every single eligible person of Spanish-American heritage who was qualified was added to the roster, and two of them even served on the grand jury for this indictment. The court sided with Greer, setting the tone for the animosity that surrounded the case.

Because of Amelia's critical health condition, she was hospitalized in Phoenix for the remainder of 1935 and this gave Gregorio an opportunity to mount a new defense. Before the initial trial and the failed motion to quash, he also filed a motion and affidavits for a change of judge. The motion was finally granted in January 1936.[94] The García's argued that the honorable Levi S. Udall, the superior court judge of Apache County, could not be objective because of his political and religious affiliations. Amelia signed an affidavit, as did Monico, testifying that Udall "because of his bias and prejudice cannot give this Defendant a fair and impartial trial."[95] Levi Udall was the descendant of David King Udall, the first Mormon bishop of the Church of Latter-day Saints appointed to build a stake near St. Johns, which at the time was known as a predominantly Hispano Catholic community. Levi inherited the leadership of the St. Johns Stake from his father. Conflicts over land between the two communities emerged and these tensions were fueled by non-Mormon Anglos who aligned themselves with the Spanish-speaking Catholics. The legacies of this nineteenth-century past colored the contemporary relations among all of these descendants. Even though Gregorio won the motion to replace Udall with the Honorable John P. Clark of Navajo County, the political tension around Amelia's case and the other defendants escalated in Apache County. Before Udall was forcibly recused from the case, he ordered the county sheriffs to arrest and retrieve Amelia from her Phoenix hospital bed. She is returned to St. Johns for a preliminary hearing, but then released on bond because of her illness.

Finally, on January 22, 1936, the third trial began and lasted two days. Amelia testified that she had been targeted by a prosecution "inspired by 'politics' and 'spite.'"[96] She insisted that the state did not show true facts, as records related to the case had been altered since she had last seen them in the summer of 1935. At the heart of her defense, she proclaimed that the state examiner A. C. Wagner bungled the audit of her records. That one night he had left open a window in the courthouse where her office was located and blank warrants had been blown across the lawn. She discovered this because her own daughter-in-law had helped to recover the paperwork.[97] Wagner agreed that he had left the window open, but he denied that any paperwork had blown away. Further, Amelia confirmed that the signatures on the warrants did not match her own. J. R. McEvoy, vice president of the First National Bank of Holbrook, also testified that he did not know who had actually submitted the warrants for deposit because he did not handle the transaction and at the time their procedure did not include crossmatching warrants with deposit slips, so there was no way to confirm exactly which deposit slip matched each warrant.[98] They relied solely on the numerical figure of the deposit as evidence.

After two days of testimony, the jury met for three-and-a-half hours and convicted Amelia of "obtaining money on false warrants."[99] Because of her ill health, she was not present in the court when the judge issued the verdict and her sentencing hearing was delayed until the end of February. In the meantime, the Apache County attorney Dodd L. Greer filed 137 lawsuits on behalf of eleven school districts in order to recover $125,000.[100] Greer named Amelia and six former county treasurers among the defendants. In addition, ten days later, he filed another dozen suits for another twenty-five thousand.[101] At a hearing on February 28, 1936, Judge Clark sentenced Amelia to twelve to fifteen months at the Florence State Prison.[102] She and Charles Weidler were the only two people convicted of the embezzlement.

Gregorio managed to stay the order by filing an immediate appeal to the Arizona Supreme Court. Amelia remained on bond until July 6, 1937, her official surrender date.

The trials of Amelia Hunt García killed her. In the months following the sentencing, she succumbed to nervous exhaustion and massive gastrointestinal complications involving her gall bladder, appendix, ulcers, and even suggestions of cancer. Monico went broke, selling off their assets to pay for her defense and her continued hospitalization. He moved into an auto court in downtown Phoenix to be near her.[103] When Amelia finally had to relinquish herself to the Florence State Prison, Warden A. J. Barnes decided in consultation with the prison physician to leave her at the hospital under guard. This caused such an uproar across the state that the *Arizona Republic* wrote an editorial opinion on the precedent set by not admitting sick inmates to the prison.[104] The warden sought the guidance of the state attorney general who confirmed that he was within his legal right to "keep a prisoner, under guard, outside the penitentiary walls."[105] At the end of October, the warden even called for a "sanity hearing" given Amelia's critical mental state. "She has hallucinations, screams and yells, and 'imagines that she is about to be killed.'"[106] She died a few days later on November 2, 1937.

Amelia Hunt García's political demise marked a turning point for Arizonenses just as the coming of the railroads in 1880 signaled the demise of the Tucsonense freighters and the 1917 Bisbee deportation of IWW miners folded Mexican unionization. García's trial, conviction, and death warned others who might challenge the Anglo authority and the boundaries of white-brown relations in these borderlands. As Gregorio argued, Amelia "was made the 'Goat' with reference to the irregularities found in the different offices in Apache County."[107] Or, to quote 1930s social commentator Will Rogers, "It doesn't take a genius to spot a goat in a flock of sheep." According to Gregorio, "Some of the good Citizens of Apache County decided to rid themselves of the only Republican who could be elected to that office term after term, and that she was not a member of their flock."[108]

Despite all that the García family suffered, Gregorio and Monico never lost sight of the importance of sustaining Mexican American civil rights. Always politically active, they continued their work—Gregorio as an attorney and Monico as a court interpreter. The State Board of Education stripped Monico of his Life Diploma and ability to work as a teacher, but that did not break his Arizonense spirit. Gregorio continued to work with local civil rights organizations in central Arizona, becoming the supreme president of the Alianza in 1950. Within two years of Amelia's death, Arizonense school trustees in Apache County began searching for new Mexican American teachers. They posted advertisements with teaching bureaus and explicitly solicited qualified bilingual, bicultural candidates to oversee their children's classrooms. Civic integration continued to provide the raw emotional fuel to sustain the few remaining school districts still controlled by Arizonense trustees and those sympathetic to Arizonense interests. In St. Johns, Amelia's supporters quietly worked to resurrect her legacy and to rebuild an Arizonense-inspired politic in their public schools. By 1940, Los Conquistadores would take the helm.

Los Conquistadores

Rosalío "Ross" Florián Muñoz imagined a kinder world, where ethnicity mattered less, intellect mattered more, and commitment to nation united all Americans—immigrants and citizens alike. Unlike the Garcías who had spent the majority of their lives in Apache County, Ross spent his life on the move, crossing the Texas-Mexico border with his parents as a young boy in 1918, later trekking to Arizona where his preacher father Reverend Esaú Pérez Muñoz ministered to Spanish-speaking communities across the state.[109] In 1938, at the age of twenty-five, Ross achieved two major goals: He became a naturalized U.S. citizen and he earned the *first* master's degree awarded by Arizona State Teachers College at Tempe.[110]

His thesis examined the correlation between intelligence and bilingualism among Mexican American children in Maricopa County.[111] Using state-of-the-art psychological assessments developed by social scientists, Muñoz evaluated the school readiness of 177 children in four schools in Phoenix and the East Valley. He measured the children's abilities to think in English and Spanish, and he assessed their vocabulary, logic, and problem-solving and sequencing skills, as well as their abilities to draw conclusions and classify ideas. He studied their innermost feelings about themselves and their worlds by creating "pupil portraits." Rudolph Pintner, a leader in the field of educational psychology and intelligence testing, developed the "pupil portrait test" to measure the social adjustment of schoolchildren.[112] Muñoz also developed a corresponding questionnaire, based on Pintner's work, to measure the students' bilingualism, literacy, family background, and social language use. He attempted to prove that bilingualism enhanced student learning, hoping that his findings might contribute to similar intelligence studies that challenged prevailing misperceptions of immigrant youth, like himself, who grew up in the Arizona public schools.

Muñoz conducted the study to address what Arizona educators considered the long-standing Mexican Problem, a characterization that he challenged as an issue of equality.[113] He did not see a Mexican Problem; rather, he saw a failure on the part of Anglo Americans and the school officials to recognize the value and humanity of ethnic Mexican people, many of whom had lived in the state for several generations. "The truth . . . ," he wrote, "is that approximately one fourth of the [Arizona] population is of Mexican nationality and that a high percentage of these Mexicans are native born and children of native-born parents."[114] He believed that they possessed "the right to call the United States their home." Even though it was incumbent for them to learn "American ways," they had the right "to retain their self-respect." Muñoz insisted that citizens, naturalized and American-born, had a responsibility to their government and its institutions, and vice versa. He defined this reciprocal notion of nation building as one of mutual exchange where teacher and child learned from one another. The child imparted cultural knowledge, and the teacher learned from and validated the child. The teacher also taught the child how to become a confident and informed American citizen through literacy in the English language. Muñoz linked citizenship responsibility to self-respect, which he ultimately defined as the democratic right to retain one's ethnicity and simultaneously advance America. Muñoz's thesis is a manifesto of sorts, a declaration of Mexican American rights, and a daring act of public writing for a young man embracing his American citizenship.

Ross Muñoz was not alone in his thinking about challenging status quo perceptions of Mexican Americans and harnessing their potential contribution to American society. As active members of Christian youth organizations associated with the Methodist Episcopal Church, South, including the Mexican Youth Conference (MYC) of the Young Men's Christian Association (YMCA), Ross and his sister Rebecca perceived themselves to be role models poised to contribute to American society. Rebecca described the era as the advent of an "intellectual awakening" and pushed their generation to take a leadership role. She wrote, "[We] find at this time a great movement taking place among those of us who have been able to take the opportunities of education and see the immense possibilities of improvement for our people as a whole, aiming to awaken our people, especially our youth to take those opportunities and thus enable themselves to become better and more productive citizens of this our country."[115] An "Arizona editor" for the

Mexican Voice, Rebecca evoked not only the MYC's message but also a spirit of activism evolving in Mexican American communities nationwide, such as El Congreso de Pueblos de Hablan Espanola (the Spanish-speaking People's Congress), which held its national civil rights assembly in Los Angeles that same year.[116] El Congreso, a consortium of unions, mutualistas, and ethnic organizations, developed an extensive pro-immigrant, antidiscrimination, and desegregation platform centered on the rights of Spanish-speaking people in the United States to live and work peacefully and free from the threat of deportation.[117]

For the Muñoz siblings, the political moment called for a new approach to Mexican American activism, not only to improve race relations but also to improve intergenerational cooperation. Together, Rebecca, Ross, and fellow students at the ASTC founded "Los Conquistadores," the first official Mexican American student club at the college. Although their club's name invoked the settler colonialism of the Spanish empire (*conquistador* translates to conqueror), they embraced this European fantasy heritage as "a form of ethnic/racial superiority over the Anglos and to affirm their identities as Americans, too."[118] Los Conquis, as they affectionately called themselves, was an incipient civil rights organization.[119] The Muñoz children argued that a central goal of Los Conquis was to improve Mexican American recruitment and retention at

Figure 13. Los Conquistadores breakfast at the Tempe Café, Arizona State Teachers College, 1938. Courtesy of Rebecca Muñoz Gutiérrez Photographs, MP SPC 323, Arizona State University Library.

Figure 14. Los Conquistadores members posing after breakfast outside the Tempe Café, Arizona State Teachers College, 1938. The students are (in front, left to right) Josephine F. Muñoz, Aurelia Gonzales, Louis Arévalo, Gilbert Aguilar, Lucinda F. Muñoz, and Carmen Reynoso; (in back, left to right) Crispin Alvarado, Alice Peralta, Albert Ramírez, and Joe Limón. Courtesy of Rebecca Muñoz Gutiérrez Photographs, MP SPC 323, Arizona State University Library.

the college. They organized annual youth conferences on civil rights, bringing high school and college students from across Arizona to Tempe to discuss the state of the Mexican American community.[120] Rebecca and her younger brother Solomon reported these activities, as well as their social and athletic events, to the *Mexican Voice*, which distributed its newsletter across Arizona, California, and New Mexico.[121] Félix J. Gutiérrez, the founder and editor of the *Mexican Voice*, encouraged this participation, having met the Muñoz siblings, possibly as early as 1934 when the YMCA first began recruiting Protestant Mexican youth.[122] They could have met even earlier, in the 1920s, when Ross joined the Phoenix YMCA and established the "United Mexicans," a successful basketball club comprised of Mexican youth from different Christian faiths. The United Mexicans played other teams in the regional YMCA basketball league. The Muñoz children participated from childhood in broad evangelism networks across the region given their parents' work in the Methodist church.

Ross and Rebecca benefited significantly from the mentorship of their faculty adviser, the foreign language professor Irma Wilson.[123] Both Ross and Rebecca majored in Spanish and developed very trusted relationships with her. Professor Wilson served as the chair of Ross's master's thesis and Ross thanked her first on his acknowledgments page.[124] She also hired Rebecca as a grading and teaching assistant for her beginning Spanish classes, and probably served as her adviser when she later began her own master's program.[125] Professor Wilson agreed to sponsor Los Conquis when the Muñoz siblings proposed the new student club in October 1937. She may have suggested that they name themselves "Los Conquis," as she had changed the name of the Spanish Club to "Los Hidalgos del Desierto," when she became its sponsor in 1923. Like the Spanish Club at Arizona State Teacher's College at Flagstaff and the Latin-American Club at the University of Arizona, Los Hidalgos had a reputation as a gathering circle for the few Mexican American students at the college.[126] Professor Wilson persuaded the students to give the club an original name in Spanish and to broaden their academic study to include Old Mexico. She also encouraged their social activities, assisted them financially with school supplies, and opened her home to them. With "Los Conquis," she helped them negotiate permission to establish, what the college considered, its first "race-based" club. Even though the college sponsored all sorts of clubs that appeared to be "white only," none of the clubs had a specific racial or ethnic focus. Even the "Inter-Racial club," which Urquides helped inaugurate in 1928, had a multiethnic membership. Solomon Muñoz remembered that the new club's name was contentious. The students wanted a name that clearly identified their ethnic heritage, but the administration steered them away from any declaration of racial identity. "The club was NOT allowed to use Mexican American!"[127] That's why, decades later, Los Conquis often laughed about the contradiction between its name and its purpose. Charles Bejarano, who joined Los Conquis long after Ross and Rebecca Muñoz had graduated, said, "We used to joke about the name of the organization. We thought it was kind of pretentious to be associated with Spaniards when our parents or grandparents were born in Mexico and our fathers did pick-and-shovel work in the mines. Just because we spoke Spanish didn't mean we were Spaniards. We were Mexican Americans. What we wanted to do was emphasize that we were Americans first, and of Mexican descent, second. We were proud to be of Mexican descent, yes. But we were born in the United States, not Mexico."[128]

At the ATSC, most of the Mexican American students participated in Los Hidalgos, but its aims did not include community awareness or any kind of consciousness raising or identity exploration. Club membership was open to students from any background; it was a coed space that any Spanish-speaking student could join. The Muñozes enjoyed participating in the club and served as officers.[129] As Ross began his master's studies, the siblings called for a new organization, one devoted solely to race politics. With Wilson's support, the siblings joined together with fellow students Hilario T. Alvarado of Miami and Tony Vicente of Jerome to write the organization's preamble and constitution. By the close of the fall semester, they had registered "Los Conquistadores" as an official campus organization and elected a leadership slate, which included Ross.

Los Conquistadores imagined "race work" as central to their organization. In some respects, their mission mirrored old-school Progressive notions of Americanization, which Professor Wilson had long espoused, but they also asserted a positive group identity and group action. They said, "We, the Spanish speaking students of [ASTC] . . . do hereby organize this club."[130] The preamble included three central aims: "to develop a better understanding between ourselves and others; to gain greater social, cultural, and intellectual values through our association with others; and to interest others in a college education, especially those of our own nationality."[131] They espoused "cross-cultural" exchange, not a one-way exchange. They expected to learn how to maneuver within American institutions as a result of this cross-cultural exchange. They also emphasized reciprocity. As they learned "American values" and taught "Mexican values," they encouraged the next generation to pursue college with them.

This final emphasis on education linked Los Conquis directly to the MYC, and its later incarnation the Mexican American Movement (MAM), which adopted the motto "Progress Through Education."[132] Historian George Sánchez wrote that the second generation became convinced that "Mexican people in the United States could succeed only through education."[133] Indeed, Ross and his siblings, as did MYC/MAM members, worked ardently to challenge Darwinistic perceptions of Mexican ignorance and to expand their social, economic, and political opportunities. Education, they believed, could transform the Mexican by opening a path out of the barrio, out of the working class, and into an American society where they could be active contributors to democracy. Critics of MAM have pointed to the irony of these lofty goals given the precarious effects that institutionalized racism had wrought upon the Mexican American community writ large.[134]

At the local level in Arizona, Los Conquis cultivated real action and support from across first-generation leadership and second-generation students. In 1938, Los Conquis pursued two specific endeavors: the establishment of an "Endowment Fund" and an annual Mexican Youth Conference. In their preamble, Los Conquis vowed to encourage Mexican American participation in higher education. Through the Endowment Fund, they solicited and raised funds to help pay college expenses for students attending the ASTC and other regional colleges in Phoenix, Flagstaff, and Tucson. As part of this effort, the students joined with the "Latin American Club of Arizona," a political organization with fifty-seven chapters across the state.[135] Founder and supreme president, Luis H. Córdova provided a "letter of introduction" to Los Conquis, specifically students Hilario T. Alvarado and Ross F. Muñoz, so that they could openly solicit funds for the endowment as they approached students and community leaders in towns across the state. Alvarado and Muñoz also carried letters of support from the assistant attorney general Albert M. García (no relation to Amelia) and from Fred Teyechea (the 1938 Conqui vice president) who worked in the County Recorder's Office in Santa Cruz County.[136] Ross and his fellow Conquis usually traveled on these junkets during school breaks.[137] During Thanksgiving 1938, María Urias remembered that Ross stopped to visit her at her parents' home in Tucson on his way to Nogales during one of these trips with his "college friends." "They were going to several towns trying to encourage Mexican students to go on to college. They were early recruiters, dedicated to improving the lot of the Mexican through education."[138]

This alliance between the Latin American Clubs and Los Conquis proved critical to moving student leaders into local community leadership. Given the level of discrimination practiced in Arizona society, Mexican American college graduates still found it difficult to secure full-time teaching appointments despite their certified college credentials and their organizational mandates for self-improvement. Ross Muñoz and María Urias (who later married) both encountered this unemployment situation when they finished school in 1938. Yet, both managed to garner teaching jobs in northeastern Arizona's Apache County as result of the active lobbying of Latin American Club vice president Benjamin López. The political scenario that unfolded in both of their hirings suggests that, despite criticism of Los Conquis's or MAM's Americanization agendas, the groups' goals did result in tangible outcomes for those inside and outside their leadership circles. Working in tandem with first-generation leadership, they narrowly circumvented the institutional racism many Mexican American educators encountered as they sought employment in the public schools, where they often found themselves locked out of jobs in predominantly white schools and communities.

In Ross's case, he felt that school districts declined to hire him because he was Mexican American. In her memoir, María remembered, "He had tried in vain to get a teaching job for which he had prepared and for which he was well qualified and had superior recommendations—such were the times—*Discrimination.*"[139] With no teaching option in the fall of 1938, Ross managed to secure a social work position with the Apache County Board of Public Welfare and served as the truant officer for St. Johns School District No. 1. The social work job required only a bachelor's degree, although Ross possessed a master's degree and had earned his teaching certification in 1934. If this was not de facto discrimination, then perhaps Ross's legal status as a resident alien precluded him from teacher employment? Arizona school law prohibited districts from employing "non-citizens" as teachers.[140] Ross became a naturalized citizen in 1938 and, by the next school year, 1939–1940, the Concho School District No. 6, also in Apache County, hired him as principal and teacher of the combined seventh and eighth grades. María wrote that the teaching job finally came because "he was well liked and respected by the people in these communities."[141] This may have been a factor in Ross's initial hiring as a social worker, but on his Endowment Fund junkets for Los Conquis, Ross probably met Benjamin López, the Latin American Club's state vice president and a St. Johns school trustee. López, himself, had majored in history and trained to become an educator at Flagstaff.[142] López probably saw himself in Ross Muñoz and in every Mexican American teacher he hired to work in Apache County.

María's experience is a perfect example of affirmative Mexican American hiring in Arizona's schools. In October 1938, she received an offer directly from López on behalf of the St. Johns trustees. The newly elected school board, which had ousted a previously white, Mormon board, adopted an informal resolution to hire as many Mexican American teachers as possible. López contacted the University of Arizona Teacher Placement Office but the director did not recommend María even though she had graduated, earned the teaching credential, and registered for placement services. At that time, María was unfamiliar with Los Conquis and MYC, there was no Mexican American club at the university, and she often lamented the lack of Mexican

American students like her on campus.[143] In her freshman year, 1933–1934, she counted five Mexican American students, including herself and her cousin José (Pepe) T. Castelán. When she received the St. Johns job offer, she learned that the Placement Office rarely promoted her application even though she "had some excellent recommendations . . . and ranked in the top two or three percent of [her] class."[144] The Placement Office nominated her for one job—"teaching reading to retarded 6th graders in Jerome, Arizona."[145] During the summer of 1938, she wrangled an interview with Mr. Rose, the superintendent of the Tucson schools, but "nothing came of that." Then, about October 1, she received the "wire" from López. When she called the Placement Office to have her dossier forwarded to St. Johns, the director Mr. Kelly told her he had not recommended her for the job. He knew St. Johns was a Mormon community, so he didn't bother to send her application because "he didn't think [she] had a chance to be hired." Since he never officially recommended her, she didn't have to pay the $25.00 finding fee. She only discovered the hidden politics behind her hire months after she started teaching at St. Johns. The Barth family, who owned most of St. Johns commerce and who also employed López, had asked a traveling school supply salesman to pay a personal visit to the University Teacher Placement Office to ask for the name of a Mexican American teacher who could play the organ. The Placement Office released María Urias's name but never bothered to notify her. López and the Barths took it upon themselves to locate her. She departed to St. Johns on October 6, 1938.[146]

In 1938 and 1939, the St. Johns School District No. 1 and the neighboring Concho School District No. 6 hired a notable cohort of young Mexican American teachers to work alongside Ross and María. From the ASTC, St. Johns hired Inez Jones Gómez (a Conqui) to teach the first grade; from Flagstaff, they hired the principal Apolinar Rodríguez who also taught seventh and eighth grades. Other teachers included William G. Lerma and Carlos Arciniega. Ross also convinced his sister Lucinda Muñoz (a Conqui) to come and teach kindergarten in St. Johns, and his friends Eleazar "Al" Arvizu (a Conqui) and Paulina Sánchez (also a Conqui) to teach in Concho.[147] Other Conquis, like their predecessors, also found work teaching in segregated schools and classrooms across the state, including Albert Cruz and Rebecca Muñoz who started her master's degree before joining the faculty at Mesa's Webster School.[148]

The cooperation between Los Conquis and the Latin American Club confirmed intergenerational collaboration and demonstrated a public, statewide, and self-proclaimed affirmation about the role of Mexican Americans in Arizona. Both groups asserted an ideology that combined notions of uplift, personal achievement, Americanization, and racial pride. The Latin American Clubs developed in 1933 as a way to promote political activism and voter participation among Spanish-speaking people in Arizona. With fifty-seven chapters across the state, the clubs brought together the most educated, the wealthiest, and the most politically active Arizonenses. Each year at its annual convention, the club endorsed a platform of candidates for statewide and local office, and its influence drew the likes of governors, senators, and representatives. The club's 1936 meeting at the Hotel Adams in downtown Phoenix opened with a welcoming by Phoenix mayor John H. Udall and a special address by Governor B. B. Moeur (a well-known Klan member). The meeting program included full-page advertisements from both gubernatorial candidates and an evening automobile parade that began at 7 p.m. and concluded at 10:45 p.m. after six receptions at downtown hotels, including at the prestigious Westward Ho. As president of the Latin American Club, Luis H. Córdova hosted the meeting, so his 1938 endorsement letter for the Conqui's Endowment Fund became a golden ticket for entry into nearly any Arizonense community in the state. Córdova's social capital also extended well into the working class, as he was a union leader and boilermaker in the Southern Pacific roundhouse.

These connections offer new evidence of the emergence of second-generation Mexican American identity and consciousness. The link between Tempe and Los Angeles, Los Conquis and MYC/MAM, are critical for reconsidering the influence of ideas and exchange among Arizonenses and Californios, and even the Hispanos and Tejanos who received copies of the *Mexican Voice*. The Muñozes's vision clearly relates to larger "race work" taking place in both states and among both first- and second-generation leadership and organizations. The collaboration among youth groups from Arizona, California, and New Mexico also reveals that these networks operated decades before the Crusade for Justice's 1969 call for the first Chicano Youth Conference. The existence of these networks exposes a recognized regional, cultural, and political affinity built on the decades-long organizing of mutual aid societies like the Alianza, as well as other self-help and religious organizations in the Southwest. Working- and middle-class Mexican Americans focused their time, energy, and savvy, to build organizational alliances on issues affecting the condition of their people across the United States. Understanding these connections helps historians uncover how Mexican American civil rights evolved over time, across generations, and across state lines prior to the notable efforts of the G.I. Generation and the Chicano Movement. Reflecting on the political work of Ross Muñoz and María Urias, their son Rosalío U. Muñoz, who in 1970 co-chaired the anti-war National Chicano Moratorium Committee, believes that these connections also help us reimagine how the "movement" for civil rights "has not died or diminished but has grown into new forms, [and] approaches . . . while confronting the problematica of new generations."[149]

During his early teaching years, Ross Muñoz remained active with Los Conquis and MYC, traveling during school breaks across Arizona on their behalf. In 1939 and 1941, Los Conquis followed up the endowment recruitment trips by organizing statewide youth conferences to bring potential high school graduates and transfer students to the ATSC in Tempe for Mexican Youth Conferences.[150] The 1939 conference brought together MYC leadership from Arizona and California, including *Mexican Voice* editor Félix Gutiérrez, future MYC president Paul Coronel, and teacher Gualberto Valadez from La Jolla. More important, Arizona's first-generation leadership and their political alliances showed up, too. The Phoenix Mexican Consul, Morelos Gonzales, and representatives from the YMCA, the ATSC, and the *División Juvenil Progreso* from Mesa, as well as numerous teachers and social workers participated in two days of meetings.[151] In 1940, Los Conquis attended the Mexican Youth Conference in San Pedro, California. They returned with such enthusiasm that they drafted a document titled "The Proposed Movement for Youth in Arizona." Historian Christine Marin described the statement as a "manifesto for educational leadership" that called for the leadership development as well as Mexican American self-critique.[152]

This note on self-critique emerged both in Los Conquis's manifesto and in other writings. According to Marin, Los Conquis "blamed Mexican American youth for failure to recognize their worth" as citizens, for hiding from public life, and "for not capitalizing" on educational opportunities.[153] They further "chastised those Mexican Americans who failed to use their education to become the leaders to combat the forces of racism that stifled efforts to reform their communities." Historian George Sánchez raised concerns about MYC/MAM's avoidance of "public exploration of the negative psychological and social consequences of racism on Mexican Americans."[154] But, in Arizona, we see this shift emerge in Ross's master's thesis and in his public school work as a principal.

The findings of Ross Muñoz's thesis reflect an underlying concern with the social condition of the Mexican child, as well as the lack of self-esteem or, as he calls it, "personal value" among Mexican Americans. He interpreted this misunderstanding as a frustration rooted in the pessimistic educational condition and poor socioeconomic reality of Arizona Mexicans. For example, in his study of 177 students in the Salt River Valley, he found that seventh and sixth graders were seven to eleven months older than the state average for children in those grades. This meant that sixth graders were eleven months behind (e.g., "retarded") in academic performance and that the seventh graders were only six months behind. This closing gap, however, was not a positive finding. The nearly half-year difference between sixth- and seventh-grade retardation did reflect an improvement in student performance, but to Ross it also signaled two conditions—teacher apathy and poor socioeconomic condition—that forced many students to drop out of school.[155] He argued that the social conditions of Mexican children must be examined, and he pushed scholars to recognize that these social conditions did not bear on the intellectual potential of the children.

Ross's findings, however, remained intellectualized. The economic need of the Mexican American community was overpowering and, like Urquides's children in Tucson, the children of St. Johns and Concho also experienced the crushing poverty of the Great Depression. The want in northern Arizona was so profound that the Works Progress Administration sent photographer Russell Lee to St. Johns in 1939 and to Concho in 1940 to document the situation in these mountain-plateau sheepherding communities. In St. Johns, men and boys queued with burlap sacks at the ready to carry home surplus commodities. In Concho, Lee focused on families and their homesteads: an "old couple of Spanish extraction" seated at the foot of their bed, adobe homes with chili ristras, a farmer carrying his toddler sons, women and children picking chili peppers and sorting beans, home altars, as well as the sprawling mesa filled with clouds as far as the eye could see. Lee even visited principal Ross Muñoz as he taught a social studies lesson on the geography of North America to seventh- and eighth-grade students.[156] More photographs showed Mexican American children at the chalkboard, reading at their desks, playing at recess, and catching the bus to the St. Johns High School. In one profile shot of Juan Candelaria, Lee noted that the well-known stockman "is considering selling several thousand acres of land" to the Farm Security Administration.[157] The situation in Concho never improved. By the end of the year, Muñoz transferred to the nearby community of St. Johns, District No. 1, likely for better pay. He left Concho in the charge of his friend and former Conqui, Eleazar V. Arvizu, who was promoted to principal.[158]

Figure 15. Principal Rosalío "Ross" F. Muñoz teaching a geography lesson about the U.S.-Mexico borderlands to Arizonense students at the Concho School, Arizona, 1940. Photograph by Russell Lee. Farm Security Administration, Office of War Information Photograph Collection, Library of Congress.

From Teacher to Soldier to Social Worker

In the summer of 1942, Tucson Unified School District (TUSD) announced that it had more teacher turnover as a result of World War II than it had ever had since the Great War.[159] Roughly 10 percent, thirty-eight of its 375 faculty members resigned. Many women quit to marry their sweethearts before they went off to war, while a number of men joined the military. In the rush to secure faculty for the coming academic year, Superintendent Robert Morrow hired twenty-six new teachers that June, including Ross F. Muñoz, who was eager to return to María's hometown. But the excitement was short lived. By the end of July, the U.S. Navy appointed Ross as a translator. The U.S. Office of Censorship in Washington, D.C., assigned him to the Cable Censorship Division of the Landwire Branch at the Bisbee, Arizona, field station.[160] He intercepted telegrams and listened to phone calls from across the Western Hemisphere. With Spanish, French, and English fluency, he also easily learned conversational Italian, Portuguese, and some German. Ross must have enjoyed his military post and the increased annual pay ($1,800), but the U.S. Naval Reserve rebuffed his efforts to join them permanently. In 1943, he received notice that his application was rejected because he did "not meet the requirements for permanent appointment in the U.S. Naval Reserve."[161] Those requirements were not elaborated in the telegram notice, but the U.S. military had a reputation for discrimination toward Mexican American soldiers.[162] Muñoz's status as a naturalized citizen could have been a factor, not to mention that his educational level would have automatically raised his rank from an enlisted soldier (Yeoman First Class) to an officer.[163] The U.S. Navy honorably discharged him in October 1945.

Over the next decade, Ross reshaped his professional career as an educator in order to find a permanent place for his growing family. He and María had several children by the end of World War II, and he hoped to be gainfully employed as a teacher or social worker, having worked in those professions in Apache County.[164] Always anxious to find the best paying job, he crisscrossed the state, moving from teaching positions in Tucson and Phoenix to county welfare positions in Flagstaff. He secured an employee scholarship from the State of Arizona to begin graduate school at the University of Southern California.[165] This was an important moment for Muñoz to resuscitate a deferred dream. When he graduated from Phoenix Junior College in 1933, he turned down a full scholarship to the University of Chicago. Had he gone, he more than likely would have advanced directly into a doctoral program; instead, he completed the bachelor's (1936) and master's (1938) degrees at Tempe. The chance to join USC revived those earlier ambitions. Just days before the start of the 1947 fall term, he received the Western Union telegram announcing that he was "Accepted by University for Graduate Standing and by Graduate School of Social Work."[166] His decision was immediate. With his G.I. Bill educational benefits in hand, he convinced the state of Arizona to grant him a paid professional leave of absence so that he could complete his studies. Ann M. Bracken, a director at the Arizona State Department of Child Welfare, desperately wanted to retain Muñoz and offered him various employment scenarios. She proposed a supervisory position headquartered at Flagstaff; he would oversee four Northern Arizona counties starting at $250/month, plus travel funding. She wrote, "I have not discussed this with Personnel or the Board—I would like your thinking on this, or suggestions. I do not wish to see you leave Arizona, but I can realize you must consider what is best for you and your family who have shared with you all the struggle." Bracken's offer was not enough.

This time, Ross and María chose educational opportunity and moved their family to Los Angeles. After completing a second master's degree in social work at USC, he joined the truancy division at the Los Angeles Unified School District. He recommitted to his religious and political activism, participating in Democratic Party politics to elect Mexican Americans to the Los Angeles City Council, including 13th district candidate Alfonso Mirabal, who ran and lost in 1953.[167] Historians credit Edward R. Roybal for mobilizing Mexican American politics in Los Angeles through his Community Service Organization (CSO), which he founded in 1947, the same year that the Muñoz family returned to Los Angeles.[168] Ross completed his Ph.D. in social work in 1957 and soon raised himself through the ranks at LAUSD to director of the Pupil Services and Attendance Branch.[169] When he retired in the 1970s, he was among the highest-ranking Latino officials in the district and celebrated for bringing "modern social work to change the way educators dealt with truancy and other problems," including child poverty.[170] More than 150,000 Mexican Americans resided in Los Angeles by midcentury; it was the largest enclave of Mexicans *fuera de México* (outside of Mexico) in the world and the largest Mexican American community in the United States. The Muñoz family had finally found home.

During the 1930s and 1940s, Arizonenses cultivated a political discourse and community action for improving children's lives through public school work. The Juan Crow realities that gripped Arizona society, however, curtailed the professional opportunities and institutional change that these college graduates had imagined. The excitement that Rebecca Muñoz expressed as she stood at the "threshold of a new era for the betterment of their people," faded in the wake of a sobering awareness that the politics of race dominated the trajectory of Arizonense lives. While it appeared that Ross and María may have fled Arizona for California horizons, it might be more appropriate to consider how Arizona abandoned them. The likelihood that Ross might ever achieve any level of professional parity with his Anglo-American colleagues seemed highly unlikely, especially when accusations unraveled lifetime careers, such as those of Monico and Amelia Hunt García, and penalized others such as María Urquides for challenging the impoverished status quo of barrio schools. Educational equality for Arizonense students and teachers remained as elusive as a desert mirage, and it would take them yet another decade to disentangle themselves from generations of racialization.

Prelude to the Chicano Movement

While World War II interrupted the lives of the Arizonenses in the same way that it did the nation, civic integration did not fade in the minds and practice of Arizonense school leaders. As war preparedness faded and soldiers returned to their families on the home front, the pressing question of the Mexican American social condition continued to weigh on the Arizonense educated elite. Teachers, social workers, politicians, and lawyers reconsidered possibilities for improving their communities and for achieving educational equality. Like their compatriots across the American Southwest whom historians have often called the "Mexican American Generation," these Arizonenses became part of a wide network of Mexican-heritage leaders across the nation who sought the full promise and equality of the American Dream.[1] Arizonenses such as teacher-turned-union activist María Urquides and teacher-turned-lawyer Ralph Estrada assumed national and state leadership in proclaiming Mexican American civil rights and dismantling school segregation in Arizona. As children of the Alianza, and now leaders in their own right, their action to challenge educational segregation, to support racial unity, and to endorse bilingual education not only informed generational politics but also exemplified the pinnacle of civic integration as they applied their lettered expertise to help solve the most pressing civil rights and educational issues affecting Mexican Americans in the nation. They contributed to larger, integrated civil rights initiatives to transform public education into an institution receptive to the academic, social, and economic needs of Mexican American children. Their work also set the terms for the emergent Chicano generation, a group that radicalized the politics of civic integration in the coming decades.

As a Tucsonense teacher and high school dean of students, María Urquides's popularity, authority, and presence grew exponentially in

Anglo-American and Mexican American communities in the postwar decades. In 1960, the Democratic Party appointed her as the only Mexican American woman to the board of the national Viva Kennedy campaign.[2] She and Ida Celaya, both educators and the only women, served on the state executive board that included a "who's who" of Arizonense politicians, newspaper editors, and lawyers, including Ralph Estrada.[3] As president of the Arizona Education Association (AEA) and a decades-long member of its Tucson chapter, Urquides pressed the National Education Association (NEA) to reconsider matters of segregation, including in its own membership, and especially race-based and language policies and practices that deterred the status of minority and immigrant children.[4] This work, in concert with teachers in Tucson who had developed a new bilingual program called "Spanish for Spanish Speakers," led to a national study and conference on the condition of Spanish-speaking children in the United States. According to historian Maritza de la Trinidad, Urquides convinced the NEA to fund a survey of educational programs for Spanish-speaking students in schools across the Southwest.[5] With $2,000, she and a team of Tucson teachers visited schools in California, Colorado, New Mexico, and Texas that investigated the educational conditions of Mexican American youth across the Southwest. They published their findings in the 1966 NEA report, *The Invisible Minority, Pero No Vencibles: Report of the NEA-Tucson Survey on the Teaching of Spanish to the Spanish-Speaking*. In lieu of age-old Americanization strategies geared to stripping the child of cultural and language identity, the report called for student-centered, culturally responsive bilingual curricula that uplifted Spanish-speaking children. The popularity of the report led the NEA to host a symposium on bilingual education in 1966 that brought scholars and politicians from across the United States to Tucson, launching a nationwide push for bilingual education. The following year, Texas senator Ralph Yarborough convinced the U.S. Congress to pass the Bilingual Education Act, as Title VII of the Elementary and Secondary Education Act of 1968, "in recognition of the special educational needs of the large numbers of children of limited English-speaking ability in the United States."[6] In the forty-six years since graduating from the Arizona State Teachers College, Urquides's shift in personal consciousness and professional pedagogy turned dramatically from promoting and practicing Americanization to advocating nationally for bilingual education. She joked publicly, "[I] often tell people that if I go to hell, it will be for spanking kids for speaking Spanish."[7] As a result of her contribution to this landmark legislation and its significant impact on the educational lives of Spanish-speaking children, she is often lauded as "the mother of bilingual education."[8]

When she retired from the Tucson Unified School District in May 1974, Urquides told a reporter for the *Arizona Daily Star* that she wished she were "just beginning to teach." Having dedicated nearly five decades to Tucson children, her work felt incomplete. Only two years into her administrative appointment as an area student services coordinator where she and her staff at Tully Elementary School (named for former teacher and superintendent Carlos Tully) identified and assisted learning disabled children in westside Tucson, she still felt a huge commitment to remain. "I really feel I would like to stay and finish," Urquides said. Because school segregation had marked so much of her personal life and professional career, it is possible that she wanted to witness this new moment.

Urquides had come so far and such a long way from 1947 when she completed her bachelor's degree at the University of Arizona. That spring, the *Arizona Daily Star* selected her for a news feature called "Woman of the Week." This honorary column included a photo and sweet write-up of her accomplishments. The paper lauded her heritage as a "daughter of Old Tucson," her civic activity, her accomplishments as a full-time teacher, and her case work at the Catholic Social Services of Arizona.[9] But the paper also poked fun at her Spanish "accent," retelling an old high school story about how she flubbed the English pronunciation of a few words in a choir solo. "Now she makes it a point to keep her small fry speaking English—and good English—in classroom and playground."[10] In one line, the newspaper put her and her students in their place. Those "small fry" were her children "at Davis Elementary School, the largest school in the district, with 720 students—98 percent of whom were of Mexican origin."[11]

This news piece marked a turning point in Urquides's career. Before 1947, her teaching and civic work focused on providing all sorts of general assistance to her Davis School students and their Oury Park neighborhood center, including the fundraising needed to support a full-time youth coordinator to keep the center open daily.[12] The Tucson School District lauded her for translating State Nutrition Committee pamphlets, which they shared with Spanish-speaking families across the city.[13] She sang (often and even on the radio) at the Alianza's Founders Day celebrations, taught catechism with Ida Celaya and the Catholic Daughters of America, canvased with the League of Women Voters, and fundraised for children's and women's programs with the Young Women's Christian Association.[14] Now, with a degree in hand and decades of volunteer experience, she made a political move to take on the leadership of the Tucson Education Association (TEA). In 1948, she represented the TEA at the NEA annual meeting in Cleveland, Ohio, and, by 1950, the TEA elected her as its president.[15]

Urquides's first order of business was to desegregate the Tucson public schools. A few years earlier, she joined the Tucson Council for Civic Unity (CCU), a multiracial and multireligious organization that called for racial unity.[16] The CCU's main project was to eliminate segregation across Arizona. The Tucson and Phoenix councils joined together to form a statewide council and they chose as board members Urquides and Tucson school superintendent Robert D. Morrow. Urquides's commitment was steadfast, especially given the support of her employer. She signed onto the CCU's articles of incorporation and went on a speaking tour, attesting to the undemocratic nature of segregation from a teacher's point of view.[17] "As long as segregation exists, we are not teaching preparation for living in a democratic world," Urquides professed.[18]

Urquides's work with the CCU allowed her to combine her concerns about race, gender, and education together in a fundamental way.[19] Not only could she publicly challenge racial and language segregation in the schools as a spokesperson, but she could do so as a professional educator. For instance, she endorsed the CCU's early decision to support African American teachers who might lose their jobs in the face of desegregation; the CCU vowed to file a lawsuit to protect their tenure if needed.[20] The CCU also formally aligned Urquides with Gregorio García, Ralph Estrada, and the Alianza. Although they knew one another and had come of age as children of the Alianza, Mexican women had no role in its business.[21] They served in an auxiliary society that supported the Supreme Council and its chapters across the state. This is why Urquides sang at their events, but now she had her own seat on the same political stage and would remain as an elected teacher union leader for decades. Urquides broke barriers not only around race, but specifically as a Mexican American woman leader of her generation. No other Mexican American woman in the nation had the same kind of authority or public resonance in the 1950s or 1960s, until the rise of the Chicana and Chicano Movements in 1965.[22]

Urquides's quest for educational justice was tied intimately to the history of Arizonenses and their desire to fulfill civic integration. When Urquides and García took the stage for the CCU, they both spoke to the values of democracy, the unfulfilled promises of the nation, and the importance of tolerance and acceptance. In October 1950, García and Urquides headlined a CCU public lecture with University of Arizona professor Dr. E. H. Spicer, Tucson superintendent Morrow, and Major Dorsey J. Watson, U.S. Army Retired, who spoke on his experience as a Negro soldier.[23] "Speaking from personal experience," García said, "I can say that the segregation of Spanish-American children in Arizona has encouraged misunderstanding, prejudice, and friction between groups, and has retarded the development and education of these children."[24]

The Alianza's participation in the CCU marked a significant shift in postwar interracial politics as its older membership and affiliated organizations, such as the Latin American Club, often relied on the privileges of whiteness, called for separation from the African American community, and endorsed politicians such as segregationist governor Benjamin B. Moeur.[25] That same October, the Alianza published an editorial in its magazine opposing racial segregation of all children in the public schools ("contra la segregación de nuestros estudiantes"), urging voters to support the statewide Initiative 318 endorsed by the CCU and the Alianza.[26] Initiative 318 called for an immediate prohibition of "segregation of students in the public schools of Arizona for reasons of race, creed, color or national origin."[27] The Alianza carefully explained that the continued segregation existed on the "pretext" that their children had a language deficiency ("deficiencias de lenguaje") that required separate instruction. They argued against this fallacy, pointing out three truths: The majority of Mexican American children can and do speak English; when these children enter school, the teachers do not assess them to determine who can and cannot speak English; and in certain schools the segregation continues beyond the eight years of primary school. The Alianza argued that the obvious and only reason for the segregation was that their children were "mexico-americanos." Since the Supreme Court of Arizona had ruled that segregation was constitutional, the only solution was to change unjust laws. Along with the NAACP, the Urban League, and the *Arizona Sun* (an African American newspaper), the Alianza endorsed Initiative 318 wholeheartedly, urging Arizonenses to vote against segregation.[28] Despite their best efforts to convince voters that segregation was never equal, not to mention that it was unchristian, the initiative ultimately failed in November 1950.

The Alianza's position on Initiative 318, however, was only one aspect of its new desegregation project called the "Guerra al Prejuicio Racial" (War Against Racial Prejudice). The Alianza maintained its solvency as a mutual aid society that sold insurance and had always kept lawyers on retainer, but with attorneys at its helm—García as suprema and Estrada as supreme attorney—they officially opened a legal unit to tackle civil rights issues. Given their decades-long professional careers in Phoenix, García and Estrada focused their legal strategy on desegregating schools in the vicinity of the valley, beginning with the towns of Tolleson, Glendale, and Winslow. In 1950, Estrada filed *Gonzales v. Sheely*, the first case to use the *Mendez v. Westminster* ruling.[29] In *Gonzales*, Mexican American parents—led by Porfirio Gonzales, Faustino Curiel, and the Comité Movimiento Unido Mexicano Contra la Discriminación (Committee of the United Mexican Movement Against Discrimination)—challenged the segregation of their children in a separate school building of Tolleson Elementary School District No. 17. A small agricultural hamlet in western Maricopa County, Tolleson had a long history of racial segregation in its town and school.[30] The district had one school building and divided the children by race into different classrooms. In a scenario similar to Tempe in the early 1900s, the district built a second school, designating one school as the "Mexican School" and the other for white children and a few English-speaking Mexican American children. The district officials insisted that language, not race, was the basis for their decision to separate the students because most of the Mexican American children did not speak English. Estrada argued that this was false because the district had no testing program to verify language ability and, more important, the segregation violated the Fourteenth Amendment. Judge David W. Ling ruled on behalf of the Arizonense parents, faulting the school district for discrimination: "Segregation of school children in separate school buildings because of racial or national origin ... constitutes a denial of the equal protection of the laws guaranteed to petitioners as citizens of the United States."[31]

The victory in *Gonzales v. Sheely* generated a domino effect that led to school desegregation in Arizona. Not only did Judge Ling's ruling rely on and bolster the growing federal case law on desegregation, but also this victory signaled to white Arizonans and to school districts across the state that segregation was no longer legally valid and would be challenged. Judge Ling announced his ruling in *Gonzales* on March 26, 1951; and days before that announcement, Tucson superintendent Morrow "promise[d] early desegregation."[32] Two months later, the Tucson school board voted to desegregate its district, and to change the name of Paul Laurence Dunbar Elementary School for black children.[33] The town of Nogales soon followed, becoming the second city to desegregate.[34] Estrada continued to file lawsuits to expand the scope of the desegregation because *Gonzales* applied only to the Tolleson district and did not challenge the "the constitutionality of the Arizona statute that

Guerra al Prejuicio Racial

PALADINES DE LA DEMOCRACIA.—He aquí a varios de los elementos que han estado tomando parte muy importante en la lucha que se viene librando en el Estado de Arizona, contra la segregación de los niños mexicanos en las escuelas. En primera línea, de izquierda a derecha, aparecen el licenciado Gustavo García, de San Antonio, Texas; el Hno. licenciado Rafael Estrada, Abogado Consultor y Gerente de la Alianza; profesor Jorge Ramírez, de la Universidad del Estado de Texas. En el mismo orden, atrás, los Hnos. Lauro R. Montaño, de la Logia 52 de Los Angeles, Calif.; Arturo Fuentes y J. I. Gandarilla, Presidente y Vicepresidente Supremos de la Alianza y el licenciado Fred Okrand, de Los Angeles, California.

Figure 16. "Guerra al Prejuicio Racial." In 1952, *Alianza* magazine published this photograph of lawyers and civil rights leaders affiliated with the school desegregation case *Gonzales v. Sheely* (1951) as part of its campaign to end racial prejudice in Arizona. From left to right: (front row) Texas attorney Gus García; attorney Ralph Estrada, University of Texas professor Jorge Ramírez; (back row) Lauro R. Montaño of Alianza Lodge No. 52, Los Angeles; Arturo Fuentes, Alianza supreme president; J. I. Gandarilla, Alianza supreme vice president; and Los Angeles ACLU attorney Fred Okrand. Chicano Research Collection, Arizona State University.

allowed the racial segregation of students in the first place."[35] The Alianza, with Estrada as lead counsel, sued towns and school districts in Arizona and California, including the Glendale city schools in *Ortiz v. Jack* (1951), the city of Winslow public recreation in *Baca v. Winslow* (1955), and the El Centro, California, schools in *Romero v. Weakley* (1955).[36]

The success of these school desegregation campaigns pushed Urquides and Estrada to the forefront of Arizonense politics and into the national limelight that would bring them the attention of the Democratic National Party. García, unfortunately, died of a heart attack in his law office in 1953, leaving the future of the Alianza in Estrada's hands.[37] Estrada took the role of the Alianza's suprema and continued la Guerra al Prejuicio Racial. Urquides gained greater leadership opportunities in the Arizona Education Association, representing the state at the national annual meetings and, at the governor's request, at the White House Conference on Children and Youth.[38] In 1959, the AEA elected Urquides as its president.[39] By 1960, Urquides and Estrada joined a cadre of Mexican American leaders from across the Southwest as members of the executive board of the national Viva Kennedy campaign. Their move into national politics created opportunities for younger, local leadership to emerge in Phoenix and Tucson. This leadership later introduced and pursued the Chicano Movement agendas around the rollout of school integration, higher education access, and the curriculum changes that would come to include the advent of Chicana and Chicano Studies in Arizona public schools.

NOTES

The following abbreviations appear in the notes:

ASA ASLAPR   Arizona State Archives, Arizona State Library, Archives and Public Records
CRC ASU   Chicano Research Collection, Arizona State University Libraries
CSRC UCLA   Chicano Studies Research Center Archives, UCLA
UA ASU   University Archives, Arizona State University Libraries

Introduction

1. Conrad James Carreón, obituary, *Arizona Republic*, February 21, 2002.

2. Bradford Luckingham, *Minorities in Phoenix: A Profile of Mexican American, Chinese American, and African American Communities, 1860–1992* (Tucson: University of Arizona Press, 1994), 46.

3. "Resolucion Presentada ala 'AEA' Terminaria con la Discriminacion [sic]," *El Mensajero*, November 14, 1941, 1, 4, 6. In 1943, Carreón became the editor and publisher of *El Mensajero*, which had been owned and operated by numerous Arizonense business leaders since its founding in 1900. See *El Mensajero*, LCCN: sn 96060814, Arizona Historical Digital Newspapers, Arizona Memory Project, ASA ASLAPR.

4. The *Arizona Republic* referred to Carreón's resolution as a "tolerance unit." See "Prescott Educator Is Elected," *Arizona Republic*, November 16, 1941, 1.

5. "1941 Los Conquistadores Conference Program" (loose document) in Veronica Castillo, "Biography of Rebecca Muñoz Gutiérrez," Small Manuscript, MM CHSM-883 (December 4, 2000), CRC ASU.

6. This Muñoz family and I are not related, although both of our families can be traced to Tamaulipas, Mexico.

7. *Arizona Republic*, December 6, 1941; "Group of People Posing on Lawn, Arizona Conference, 1941," Image 95, Rebecca Muñoz Gutiérrez Photographs, 1920–1959, MP SPC 323, CRC ASU. The scrapbook notes identify James Carreón and Gonzales Morelos in the photo. Other conference attendees included ASTC education chair Dr. Samuel Burkhard, ASTC professor Irma Wilson, and ASTC dean Dr. John Odus Grimes.

8. Veronica Castillo, "Biography of Rebecca Muñoz Gutiérrez," Small Manuscript, MM CHSM-883 (December 4, 2000), CRC ASU.

9. Rosalío F. Muñoz, Resume, Ricardo Muñoz Papers, Box 34, Folder 14, CSRC UCLA. Muñoz spoke fluent English, French, and Spanish, as well as conversational German, Italian, and Portuguese.

10. *Arizona Republic,* December 16, 1941; December 24, 1941; December 30, 1941.

11. Victoria-María MacDonald, ed., *Latino Education in the United States: A Narrated History from 1513–2000* (New York: Palgrave Macmillan, 2004), 68; Samuel Pressly McCrea, "Establishment of the Arizona School System" (master's thesis, Stanford University, 1902), in the *Biennial Report of Superintendent of Public Instruction of Territory of Arizona, 1907–1908* (Phoenix, 1908), 84, 96, 100; Thomas E. Sheridan, *Los Tucsonenses: The Mexican Community in Tucson, 1854–1941* (Tucson: University of Arizona Press, 1986), 46–53.

12. Carl F. Kaestle, *Pillars of the Republic: Common Schools and American Society, 1780–1860* (New York: Hill and Wang, 1983), 97–98; Clif Stratton, *Education for Empire: American Schools, Race, and the Paths of Good Citizenship* (Berkeley: University of California Press, 2016), 178–182, 189; Mirelsie Velázquez, *Puerto Rican Chicago, Schooling the City, 1940–1977* (Champaign: University of Illinois, 2022), 8–11.

13. School district petitions are archived by county. For example, *see* "Petition for School District," DS by Rafael Romero *et al.*, March 1, 1890, Petitions 1887–1897; School Records-Reports 1886–1919, Box 2; Superintendent of Schools; Apache County, RG 100, ASA ASLAPR.

14. Philis Barragán Goetz, *Reading, Writing, and Revolution: Escuelitas and the Emergence of a Mexican American Identity in Texas* (Austin: University of Texas Press, 2020); Rubén Donato and Jarrod Hansen, *The Other American Dilemma: Schools, Mexicans, and the Nature of Jim Crow, 1912–1953* (Albany: State University of New York Press, 2021).

15. I thank Vicki L. Ruiz for coining this term.

16. Katherine Benton-Cohen, *Borderline Americans: Racial Division and Labor War in the Arizona Borderlands* (Cambridge, Mass.: Harvard University Press, 2009), 156–162; Gerald L. Cadava, *Standing on Common Ground: The Making of a Sunbelt Borderland* (Cambridge, Mass.: Harvard University Press, 2013), 64, 79, 92; Anita Huizar-Hernández, *Forging Arizona: A History of the Peralta Land Grant and Racial Identity in the West* (New Brunswick, N.J.: Rutgers University Press, 2019), 7–8; Eric V. Meeks, *Border Citizens: The Making of Indians, Mexicans, and Anglos in Arizona* (Austin: University of Texas Press, 2007), 30–31; James E. Officer, *Hispanic Arizona, 1536–1856* (Tucson: University of Arizona Press, 1987), 91–294; Sheridan, *Los Tucsonenses,* 70.

17. Biographical Note, Mariano G. Samaniego Family Papers, MS 0706, Arizona Historical Society-Tucson; Manuel G. Gonzales, "Mariano G. Samaniego," *Journal of Arizona History* 31, no. 2 (Summer 1990): 141–160; Sheridan, *Los Tucsonenses,* 48–50.

18. Sheridan, *Los Tucsonenses,* 49.

19. Sheridan, *Los Tucsonenses,* 48; Alyssa Bentz, "How a Mexican Immigrant Became a Legend in Arizona," Wells Fargo Stories, https://stories.wf.com/mexican-immigrant -became-legend-arizona/; Jeff Biggers, "A Mexican Immigrant's Act of Honor," *New York Times,* February 14, 2002, https://opinionator.blogs.nytimes.com/2012/02/14/a-mexican

-immigrants-act-of-honor/. Sheridan notes that Tully, Ochoa & Co., paid $3,300 in taxes, making them the "largest taxpayer in Pima County."

20. Teresa Palomo Acosta, "Alianza Hispano-Americana," *Handbook of Texas Online*, Handbook of Texas Online, November 1, 1994, www.tshaonline.org/handbook /entries/alianza-hispano-americana; Kaye Lynn Briegel, "Alianza Hispano-Americana, 1894-1965" (PhD diss., University of Southern California, 1974) 1, 214; Sheridan, *Los Tucsonenses*, 167-175.

21. Jaime R. Águila and F. Arturo Rosales, "Lost Land and México Lindo: Origins of Mexicans in Arizona's Salt River Valley, 1865-1910," in *Mexican Workers and the Making of Arizona*, ed. Luis F. B. Plascencia and Gloria H. Cuádraz (Tucson: University of Arizona Press, 2018), 74-76.

22. For an assessment of Mexican American discrimination in Arizona, see Benton-Cohen, *Borderline Americans*; Cadava, *Standing on Common Ground*; Sheridan, *Los Tucsonenses*; Linda Gordon, *The Great Arizona Orphan Abduction* (Cambridge, Mass.: Harvard University Press, 1999); Josiah McC. Heyman, *Life and Labor on the Border: Working People of Northeastern Sonora, Mexico, 1886-1986* (Tucson: University of Arizona Press, 1991); Luckingham, *Minorities in Phoenix*; Meeks, *Border Citizens*; Plascencia and Cuádraz, eds., *Mexican Workers and the Making of Arizona*; and F. Arturo Rosales, *Pobre Raza! Violence, Justice, and Mobilization Among México Lindo Immigrants, 1900-1936* (Austin: University of Texas Press, 1999).

23. Mark Reisler, *By the Sweat of Their Brow: Mexican Immigrant Labor in the United States, 1900-1940* (Westport, Conn.: Greenwood Press, 1976), 144.

24. Gilbert G. González, *Chicano Education in the Era of Segregation* (Philadelphia: Balch Institute Press, 1990), xii-xiv, 87-109. See, in particular, chapter 4, "Training for Occupational Efficiency: Vocational Education."

25. For a discussion of the "question" or "problem" in the nineteenth century, see Holly Case, *The Age of Questions: or, A First Attempt at an Aggregate History of the Eastern, Social, Woman, American, Jewish, Polish, Bullion, Tuberculosis, and Many Other Questions over the Nineteenth Century, and Beyond* (Princeton, N.J.: Princeton University Press, 2018).

26. Gilbert G. González, *Culture of Empire: American Writers, Mexico, and Mexican Immigrants, 1880-1930* (Austin: University of Texas Press, 2004), 11; Lozano, *An American Language*, 143, 171-173; Stratton, *Education for Empire*, 178-182, 189.

27. González, *Chicano Education in the Era of Segregation*, 87-109.

28. *El Tucsonense*, August 30, 1916; March 17, 1927; *El Mensajero*, October 6, 1943.

29. Ralph Estrada, "The Mexican-American Minority," *Alianza* (February 1962): 13-14.

30. Katherine Benton-Cohen, "Other Immigrants: Mexicans and the Dillingham Commission of 1907-1911," *Journal of American Ethnic History* 30, no. 2 (Winter 2011): 33; Cybelle Fox and Thomas Guglielmo, "Defining America's Racial Boundaries: Blacks, Mexicans, and European Immigrants, 1890-1945," *American Journal of Sociology* 18, no. 2 (September 2012): 327-379; Thomas Guglielmo, "Fighting for Caucasian Rights: Mexicans, Mexican Americans, and the Transnational Struggle for Civil Rights in World War II Texas," *Journal of American History* 92, no. 4 (2006): 1212-1237.

31. Katherine Benton-Cohen, *Inventing the Immigration Problem: The Dillingham Commission and Its Legacy* (Cambridge, Mass.: Harvard University Press, 2018), 7.

32. Officer, *Hispanic Arizona*, 25–27.

33. Thomas E. Sheridan, *Arizona: A History*, rev. ed. (Tucson: University of Arizona Press, 2012), 137; Madeline Ferrin Paré, *Arizona Pageant: A Short History of the State* (Phoenix: Arizona Historical Foundation, 1965), 190.

34. Henry F. Dobyns, *Tubac Through Four Centuries: An Historical Resume and Analysis* (Phoenix: Arizona State Park Boards, 1959; 1995 Reformat), web version accessible at www.parentseyes.arizona.edu/tubac/; Carl Hayden, "Sabino Otero," Hayden Arizona Pioneer Biographies Collection, ASU, www.asu.edu/lib/archives/azbio/bios/OTEROS .PDF; *El Tucsonense*, May 5, 1923; Officer, *Hispanic Arizona*, 66, 292, 346nn37–38; George H. Kelly, "Providing Education in Arizona," *Arizona Historical Review* 2, no. 3 (October 1929): 101–106.

35. Officer, *Hispanic Arizona*, 17, 22; *see also* James E. Officer and Henry F. Dobyns, "Teodoro Ramirez: Early Citizen of Tucson," *Journal of Arizona History* 25, no. 3 (Autumn 1984): 221–244; Victor R. Stoner and Henry F. Dobyns, "Fray Pedro Antonio de Arriquibar, Chaplain of the Royal Fort at Tucson," *Arizona and the West (Journal of the Southwest)* 1, no. 1 (Spring 1959): 71–79.

36. Officer, *Hispanic Arizona*, 19–20; 335n69.

37. Gabriela F. Arredondo, *Mexican Chicago: Race, Identity and Nation, 1916–1939* (Urbana: University of Illinois Press, 2008), 17; Asunción Lavrin, "Women in Twentieth Century Latin American Society," in *Cambridge History of Latin America*, Vol. 4, ed. Leslie Bethell (Cambridge: Cambridge University Press, 1994), 503; MacDonald, *Latino Education in the United States*, 1–21, 38–43. See also Mary Kay Vaughan, *Cultural Politics in Revolution: Teachers, Peasants, and Schools in Mexico, 1930–1940* (Tucson: University of Arizona Press, 1997), and Vaughan, *The State, Education and Social Class in Mexico, 1880–1928* (DeKalb: Northern Illinois University Press, 1982).

38. Officer, *Hispanic Arizona*, 275–277.

39. McCrea, "Establishment of the Arizona School System" 78. McCrea attributes his interpretation to the *Journals of the Legislative Assembly of the Territory of Arizona* (1864). He also published his thesis in digest form as "History of Arizona Education" in *Educational Conditions in Arizona (Report of a Survey by the United States Bureau of Education)*, U.S. Department of the Interior, Office of Education (Washington, D.C., 1918 [Bulletin, 1917, No. 44]).

40. MacDonald, *Latino Education in the United States*, 71–73.

41. Plascencia and Cuádraz, *Mexican Workers and the Making of Arizona*, 9.

42. "[Antonio A. Celaya,] Mexican, One of the People of This Great United States," in *Immigration and Assimilation*, Hannibal Gerald Duncan (Boston: D. C. Heath, 1933), 757. I identified Celaya based on facts revealed in this anonymous oral history. Duncan reprinted nine interviews by other scholars; this one may be the work of anthropologist Manuel Gamio who frequented Arizona.

43. Lydia R. Otero, *In the Shadows of the Freeway: Growing Up Brown & Queer* (Tucson, Ariz.: Planet Earth Press, 2019), 6, 27–28.

44. Rosalío F. Muñoz, "Dad on Family in Miami," n.d., unpublished manuscript about the life of Rev. Esaú Pérez Muñoz; typed, electronic copy provided to author by the Muñoz family.

45. Historian Rosina Lozano defines "treaty citizens" as those Mexicans who chose to remain in the United States after the Mexican-American War and who were protected by the 1848 Treaty of Guadalupe Hidalgo or the Treaty of La Mesilla, as it was known in Mexico. Rosina Lozano, *An American Language: The History of Spanish in the United States* (Berkeley: University of California Press, 2018), 5.

46. Águila and Rosales, "Lost Land and México Lindo," 72-74.

47. For examples, see Laura R. Barraclough, *Charros: How Mexican Cowboys Are Remapping Race and American Identity* (Berkeley: University of California Press, 2019), 39, 44; Meeks, *Border Citizens*, 10; Mae M. Ngai, *Impossible Subjects: Illegal Aliens and the Making of Modern America* (Princeton, N.J.: Princeton University Press, 2004), 3.

48. Vicki L. Ruiz, *From Out of the Shadows: Mexican Women in Twentieth-Century America* (New York: Oxford University Press, 1998), xvi.

49. For examples of how immigrants, women, and ethnic minorities pursued citizenship, see Evelyn Nakano Glenn, *Unequal Freedom: How Race and Gender Shaped American Citizenship and Labor* (Cambridge, Mass.: Harvard University Press, 1999); Felipe Gonzales, *Política: Nuevomexicanos and American Political Incorporation, 1821-1910* (Lincoln: University of Nebraska Press, 2016); Linda Kerber, *No Constitutional Right to Be Ladies: Women and the Obligations of Citizenship* (New York: Hill and Wang, 1998); Ngai, *Impossible Subjects*; Natalia Molina, *How Race Is Made in America: Immigration, Citizenship, and the Historical Power of Racial Scripts* (Berkeley: University of California Press, 2014); Luis F. B. Plascencia, *Disenchanting Citizenship: Mexican Migrants and the Boundaries of Belonging* (New Brunswick, N.J.: Rutgers University Press, 2012); Ana Elizabeth Rosas, "Historical Paths to Mexican American Citizenship," *Mexican Studies/ Estudios Mexicanos* 24, no.1 (Winter 2008): 147-167.

50. Benton-Cohen, *Borderline Americans*, 149-176. In chapter 5, "Mexicans and Mormons in the San Pedro River Valley," she delineates how race relations shaped school politics in four communities.

51. *Arizona Republic*, March 15, 1893; March 23, 1893. The seventeenth legislative assembly debated two bills to introduce Spanish-language instruction in the public schools and higher education institutions, alongside another to remove English-language requirements for elected officials. All three failed.

52. "Jaime Crow" is the literal translation of "Jim Crow" and several scholars use this translation to refer to white/brown segregation. In popular media, the *Nation* adopted the term "Juan Crow" and I prefer this term for its accessibility and popularity in the scholarship. Roberto Lovato, "Juan Crow in Georgia," *Nation*, May 26, 2008.

53. Michelle Alexander, *The New Jim Crow: Mass Incarceration in the Age of Colorblindness* (New York: New Press, 2012), 12; Laura E. Gómez, *Manifest Destinies: The Making of the Mexican American Race* (New York: New York University Press, 2007).

54. *St. Johns Herald*, November 17, 1927.

55. Arizona women were granted suffrage in July 1912, after U.S. statehood. For a discussion of suffrage and statehood, see David Berman, *Politics, Labor, and the War on Big Business: The Path of Reform in Arizona, 1890-1920* (Boulder: University Press of Colorado, 2012); Lozano, *An American Language*, 153-154; Sheridan, *Arizona*, 185.

56. Lozano, *An American Language*, 100; Stephen B. Weeks, "History of Public School Education in Arizona," Bulletin No. 17, Bureau of Education, Department of the Interior (Washington, D.C.: Government Printing Office, 1918), 46, 88; Arizona Territory Session Laws, no. 33, sec. 58 (1883); Arizona Territory Session Laws, no. 75, sec. 80 (1885); Arizona Territory Revised Statutes, no. 1552, sec. 79 (1887).

57. Arizona Territory Revised Statutes, no. 2169, sec. 7 (1887). This ban on non-English speakers extended to grand and petit juries.

58. Arizona Territory Session Laws, no. 21 (1891); Elise M. Dubord, "Language Policy and the Drawing of Social Boundaries: Public and Private Schools in Territorial Tucson," *Spanish in Context* 7, no. 1 (2010): 34; Lozano, *An American Language*, 99-100.

59. Molina, *How Race Is Made in America*, 6-11; Molina, "The Power of Racial Scripts: What the History of Mexican Immigration to the United States Teaches Us About Relational Notions of Race," *Latino Studies* 8, no. 2 (2010): 157.

60. Laura E. Gómez, *Inventing Latinos: A New Story of American Racism* (New York: New Press, 2020), 6.

61. R. E. Somers, "Mexican Indifference or Interest!" *Arizona Teacher and Home Journal* 11, no. 4 (1923): 6-8.

62. Mrs. M. R. Peralta, Tempe, Arizona, to Governor George W. P. Hunt, Phoenix, Arizona, January 22, 1925, and January 28, 1925, Arizona Governor's Office, Governors George W. P. Hunt, Thomas Campbell, and John C. Phillips, SG 8, Box 3, folder 29: Segregation in Schools: Correspondence, 1925, ASA ASLAPR.

63. Mrs. Peralta to Governor Hunt, January 22 and January 28, 1925.

64. Rosalío F. Muñoz, "Dad on Family in Miami," excerpt from unpublished, untitled manuscript about the life of Rev. Esaú Pérez Muñoz; typed, electronic copy provided to author by the Muñoz family.

65. The dissertation includes appendixes with information on more than 150 students and 75 teachers. Laura K. Muñoz, "Desert Dreams: Mexican American Education in Arizona, 1870-1930" (PhD diss., Arizona State University, 2006).

66. Rebecca Muñoz Gutiérrez Photographs, 1920-1959, MP SPC 323 & 324, CRC ASU.

67. Ricardo Muñoz Papers, 1900-2005, CSRC.64, CSRC UCLA; Rosalío Muñoz Papers, 1900-2015, CSRC.93, CSRC UCLA.

68. Monica Muñoz Martinez, *The Injustice Never Leaves You: Anti-Mexican Violence in Texas* (Cambridge, Mass.: Harvard University Press, 2018), 27.

69. Relevant works in Chicano educational history include Carlos Kevin Blanton, *The Strange Career of Bilingual Education in Texas, 1836-1981* (College Station: Texas A&M University Press, 2004); Blanton, *George I. Sánchez: The Long Fight for Mexican American Integration* (New Haven, Conn.: Yale University Press, 2014); Thomas P. Carter,

Mexican Americans in School: A History of Educational Neglect (New York, 1970); Rubén Donato, *The Other Struggle for Equal Schools: Mexican Americans During the Civil Rights Era* (Albany: State University of New York Press, 1997); Donato, *Mexicans and Hispanos in Colorado Schools and Communities, 1920-1960* (Albany: State University of New York Press, 2007); Donato and Hanson, *The Other American Dilemma*; Darius V. Echeverría, *Aztlán Arizona Mexican American Educational Empowerment, 1968-1978* (Tucson: University of Arizona Press, 2014); Ruben Flores, *Backroads Pragmatists: Mexico's Melting Pot and Civil Rights in the United States* (Philadelphia: University of Pennsylvania Press, 2014); David G. García, *Strategies of Segregation: Race, Residence, and the Struggle for Educational Equality* (Berkeley: University of California Press, 2018); Lynne Marie Getz, *Schools of Their Own: The Education of Hispanos in New Mexico, 1850-1940* (Albuquerque: University of Press, 1997); Goetz, *Reading, Writing, and Revolution*; Gilbert G. González, *Chicano Education in the Era of Segregation* and *Culture of Empire*; Gilbert G. González and Raul A. Fernández, *A Century of Chicano History: Empire, Nations, and Migration* (New York: Routledge, 2003); Gonzalo Guzmán, "'Things Change You Know': Schools as the Architects of the Mexican Race in Depression-Era Wyoming," *History of Education Quarterly* 61 (2021): 392-422; Lozano, *An American Language*; Herschel T. Manuel, *The Education of Spanish-Speaking Children in Texas* (Austin: University of Texas Press, 1930); MacDonald, ed., *Latino Education in the United States*; John M. Nieto-Phillips, *The Language of Blood: The Making of Spanish-American Identity in New Mexico, 1880s-1930s* (Albuquerque: University of New Mexico Press, 2008); Guadalupe San Miguel Jr., *"Let Them All Take Heed": Mexican Americans and the Campaign for Educational Equality in Texas, 1910-1981* (Austin: University of Texas Press, 1987); Guadalupe San Miguel Jr. and Rubén Donato, "Latino Education in Twentieth-Century America: A Brief History," in *The Handbook of Latinos and Education: Theory, Research and Practice*, ed. Enrique G. Murrillo Jr. et al. (New York: Routledge, 2010); George I. Sánchez, *Forgotten People: A Study of New Mexicans* (Albuquerque: University of New Mexico Press, 1940); Kathryn Schumaker, *Troublemakers: Students' Rights and Racial Justice in the Long 1960s* (New York: New York University Press, 2019); and Richard Valencia, *Chicano Students and the Courts: The Mexican American Legal Struggle for Educational Equity* (New York: New York University Press, 2008).

Arizona borderland histories pertinent to the Mexican/Chicano educational past include Benton-Cohen, *Borderline Americans*; Linda Gordon, *The Great Arizona Orphan Abduction*; Josiah McC. Heyman, *Life and Labor on the Border*; Luckingham, *Minorities in Phoenix*; Christine Marin, "Courting Success and Realizing the American Dream: Arizona's Mighty Miami High School Championship Basketball Team, 1951," *International Journal of the History of Sport* 26, no. 7 (June 2009): 924-946; Marin, "'GET RID OF THE SHACKS!' West Live Oak Street Redevelopment in Miami, Arizona, 1946-1952," *Journal of Arizona History* 56, no. 2 (Summer 2015): 205-226; Eric V. Meeks, *Border Citizens*; Katherine G. Morrissey and Kirsten M. Jensen, *Picturing Arizona: The Photographic Record of the 1930s* (Tucson: University of Arizona Press, 2005); Plascencia and Cuádraz, eds., *Mexican Workers and the Making of Arizona*; Rosales, *¡Pobre Raza!*;

Sheridan, *Los Tucsonenses*; Samuel Truett, *Fugitive Landscapes: The Forgotten History of the U.S.-Mexico Borderlands* (New Haven, Conn.: Yale University Press, 2006).

70. Mario T. García, *The Chicano Generation: Testimonios of the Movement* (Berkeley: University of California Press, 2015), 212; Carlos Muñoz, *Youth, Identity, Power: The Chicano Movement* (New York: Verso, 1989), 34; Lorena Oropeza, *¡Raza Sí! ¡Guerra No¡ Chicano Protest and Patriotism During the Viet Nam War Era* (Berkeley: University of California Press, 2005), 118, 223; George J. Sánchez, *Becoming Mexican American: Ethnicity, Culture, and Identity in Chicano Los Angeles, 1900–1945* (New York: Oxford University Press, 1993), 262.

71. Veronica Castillo to Christine Marin, email correspondence, March 22, 2000 (in possession of the author).

72. Alan J. Daly, *Social Network Theory and Educational Change* (Cambridge, Mass.: Harvard Education Press, 2010).

73. Vicki L. Ruiz, "Class Acts: Latina Feminist Traditions, 1900–1930 (AHA Presidential Address)," American Historical Review 121, no. 1 (February 2016): 15–16.

74. Rosales, *¡Pobre Raza!*, 135.

Chapter 1

1. "Kirkland-McKinney Ditch," Tempe Historic Property Register, City of Tempe, March 25, 2015, available online at www.tempe.gov/government/community -development/historic-preservation/historic-preservation-facilities-directory; *Arizona Weekly Citizen* (Tucson), November 11, 1871, 2; *Santa Fe New Mexican*, November 24, 1871, 4; Esther Margaret Carrillo Canchola, "Our Sotelo Roots" (unpublished manuscript, MM CHSM-917, 1985, CRC ASU), 6-B, 7-D, and 4-E; Christine Marin, "Manuela Sánchez Sotelo and María Sotelo Miller" in *Arizona Latina Trailblazers: Stories of Courage, Hope and Determination* (Phoenix, Ariz.: Latino Perspectives Media and the Raul H. Castro Institute, 2011), 22–29; Scott Solliday, "Hispanic Genealogy in Tempe," in *Memories of Old Settlers of Tempe*, ed. Joel A. Benedict, Irene A. Benedict, and Elizabeth Hampton James (Tempe, Ariz.: Old Settlers Association, 1996), 8–9; Manuela Sotelo, Probate Record, May 27, 1902, Maricopa, Arizona, Case number 756, Case Files, P0727-P0764, Probate Records, 1870-1930, Arizona, Superior Court (Maricopa County); Scott Solliday, "The Journey to Rio Salado: Hispanic Migrations to Tempe, Arizona" (master's thesis, Arizona State University, 1993), 56, 62–63. According to Canchola, Tiburcio died of a heart attack in Florence en route to Tempe with Manuela and the family. Newspapers reported the death of Feliciano Sotelo, a federal postal agent thought to be killed by Apaches on a U.S. mail route near Tucson. His government life insurance paid for the Sotelo family's move to Tempe. José later drowned attempting to cross the flooded Salt River on horseback.

2. Christine Marin, "Trailblazers 2011: Manuela Sánchez Sotelo and María Sotelo Miller," in *Latino Perspectives Magazine* 7, no. 7 (March 2011): 22–23; Marin, "Manuela Sánchez Sotelo: The Mexican Mother of Tempe, Pioneer Homesteader, Goodwill Ambassador,"

Arizona Women's History Alliance (August 12, 2020), www.azwomenshistoryalliance.org /manuela-sanchez-sotelo-the-mexican-mother-of-tempe-pioneer-homesteader-goodwill -ambassador/.

3. Canchola, "Our Sotelo Roots", 4-E.

4. Canchola, "Our Sotelo Roots," 4-F; Christine Marin, Tempe, Arizona, to Zona Y. (Barker) Bower, La Verne, California, letter, July 12, 2011, in author's possession.

5. Monica Muñoz Martinez, *The Injustice Never Leaves You: Anti-Mexican Violence in Texas* (Cambridge, Mass.: Harvard University Press, 2018), 27, 159; *see also* Michel-Rolph Trouillot, *Silencing the Past: Power and the Production of History*, 2nd rev. ed. (Boston: Beacon Press, 2015).

6. Canchola, "Our Sotelo Roots," 4-F. According to Canchola, the ASU University Archives are missing land-acquisition records from the period of 1885 to 1911.

7. James E. Officer, *Hispanic Arizona, 1536-1856* (Tucson: University of Arizona Press, 1987), 275-278. The Treaty of Mesilla, which the U.S. Congress ratified in 1854, is also known as the Gadsden Treaty Purchase. The first version of the treaty was signed December 30, 1853, and the U.S. survey team entered the northern region of the state of Sonora, Mexico, to begin the annexation in January 1854.

8. Jaime R. Águila and F. Arturo Rosales, "Lost Land and México Lindo: Origins of Mexicans in Arizona's Salt River Valley, 1865-1910," in *Mexican Workers and the Making of Arizona*, ed. Luis F. B. Plascencia and Gloria H. Cuádraz (Tucson: University of Arizona Press, 2018), 70; Daniel D. Arreola and Rio Hartwell, "Phoenix Population Origins, 1870-1900," *Geographical Review* 104, no. 4 (2014): 439-458. Águila and Rosales estimate from the 1870 Census that Mexicans in Maricopa County worked in only four occupations—as farmers, miners, laborers, or service workers.

9. David R. Dean and Jean A. Reynolds, *Hispanic Historic Property Survey: Final Report* (City of Phoenix, 2006), 8.

10. Joe Torres, oral history, interview by Pete R. Dimas, May 8, 2006, Veterans Hall of Fame Collection, Braun Sacred Heart Center, Phoenix, www.braunsacredheartcenter .org/joe-torres.html. Joe Torres was a force in Phoenix politics as a member of Local 383, Laborers International Union of North America, American Legion Post No. 41, and Chicanos Por La Causa, a Phoenix group organized in 1969 to fight racial discrimination against Mexican Americans.

11. Vicki L. Ruiz, *From Out of the Shadows: Mexican Women in Twentieth-Century America* (New York: Oxford University Press, 1998), xi, 25-27.

12. Katherine Benton-Cohen, *Borderline Americans: Racial Division and Labor War in the Arizona Borderlands* (Cambridge, Mass.: Harvard University Press, 2009), 149-176; Thomas E. Sheridan, *Los Tucsonenses: The Mexican Community in Tucson, 1854-1941* (Tucson: University of Arizona Press, 1986), 45-49.

13. Águila and Rosales, "Lost Land and México Lindo," 65-72.

14. John P. Hoyt, comp. *The Compiled Laws of the Territory of Arizona, 1894-1877* (Detroit, Mich.: Richmond, Backus & Co., Printers, 1877), 231; No. 33 Sec. 35, *Arizona*

Session Laws, (1883), 44; Benton-Cohen, *Borderline Americans*, 30-31; Amy de Haan, "Arizona Women Argue for the Vote: The 1912 Initiative Campaign for Women's Suffrage," *Journal of Arizona History* 45, no. 4 (Winter 2004): 378; Lozano, *An American Language*, 154; Heidi J. Osselaer, "Arizona's Woman Suffrage Movement," *Western Legal History* 30, nos. 1-2 (2019): 82; Heidi J. Osselaer, *Winning Their Place: Arizona Women in Politics, 1883-1950* (Tucson: University of Arizona Press, 2009), 22; Thomas E. Sheridan, *Arizona: A History*, rev. ed. (Tucson: University of Arizona Press, 2012), 185.

15. Marin, "Manuela Sánchez Sotelo and María Sotelo Miller," 22-23.

16. Canchola, "Our Sotelo Roots," 7.

17. Anita E. Huizar-Hernández, "'The Present Past: Recovering Native American, Mexican-American, and Anglo Narratives of Territorial Arizona 1848-1912" (PhD diss., University of California, San Diego, 2016); Marie Zander, "The Life of an Arizona Pioneer [María Sotelo]" in Canchola, "Our Sotelo Roots," 7-F.

18. Solliday, "'The Journey to Rio Salado: Hispanic Migrations to Tempe, Arizona," 70-73.

19. Benton-Cohen, *Borderline Americans*, 36; Sal Acosta, *Sanctioning Matrimony: Western Expansion and Interethnic Marriage in the Arizona Borderlands* (Tucson: University of Arizona Press, 2016), 16-17.

Benton-Cohen calls these Anglo men and their Mexican wives "intermarriers." She explains that this was not a trend, but a reality of Arizonense life. Nearly one-fourth of Pima County marriages between 1872 and 1879 were "between Anglos and people with Spanish surnames" and 50 percent of the founders of the Arizona Pioneers Historical Society "married Mexican women, most from prominent Tucson families." Acosta strategically notes that most of these intermarriages were not matches between the white or Mexican elite, as Sotelo and Miller were regarded, but among the working classes and across race, including whites, Mexicans, Blacks, and Chinese.

20. "Maríana Gonzales Priest," Tempe History Museum, accessed June 20, 2015, www.tempe.gov/government/community-services/tempe-history-museum/history -and-research/mariana-gonzales-priest; "Mariano Gonzales," Tempe History Museum, accessed June 20, 2015 www.tempe.gov/government/community-services/tempe-history -museum/history-and-research/mariano-gonzales; "Notice of Sole Tradership" (public notice of Mariana Priest's stock and farming business), *Weekly Republican* (Phoenix), January 26, 1883. Mariano Gonzales's oldest daughter Carmel also married a Euro-American, James Lindsey; their only child Carmen Carmelita Lindsey married Ramon Valenzuela.

21. Santos Vega, *Mexicans in Tempe* (Charleston, S.C.: Arcadia Publishing, 2009), 10.

22. *Educational Conditions in Arizona, (Report of a Survey by the United States Bureau of Education)*, U.S. Department of the Interior, Office of Education (Washington, D.C., 1918 [Bulletin, 1917, No. 44]), 22-23; Ariz. Assembly Journal, 13th sess. (1885), 590, 738, 826. *See also* Ernest J. Hopkins and Alfred Thomas Jr., *The Arizona State University Story* (Phoenix: Southwest Publishing Co., 1960). Hopkins and Thomas explain

the controversy over the 1885 legislature's failure to give the institution an official name. As a result, the Normal School (as it was known initially) had many names, but it was known as the Tempe Normal School (TNS) from 1901 to 1925 and as the Arizona State Teachers College (ASTC) at Tempe from 1928 to 1945.

23. Canchola, "Our Sotelo Roots," 4-F; "James T. Priest," *City of Tempe, Arizona,* accessed June 20, 2015, www.tempe.gov/government/community-services/tempe-history -museum/history-and-research/james-t-priest; Hopkins and Thomas, *The Arizona State University Story,* 51.

24. "List of Students" in *Arizona Territorial Normal School Catalogue* (1886-1900), UA ASU, Archival Collection 0.3 (hereafter "List of Students"). For Clara Miller, see "List of Students" (1889), 7. For Anna Manuela Miller, see "List of Students" (1893), 25.

25. "Anna Manuela Miller," a diploma issued by the Arizona Territorial Normal School, Tempe, Arizona, in *Arizona State University: A Documentary History of the First Seventy-Five Years, 1885-1960,* Vol. 1, ed. Alfred Thomas Jr. (Tempe, Ariz.: Alfred Thomas Jr., 1960), 169. The sisters' names changed to reflect their marriages: Anna Manuela Miller Yeager Raub and Clara María Miller Zander.

26. F. O. Bishop, "A History of Teacher Certification in Arizona Under Territorial and Statehood Days" (master's thesis, University of New Mexico, 1939), 51-52.

27. U.S. Department of the Interior, Bureau of Education, *Report of the Commissioner of Education Made to the Secretary of the Interior for the Year 1870 with Accompanying Papers* (Washington, D.C.: Government Printing Office, 1870), 318; Bishop, "A History of Teacher Certification in Arizona Under Territorial and Statehood Days," 44, 44n5.

28. *Arizona Territorial Legislative Journals* (1871), 44.

29. Mariano Aguirre in "List of Students" (1889); Aurelia Borques [sic] in "List of Students" (1892, 1893); Samuel Pressly McCrea, "Establishment of the Arizona School System" (master's thesis, Stanford University, 1902), in the *Biennial Report of Superintendent of Public Instruction of the Territory of Arizona, 1907-1908* (Phoenix: Arizona Department of Public Instruction, 1908); *Arizona Republic,* September 4, 1891; *Tucson Citizen,* January 25, 1915. McCrea's work also appeared in digest form as the "History of Arizona Education" in *Educational Conditions in Arizona,* 15-32.

30. Bishop, "A History of Teacher Certification in Arizona Under Territorial and Statehood Days," 44.

31. *Mohave County Miner,* September 2, 1893.

32. Sheridan, *Los Tucsonenses,* 255.

33. Nicolás Kanellos and Helvetia Martell, *Hispanic Periodicals in the United States, Origins to 1960: A Brief History and Comprehensive Bibliography* (Houston, Tex.: Arte Público Press, 2000), 96-99, 278-280. By Kanellos and Martell's count, the Arizonenses published 147 Spanish-language newspapers between 1848 and 2000.

34. *Tucson Citizen,* November 4, 1903, 5:3; "Population," *1900 Census: Abstract of the Twelfth Census,* U.S. Census Bureau (Washington, D.C.: Government Printing

Office, 1902), 32, www.census.gov/library/publications/1902/dec/abstract.html (webpage revised January 5, 2022). The total Arizona population in 1900 was 122,931. For a
sampling of Arizona's Spanish-language newspapers, see the Arizona Historical Digital
Newspapers, Arizona Memory Project at https://azmemory.azlibrary.gov/.

35. Patricia Preciado Martin, "Ramona Benítez Franco," in *Beloved Land: An Oral
History of Mexican Americans in Southern Arizona* (Tucson: University of Arizona Press,
2004), 34; Officer, *Hispanic Arizona*, 17, 78.

36. "Petition for school district," DS by Rafael Romero et al., March 1, 1890, Petitions 1887–1897; School Records Reports 1886–1919, Box 2; Superintendent of Schools;
Apache County, RG 100; ASA ASLAPR. Based on the Certificates of Elections of Trustees and Teacher's Monthly Reports (filed in Box 1), evidence suggests this is a petition for Leeds School District No. 12. County superintendents recycled school districts'
numbers, and a former school district No. 12 existed in 1883. The petitioners, along with
the number of school-aged children in their households, included Rafael Romero, 3;
Dionicio Montoya, 1; Manuel Mestas, José D. Ruby, 1, Pedro Gonzales, 1; José Ygnasio
Cordova, Ant. J. Chabez, 3; C. Nabarette, 1; Rito Amador, 3; Santa Roza Lusero; Alejo
Espinoza, 4; J. Ma. (José María) Jaramillo, 4; Gabriel García, 5; Rosendo Montano, 1;
Porfirio Gonzales, 5; Juan A. Lial, 3; Quirino Jaramillo, 2; Refugio Salazar, 1; Ambrocio
Gonzales, 2; A. O. Mcintosh, 3; and Juan Jaramillo, 1.

37. Gloria Anzaldúa, "Let us be the healing of the wound: The Coylxauhqui impera-
tive—la sombra y el sueño," in *The Gloria Anzaldúa Reader*, ed. AnaLouise Keating
(Durham, N.C.: Duke University Press, 2009), 292, 310–311. Gloria Anzaldúa defines
conocimientos as "knowledge and insights," and the path to this conocimiento usually
includes a "choque" (a crack or "shift in perception"), which here at this moment in
Arizona is the Mexican-American War and its fallout.

38. Victoria-María MacDonald, ed., *Latino Education in the United States: A Narrated History from 1513–2000* (New York: Palgrave Macmillan, 2004), 66.

39. Canchola, "Our Sotelo Roots," 1-D.

40. Rosina Lozano, *An American Language: The History of Spanish in the United
States* (Berkeley: University of California Press, 2018), 5–6, 61.

41. Canchola, "Our Sotelo Roots," 1-A; Henry F. Dobyns, *Tubac Through Four Centuries: An Historical Resume and Analysis* (Phoenix: Arizona State Park Boards, 1959;
1995 Reformat), web version accessible at www.parentseyes.arizona.edu/tubac/; Officer *Hispanic Arizona* 91. Lt. Sotelo's name appears as both "Ygnacio" and "Ignacio" in
records. Canchola's version of events triangulates a variety of sources, including Dobyns.
Her work represents what historian Monica Muñoz Martinez calls "vernacular history-
making." See Monica Muñoz Martinez, *The Injustice Never Leaves You*, 27, 159.

42. Officer, *Hispanic Arizona*, 352n43.

43. Canchola, "Our Sotelo Roots," 1-D; Karl Jacoby, *Shadows at Dawn: A Borderlands Massacre and the Violence of History* (New York: Penguin Press, 2008), 62.

44. Canchola, "Our Sotelo Roots," 1-F.

45. Anita Huizar-Hernández, "The Specter of Statehood: Inventing Arizona in Charles D. Poston's *Building a State in Apache Land* [Tempe, Ariz.: Aztec Press, 1963, reprint] and Marie Clara Zander's 'The Life of an Arizona Pioneer,'" *MELUS: Multi-Ethnic Literature of the U.S.* 42, no 2 (Summer 2017): 67; Solliday, "The Journey to Rio Salado," 38. Both authors cite Zander's unpublished manuscript, "The Life of an Arizona Pioneer [María Sotelo]." *See also* Anita Huizar-Hernández, *Forging Arizona: A History of the Peralta Land Grant and Racial Identity in the West* (New Brunswick, N.J.: Rutgers University Press, 2019).

46. Águila and Rosales, "Lost Land and México Lindo," 66–67.

47. Solliday, "The Journey to Rio Salado," 73.

48. Águila and Rosales, "Lost Land and México Lindo," 67; Irene Góomez Hormell, oral history (OH-130A), interview by Diane Matsch, February 13, 1993, Tempe History Museum; Andie Flores and Morgan Riffle, "Mickey Mouse Neighborhood," in "A People's Guide to Maricopa County," ed. Wendy Cheng (December 5, 2012), https://peoplesguidetomaricopa2.blogspot.com/2012/12/mickey-mouse-neighborhood.html; Vega, *Mexicans in Tempe*, 9, 27. In the 1950s, the town of Tempe and ASU purchased the Mickey Mouse barrio through eminent domain and built the stadium and the university dormitories Manzanita Hall and San Pablo Hall. The nickname is attributed to Floyd "Chino" Soto, who lived there and whose childhood friends teased him, saying that from the top of the hill (probably the side of the butte) it looked like a "ratonería" or "mouse's hole." According to his niece Irene Gómez Hormell, Soto's response was "It's okay. Mickey Mouse lives here."

49. Arizona Territory Legislative Journals (1864), 176–177.

50. Arizona Territory Legislative Journals (1864), 176–177; *A Brief Sketch of the Mission of San Xavier del Bac with a Description of Its Church* (San Francisco: Thomas' Steam Printing House, 1880), 15–16. While the territorial legislature described the students at San Xavier del Bac as "Mexican and Indian," other reports indicate that federal Indian agents asked the priests to open a school for the Tohono O'odham, which they operated until 1876 when the agencies of the Akimel O'odham (Pima) and Tohono O'Oodham (Papago) were consolidated.

51. Sheridan, *Los Tucsonenses*, 46; *Arizona Weekly Citizen* (Tucson), November 16, 1870.

52. U.S. Department of the Interior, Bureau of Education, *Report of the Commissioner of Education Made to the Secretary of the Interior for the Year 1870 with Accompanying Papers* (Washington, D.C.: Government Printing Office, 1872), 377.

53. "Report of the Governor to the Territorial Board of Education of the Conditions of the School in the Year 1873," File 343, Superintendent of Public Instruction, Box 22, Secretary of the Territory, Record Group 6, ASA ASLAPR.

54. Sheridan, *Los Tucsonenses*, 278n28.

55. "Schools of Tucson," *Tucson City Directory* (San Francisco: G. W. Barter, 1881), 34, 100.

56. *El Fronterizo*, December 21, 1879; February 12, 1880; January 9, 1881 (CRC ASU Newspaper Card File: Education).

57. *Tucson Citizen*, August 24, 1882; September 1, 1882.

58. "Schools of Tucson," *Tucson City Directory* (1881), 33.

59. *Arizona Territorial Legislative Journals* (1868), 148.

60. Dean and Reynolds, *Hispanic Historic Property Survey*, 25.

61. *Arizona Session Laws* (1879), 126; *Arizona Revised Statutes* (1913), 916–917. In 1913, the two-mile distance between schoolhouses was extended to four miles.

62. Arreola and Hartwell, "Phoenix Population Origins, 1870–1900," 446–447, 449, 454.

63. Dora O. Quesada, "Dora's World by the Hassayampa," unpublished manuscript, produced in association with the First Families of Arizona, an Auxiliary of the Phoenix Museum of History (Wickenburg, Ariz., 1995), 3.

64. Quesada, "Dora's World," 12.

65. Quesada, "Dora's World," 36.

66. Minutes (January 12, 1881), Minutes, Book 1 (1871–1881), Superintendent of Schools, Maricopa County, RG 107, CRC ASU, 34. Vulture Mine and Wickenburg were both called School District No. 9.

67. Quesada, "Dora's World," 38.

68. Historical Information, Wickenburg Unified School District No. 9, www .wickenburgschools.org/domain/108.

69. Alicia Quesada, interview by the author, February 16, 2004. For the history of escuelitas, see Philis M. Barragán Goetz, *Reading, Writing, and Revolution: Escuelitas and the Emergence of a Mexican American Identity in Texas* (Austin: University of Texas Press, 2020).

70. Julia Macias Brooks, "Ygnacio Garcia–Community Donor, Early Pioneer," Wickenburg Unified School District No. 9, available at www.wickenburgschools.org /domain/108; Wickenburg Unified School District No. 9, "Arizona MPS Garcia School," National Register of Historic Places Nomination Form (Washington, D.C.: U.S. Department of the Interior, National Park Service, 1982).

71. Alicia Quesada, "Incidents in the Life of Alicia Otilia Quesada," unpublished manuscript, produced in association with the First Families of Arizona, an Auxiliary of the Phoenix Museum of History (Wickenburg, Ariz., 1995), 51.

72. Rose E. Fowler, "Biographical Sketch of Grandma Wright," n.d., loose document, Box 44, Folder 21, Ricardo Muñoz Papers, CSRC UCLA; *Arizona Daily Star*, June 6, 1991; November 19, 2013.

73. Martin, "Ramona Benítez Franco," in *Beloved Land*, 33–34.

74. *Tucson Citizen*, September 12, 1906.

75. *Arizona Daily Citizen*, September 24, 1887 (CRC ASU Newspaper Card File, Subject: Education).

76. Elise M. DuBord, "Language Policy and the Drawing of Social Boundaries: Public and Private Schools in Territorial Tucson," *Spanish in Context* 7, no. 1 (2010): 27; Sheridan, *Los Tucsonenses*, 47.

77. *El Fronterizo*, February 29, 1880, 5:4 (CRC ASU Newspaper Card File, Subject: Education).

78. Sec. 58, *Arizona Session Laws* (1883), 49.

79. Title 19, Chapter 9, No. 2213 (Sec. 84) "English," *Arizona Revised Statutes* (1901), 602; Article XX (Ordinance 7), Constitution of the State of Arizona in *Arizona Revised Statutes* (1913), 171; Title 11, paragraph 2769, *Arizona Revised Statutes* (1913), 932; Sec. 80, *Arizona Session Laws* (1885), 157.

80. Sheridan, *Los Tucsonenses*, 47.

81. Bradford Luckingham, *Minorities in Phoenix: A Profile of Mexican American, Chinese American, and African American Communities, 1860-1992* (Tucson: University of Arizona Press, 1994), 23-24, 29; James D. McBride, "Liga Protectora Latina: A Mexican American Benevolent Society in Arizona," *Journal of the West* 14, no. 4 (1975): 83.

82. McBride, "Liga Protectora Latina," 83; "Estatutos de la Liga Protectora Latina (photocopy)," September 1920, CHSM-318, CRC ASU.

83. Martin, "Carlotta Parra Rodríguez Sotomayor," in *Beloved Land*, 4.

84. Martin, "Carlotta Parra Rodríguez Sotomayor," in *Beloved Land*, 4.

85. For a discussion of Mexican educational activities under Spanish rule and within Norteño society, *see* Ana María Alonso, *Thread of Blood: Colonialism, Revolution, and Gender on Mexico's Northern Frontier* (Tucson: University of Arizona Press, 1995), 7, 15-16; MacDonald, *Latino Education in the United States*, 9; Sheridan, *Los Tucsonenses*, 2; Weber, *The Spanish Mexican Frontier in North America* (New Haven, Conn.: Yale University Press, 1992), 332.

86. MacDonald, *Latino Education in the United States*, 9.

87. Geraldo L. Cadava, *Standing on Common Ground: The Making of a Sunbelt Borderland* (Cambridge, Mass.: Harvard University Press, 2013), 7-20.

88. Arreola and Hartwell, "Phoenix Population Origins, 1870-1900," 454.

89. Glenn, *Unequal Freedom*, 19, 270n4.

90. See the chapter, "Los Vecinos," in Jacoby, *Shadows at Dawn*, 48-93; *see also* Carlos G. Vélez-Ibañez and Josiah Heyman, eds., *The U.S.-Mexico Transborder Region: Cultural Dynamics and Historical Interactions* (Tucson: University of Arizona Press, 2017).

91. Alonso, *Thread of Blood*, 16, 33.

92. Carl Hayden, "Sabino Otero," Hayden Arizona Pioneer Biographies Collection, ASU, www.asu.edu/lib/archives/azbio/bios/OTEROS.PDF; *Arizona Daily Star*, October 24, 2010; Officer, *Hispanic Arizona*, 66, 292, 346nn37-38; Sheridan, *El Tucsonense*, May 5, 1923.

93. Dobyns, *Tubac Through Four Centuries*, at www.parentseyes.arizona.edu/tubac/.

94. The English translation that appeared on the reverse of this Spanish notice reads: "St. Cosme Ariz. [Walnut Grove, Ariz.] June 9th, 1892. This is to let all the people know that a[n] Election gone [sic] be at the school house to vote school Trustees on the 25th of this month and the Election will be open at 10 o'clock in the morning. [Signed]

Marcos Baca, Francisco Sais." School election notice, St. Cosme [Walnut Grove], Ariz.; DS by Marcos Baca and Francisco Saís; June 9, 1892; Certificates of Elections–Trustees, 1891-1900, School Records–Reports 1886-1919, Box 2; Superintendent of Schools; Apache County, RG 100; ASA ASLAPR.

95. Sheridan, *Los Tucsonenses*, 2, 42.

96. Martin, "Luis Acuña Gastellum," in *Beloved Land*, 125; Luis A. Gastellum, "Memories of My Youth at Tubac: From the Old Homestead to Adulthood," *Journal of Arizona History* 36, no. 1 (Spring 1995), 7-11.

97. Martin, "Luis Acuña Gastellum," in *Beloved Land*, 125.

98. "The Luisa Rojas House: Memories," *Monthly Arizonan* (February 1993), n.p.; *Arizona Daily Star*, May 12, 1989.

99. Sheridan, *Los Tucsonenses*, 47.

100. *Arizona Session Laws* (1879), 126.

101. "Statistics—July 1, 1889, to June 30, 1890 [table]," in *Biennial Report of Superintendent of Public Instruction of the Territory of Arizona, 1889-1890* (Phoenix: Arizona Department of Public Instruction, 1890), 37.

102. Minute Book, No. 2 (1883-1914), RG 107 Maricopa County, Superintendent of Schools, Records, 1883-1931, 1951, ASA ASLAPR.

103. Águila and Rosales, "Lost Land and México Lindo," 79; *Arizona Republic*, February 9, 1899. Frederick Balsz married Eliza Tapia of Sacramento, California, and Soledad Bracamonte of Arizona, who was the mother of nine of his children.

104. *Arizona Republic*, April 18, 1941; *Phoenix Gazette*, March 10, 1965. The two newspapers report the founding of the school in different years, either 1875 or 1888.

105. Kathy Smith Franklin, "A Spirit of Mercy: The Sisters of Mercy and the Founding of St. Joseph's Hospital in Phoenix, 1892-1912," *Journal of Arizona History* 39, no. 3 (Autumn 1998): 269.

106. *Arizona Republic*, February 18, 1892; August 27, 1892; September 7, 1892; June 14, 1894; June 15, 1894.

107. *Arizona Republic*, March 8, 1894.

108. *Arizona Republic*, July 26, 1894.

109. Minutes, Book 2 (1883-1914), Superintendent of Schools, Maricopa County, School Board Minutes, RG 107, ASA ASLAPR, 85.

110. Teacher's Monthly Reports, School Records–Reports 1886-1919, Boxes 1-2; Superintendent of Schools; Apache County, RG 100; ASA ASLAPR. These boxes include monthly report data from twenty-two school districts, including St. Johns No. 1, Springerville No. 2, Eager No. 3, Nutrioso No. 4, San José del Tule "El Tule" No. 5, Concho No. 6, Alpine No. 7, Taylor No. 8, Snowflake No. 9, Woodruff No. 10, St. Josephs No. 11, Leeds No. 12, Hunt No. 13, Holbrook No. 14, Alpine No. 15, Pinetop No. 16, Adairville and/or Stanton (in Concho) No. 17, Amity and/or Chambers No. 18, Cedro and/or Show Low No. 19, Winslow No. 20, Walnut Grove/San Cosme and/or Bonita Canyon No. 21, and Erastus No. 24. Mexican parents influenced the schools

at St. Johns No. 1, El Tule No. 5, Concho No. 6, Leeds No. 12, Springerville No. 2, and Walnut Grove No. 21.

111. "Amelia Hunt García," *History of Arizona*, Vol. 4, ed. Richard E. Sloan (Phoenix, Ariz.: Record Publishing Company, 1930), 484. Amelia Hunt was the daughter of U.S. Army Captain James Clark Hunt and Hispana Juanita Rubi García. The Hunts' ranch was near St. Joseph, Arizona, Yavapai County. The town is known today as Joseph City, the oldest Mormon settlement in Arizona, and is part of the reconfigured Navajo County.

112. *Weekly Journal-Miner* (Prescott, Ariz.), July 3, 1889.

113. *St. Johns Herald*, May 26, 1892; October 20,1892; Louis A. Hieb, "John Lorenzo Hubbell (1853-1930), trader to the Navajos," *American National Biography*, March 22, 2019, www.anb.org/view/10.1093/anb/9780198606697.001.0001/anb-9780198606697-e -1000827. Amelia Hunt's mother, Juanita Rubi García, may have been related to Lena Rubi or Lorenzo Hubbell as all three descended from Spanish–New Mexican families in northwestern New Mexico near the Pajarito Land Grant. Also, Lorenzo Hubbell likely knew Amelia's father as they were among the founders of El Vadito/St. Johns, Arizona.

114. Minutes, Teacher's Institutes, St. Johns, Apache County, School Records–Reports 1886-1919, Box 2, RG 100 Superintendent of Schools, ASA ASLAPR, 2.

115. St. Johns No. 1 Teacher's Monthly Report, DS by Monico García, December 5, 1894, Box 1; Test scores for Monico García, Second Grade Territorial Certificates, March 3, 1897, Box 2, Affidavit of Raymundo Angel by District Attorney Alfred Ruiz, 28 September 1897, Box 2; Apache County, School Records–Reports 1886-1919, RG 100 Superintendent of Schools, ASA ASLAPR; "Territorial Board of Examiners," in *Biennial Report of the Superintendent of Public Instruction of the Territory of Arizona* (Phoenix: Arizona Department of Public Instruction, 1890), Folder 345, Box 22, RG6 Secretary of the Territory, 1871-1909, ASA ASLAPR.

116. *St. Johns Herald*, February 26, 1898.

117. *Arizona Republic*, January 18, 1898.

118. "St. Mary's Church—Our Lady of Mount Carmel Catholic Church," Arizona, National Register of Historic Places and National Historic Landmarks Program Records, 2013-2017, Records of the National Park Service, 1785-2006, https://catalog .archives.gov/id/75610005. The Arizonense families of San Pablo/Tempe founded this church in 1881.

119. *Arizona Republic*, July 5, 1898.

120. *Arizona Republic*, April 14, 1898; July 1, 1898.

121. *Arizona Republic*, December 14, 1898.

122. Dr. René Díaz-Lefebvre, in conversation with the author, 2005. Díaz-Lefebvre is Ochoa's grandson and a psychology professor at Glendale Community College.

123. Sheridan, *Los Tucsonenses*, 218.

124. For a history of Barrio Libre, *see* Lydia Otero, *La Calle: Spatial Conflicts and Urban Renewal in a Southwest City* (Tucson: University of Arizona Press, 2010).

125. *Arizona Weekly Citizen*, May 18, 1889.

126. María Ángeles García Aranda, "La enseñanza de español el Club de mujeres Ebell de Los Ángeles: La labor de Aurelia Bórquez (1914-1917), *Signo y Seña* 38 (July-December, 2021): 40.

127. "Language [New Books]," *Branch Library News* 6 (1919): 13; Aurelia Borquez de Whenthoff, *Elementary Spanish Reader* (Los Angeles: Aurelia Borquez, 1917); Borquez de Whenthoff, *A Series of Spanish Conversations in the Conjugational Order: A Series of Commercial Letters and Short Stories* (Los Angeles: Aurelia Borquez, 1916); Borquez, *Leyendas históricas mexicanas costumbres y mitología* (Los Angeles: Aurelia Borquez, 1915). Borquez did not use an accent in her last name in any of her publications.

128. McCrea, "Establishment of the Arizona School System," 95.

129. Glenn, *Unequal Freedom*, 147, 160; Ian Haney López, *White by Law: The Legal Construction of Race*, rev. and updated, 10th anniv. ed. (New York, 2006), 1, 27–28.

130. McCrea, "Establishment of the Arizona School System," 82.

131. "Message of Governor McCormick to the Fourth Legislature of Arizona [September 9, 1867]," *Arizona Territory Legislative Journals* (1867), 42-43; *Arizona Territory Legislative Journals* (1864), 176-177; McCrea, "Establishment of the Arizona School System," 78.

132. Sheridan, *Los Tucsonenses*, 217.

133. "Schools of Tucson," *Tucson City Directory* (1881), 33. P. R. Tully married two Mexican Catholic women: María Trinidad Conklin of New Mexico who died in a house fire in 1874, and then Dolores Siqueiros Juarez of Old Mexico whom he wed in October 1881.

134. McCrea, "Establishment of the Arizona School System," 100.

135. J. Morris Richards, "Nasianceno Gonzales," in *History of the Arizona State Legislature, 1912-1967*, Vol. 19 Biographies (Phoenix: Arizona Legislative Council), 329; *Holbrook News*, May 17, 1912.

136. Gilbert G. González, *Culture of Empire: American Writers Mexico and Mexican Immigrants, 1880-1930* (Austin: University of Texas Press, 2004), 164; MacDonald, *Latino Education in the United States*, 57–58, 66; Sheridan, *Los Tucsonenses*, 217.

137. "District Superintendents—1867-Present," Tucson Unified School District (webpage), www.tusd1.org/Information/History/District-Superintendents.

138. Mary Melcher, "Josephine Brawley Hughes," Arizona Women's History Alliance, www.azwomenshistoryalliance.org/josephine-brawley-hughes-biography (accessed March 29, 2023); Arizona Women's Hall of Fame, "Josephine Brawley Hughes," Carnegie Center, Arizona State Library, Archives and Public Records, Phoenix, Arizona, www.azwhf.org/copy-of-hallie-bost-wright-hopkins-1 (accessed March 29, 2023). Called "Mrs. L.C. Hughes," Josephine Brawley taught a free public school for girls in the Old Pioneer Brewery in 1873 during the time that her husband served as the ex officio county school superintendent.

139. L. C. Hughes, "Annual Report of the County Superintendent of Public Schools for Pima County [Arizona Territory] for the Year 1872," Annual Reports, Superintendent

of Schools, Pima County, RG 110, AAHD, 2–3 (hereafter cited as "Annual Report, Pima County, 1872"); MacDonald, *Latino Education in the United States*, 67.

140. David Tyack, *Seeking Common Ground: Public Schools in a Diverse Society* (Cambridge, Mass.: Harvard University Press, 2003), 9–14.

141. "Annual Report, Pima County, 1872," 2–3.

142. "Annual Report, Pima County, 1872," 3.

143. "Annual Report, Pima County, 1872," 6.

144. John Spring to William J. Osborn, December 11, 1874, File 343, Superintendent of Public Instruction, Box 22, Secretary of the Territory, Record Group 6, ASA ASLAPR.

145. *Arizona Daily Star*, May 2, 1943; September 19, 2010. Ignacio Bonilla's sister Soledad later married the former governor Anson P. K. Safford. Bonillas did not graduate from MIT, but he had enough education to work as an engineer for the Mexican government. He joined the Mexican Revolution as a member of Venustiano Carranza's cabinet and became the first Mexican ambassador to the United States. Carranza chose Bonillas to run for president in the 1920 elections. The Tucson School District named a high school for him in 1953.

146. *Arizona Session Laws* (1883); McCrea, "Establishment of the Arizona School System," 78; Aileen Pace Nilsen *et al.*, *Dust in Our Desks: Territory Days to the Present in Arizona Schools* (Tempe: Arizona State University, College of Education, 1985), 26. See also William Poetz, "Early History of Education in Arizona Territory," unpublished paper, 1970, Arizona Collection, Department of Archives and Manuscripts, Arizona State University, Tempe, 2–3.

147. Elise M. DuBord, "Mexican Elites and Language Policy in Tucson's First Schools," *Divergencias: Revista de Estudios Lingüísticos y Literarios* 1, no. 1 (Fall 2003), 5; Sheridan, *Los Tucsonenses*, 47.

148. "Message of Governor McCormick to the Fifth Legislative Assembly (November 16, 1868)," *Arizona Territory Legislative Journals* (1869), 39. The assembly voted to print the governor's message in English and Spanish.

149. Sheridan, *Los Tucsonenses*, 47.

150. DuBord, "Language Policy and the Drawing of Social Boundaries," 32; Lozano, *An American Language*, 99.

151. *Arizona Session Laws* (1875), 40–42; *Arizona Session Laws* (1877), 19.

152. *Arizona Session Laws* (1879), 79.

153. Sheridan, *Los Tucsonenses*, 147. Tully earned the high school diploma in 1869.

154. Frank C. Lockwood, *Tucson: The Old Pueblo*, repr. ed. (Tucson, Ariz.: Santa Cruz Valley Press, 2005), 75; Sheridan, *Los Tucsonenses*, 47n28, 278; Sheridan, *Arizona*, 135. William S. Oury was a former Texas Ranger, a Confederate sympathizer, and a leader of the 1871 Camp Grant Massacre of 144 Apaches (Aravaipas and Pinals). *See* Chip Cowell-Chanthaphonh, *Massacre at Camp Grant: Forgetting and Remembering Apache History* (Tucson: University of Arizona Press, 2015).

155. "Schools of Tucson," *Tucson City Directory* (1881), 33. P. R. Tully's wives were María Trinidad Conklin of New Mexico, who died in a house fire, and Dolores Saquiros Juarez of Old Mexico.

156. DuBord, "Mexican Elites and Language Policy," 12–13 [quoting G. C. Hall, *Annual Report of the Principal of the Public Schools* (Tucson: Arizona Publishing Co.'s Steam Print, 1882), n.p., and *Las Dos Repúblicas*, May 18, 1878].

157. Gordon, *The Great Arizona Orphan Abduction*, 332n4; Jacoby, *Shadows at Dawn*, 70. Jacoby discusses numerous language issues throughout his assessment of the 1871 Camp Grant Massacre.

158. Gordon, *The Great Arizona Orphan Abduction*, 46; DuBord, "Language Policy and the Drawing of Social Boundaries," 28.

159. *El Fronterizo*, January 18, 1880, 3:1 (CRC ASU Newspaper Card File, Subject: Education, translated).

160. Quesada, "Dora's World," 1.

161. Glenn, *Unequal Freedom*, 2; see also Benton-Cohen's *Borderline Americans* and Gordon's *The Great Arizona Orphan Abduction*, for local studies of Cochise and Graham counties, respectively.

162. Dean and Reynolds, *Hispanic Historic Property Survey*, 8.

163. J. T. Alsap to Governor A. P. K. Safford, June 25, 1872, Minutes, Book 1 (1871–1881), Superintendent of Schools, Maricopa County, RG 107, ASA ASLAPR.

164. Luckingham, *Minorities in Phoenix*, 18.

165. Luckingham, *Minorities in Phoenix*, 18; Gordon, *The Great Arizona Orphan Abduction*, 268. Gordon defined vigilante racism toward Arizona Mexicans a "racial double standard about punishment—white bad men got trials, Mexicans just got hanged."

166. School Census Report of Maricopa County, 1874, Superintendent of Schools, RG 107, ASA ASLAPR. The author counted the total number of Spanish-surnamed children (199) listed in the census. The census taker reported that no children in 1874 attended private school, as none existed.

167. School Census Report of Maricopa County, 1874. One Chinese girl, the daughter of Quong You, also appeared in the record, but she did not attend school.

168. School Census Report of Maricopa County, 1874. In the 1882 Arizona Territorial Census, Maricopa County, Trinidad Escalante is listed as born in Mexico. Four of her children, Georgia, Lily, Berry, and John, are also listed.

169. School Census Report of Maricopa County, 1874. Luckingham, *Minorities in Phoenix*, 16. J. W. Swilling appears on census rosters for School Districts No. 1 and No. 2, suggesting duplication or a possible second family. Since the numbers matched, I counted the children only once.

170. *Arizona Republic*, October 1, 1901; September 28, 1892; Lynne Marie Getz, *Schools of Their Own: The Education of Hispanos in New Mexico, 1850–1940* (Albuquerque: University of New Mexico Press, 1997), 40–47; Luckingham, *Minorities in Phoenix*, 20; Dean and Reynolds, *Hispanic Historic Property Survey*, 12; Charlotte Whaley, *Nina*

Otero-Warren of Santa Fe (Albuquerque: University of New Mexico Press), 47. Lucking-ham says that Jesús Otero (1831–1901) was the brother of the future territorial governor of New Mexico, Miguel A. Otero. *Arizona Republic* refers to their relation as "cousins" (perhaps, first cousins, or primos hermanos). Both Miguel Sr. (1829–1882) and his son, Miguel A. Otero Jr. (1859–1944), served as governors of New Mexico. The elder Miguel is much closer in age to Jesús and served as acting governor in 1861. Miguel Jr. served as governor from 1897 through 1906. According to Getz, Miguel A. Otero Jr. was Nina Otero-Warren's uncle, although Whaley calls them second cousins. Nonetheless, it is fair to say that the trio are related across several family generations.

171. *Arizona Republic*, June 20, 1896.

172. MacDonald, *Latino Education in the United States*, 67; Madeline Ferrin Paré, *Arizona Pageant: A Short History of the State* (Phoenix: Arizona Historical Foundation, 1965), 247.

173. Paré, *Arizona Pageant*, 247–248.

174. Sylvia Neely, "Arizona Territory's First Graded Public School: The Prescott Free Academy," *Days Past Articles*, Sharlot Hall Library and Archives (Prescott, Ariz.), August 29, 1999, available at https://la.sharlothallmuseum.org/index.php/blog/cat/1999DP/post/arizona-territory-first-graded-public-school/.

175. Jessie Benton Frémont, "My Arizona Class," in *How to Learn and Earn, or, Half Hours in Some Helpful Schools*," ed. Jessie Benton Frémont (Boston, 1884), 449. Also available online at http://pds.lib.harvard.edu/pds/view/3370015.

176. Frémont, "My Arizona Class," 444, 463. Frémont wrote that, among Euro-American settlers in Arizona, "it was the accepted phrase to speak of themselves as outside the world, while going to California, or anywhere, was called 'going inside.'"

177. Ada Ekey became Mrs. George P. Jones but was sometimes referred to as Ada Jones or Mrs. Ada Jones.

178. Ada Jones, "The Early Schools of Nogales, Arizona," [manuscript] n.d. (circa 1939), Alta Pimeria Historical Society, Nogales, Arizona, 9; Jamalle Karam Simon, "Nogales Schools, 1886–1982," *Nogales News*, n.d. (circa October 1980).

179. Jones, "The Early Schools of Nogales, Arizona," 9.

180. Jones, "The Early Schools of Nogales, Arizona," 1; Simon, "Nogales Schools, 1886–1980." Jones also noted that she had attended public school in Nogales in 1886.

181. Jones, "The Early Schools of Nogales, Arizona," 11.

182. Jones, "The Early Schools of Nogales, Arizona," 16. Ada Jones recollects that Rodríguez became a "future President of Mexico." In reality, the Mexican Congress appointed him interim president for the years 1932–1934.

183. Jones, "The Early Schools of Nogales, Arizona," 16.

184. Jones, "The Early Schools of Nogales, Arizona," 12.

185. Benton-Cohen, *Borderline Americans*, 162–167.

186. Arreola and Hartwell, "Phoenix Population Origins, 1870–1900," 450.

187. Arreola and Hartwell, "Phoenix Population Origins, 1870–1900," 452.

188. *Arizona Republic*, August 16, 1899.

189. MacDonald, *Latino Education in the United States*, 39–42, 59–71; Benton-Cohen, *Borderline Americans*, 162.

Chapter 2

Epigraph: Ida Celaya, "El Adios de una Senior," *The Sahuaro* (Tempe: Senior Class, Tempe Normal School of Arizona, 1917), n.p. The original poem is written in Spanish; the English translation is mine.

1. *Arizona Daily Star*, August 9, 1992; Elizabeth Quiroz Gónzalez, "The Education and Public Career of María L. Urquides: A Case Study of a Mexican American Community Leader" (PhD diss., University of Arizona, 1986), 33–56.

2. The Normal School underwent many name changes from its founding in 1885 to 1958 when it became Arizona State University. This chapter refers to the institution as the Normal School, the Tempe Normal School (1901–1925) and the Arizona State Teachers College at Tempe (1928–1945). In 1926 and 1927, the institution was named the Tempe State Teachers College (TSTC).

3. Gónzalez, "The Education and Public Career of María L. Urquides," 43.

4. *Arizona Daily Star*, May 31, 1974.

5. Gónzalez, "The Education and Public Career of María L. Urquides," 44.

6. *Arizona Republic*, October 6, 2001. René Díaz-Lefebvre shared this dicho in the telling of his family's Arizona history. Teacher Petra Ochoa Díaz is his maternal grandmother.

7. Rubén Donato and Jarrod S. Hanson, "Legally White, Socially 'Mexican': The Politics of de Jure and de Facto School Segregation in the American Southwest," *Harvard Educational Review* 82, no. 2 (2012): 208; Laura E. Gómez, *Manifest Destinies: The Making of the Mexican American Race*, 2nd ed. (New York: New York University Press, 2018), 3, 12–13, 88, 166; Rosina Lozano, *An American Language: The History of Spanish in the United States* (Berkeley: University of California Press, 2018), 61.

8. Victoria-María MacDonald and Gonzalo Guzmán, "Revolution and World War I Civil Rights?: Transnational Relations and Mexican Consul Records in Mexican American Educational History, 1910–1929," *Education's Histories* 4 (December 28, 2017), https://scholarworks.umt.edu/eduhist/vol4/iss1/5/. In 1925, police rescued four Mexican American boys and locked down a junior high school in Kansas City, Kansas, after parents led by the PTA threatened mob violence. Even with the intervention of the Mexican consulate and the U.S. secretary of state, Kansas politicians and school officials refused to admit the youth. The Mexican parents had no choice but to enroll their sons in a Catholic school or be fined and/or jailed for violating compulsory education laws.

9. Victoria-María MacDonald, "The Fractured Pipeline: Mexican American Access to High Schooling, 1920–1954," unpublished manuscript in the author's possession and used with permission, 17; Ruth Tuck, *Not with the Fist: Mexican-Americans in a Southwest City* (New York: Harcourt Brace, 1946), 198.

10. Historians of the pre-Chicano Rights era have indicated that eighth grade was the typical highest level among southwestern Mexican Americans and this literature often points to a predominant discourse of school failure and under-education among Mexican American youth. However, as this Arizona history emphasizes, local, state, and federal record invisibility of Mexican Americans during this era discouraged historians from examining the pre-movimiento entrance of Chicanos into high school and junior colleges in the pre- and post-World War II decades. David Montejano in *Quixote's Soldiers: A Local History of the Chicano Movement, 1966–1981* (Austin: University of Texas Press, 2010) also describes the Chicano youth culture of San Antonian Chicano youth pushing their way into public high schools and junior colleges in the late 1950s and early 1960s. In 1964, the Ford Foundation gave the first large-scale, multiyear grant to the University of California, Los Angeles, to study the Mexican American population. One of the publications from that grant, "The Mexican American Studies Project," included a chapter on education, noting also the uneven, but slow increase of Mexican Americans into high schooling in samples from the 1950 and 1960 federal censuses. Victoria-María MacDonald is the only historian to date who has written exclusively on this topic, and I have relied on her work in this chapter, most notably "The Fractured Pipeline." See also Victoria-María MacDonald, "Compromising La Causa?" The Ford Foundation and Chicano Intellectual Nationalism in the Creation of Chicano History, 1963-1977," *History of Education Quarterly* 52, no. 2 (May 2012): 251–281.

11. MacDonald, "The Fractured Pipeline," 5; Victoria-María MacDonald and Alice Cook, "Before Chicana Civil Rights: Three Generations of Mexican American Women in Higher Education in the Southwest, 1920–1965," in *Women's Higher Education in the United States: New Historical Perspectives,* ed. Margaret Nash (New York: Palgrave Macmillan, 2017), 237; MacDonald to Muñoz, in conversation with the author.

12. U.S. Department of the Interior, Office of Education, *Educational Conditions in Arizona (Report of a Survey by the United States Bureau of Education)* (Washington, D.C., 1918 [Bulletin, 1917, No. 44]), 120, 139; "State School Survey," *Arizona Teacher and Home Journal* (hereafter *ATHJ*) 13, no. 9 (May 1925): 22-26; C. Ralph Tupper, *A Survey of the Arizona Public School System: A Study of the Elementary and Secondary Public Schools of the State*, Arizona State Board of Education (Phoenix, Ariz.: Gazette Print. Co., 1925), 23. Tupper's state survey examined a decade of census and attendance records.

13. Tupper, *A Survey of the Arizona Public School System*, 51. According to Tupper's assessment of the 1920 U.S. Census, Arizona ranked fifth in the nation for the proportional size of its foreign-born population, of which 75 percent claimed Mexico as a country of origin. In the Southwest, Arizona ranked first with the largest percentage of foreign born Mexicans (75 percent), compared to Texas with 69 percent, followed by New Mexico and Oklahoma.

14. "State School Survey," ATHJ 13, no. 9 (May 1925): 22-26.

15. U.S. Department of the Interior, *Educational Conditions in Arizona*, 116–119. Educators of the era determined that these overage Mexican American children suffered

from the "injury of retardation" (slowness or backwardness) or "excessive retardation" (three or more years behind grade level), which caused them to "leave school early and are therefore deprived of an education."

16. Maritza De La Trinidad, "Mexican Americans and the Push for Culturally Relevant Education: The Bilingual Education Movement in Tucson, 1958–1969," *History of Education* 44, no. 3 (2015): 323.

17. U.S. Department of the Interior, *Educational Conditions in Arizona*, 94.

18. Tupper, *A Survey of the Arizona Public School System*, 25, 27–28.

19. Eve Tuck, "Suspending Damage: A Letter to Communities," *Harvard Educational Review* 79, no. 3 (Fall 2009): 422. Indigenous scholars introduced the term "survivance" to explain how they and their ancestors created space and renewal in the face of genocide. Based on the work of Vine Deloria Jr. [*We Talk, You Listen: New Tribes, New Turf* (New York: Macmillan, 1970)], Bryan McKinley Jones Brayboy says, "Survivance, which combines survival and resistance, calls for adaptation and strategic accommodation in order to survive and develop the processes that contribute to community growth," in "Toward a Tribal Critical Race Theory in Education," *Urban Review* 37, no. 5 (December 2005): 435. *See also* Gerald Vizenor, *Manifest Manners: Narratives on Postindian Survivance* (Lincoln: University of Nebraska Press, 1999); and Malie Villegas et al., eds. *Indigenous Knowledge and Education: Sites of Struggle, Strength, and Survivance* (Cambridge, Mass.: Harvard Educational Review, 2008).

20. Katherine Benton-Cohen, "Other Immigrants: Mexicans and the Dillingham Commission of 1907–1911," *Journal of American Ethnic History* 30, no. 2 (Winter 2011): 33.

21. *Arizona Daily Star*, August 9, 1992.

22. *See* Gloria Anzaldúa, *Borderlands/La Frontera: The New Mestiza* (San Francisco: Aunt Lute Books, 1987), 44; Emma Pérez, *The Decolonial Imaginary: Writing Chicanas into History* (Bloomington: Indiana University Press, 1999), xvi, 142n7; *see also* Chela Sandoval, *Methodology of the Oppressed* (Minneapolis: University of Minnesota, 2000).

23. Register of Non-Degree Graduates, 1887–1936, No. 0.13, UA ASU, Hayden Library, Arizona State University, Tempe (hereafter cited as "Register of Non-Degree Graduates, 1887–1936"); "Appendix D: Mexican American, African American and Asian American Alumni of the Tempe Normal School," in Laura K. Muñoz, "Desert Dreams: Mexican American Education in Arizona, 1870–1930" (PhD diss., Arizona State University, 2006), 337–342 [hereafter cited as "Appendix D"]; James Gregory, "Arizona Migration History, 1860–2018," America's Great Migrations Project, part of The Great Depression in Washington State Project [digital humanities project], https://depts.washington.edu/moving1/Arizona.shtml (accessed April 1, 2023). Gregory estimates that a third of Arizona's population was ethnic Mexican, 20 percent were Native American, and nearly 50 percent were non-Hispanic white.

24. See "Appendix D." Using a variety of sources, including attendance records, diploma lists, yearbooks, and student transcripts, I compiled a list of 165

ethnic-minority students—including 151 Mexican Americans, 8 African Americans, and 6 Asians or Asian Americans—who attended TNS from the 1890s to the 1930s. I identified the majority of these students by searching for Hispanic surnames in the "Register of Non-Degree Graduates, 1887–1936." This register lists graduates who earned one-, two-, and three-year teacher-training diplomas that TNS granted as terminal degrees before and after the baccalaureate, which it began issuing in 1926. Yearbooks and "student lists" from the course catalogs further substantiate matriculation for those students who did not complete any degree. In addition, another 19 students sat for senior portraits that were printed in class yearbooks, but I have not confirmed their graduation against registrar records. Potentially, 91 of 151 (60 percent) Mexican American or Spanish-surnamed students may have completed the two-year diploma. For a comparison to the late twentieth century, *see* Amaury Nora, "Access to Higher Education for Hispanic Students: Real or Illusory?" in *The Majority in the Minority: Expanding Representation of Latina/o Faculty, Administrators and Students in Higher Education*, ed. Jeanett Castellanos and Lee Jones (Sterling, Va.: Stylus Publishing, 2003), 51.

25. Tuck, "Suspending Damage," 420.

26. *The Papoose* (Globe High School Yearbook, 1916), 22.

27. Carl F. Kaestle, *Pillars of the Republic: Common Schools and American Society, 1760–1983* (New York: Hill & Wang, 1983); Nancy Beadie and Joy Williamson-Lott et al., "Gateways to the West, Part I: Education in the Shaping of the West," *History of Education Quarterly* 56, no. 3 (2016): 430; Robert Lee and Tristan Ahtone, "Land-Grab Universities: Expropriated Indigenous Land Is the Foundation of the Land-Grant University System," *High Country News*, March 30, 2020 [digital project], www.hcn.org /issues/52.4/indigenous-affairs-education-land-grab-universities; Margaret A. Nash, "Entangled Pasts: Land-Grant Colleges and American Indian Dispossession," *History of Education Quarterly*, 59, no. 4 (2019): 437–467.

28. *Arizona Territory Session Laws* (1871), 68–80; *Arizona Territory Legislative Journals* (1871), 308. The law was titled "AN ACT To establish public schools in the Territory of Arizona," but it was known informally as the Safford-Ochoa Act for the territorial governor Anson P. K. Safford who endorsed it and the Tucson legislator Estevan Ochoa who proposed it.

29. *Arizona Territory Session Laws* (1895), 40–42; *Arizona Territory Legislative Journals* (1871), 392, 404. The law was titled, "AN ACT To Provide for the Establishment and Maintainance [sic] of High Schools in the Territory of Arizona," and proposed by J. A. Marshall of Phoenix.

30. *The School Laws of Arizona* (Superintendent of Public Instruction, 1887), 52.

31. *Report of the Acting Governor of Arizona to the Secretary of the Interior* (Washington, D.C.: Government Printing Office, 1891), 27.

32. *Tucson Citizen*, January 1, 1890; James W. McClintock, *Mormon Settlement in Arizona; A Record of Peaceful Conquest of the Desert* (Phoenix, Ariz.: Manufacturing Stationers, 1921), 265. The Church of Jesus Christ of Latter-day Saints also operated

academies at Snowflake and Thatcher as early as 1889, and at its Mexican colony at Ciudad Juárez, Chihuahua.

33. *Tombstone Weekly Epitaph*, October 15, 1893.

34. *Arizona Republic*, October 4, 1893; October 25, 1893; February 6, 1894; February 7, 1894.

35. *Arizona Republic*, October 4, 1893.

36. *Arizona Republic*, March 4, 1893; March 16, 1893.

37. *Biennial Report of the Superintendent of Education for the Years 1893–1894, to the Governor of Arizona* (Phoenix, Ariz.: Mesa Free Press, 1895), 39.

38. *Report of the Superintendent of Public Instruction of the State of Arizona, for the School Years Ending June 30, 1917, and June 30, 1918* (Phoenix: Arizona Department of Education, 1918), 31–32.

39. Alva Otis Neal, *Arizona High Schools* (Tucson: University of Arizona Extension Division, University Station, 1921), 12. Tempe Normal is listed as an accredited high school offering a four-year course, which is accepted for admission to the University of Arizona.

40. *Report of the Acting Governor of Arizona to the Secretary of the Interior* (Washington, D.C.: Government Printing Office, 1891), 32.

41. Jurgen Herbst, *The Once and Future School: Three Hundred and Fifty Years of American Secondary Education* (New York: Routledge, 1996); Edward A. Krug, *The Shaping of the American High School* (Madison: University of Wisconsin Press, 1969).

42. Michael B. Katz, *The Irony of Early School Reform: Educational Innovation in Mid-Nineteenth Century Massachusetts* (Cambridge, Mass.: Harvard University Press, 1968; reis. New York: Teachers College Press, 2001); Maris Vinovskis, *The Origins of Public High Schools: A Reexamination of the Beverly High School Controversy* (Madison: University of Wisconsin Press, 1985).

43. John L. Rury, *Education and Social Change: Contours in the History of American Schooling*, 6th ed. (New York: Routledge, 2019).

44. *Arizona Republic*, October 17, 1895.

45. *Arizona Republic*, May 5, 1896.

46. Local newspapers provide citizens' views of the pros and cons of voting in *single-district high schools* (such as the Tucson Unified School District, which included schools for grades K-12) versus *union high school districts* (such as the Phoenix Union High School District, which included only grades 9-12). Both types of districts still exist in Arizona. Consider this front-page headline in the *Arizona Republic* (March 28, 1895): "WANT IT ALONE. Mass Meeting in Matter of the High School. Favors a Distinct District for Phoenix. Arguments for and Against a Union High School. Opponents Fear That a Union District Would Be Unwieldy and Unmanageable." Other territory-wide examples include "High School for County Is New Project," *Daily Arizona Silver Belt* (Globe, Ariz.), February 22, 1910; "Committee Will Advise for City High School, Outlying Districts Reject Idea of Institution for County," *Daily Arizona*

Silver Belt (Globe, Ariz.), April 26, 1910; "High School for Safford," *Guardian* (Safford, Ariz.), September 25, 1903.

During the 1980s–1990s, scholars produced considerable work on the American high school, focusing on issues of social class and European immigration, including ethnic white and Jewish students. These authors employed varied methodologies, and include David Hogan, *Class and Reform: School and Society in Chicago, 1880–1930* (Philadelphia: University of Pennsylvania Press, 1985); David F. Labaree, *The Making of an American High School: The Credentials Market and the Central High School of Philadelphia, 1838–1939* (New Haven, Conn.: Yale University Press, 1988); Joel Perlmann, *Ethnic Differences: Schooling and Social Structure Among the Irish, Italians, Jews, and Blacks in an American City, 1880–1935* (New York: Cambridge University Press, 1989); William J. Reese, *The Origins of the American High School* (New Haven, Conn.: Yale University Press, 1995); and Reed Ueda, *Avenues to Adulthood: The Origins of the High School and Social Mobility in an American Suburb* (New York: Cambridge University Press, 1987).

47. *Arizona Republic*, April 8, 1895; *Report of the Superintendent of Public Instruction* (1905–1906), 31.

48. *Arizona Republic*, May 27, 1896; *Report of the Superintendent of Public Instruction* (1932–1934), 23; Samuel Pressly McCrea, "The Establishment of the Arizona School System" (master's thesis, Stanford University, 1902), 68.

49. "History of Tucson High School," Tucson High Badger Foundation, www .badgerfoundation.org/history-of-tucson-high/.

50. Neal, *Arizona High Schools*, 14; *Report of the Superintendent of Public Instruction* (1912–1914), 46–67. In 1912, there were no high schools in Coconino, Graham, Mohave, and Pinal Counties.

51. *Arizona Republic*, August 29, 1930; Bradford Luckingham, *Phoenix: The History of a Southwestern Metropolis* (Tucson: University of Arizona Press, 1989), 88; "Phoenix Union High School District History," Phoenix Union High School District, accessed March 20, 2019, at www.pxu.org/Page/194.

52. Dora Quesada, "Dora's World by the Hassayampa," unpublished manuscript, 46.

53. *Arizona Daily Star*, September 7, 1909; Thomas E. Sheridan, *Los Tucsonenses: The Mexican Community in Tucson, 1854–1941* (Tucson: University of Arizona Press, 1986), 97.

54. *Los Angeles Times*, June 25, 1896.

55. *Arizona Sentinel*, July 28, 1984; August 10, 1894.

56. *Arizona Republic*, June 16, 1965; "Biography of James M. Barney," CB Biography, ASU Hayden Arizona Collection (Call No. CB EPH BO-1, Id. No. 35215).

57. *St. Johns Herald*, September 2, 1915.

58. Victoria-María MacDonald, ed., *Latino Education in U.S. History: A Narrated History from 1513–2000* (New York: Palgrave Macmillan, 2004), 73.

59. "Sister Clara Otero," Arizona Women's Hall of Fame, accessed at www.azwhf.org /copy-of-minna-vrang-orme.

60. Sister Regina (Amelia Diaz), Tucson, Ariz., to Dr. René Díaz-Lefebvre, Phoenix, Ariz., July 16, 1979, letter explaining family roots, Díaz-Lefebvre Photograph Collection, CRC ASU. Sister Gertrude also served as Mother Superior. See also Raquel Rubio Goldsmith, "Shipwrecked in the Desert: A Short History of the Mexican Sisters of the House of the Providence in Douglas, Arizona, 1927-1949," in *Women on the U.S.-Mexico Border: Responses to Change*, eds. Vicki L. Ruiz and Susan Tiano (Boston: Allen & Unwin, 1897), 177-195. These sisters also operated a private, after-school program that included daycare, Spanish-language lessons, and catechism for Mexican American youth.

61. Jaime R. Águila and F. Arturo Rosales, "Lost Land and México Lindo: Origins of Mexicans in Arizona's Salt River Valley, 1865-1910," in *Mexican Workers and the Making of Arizona*, eds. Luis F. B. Plascencia and Gloria H. Cuádraz (Tucson: University of Arizona Press, 2018), 83.

62. Sheridan, *Los Tucsonenses*, 112, 115, 148, and 168.

63. Kaye Lynn Briegel, "Alianza Hispano-Americana, 1894-1965: A Mexican American Fraternal Insurance Society" (PhD diss., University of Southern California, 1974), 50.

64. "Register for 1904-5," in *Territorial Normal School of Arizona Catalogue* 20 (1905), 54.

65. Christine Ogren, *The American State Normal School: An Instrument of Great Good* (New York: Palgrave Macmillan, 2005), 67.

66. Ogren, *The American State Normal School*, 65.

67. Ogren, *The American State Normal School*, 67-68.

68. Ogren, *The American State Normal School*, 68.

69. Ogren, *The American State Normal School*, 68.

70. Jo Connors, *Who's Who in Arizona* (Tucson, Ariz.: J. Connors, 1913), 587.

71. *St. Johns Herald*, November 15, 1894; March 6, 1897.

72. *St. Johns Herald*, November 15, 1894; March 6, 1897.

73. *St. Johns Herald*, July 29, 1899; June 16, 1900.

74. *St. Johns Herald*, March 3, 1900.

75. *St. Johns Herald*, May 29, 1919; December 25, 1919; "Graduates," in *Northern Arizona State Teacher College Bulletin Catalogue*, 1927-1928 (Flagstaff, Ariz.), 71. Adela García, the daughter of Monico and Amelia Hunt García, is identified as a student at the Northern Arizona Normal School at Flagstaff in 1919. Their son, James (a.k.a. Jimmie) is identified as a summer student with Monico in 1924 and 1925. Monico García is listed as a 1926 summer graduate.

76. *St. Johns Herald*, May 8, 1919.

77. "Alumni (Roster)," *The Hieroglyphics* (Tempe Union High School, 1927), n.p. Ophelia Celaya is the sister of TNS graduate Ida Celaya and they are the daughters of Tempe grocer Antonio A. Celaya. Mariano Martinez, a.k.a. Marion B. Martinez, listed himself as a physician in Omaha, Nebraska, in 1927. He attended Creighton University, the same school that trained Dr. Hector P. García, founder of the American G.I. Forum. See "Freshman Medics," *The Blue Jay* (Creighton University, 1926), 128.

78. *The Phoenician* (Phoenix Union High School Yearbook, 1911), 55.

79. Elizabeth Muñoz Grijalva, "Elizabeth Muñoz Grijalva; 1972," unpublished manuscript, 1972, MM Small Manuscripts, MM CHSM-154, CRC ASU, 4-5.

80. Veronica Castillo, "Biography of Rebecca Muñoz Gutiérrez," unpublished manuscript, December 4, 2000, MM Small Manuscripts, MM CHSM-883, ASU CRC, n.p.

81. Castillo, "Biography of Rebecca Muñoz Gutiérrez," n.p.

82. Ian Haney López, *White by Law: The Legal Construction of Race*, rev. and updated, 10th anniv. ed. (New York: New York University Press, 2006), 1, 27–28; MacDonald and Cook, "Before Chicana Civil Rights," 247.

83. MacDonald and Cook, "Before Chicana Civil Rights," 237–238.

84. Angela Valenzuela, *Subtractive Schooling: U.S.-Mexican Youth and the Politics of Caring* (Albany: State University of New York Press, 1999).

85. Tupper, *A Survey of the Arizona Public School System*, 51.

86. Tupper, *A Survey of the Arizona Public School System*, 53.

87. Tupper, *A Survey of the Arizona Public School System*, 51.

88. Tupper, *A Survey of the Arizona Public School System*, 53; also quoted in Annie Reynolds, *The Education of Spanish-Speaking Children in Five Southwestern States*, Bulletin 1933, No. 11 (Washington, D.C.: U.S. Department of the Interior, Office of Education, 1933), 38.

89. MacDonald, "The Fractured Pipeline," 2.

90. S. L. M. Martinez, "The Education of Mexican Descent Youth in the Southwest, 1940–1980: An Exploratory Analysis of Enrollment and Achievement in the High School Movement" (PhD diss., University of Kansas, 2007).

91. MacDonald, "The Fractured Pipeline," 9.

92. MacDonald, "The Fractured Pipeline," 1.

93. Office of Censorship, Tucson, Arizona, to Rosalío F. Muñoz, Bisbee, Arizona, (correspondence regarding admission to citizenship), September 17, 1942, Ricardo Muñoz Papers, CSRC UCLA. For access to birth certificates for the American-born children, see Arizona Genealogy Record Search, a historical database operated by the State of Arizona Department of Health Services, www.azdhs.gov/licensing/vital-records/genealogy/index.php.

94. Maricopa School Census, Marshalls Report, Dist. No. 17 (n.p.; Image 413 of 1196, lines 12-15), Arizona, School Census Records, 1910-1917, ASA ASLAPR; "Jessie Z. Barney," Enumeration District 7-29, Phoenix, Maricopa County, U.S. Census 1930, Sheet 14 A/page 186, line 20.

95. *The Phoenician*, Phoenix Union High School Yearbook (Phoenix, Ariz., 1920), 73-76.

96. *The Phoenician*, Phoenix Union High School Yearbook (Phoenix, Ariz., 1911 and 1913), n.p.

97. 1910, 1920, and 1930 U.S. Censuses; "Proposals Remembered," *Arizona Republic*, June 16, 1974; Ramón R. Denogean, oral history interview by Cecilia Denogean

Esquer, Phoenix, Arizona, November 11, 1971, Cecilia Denogean Esquer Collection, ASU CRC.

98. *Arizona Republic*, September 27, 1895; November 21, 1933; September 11, 1935; May 31, 1935; September 19, 1936; November 22, 1936. In September 1936, 4,414 students enrolled at PUHS, whereas 91 students enrolled in the fall of 1896.

99. "Foreword," *The Phoenician*, Phoenix Union High School Yearbook (Phoenix, Ariz., 1935), n.p.

100. *The Phoenician*, Phoenix Union High School Yearbook (Phoenix, Ariz., 1913), n.p. In 1913, Alex is a junior, while Oscar and Felix are listed as sophomores.

101. Alex and Jesusa Rosas, *Phoenix City and Salt River Valley Directory* (Phoenix: Arizona Directory Company, 1916), 287.

102. Felix Rosas, *Phoenix City and Salt River Valley Directory* (Phoenix: Arizona Directory Company, 1916), 287.

103. *New York Times*, October 13, 1933; November 21, 1933; March 14, 1934; March 20, 1935.

104. Historian Carlos Blanton wrote the first comprehensive biography of scholar George I. Sánchez; however, Blanton does not cover Sánchez's schooling at Winslow. *See* Carlos Kevin Blanton, *George I. Sánchez: The Long Fight for Mexican American Integration* (New Haven, Conn.: Yale University Press, 2014), 18.

105. Official Register of Electors, South Jerome Precinct, Yavapai County, Arizona, 1918, 193, 253, ASA ASLAPR; "Miner Struck over Head in Row at Camp," *Weekly Journal-Miner* (Prescott, Ariz.), May 31, 1922; Blanton, *George I. Sánchez*, 16–17; John H. Lindquist, "The Jerome Deportation of 1917," *Arizona and the West* 11, no. 3 (Autumn 1969), 238; James D. McBride, "The Liga Protectora Latina: A Mexican American Benevolent Society in Arizona," *Journal of the West* 14 (October 1975), 85. Telesforo Sánchez filed charges against a fellow miner named José Salas who assaulted him with a carbide lamp; this may be the same José Salas who boarded with the Sánchez family in Jerome, according to the 1920 Census. Blanton suggests that Sánchez was a member of the Industrial Workers of the World. He also may have been a member of the Liga Protectora Latina, which organized 500 Mexican workers at the United Verde mine.

106. *Winslow Mail*, December 9, 1921; December 23, 1921; January 13, 1922; January 20, 1922; February 10, 1922; May 5, 1922. *The Sandstorm* (Winslow High School Yearbook, 1922), 9.

107. *Winslow Mail*, February 10, 1922.

108. *The Sandstorm* (Winslow High School Yearbook, 1922), 14–17, 24–28; U.S. Department of the Interior, *Educational Conditions in Arizona*, 120, 139.

109. Mary King, "Languages," *The Sandstorm* (Winslow High School Yearbook, 1922), 47.

110. Laura K. Muñoz, "Ralph Estrada and the War Against Racial Prejudice in Arizona," in *Leaders of the Mexican American Generation: Biographical Essays*, ed. Anthony Quiroz (Denver: University of Colorado Press, 2015), 283–284; *Arizona Republic*, December 6, 1941; "Photograph: Grady Gammage, Tom García, and Moreles Gonzales

at Restaurant Table," n.d. [circa December 1941], Call No. MP SPC 323:98, n.d., Rebecca Muñoz Gutierrez Photographs, ASU CRC. Gammage regularly attended Los Conquistadores events, including this breakfast (circa December 1941) in Tempe. All three participated in the 1941 Conquis annual conference in Tempe. Gonzales was the Mexican Consul at Phoenix and García was a youth director in California. Gammage also mentored teacher Ralph Estrada when they both worked in the Winslow schools.

111. *The Mucker* (Jerome High School Yearbook, 1924), n.p. Cuca Tisnado is described by the following quote: "Why, she defies me like Turk to Christian."

112. *La Cuesta* (Arizona State Teachers College at Flagstaff, Yearbook, 1926), 32. The full Tisnado family and their origins are identified in the obituary of the matriarch Refugio Rivera de Tisnado, *El Sol*, April 17, 1953. Cuca Tisnado Culling lived in Phoenix; her sister Aurora Tisnado McKinnis, in Los Angeles.

113. *La Cuesta* (Arizona State Teachers College at Flagstaff Yearbook, 1929), 44.

114. *Arizona Daily Star*, June 6, 1991; August 19, 2002.

115. María Urias Muñoz, "Ignacia Theresa Terrazas de Urias—My Mother," unpublished manuscript, September 23, 1995, Box 82, "Rosalio and María," Ricardo Muñoz Papers, CSRC UCLA; Antonio G. Urias, obituary, *El Tucsonense*, January 24, 1934, Scrapbook, Ricardo Muñoz Papers, CSRC UCLA.

116. Autograph Book, various entries to María Urias, May 1928, Ricardo Muñoz Papers, CSRC UCLA.

117. *Desert* (University of Arizona Yearbook, 1937), 59.

118. *The Sahuaro* (TNS Yearbook, 1926), n.p. Evangeline started at the TNS in 1925 and her sister Genevieve in 1926. This means they likely attended Ray High School as early as 1921 and 1922.

119. See "Sonora, Arizona, 1907–1965," online exhibit, ASU Libraries, www.asu.edu /lib/archives/sonoraAZ.htm.

120. Gónzalez, "The Education and Public Career of María L. Urquides," 44.

121. Ruby Estrada, interview by María Hernández, August 4, 1981, Arizona Collection, ASU Libraries; Vicki L. Ruiz, *From Out of the Shadows: Mexican Women in Twentieth-Century America* (New York: Oxford University Press, 1998), 54; *Arizona Republic*, January 21, 2011. Ruby Estrada (née López) attended the TNS after graduating from Ray High School in 1928; she married Ralph Estrada in 1932.

122. R. E. Somers, "Mexican Indifference or Interest!" *ATHJ* 11, no. 4 (April 1923): 6–8.

123. Josiah Heyman, "The Oral History of the Mexican American Community of Douglas, Arizona, 1901–1942," *Journal of the Southwest* 35, no. 2 (1993): 199–200; Allen Pace Nilsen et al., *Dust in Our Desks: Territory Days to the Present in Arizona Schools* (Tempe: Arizona State University, College of Education, 1985), 22. The Faras sisters were well known as teachers in Pirtleville, an unincorporated area outside Douglas, Arizona. The Pirtleville School was renamed in their honor.

124. Register of Non-Degree Graduates, 1887–1936; Pamela Claire Hronek, "Women and Normal Schools: Tempe Normal, a Case Study, 1885–1925" (PhD diss.,

Arizona State University, 1985), 96. TNS issued a two-year teaching diploma, or non-baccalaureate degree, similar to the modern associate degree offered by community colleges. The ASU registrar called students who earned these diplomas "non-degree graduates" because, even though these students officially graduated and the college called them "graduates," these students did not earn the four-year bachelor's degree.

125. "List of Students," *Territorial Normal School of Arizona Catalogue*, 1888-1889, UA ASU, 7.

126. "Appendix D."

For a critique on the use of Hispanic surnames as an ethnic signifier of student identity and for comparisons to the late twentieth century, *see* Victoria-María MacDonald and Teresa García, "Historical Perspectives on Latino Access to Higher Education, 1848-1990," and Amaury Nora, "Access to Higher Education for Hispanic Students: Real or Illusory?" in *The Majority in the Minority: Expanding Representation of Latina/o Faculty, Administrators and Students in Higher Education*, ed. Jeanette Castellanos and Lee Jones (Sterling, Va.: Stylus Publishing, 2003).

127. "The New ASU Story: Academic Programs," online exhibit, Department of Archives and Manuscripts, Hayden Library, Arizona State University, Tempe, accessed December 30, 2005, available at www.asu.edu/lib/archives/asustory/acpro.htm.

128. Alfred Thomas Jr., *Arizona State University: A Documentary History of the First Seventy-Five Years, 1885-1960*, Vol. 2, ed. Alfred Thomas Jr. (Tempe, Ariz.: Alfred Thomas Jr., 1960), 21.

129. "Normal Biennial Report to 23rd Legislature, 1902-1903 and 1903-1904," 4.

130. Register of Non-Degree Graduates, 1887-1936.

131. "Normal School of Arizona Wins," football team photo, UP UPC ASUA 66 1890s No. 33, Photograph Collection, ASU; Charles Sigala, oral history interview by Scott Solliday, April 22, 1994, OH-141, Barrios Oral History Project, Tempe Historical Museum. For football coverage of Sigala, see *Arizona Republic*, October 22, 1899; November 18, 1899; December 5, 1899. See also the Charles Sigala Collection, RG 49, THM, Arizona. Charles is Chris Sigala's son. Chris Sigala also served in several leadership positions for the Tempe Lodge No. 1 of the *Liga Protectora Latina*. See, McBride, "The Liga Protectora Latina," 83-88; see also, *Arizona Republic*, June 29, 1915.

132. *The Sahuaro* (TNS Yearbook, 1917), n.p.

133. Training Department Register, *Territorial Normal School of Arizona Catalogue* 21 (1906): 54; Register, *Territorial Normal School of Arizona Catalogue*, 22-25 (1907-1910). The girls' names appear as "Anna Casanega" and "Nellie Casanega" in the alphabetized list. They also may have been related to three other female students from the Tubac/Calabasas/Nogales area, including Flora Casanega (1914), Emma Casanega (1915-1918), and Lorraine J. Casanega (1931-1936).

134. *Border Vidette*, December 17, 1898; September 20, 1902; September 17, 1904; March 2, 1907; August 31, 1907; Lorraine Casanega, Birth Certificate, Arizona Genealogy Record Search.

135. "Course of Study by Hiram Bradford Farmer," Territorial Normal School of Arizona, 0.3 Catalog 1886-1887, UA ASU.

136. *Tempe Normal School of Arizona Catalogue* 28 (1913-1914), 14.

137. Based on the published Catalogue rates, I calculated $15 for tuition and $80 for four months' board, for a total of $95 per child.

138. Concepción Mazón (signature), 1901, Section M, Student Contracts & Appointments Ledger, Tempe Normal School, 1906-1914, MSS 147, Box 0, Folder 8/ vol 0, UA ASU.

139. Thomas E. Sheridan, *Arizona: A History* (Tucson: University of Arizona Press, 1995), 170.

140. "Check 26 [paid] to Ramon Samora," August 27, 1897, Financial Correspondence Ledger, Tempe Normal School, June 1889-June 1898, MSS 147 Box 2, Folder 10, vol. 0, Arizona Territorial Normal School, UA ASU, n.p.

141. "Rosa Jaime," Labor Section, General Ledger, Tempe Normal School, 1906-1914, MSS 147, Box 3, Folder 10, vol. 0, UA. The general ledgers contain various sections, such as "Labor," that list the names, dates, assignments, and amount paid to each worker. Rosa Jaime appears on the ledger throughout the 1906-1907 academic year: October 1, 1906, $12 for washing; November 8, 1906, $12 for dining room; December 8, 1906, $12 for dining room; January 31, 1907, $12 for dining room; February 28, 1907, $12 for dining room; and March 31, 1907, $12 for dining room.

142. Register of Non-Degree Graduates; Rosa Pauline Jaime, Tempe Normal School of Arizona Diploma; Rosa Jaime, Arizona State University Life Diploma; and Rosa Jaime Deck, California State Board of Education Life Diploma, in Rosa Paula Jaime File, Diploma Collection, Accession No. 1993-01232, Box 1, UA ASU. Rosa Jaime's married name appears as "Deck" on her California Life Diploma but as "Dick" on all TNS sources. For example, from 1910 through 1913, her name is cited as "Rosa Jaime (Mrs. Fred Dick)" in the "Alumni Registers" printed in the TNS annual catalog. See "Alumni Register," *Territorial Normal School of Arizona Catalogue*, 1910-1913, vols. 25-28.

143. William Andrew O'Connor, Birth Certificate, Arizona Genealogy Record Search.

144. "Seizt-Miller, Marriage of a Popular Tempe Girl Yesterday Afternoon," newspaper clipping, Ruby Olive Haigler Wood Papers, 1903-1965, USM-178, UA ASU.

145. *Arizona Republic*, May 13, 1911; July 26, 1911; July 28, 1911; *Graham Guardian*, August 4, 1911; *Tucson Citizen* July 27, 1911; *Williams News*, May 13, 1911. The accused was listed as both "Alejandro Gallegos" and "Alexander Deyardo," and was sentenced to death. He was executed at Florence, Arizona, despite pleas from Yaeger's family for a gubernatorial commutation.

146. For lynching of Mexican Americans in the Southwest, *see* William D. Carrigan and Clive Webb, *Forgotten Dead: Mob Violence Against Mexicans in the United States, 1848-1928* (New York: Oxford University Press, 2013); Monica Muñoz Martinez, *The Injustice Never Leaves You: Anti-Mexican Violence in Texas* (Cambridge, Mass.: Harvard

University Press, 2018); F. Arturo Rosales, *¡Pobre Raza!: Violence, Justice, and Mobilization Among Mexico Lindo Immigrants, 1900–1936* (Austin: University of Texas Press, 1999).

147. "Social capital" refers to the perceived wealth (economic, cultural, or symbolic) or potential success that individuals within groups attribute to one another based on association. Sociologists Alejandro Portes and Patricia Landolt define the term as "the ability to secure resources by virtue of membership in social networks or larger social structures." See Alejandro Portes and Patricia Landolt, "Social Capital: Promise and Pitfalls of Its Role in Development," *Journal of Latin American Studies* 32, no. 2 (May 2000): 529–547; Alejandro Portes, "Two Meanings of Social Capital," *Sociological Forum* 15, no.1 (March 2000): 1–12; Alejandro Portes and Rubén Rumbaut, *Immigrant America: A Portrait* (Berkeley: University of California Press, 1990). For an analysis of social capital among Mexican American youth in Arizona, see Cynthia L. Bejarano, *¿Qué onda? Urban Youth Cultures and Border Identity* (Tucson: University of Arizona Press, 2005), 12–13.

148. Ralph Frank Gómez, Birth Certificate, Arizona Genealogy Record Search.

149. Inez Jones Gómez, Birth Certificate, Arizona Genealogy Record Search.

150. Alexandra Minna Stern, *Eugenic Nation: Faults and Frontiers in Better Breeding in Modern America* (Berkeley: University of California Press, 2005), 21.

151. "Inez Gómez," *The Sahuaro* (ASTC Yearbook, 1934), 51; "Katherine Gómez" (obituary), *Arizona Republic*, April 18, 1947; "Mary Gómez," *The Sahuaro* (ASTC Yearbook, 1927), n.p.

152. *Biennial Report of the Superintendent of Public Instruction for the Territory of Arizona, 1907–1908* (Phoenix, Ariz.: Office of the Superintendent of Public Instruction, 1908), 13.

153. Thomas, *Arizona State University*, Vol. 2, 125–126; "G. L. Fernández," photograph, *Picadillo* Yearbook, 1911, 10; "Gracia L. Fernández," signature, Teacher's Certificate Register, 1905–1916, Records 1883–1931, Superintendent of Schools, RG 107 Maricopa County, ASA ASLAPR. The registry entry for Fernández shows that she took the teacher's certificate exam on December 8, 1900, and that she renewed her certificate exactly four years later, on December 8, 1904.

154. *Bangor (Maine) Daily News*, July 22, 1902; *Holbrook Argus*, October 20, 1900. Fernandez's father, Fernando, was a Spanish immigrant; her mother, Francina Gilman, was born in Maine.

155. Lela Gardinier, Shelter Island, N.Y., to Superintendent John T. Hogue, St. Johns, Ariz., August 19, 1902, letter regarding the teaching contract from El Tule and Concho schools mentions Miss Fernández, Correspondence 1887–1896, Box 2 School Records—Reports 1886–1919, Superintendent of Schools, Apache County RG 100, ASA ASLAPR; Miss Gracia L. Fernández, signature, circa 1900–1901 and April 21, 1901, Teacher's Monthly Reports, El Tule No. 5, Box 2 School Records—Reports 1886–1919, Superintendent of Schools, Apache County RG100, ASA ASLAPR; Gracia L. Fernández, December 8, 1900, Teacher's Certificate Register,1905–1916, Superintendent of School Records, 1883–1931, Maricopa County RG 107, AAHD.

156. Fernández relinquished the librarianship in 1909-1910 and she also taught "Spelling and Word Analysis" in 1911-1912.

157. Historian Matthew C. Whitaker describes "race work" as the active pursuit of the "reclamation and social, economic, political, and cultural advancement of people of African descent," with a gendered framework that includes gender equality as an intertwined struggle for black liberation. Those individuals who pursue "race work" are usually called "race men" and "race women." I use the term to affirm that Mexican Americans and Latinos espoused a similar ethnic and gender consciousness in the self-promotion, preservation, and uplift of their fellow ethnics. See Matthew C. Whitaker, *Race Work: The Rise of Civil Rights in the Urban West* (Lincoln: University of Nebraska Press, 2005), 2-3; Hazel V. Carby, *Race Men* (Cambridge, Mass.: Harvard University Press, 1998), 11-12.

158. *Territorial Normal School of Arizona Bulletin*, 1911-1912, 52. Fernández expanded this rationale from that noted in the 1907-1908 course bulletin (page 37), which emphasized the need for a foreign-language requirement and for teachers familiar with the Spanish language.

159. Lynne Marie Getz, *Schools of Their Own: The Education of Hispanos in New Mexico, 1850-1940* (Albuquerque: University of New Mexico Press, 1997), 22.

160. "Eliza Loroña," January 22, 1908, Registration and Enrollment.

161. Glenda Elizabeth Gilmore, *Gender and Jim Crow: Women and the Politics of White Supremacy in North Carolina, 1896-1920* (Chapel Hill: University of North Carolina Press, 1996), 31, 39, 62-63; Annelise Orleck, *Common Sense and a Little Fire: Women and Working-Class Politics in the United States, 1900-1965* (Chapel Hill: University of North Carolina Press, 1995); Ogren, *The American State Normal School*, 77; Tey Diana Rebolledo, ed., *Nuestra Mujeres: Hispanas of New Mexico, Their Images and Their Lives, 1582-1992* (Albuquerque, N. Mex.: El Norte Publications, 1992), 95-135; Judy Yung, *Unbound Feet: A Social History of Chinese Women in San Francisco* (Berkeley: University of California Press, 1995), 69, 105, 147.

162. John M. Nieto-Phillips, *The Language of Blood: The Making of Spanish-American Identity in New Mexico, 1880s-1930s* (Albuquerque: University of New Mexico Press, 2008), 203.

163. *Territorial Normal School of Arizona Bulletin*, 1907-1908, 36.

164. *Bulletin*, 1910-1911, 44.

165. *Bulletin*, 1908-1909, 36.

166. "Information Files, Faculty: Salmans, Edith," UA ASU.

167. Concepción "Chonita" Faras, "Sueños de España," in *The Arc Light* (Tempe: Seniors of Tempe Normal School of Arizona, 1913), 130.

168. "Spanish," *TNS Catalogue* 27 (1912-1913), 51; "Drama, The Spanish Play," *The Quindecem* (TNS Yearbook, 1915), 85. In 1915, Miss Salmans and the Spanish class produced a play called "Los Pantalones."

169. Ida Celaya, "El Adios de Una Senior," in *The Sahuaro* (TNS Yearbook, 1917), n.p.

170. Ascunción Lavrin, "Women in Twentieth Century Latin American Society," in *The Cambridge History of Latin America*, Vol. 6 (Cambridge: Cambridge University

Press, 1995), 506; Francesca Miller, *Latin American Women and the Search for Social Justice* (Hanover, N.H.: University Press of New England, 1991), 43; Steven Palmer and Gladys Rojas Chaves, "Educating Señorita: Teacher Training, Social Mobility, and the Birth of Costa Rican Feminism," *Hispanic American Historical Review* 78, no. 1 (1998): 47. *See* Lavrin for a discussion of how the dialogue among Domingo F. Sarmiento and Horace and Mary Mann led to the 1869 founding of Argentina's first teacher training institute at Paraná.

171. Ogren, *The American State Normal School*, 66. Based on my count of Spanish surnames in TNS yearbooks and the Register of Non-Degree Graduates from 1888 through 1920, I estimate that at least forty-eight Mexican American women compared to twenty-two Mexican American men enrolled at TNS.

172. *El Escudo* (TNS Yearbook, 1914), 79; *The Quindecem* (TNS Yearbook, 1915), 51-54; *The Sahuaro* (TNS Yearbook, 1916), 67, 73. The TNS Yearbook had six names before 1916, the year it became "The Sahuaro."

173. Benton James's mother, Mrs. Jessie James, founded the Arizona chapter of the Federation of Colored Women's Clubs and promoted equal education laws that led to the founding of Phoenix's Carver High School and the admission of African American students at the TNS. Senior portraits of Benton James and Rafael Estrada, *The Sahuaro* (TNS Yearbook, 1923), n.p.; Crudup, "African Americans in Arizona," 323.

174. Bob Jacobsen, "ASU Held Hope, Anguish for African Americans," *ASU Vision* 6, no. 1 (Fall 2002).

175. "Appendix D."

176. Ogren, *The American State Normal School*, 66.

177. Louis Barrera, Attendance Records, Section B, n.p.

178. John R. Birchett, "The Alumni Association, The Relation of the Alumni Association to the Normal," *Normal Magazine*, Vol. 0 (1904), 43-47.

179. Barry Edward Lamb, "The Making of a Chicano Civil Rights Activist" (master's thesis, Arizona State University, 1988), 66. Rafael Estrada left teaching in 1936 when he entered law school at the University of Arizona in Tucson.

180. "Appendix D" identifies all Spanish Club members, as well members of Los Conquistadores (1937). The students used the term "Spanish Club" interchangeably with the formal organizational name, especially since the club operated under several names but always under the auspice of the Spanish professor. The club names included El Club Hispánico (1917), El Club Español (1922), and Los Hidalgos del Desierto (1923).

181. "Clionian Society," *The Quindecem*, 1917, n.p.; "Clionian Society," *The Quindecem*, 1915, 69.

182. Ogren, *The American State Normal School*, 108-118.

183. Ogren, *The American State Normal School*, 111.

184. "Appendix D." I reviewed club associations for each student and found few exceptions to their memberships in the Spanish club or sports teams/athletic clubs. Instead of literary clubs or fraternities and sororities, the students did join academic and social clubs. Two notable exceptions include Concepción Mazón and Caroline

Contreras. Concepción Mazón initially joined the Alpha Literary Society in 1900, but after attending the first two meetings left the society. The society scrapbook shows her name scratched out of the roster. Caroline Contreras, class of 1929 and 1931, was a member of the Phi Beta Epsilon literary society and its vice president in 1928 and treasurer in 1929. An analysis of Contreras's academic career and other students' extracurricular activities follows in the text. See Alpha Literary Society Scrapbook, 1900–1910, UA ASU; "Phi Beta Epsilon," *The Sahuaro* (ASTC Yearbook, 1929), UA ASU, n.p.

185. "Los Hidalgos del Desierto," *The Sahuaro* (ASTC Yearbook, 1929), n.p. My translation: "Yes it's certain/true, We're jovial/ glad and social/ we're Noblemen/Noblewomen of the Desert." Interestingly, Christine Ogren also interprets normal school students' references to themselves as "nobility" as an effort to align themselves with the middle class, except she examines a similar phenomenon among men at San José State University in San José, California. Also, Arizona historian Christine Marin translates "Los Hidalgos del Desierto" as "Lords of the Desert." See Ogren's chapter, "'Noble' Men and 'Not Necessarily Bloomer Women': The Public Sphere, Gender Attitudes and Life Choices," in *The American State Normal School*. See Christine Marin, "Arizona Highways: The G.I. Generation, Migration and Mexican Americans," unpublished manuscript, collection of the author, 5.

186. *The Sahuaro* (ASTC Yearbook, 1934).

187. "El Club Hispánico," "El Club Español," and "Los Hidalgos del Desierto," *The Sahuaro* (TNS Yearbook, 1917–1925).

188. *The Sahuaro* (TNS Yearbook, 1917), n.p.; Charles Sigala interview.

189. Senior portrait of James Barney, *The Sahuaro* (TSTC Yearbook, 1926), n.p. Barney's mother, Jessie Zazueta, hailed from Ray, Arizona, while his father, also named James Barney, possessed a mixed-racial background, graduated from Stanford University (where he met his longtime friend Senator Carl Hayden), and was a well-known and published Arizona historian. See Biography of Jessie Barney and Biography of James Barney, Arizona Collection, ASU.

190. Senior portrait of María L. Urquides, *The Sahuaro* (ASTC Yearbook, 1928), n.p.

191. *The Sahuaro* (TNS Yearbook, 1925), n.p.

192. Ogren, *The American State Normal School*, 175–177. Ogren suggests that normal school women supported individual rights in concert with "modern feminism" even though most did not identify with the movement and held rather ambivalent gender attitudes.

193. McBride, "The Liga Protectora Latina," 83; Ophelia Celaya, "Biography of Ophelia Marion Celaya," CB Biography, ASU Hayden Arizona Collection (Call No. CB BIO CEL, OPH, Id. No. 20534).

194. "Appendix D"; Sheridan, *Los Tucsonenses*, 116–117.

195. *The Sahuaro* (ASTC Yearbook, 1929), n.p.

196. In 1873, Mexican American laborers built the adobe structure called the Charles T. Hayden House, a.k.a "La Casa Vieja" (the old house) for Tempe founder Charles T. Hayden, who lived there with his wife and children until 1889 when they

moved to a new home on a nearby ranch. Arizona Senator Carl Hayden and his sisters Mary and Sally Hayden, a TNS professor, continued to own the home, which served as both a boardinghouse and restaurant. Professor Hayden often found jobs at the restaurant for TNS students, including María Urquides who sang Spanish songs to dining patrons. Built near the edge of the Rio Salado River, the restaurant today remains a popular Tempe landmark and is on the National Register of Historic Places (Building #84000173, listed on May 7, 1984).

197. *The Sahuaro* (ASTC Yearbook, 1934), 67.

198. *The Sahuaro* (ASTC Yearbook, 1928, 1929), n.p.

199. For an analysis of sports and Mexican American students, see José M. Alamillo, *Deportes: The Making of a Sporting Mexican Diaspora* (New Brunswick, N.J.: Rutgers University Press, 2020); Jorge Iber, et al., *Latinos in U.S. Sport: A History of Isolation, Cultural Identity and Acceptance* (Champaign, IL: Human Kinetics, 2011); Ignacio M. García, *When Mexicans Could Play Ball: Basketball, Race, and Identity in San Antonio, 1928-1945* (Austin: University of Texas Press, 2013); Christine Marin, "Courting Success and Realizing the American Dream: Arizona's Mighty Miami High School Championship Basketball Team, 1951," *International Journal of the History of Sport* 26, no. 7 (June 2009): 924-946.H

200. "Captain Estrada," Football Section, *The Sahuaro* (TNS Yearbook, 1923), n.p. Estrada signed the 1923 copy of *The Sahuaro* in the University Archives.

201. James Barney, *The Sahuaro* (ASTC Yearbook, 1927, 1928), n.p.

202. *Arizona Republic*, March 5, 1933; Carlos Jimenez, *The Sahuaro* (ASTC Yearbook, 1930, 1931, 1932), n.p.

203. Academic Statistics, Call 0.13, UA ASU.

204. *The Sahuaro* (TNS Yearbook, 1923), n.p.; "Della Eckardt" [student record, 1921-1924], Registration and Enrollment. The yearbook described Eckardt in this quote: "Although possessed of a dark beauty and soft charm of Spain, she is not possessed of a Spanish name." Between 1921 and 1923, Eckardt's parents resided in Tucson, Arizona; Andrade, California; Santa Ana, California, and San Cristobal, Pinar del Rio, Cuba.

205. Gónzalez, "The Education and Public Career of María L. Urquides," 47; *Arizona Republic*, October 13, 1927. Vera Chase presented a paper on the "Problems of the Non-English Speaking Child," at the 1927 meeting of the Arizona Education Association in Nogales.

206. "Who's Who, Our Societies," *The Sahuaro* (TNS Yearbook, 1924), n.p.

207. *The Sahuaro* (ASTC Yearbook, 1930), n.p.

208. "Matthews Hall," *The Sahuaro* (ASTC Yearbook, 1934), 155.

209. Gónzalez, "The Education and Public Career of María L. Urquides," 45; Hronek, "Women and Normal Schools," 111; Jacobsen, "ASU Held Hope." See also Mary Aickin Rothschild, *Doing What the Day Brought: An Oral History of Arizona Women* (Tucson: University of Arizona Press, 1992).

210. Raymond Johnson Flores, interview by Christine Marin, June 17, 1998; August 30, 1999; September 9, 1999, Tempe, Arizona, private collection of Christine

Marin; Jared Smith, "The African American Experience in Tempe" (Tempe History Museum, 2013), 18-19.

211. "Appendix D"; *The Sahuaro* (ASTC Yearbook, 1928), n.p. The African American members of the Inter-Racial Club included Madelina Cook, Catherine Garrett, Sarah Garrett, and Mozelle Mack. They listed their club affiliation next to their senior portraits.

212. Gónzalez, "The Education and Public Career of María L. Urquides," 48.

213. Gónzalez, "The Education and Public Career of María L. Urquides," 48.

214. Marin, "Arizona Highways: The G.I. Generation, Migration and Mexican Americans," 5.

215. Marin, "Arizona Highways: The G.I. Generation, Migration and Mexican Americans," 5-6n11.

216. "Prophecy," *The Arc Light* (TNS Yearbook, 1913), 55.

217. "Prophecy," *The Sahuaro* (TNS Yearbook, 1919), 56.

Chapter 3

1. Evan Skinner to John C. Monahan, December 31, 1916, file 501, Arizona, Local School Surveys, Historical Files, Records of the Office of the Commissioner of Education (1870-1979), Records of the Office of Education, RG 12; National Archives, College Park, Md. (hereafter cited as RG 12, NA).

2. U.S. Department of the Interior, Office of Education, *Educational Conditions in Arizona (Report of a Survey by the United States Bureau of Education)* (Washington, D.C., 1918 [Bulletin, 1917, No. 44]) (hereafter cited as *Educational Conditions in Arizona*).

3. Skinner to Monahan.

4. *Educational Conditions in Arizona*, 14.

5. *Educational Conditions in Arizona*, 14.

6. Gilbert G. González, *Culture of Empire: American Writers, Mexico, and Mexican Immigrants, 1880-1930* (Austin, University of Texas Press, 2004), 171.

7. Lillian Ruth Higgins, "A Flower Project," *Arizona Teacher and Home Journal* (hereafter cited as *ATHJ*) (March 1927): 230.

8. Grace Gainsley, "Teaching Mexican Children," *ATHJ* 5, no. 3 (April 1916): 10.

9. C. Louise Boehringer, "Editorial Comment: Americanization," *ATHJ* 11, no. 3 (October 1922): 7.

10. González, *Culture of Empire*, 174-176.

11. David Tyack, *The One Best System: A History of American Urban Education* (Cambridge, Mass.: Harvard University Press, 1974), 234-235. This delineation— assimilation to Americanization—follows David Tyack's differentiation of "Americanization" in the nineteenth century as a "general pattern of socialization" versus the "common competence" required by urban-industrial citizens of twentieth-century society. The twentieth-century immigrant "not only had to learn new skills but also had to shed an old culture." I use Tyack's definition, which differs from historian Gilbert González's definition of assimilation as theory and Americanization as its practice.

12. *Educational Conditions in Arizona*, 14, 43, 108-109, 120, 139. Enrollment designates only those students (49,051) who attended schools versus the total number of children (61,633) aged six to twenty-one who were eligible to attend. The twelve cities (from North to South) included Flagstaff, Winslow, Prescott, Phoenix, Tempe, Mesa, Globe, Clifton, Tucson, Bisbee, Douglas, and Nogales. Maricopa County included the towns of Phoenix, Tempe, and Mesa, and it had the largest number of schoolchildren in 1915-1916. Cochise County, located on the U.S.-Mexico border, included the towns of Bisbee and Douglas, and had the second-largest number of schoolchildren that year.

13. *Educational Conditions in Arizona*, 120n7.

14. Katherine Benton-Cohen, *Borderline Americans: Racial Division and Labor War in the Arizona Borderlands* (Cambridge, Mass.: Harvard University Press, 2009), 160-161; Bradford Luckingham, *Minorities in Phoenix: A Profile of Mexican American, Chinese American, and African American Communities, 1860-1992* (Tucson: University of Arizona Press, 1994), 16-17; Samuel Pressly McCrea, "Establishment of the Arizona School System" (master's thesis, Stanford University, 1902), in the *Biennial Report of the Superintendent of Public Instruction of the Territory of Arizona, 1907-1908* (Phoenix: Arizona Department of Public Instruction, 1908), 82n3; Thomas E. Sheridan, *Los Tucsonenses: The Mexican Community in Tucson, 1854-1941* (Tucson: University of Arizona Press, 1986), 218; and Sheridan, *Arizona: A History*, rev. ed. (Tucson: University of Arizona Press, 2012), 38. McCrea cites the 1870 census. From a total population of 9,658, "4,339 were born in Mexico, and 1,319 in other foreign countries. There were only 3,849 persons born in the United States, and of these 1,290 were born in Arizona of Mexican descent parents." About 58 percent of Arizona's population claimed Mexican heritage by birth or descent. Sheridan reports that in the nineteenth century Arizona's "non-Indian" population was mostly Mexican and that by the twentieth century "Mexicans usually formed the largest ethnic group in the public school system." Benton-Cohen notes that children born of mixed—"Anglo" and "Mexican"—marriages were often counted as "Mexican," adding to the population statistic.

15. *Educational Conditions in Arizona*, 11-13.

16. Southwestern scholarship that addresses the impact of U.S. economic development on Mexican American populations includes Albert Camarillo, *Chicanos in a Changing Society*, repr. ed. (Dallas, Tex.: Southern Methodist University Press, 2005); Benton-Cohen, *Borderline Americans*; Arnoldo de León, *The Tejano Community, 1836-1900* (Dallas, Tex.: Southern Methodist University Press, 1997); Sarah Deutsch, *No Separate Refuge: Culture, Class, and Gender on an Anglo-Hispanic Frontier in the American Southwest, 1880-1940* (New York: Oxford University Press, 1987); Evelyn Nakano Glenn, *Unequal Freedom: How Race and Gender Shaped American Citizenship and Labor* (Cambridge, Mass.: Harvard University Press, 2002); Linda Gordon, *The Great Arizona Orphan Abduction* (Cambridge, Mass.: Harvard University Press, 1999); David G. Gutiérrez, *Walls and Mirrors: Mexican Americans, Mexican Immigrants, and the Politics of Ethnicity* (Berkeley: University of California Press, 1995); Lizbeth Haas, *Conquests and Historical Identities in California, 1769-1936* (Berkeley: University of California Press,

1995); Luckingham, *Minorities in Phoenix*; Carey McWilliams, *North from Mexico: The Spanish-Speaking People of the United States* (Philadelphia: J. B. Lippincott, 1949); David Montejano, *Anglos and Mexicans in the Making of Texas, 1836-1986* (Austin: University of Texas Press, 1987); Leonard Pitt, *The Decline of the Californios: A Social History of the Spanish-Speaking Californians, 1846-1890* (Berkeley: University of California Press, 1970); Vicki L. Ruiz, *From Out of the Shadows: Mexican Women in Twentieth-Century America* (New York: Oxford University Press, 1998); Sheridan, *Los Tucsonenses*; Samuel Truett, *Fugitive Landscapes: The Forgotten History of the U.S.-Mexico Borderlands* (New Haven, Conn.: Yale University Press, 2006).

17. Historian Gilbert González already has shown that Americanization within Mexican American education stemmed from U.S. imperialism, and he links the "culture of empire" (U.S. economic colonization of Mexico and its people) to specific "domestic public policy applied to the Mexican immigrant community" within the United States, such as race-based school segregation and I.Q. testing. My goal here is to expose this same policy and program implementation in Arizona from a domestic perspective. See González, *Culture of Empire*, 10-11, 154-155; and Gilbert G. González and Raul A. Fernández, *A Century of Chicano History: Empire, Nations, and Migrations* (New York: Routledge, 2003), 83.

18. Luckingham, *Minorities in Phoenix*, 49-50, 133-134, 161-162; Eric V. Meeks, *Border Citizens: The Making of Indians, Mexicans, and Anglos in Arizona* (Austin: University of Texas Press, 2007), 161, 176-179; Herman Robert Lucero, *"Plessy* to *Brown*: Education of Mexican Americans in Arizona Public Schools During the Era of Segregation" (PhD diss., University of Arizona, 2004); Vicki L. Ruiz, "Tapestries of Resistance: Episodes of School Segregation and Desegregation in the Western United States," in *From the Grassroots to the Supreme Court: Brown v. Board of Education and American Democracy*, ed. Peter F. Lau (Durham, N.C.: Duke University Press, 2004), 44-67.

Some historians of education recently have challenged the notion and categorization of "de facto" segregation as "fiction" because all segregation is based on legal precedent. See the work of Ansley Erickson, *Making the Unequal Metropolis: School Desegregation and Its Limits* (Chicago: University of Chicago Press, 2016), and Matthew D. Lassiter, *The Silent Majority: Suburban Politics in the Sunbelt South* (Princeton, N.J.: Princeton University Press, 2006).

19. Paragraph 2750, *Revised Statutes of Arizona* (1913).

20. Sheridan, *Arizona*, 169. González and Fernández, *A Century of Chicano History*, 42-43: Gordon, *The Great Arizona Orphan Abduction*, 48-49.

21. *Biennial Report of the Superintendent of Public Instruction of the Territory of Arizona, 1905-1906* (Phoenix, Ariz., H. H. McNeil Co., 1906), 95.

22. Glenn, *Unequal Freedom*, 163; Gordon, *The Great Arizona Orphan Abduction*, 50-51, 101-105; Sheridan, *Arizona*, 168-169.

23. Glenn, *Unequal Freedom*, 163-164; Gordon, *The Great Arizona Orphan Abduction*, 104; John Higham, *Strangers in the Land: Patterns of American Nativism, 1860-1925*, 3rd printing (New Brunswick, N.J.: Rutgers University Press, 1994), 132.

24. Sheridan, *Los Tucsonenses*, 54, 78-83.

25. Gordon, *The Great Arizona Orphan Abduction*, 87; Sheridan, *Arizona*, 169–170.

26. Luckingham, *Minorities in Phoenix*, 25.

27. "Grant School, Phoenix," Image 04-1097, Historic Photographs, ASA ASLAPR; *Phoenix City Directory* (Dallas, 1921), 72, 276. Grant School was located at 4th Avenue and West Grant Street and seven blocks south of Washington Street, which is still used by city planners as the north/south divide.

28. Tyack, "Part IV, Centralization and the Corporate Model: Contests for Control of Urban Schools, 1890–1940," in *The One Best System*, 126–176, 133–134. Robert Lindley Long's educational career closely matches the trajectories of prominent schoolmen of his era, such as the presidents of Harvard University, Columbia University, and the University of Chicago. Tyack writes, "It was common for [university] presidents to become city superintendents and vice versa" as part of this "expert" reorganization of the urban schools.

29. *Biennial Report of the Superintendent of Public Instruction for the Territory of Arizona, 1885–1886* (Prescott, Ariz.: Courier Book and Job Printing Establishment, 1887), 20, 25–27, 62; *Biennial Report of the Superintendent of Public Instruction for the Territory of Arizona, 1899–1900* (Phoenix, Ariz.: H. H. McNeil Co., 1900), 28; McCrea, "Establishment of the Arizona School System," 107, 116, 131–132; *School Laws of Arizona Territory* (1887), 50-60. Teachers earned their certification either by exam or by proof of graduation from a normal school, college, or university, and they were expected to use general knowledge of academic subjects to independently organize lesson plans. For example, to garner a "second grade" certificate (the lowest credential offered), teacher applicants had to demonstrate 75-85 percent proficiency in the following subjects: Grammar, Orthography (penmanship), Arithmetic, U.S. History, Defining (Word Analysis), Geography, School Law, Mental Arithmetic, Methods of Teaching, Composition, Reading, Physiology, Algebra, and Natural Philosophy.

30. McCrea, "Establishment of the Arizona School System," 132; *Biennial Report of the Superintendent of Public Instruction for the Territory of Arizona, 1885–1886* (Prescott, Ariz.: Courier Book and Job Printing Establishment, 1887), 11; *Biennial Report of the Superintendent of Public Instruction for the Territory of Arizona, 1905–1906* (Phoenix, Ariz., H. H. McNeil Co., 1906), 4.

Superintendent Robert Lindley Long served intermittently from 1885 through 1909; he created a Territorial Board of Examiners and a system of county boards of examiners to oversee teacher licensing in 1885. Under Long, all teachers had to recertify or lose their jobs. In 1899, he rewrote and distributed 1,500 copies of the territory's revised course of study for the public schools and, as Tempe Normal School principal, also revised the course of study for future teachers. In 1916, he moved to Washington, D.C., and served as a consultant to the U.S. Bureau of Education survey team. See *Educational Conditions in Arizona*, 10.

31. Stephen Kent Amerman, *Urban Indians in Phoenix Indian Schools* (Lincoln: University of Nebraska, 2010).

32. Springerville School District No. 2, 1936, Teacher's Monthly Reports, School Reports—Records, 1886–1919, Boxes 1–2, Superintendent of Schools, Apache County,

RG 100, ASA ASLAPR. Although these boxes were labeled "1886-1919," occasionally data beyond these dates was available in some school district files. "Indian" here refers to immigrants from East Asian countries.

33. *Biennial Report of the Superintendent of Public Instruction for the Territory of Arizona, 1885-1886* (Prescott, Ariz.: Courier Book and Job Printing Establishment, 1887), 10; *Arizona Session Laws* (1879), 126; *Arizona Revised Statutes* (1913), 916-917; Glenn, *Unequal Freedom*, 20; Tyack, *The One Best System*, 114, 148. Glenn and Tyack describe how citizenship and its privileges such as educational opportunity become subject to local community "rules and social practices."

34. Benton-Cohen, *Borderline Americans*, 163. Benton-Cohen details the race and class conflict between Mexicans and Mormons over school autonomy in Arizona's San Pedro River Valley.

35. *Educational Conditions in Arizona*, 43; *Biennial Report of the Superintendent of Public Instruction for the Territory of Arizona, 1895-1896* (Phoenix, Ariz.: Arizona Department of Public Instruction, 1897), 20.

36. Ronald D. Cohen and Raymond A. Mohl, *The Paradox of Progressive Education: The Gary Plan and Urban Schooling* (Port Washington, N.Y.: Kennikat, 1979), 4; Tyack, *The One Best System*, 127, 139.

37. The Church of Jesus Christ of Latter-day Saints regulates its membership through geographic regions called "stakes." A stake, about the size of a town, is divided into wards and branches. A group of stakes constitute a temple. In 2010, Arizona had three temples, including one at Snowflake, and ninety-four stakes. See www.ldschurchtemples .com/temples/.

38. "Robert C. Smith," obituary, *Snowflake Herald*, April 16, 1920; *The Snowflake Herald*, OCLC No. 13362122, Arizona Historical Digital Newspapers, ASLAPR, https:// azmemory.azlibrary.gov/nodes/view/469.

39. *Biennial Report of the Superintendent of Public Instruction for the Territory of Arizona, 1907-1908* (Phoenix: Arizona Department of Public Instruction, 1908), 22.

40. Sheridan, *Arizona*, 196-198; David King Udall and Pearl Udall Nelson, *Arizona Pioneer Mormon: David King Udall: His Story and His Family, 1851-1938* (Tucson: University of Arizona Press, 1959).

41. The New Mexico Supreme Court published four opinions involving Alfred Ruiz, who represented appellants in all four cases. For an example, see *State ex rel. Lorenzino v. County Comm'rs*, 20 N.M. 67, 1915-NMSC-010, 145 P. 1083, 1915 N.M. LEXIS 8 (Supreme Court of New Mexico January 14, 1915).

42. *Biennial Report of the Superintendent of Public Instruction for the Territory of Arizona, 1907-1908* (Phoenix: Arizona Department of Public Instruction, 1908), 13.

43. *Biennial Report of the Superintendent of Public Instruction for the Territory of Arizona, 1907-1908* (Phoenix: Arizona Department of Public Instruction, 1908), 13.

44. Miss Gracia L. Fernández, Mrs. Amelia Hunt García, and Mr. Abel Ortega, signatures on file, Teacher's Monthly Reports, Box 2 School Records—Reports (1886-1919), Superintendent of Schools, Apache County, RG 100, ASA ASLAPR.

45. "G. L. Fernández," photograph, *Picadillo* Yearbook (Tempe, Ariz., 1911), 10; *Sun-Journal* (Lewistown, Maine), June 22, 1897; *Portland Daily Press*, June 23, 1897.

46. *Biennial Report of the Superintendent of Public Instruction for the Territory of Arizona, 1907-1908* (Phoenix: Arizona Department of Public Instruction, 1908), 13.

47. *Biennial Report of the Superintendent of Public Instruction for the Territory of Arizona, 1905-1906* (Phoenix, Ariz., H. H. McNeil Co., 1906), 12; Victoria-María Mac-Donald, ed., *Latino Education in the United States: A Narrated History from 1513-2000* (New York: Palgrave MacMillan, 2004), 68, 85-86.

48. *Biennial Report of the Superintendent of Public Instruction for the Territory of Arizona, 1905-1906* (Phoenix, Ariz., H. H. McNeil Co., 1906), 12.

49. *Biennial Report of the Superintendent of Public Instruction for the Territory of Arizona, 1905-1906* (Phoenix, Ariz., H. H. McNeil Co., 1906), 13-14, 49. In his narrative, John T. Hogue provided the average daily attendance figures (seventy for 1905 and 52 for 1906) for Concho No. 6. Assuming that the average number of students "belonging" remained consistent across the 1904-1905 and 1905-1906 school years, I approximated the percentages from the 1905-1906 Apache County school statistics included in the report.

50. *Biennial Report of the Superintendent of Public Instruction for the Territory of Arizona, 1907-1908* (Phoenix: Arizona Department of Public Instruction, 1908), 23.

51. *Biennial Report of the Superintendent of Public Instruction for the Territory of Arizona., 1907-1908* (Phoenix: Arizona Department of Public Instruction, 1908), 22.

52. Glenn, *Unequal Freedom*, 163.

53. "Navajo [County]," *ATHJ* 5, no. 1 (February 1916): 34.

54. Glenn, *Unequal Freedom*, 147.

55. Cohen and Mohl, *The Paradox of Progressive Education*, 4; Glenn, *Unequal Freedom*, 181.

56. Joseph F. Park, "The 1903 'Mexican Affair' at Clifton," *Journal of Arizona History* 18 (Summer 1977): 1.

57. Sheridan, *Arizona*, 170.

58. Sheridan, *Arizona*, 156.

59. *Educational Conditions in Arizona*, 14.

60. *Educational Conditions in Arizona*, 14; Glenn, *Unequal Freedom*, 154.

61. Gordon, *The Great Arizona Orphan Abduction*, 102; Park, "The 1903 'Mexican Affair' at Clifton," 9; Sheridan, *Arizona*, 170.

62. Gordon, *The Great Arizona Orphan Abduction*, 241.

63. Park, "The 1903 'Mexican Affair' at Clifton," 1; Gordon, *The Great Arizona Orphan Abduction*, 242. The U.S. Army, Arizona Rangers, and local sheriffs quelled the strike, but rains and flooding during the strike destroyed sections of the twin towns, including a Mexican neighborhood along Chase Creek and a brand-new schoolhouse.

64. Gordon, *The Great Arizona Orphan Abduction*, 242.

65. Gordon, *The Great Arizona Orphan Abduction*, 175.

66. Gordon, *The Great Arizona Orphan Abduction*, 194.

67. "Improvements at Ray," *ATHJ* 8, no. 1 (September 1919): 26.

68. Clare Sheridan, "Contested Citizenship: National Identity and the Mexican Immigration Debates of the 1920s," *Journal of American Ethnic History* 21 (Spring 2002): 13-14.

69. Gordon, *The Great Arizona Orphan Abduction*, 243.

70. Sheridan, *Arizona*, 174; Linda Noel, "'I Am an American': Nativos, Anglos, and the Statehood Debates of Arizona and New Mexico," paper presented at the annual meeting of the Pacific Coast Branch of the American Historical Association, Albuquerque, August 6-8, 2009.

71. Sheridan, *Arizona*, 178.

72. Sheridan, *Arizona*, 177.

73. Sheridan, *Arizona*, 179; Higham, *Strangers in the Land*, 183.

74. Sheridan, *Arizona*, 264.

75. Mark Reisler, *By the Sweat of Their Brow: Mexican Immigrant Labor in the United States, 1900-1940* (Westport, Conn.: Greenwood Press, 1976), 144; Sheridan, "Contested Citizenship," 13-14.

76. *Educational Conditions in Arizona*, 9; "State Study," *ATHJ* 7, no. 1 (February 1917): 11-13. The study began in the fall of 1916 and the *ATHJ* published the initial findings in February 1917, although a Bureau press release circulated in January 1917.

77. *Educational Conditions in Arizona*, 9, 122. "State Study," *ATHJ* 7, no. 1 (February 1917): 11-13.

78. "Surveying the Schools of Arizona," *ATHJ* 6, no. 2 (October 1916): 9-10. Katherine Margaret O'Brien Cook wrote more than seventy-five reports for the U.S. Bureau of Education in the 1910s through the 1930s. Prior to working at the Bureau, she worked as a teacher, county superintendent, and state superintendent in Colorado. She later was head of the Bureau's Division of Special Problems and an "expert" on the education of U.S. minority and non-English-speaking children, including Native Americans and Alaskan Indians, African Americans, Puerto Ricans, Mexicans, Mexican Americans, Filipinos, and Pacific Islanders. Mr. Deffenbaugh also taught and served as a city superintendent for fifteen years.

79. W. S. Deffenbaugh to Katherine M. Cook, February 2, 1917, RG 12, NA. The National Archives noted that most Arizona records from File No. 501 were destroyed, so Deffenbaugh's opinions about Mexican segregation are limited.

80. Specialist in Rural Education to Mrs. J. Billingsley, March 1, 1917, RG 12, NA.

81. *Educational Conditions in Arizona*, 112-113.

82. *Educational Conditions in Arizona*, 120. See footnote 7 for a list of the twelve cities.

83. *Educational Conditions in Arizona*, 112.

84. Also known as the *Arizona Teacher*, this monthly journal represented the views of the Arizona State Teachers' Association (later called the Arizona Education Association) and the Arizona Parent-Teacher Association. The publication ran monthly (summers excepted) from February 1914 to May 1940. See *Arizona Teacher and Home Journal* (Phoenix, Ariz., 1914-1940).

85. Tyack, *The One Best System*, 191.

86. Tyack, *The One Best System*, 191.

87. *Educational Conditions in Arizona*, 9.

88. Helen Roberts, "Education of the Non-English Speaking Child," *ATHJ* 5, no. 5 (June 1916): 8.

89. Frances S. Goff, "The Rodee Method of Teaching English to Mexican Children," *Journal of Education* 102, no. 5 (August 20,1925), 128–130; Nona Rodee, *Teaching Beginners to Speak English: A Course of Study for Non-English Speaking Children and a Manual for Teacher* (Tucson, Ariz.: Tucson Public Schools, 1923); *Arizona Republic*, September 27, 1925.

90. Goff, "The Rodee Method of Teaching English to Mexican Children," 130.

91. R. E. Somers, "Mexican Indifference or Interest!" *ATHJ* 11, no. 4 (1923): 6–8.

92. *Biennial Report of the Superintendent of Public Instruction for the Territory of Arizona, 1905–1906* (Phoenix, Ariz., H. H. McNeil Co., 1906), 8.

93. *Biennial Report of the Superintendent of Public Instruction for the Territory of Arizona, 1907–1908* (Phoenix: Arizona Department of Public Instruction, 1908), 3, 15–18; Aileen Pace Nilsen et al., *Dust in Our Desks: Territory Days to the Present in Arizona Schools* (Tempe: Arizona State University, College of Education, 1985), 23.

94. "Photograph of students picking cotton at the Arizona Industrial School in Benson" (1910) Historic Photographs, ASA ASLAPR.

95. *Biennial Report of the Superintendent of Public Instruction of the Territory of Arizona, 1905–1906* (Phoenix, Ariz., H. H. McNeil Co., 1906), 15.

96. *Biennial Report of the Superintendent of Public Instruction for the Territory of Arizona, 1907–1908* (Phoenix: Arizona Department of Public Instruction, 1908), 16.

97. Gordon, *The Great Arizona Orphan Abduction*, 132.

98. Somers, "Mexican Indifference or Interest!" 7.

99. *Educational Conditions in Arizona*, 122.

100. Somers, "Mexican Indifference or Interest!" 6–7.

101. Minnie Lintz, "Cochise [County]," *ATHJ* 5, no. 1 (February 1916): 33; Roberts, "Education of the Non-English Speaking Child," 11.

102. *Educational Conditions in Arizona*, 116.

103. "Maricopa County," *ATHJ* 11, no. 3 (October 1922): 34.

104. Gainsley, "Teaching Mexican Children," 10.

105. Gainsley, "Teaching Mexican Children," 10.

106. Gainsley, "Teaching Mexican Children," 10.

107. "Fifteenth Street School," *ATHJ* 9, no. 8 (April 1921): 25.

108. Gainsley, "Teaching Mexican Children," 10.

109. Sara M. Lovejoy, "A School Teacher's Philosophy," *ATHJ* 3, no. 4 (May 1915): 19.

110. Somers, "Mexican Indifference or Interest!" 7.

111. Somers, "Mexican Indifference or Interest!" 7.

112. C. Louis Boehringer, "School Legislation in Arizona," *ATHJ* 10, no. 8 (April 1922): 6. House Bill 54 extended the authority of attendance officers, deputizing these officers for the benefit of rural school districts.

113. Boehringer, "School Legislation in Arizona," *ATHJ* 10, no. 8 (April 1922): 6.

114. Higgins, "A Flower Project," 230.

115. *Maricopa County v. Porfirio Miranda and Luis Ledesma*, No. 981 (J.P. Crim. Ct. Ariz. March 5, 1920); *Maricopa County v. Feberano Martínez*, No. 37 (J.P. Crim. Ct. Ariz. March 7, 1921); *Maricopa County v. Orculano Ledesma*, No. 39 (J.P. Crim. Ct. Ariz. March 11, 1921); *Maricopa County v. Juan Estrada*, No. 41 (J.P. Crim. Ct. Ariz. March 24, 1921); *Maricopa County v. Jesus López*, No. 99 (J.P. Crim. Ct. Ariz. Oct. 17, 1921); and *Maricopa County v. Porfirio Romo*, No. 116 (J.P. Crim. Ct. Ariz. Jan. 25, 1921).

116. R. Romo (female), Arizona State Board of Health, Bureau of Vital Statistics, Original Certificate of Birth, No. 229 (May 21, 1924). A 1924 birth certificate for a girl born in Tempe, Arizona, to a "Porfiro Romo" lists his occupation as "Lab" (short for Laborer) from "Old Mex" (Old Mexico) and indicates that he and his wife (Romo Lopez) had two older living children.

117. "Bisbee," *ATHJ* 8, no. 4 (December 1919): 21.

118. "A Tour of Southern Arizona Schools," *ATHJ* 12, no. 7 (March 1924): 18.

119. Charles F. Philbrook, "Bisbee Public Schools," *ATHJ* 7, no. 1 (February 1917): 15-17; *Educational Conditions in Arizona*, 104-105.

120. "Bisbee," *ATHJ* 8, no. 4 (December 1919): 21; Cohen and Mohl, *The Paradox of Progressive Education*, 5.

121. Cohen and Mohl, *The Paradox of Progressive Education*, 7-8.

122. *Educational Conditions in Arizona*, 9.

123. *Educational Conditions in Arizona*, 113.

124. *Educational Conditions in Arizona*, 119.

125. *Educational Conditions in Arizona*, 108, 116, 122. The children's ages ranged from five to thirteen in the first grade, from six to fourteen in the second grade, and six to sixteen in the third grade.

126. *Educational Conditions in Arizona*, 116.

127. *Educational Conditions in Arizona*, 121.

128. *Educational Conditions in Arizona*, 121.

129. "Cochise (County)," *ATHJ* 5, no. 1 (February 1916): 33.

130. *Educational Conditions in Arizona*, 122.

131. "Cochise County Notes—Bisbee," *ATHJ* 9, no. 2 (October 1920): 23; Benton-Cohen, *Borderline Americans*, 230-231.

132. *Educational Conditions in Arizona*, 122.

133. González, *Culture of Empire*, 166.

134. Tyack, *The One Best System*, 208.

135. "Result of Questionnaire Sent to Teachers of the Foreign-Speaking Element," *ATHJ* 14, no. 10 (June 1926): 18-19.

136. Roberts, "Education of the Non-English Speaking Child," 10.

137. Roberts, "Education of the Non-English Speaking Child," 10.

138. *Educational Conditions in Arizona*, 122.

139. *Educational Conditions in Arizona*, 128; González, *Culture of Empire*, 157, 175, 219n8, 222n58. The Arizona Department of Education eventually tailored sections of

the "Course of Study for Elementary Schools of Arizona" to bilingual and Spanish-speaking children in the 1930s. These sections reiterated an emphasis on vocational courses, as the children were expected to drop out of school, marry early, and work.

140. C. R. Tupper, "The Use of Intelligence Tests in the Schools of a Small City," in *Intelligence Tests and School Reorganization*, ed. Lewis M. Terman, et al. (Yonkers-on-Hudson, N.Y.: World Book Co., 1923), 92; Tyack, *The One Best System*, 210–211. The National Education Association sponsored Terman's edited work as a "subcommittee report to the Commission on Revision of Elementary Education." See also Christine Marin, "Always a Struggle: Mexican Americans in Miami, Arizona, 1909–1951" (PhD diss., Arizona State University, 2005), which includes a chapter on Tupper.

141. Tupper, "The Use of Intelligence Tests in the Schools of a Small City," 93.

142. *Educational Conditions in Arizona*, 124.

143. Lewis Madison Terman, *The Measurement of Intelligence: An Explanation of and a Complete Guide for the Use of the Stanford Revision and Extension of the Binet-Simon Intelligence Scale* (Boston: Houghton Mifflin Co., 1916), 92.

144. *Arizona Record*, June 2, 1936. Bullion Plaza School operated as a segregated "Mexican school" from 1923 to 1950. In 1936, it enrolled 571 students. See also Bullion Plaza Cultural Center and Museum, https://bullionplazamuseum.org/.

145. Tupper, "The Use of Intelligence Tests in the Schools of a Small City," 102.

146. Tupper, "The Use of Intelligence Tests in the Schools of a Small City," 93.

147. Tyack, *The One Best System*, 211.

148. González, *Culture of Empire*, 162–163.

149. Tupper, "The Use of Intelligence Tests in the Schools of a Small City," 99.

150. Nona Rodee, "Americanization in the Tucson City Schools," *ATHJ* 12, no. 2 (October 1923), 9.

151. Rodee, "Americanization in the Tucson City Schools," 9.

152. Wayne McFrederick, "The Gilbert Mexican School," n.d., (a teacher's recollection), n.d., CRC ASU; Maritza De La Trinidad, "The Segregation of Mexican Americans in the Tucson Public Schools," *Arizona Report* 4, no. 2 (Spring 2000): 1, 6–7; see also Maritza De La Trinidad, "Collective Outrage: Mexican American Activism and the Quest for Educational Equality and Reform, 1950–1990" (PhD diss., University of Arizona, 2008).

153. Bonnie Henry, "María Urquides Has Lived a Revolution in 84 Years," *Arizona Daily Star*, August 9, 1982.

154. *Arizona Educational Directory* [1928–1929] (Phoenix: Arizona State Department of Education), 170–173.

155. *Arizona Educational Directory* [1928–1929], 117–119.

156. Sheridan, *Los Tucsonenses*, 224; Maritza De La Trinidad, "Mexican Americans and the Push for Culturally Relevant Education: The Bilingual Education Movement in Tucson, 1958–1969, *History of Education*, 44, no. 3 (2015): 316–338.

157. *Arizona Educational Directory* [1928–1929], 157.

158. Higgins, "A Flower Project," 230.

159. Higgins, "A Flower Project," 230.

160. Higgins, "A Flower Project," 230.

161. Boehringer, "Editorial Comment: Americanization," 7.

Chapter 4

1. *Adolpho Romo v. William E. Laird et al.*, no. 21617 (Sup. Ct. Ariz. October 5, 1925); Laura K. Muñoz, "Separate but Equal? A Case Study of *Romo v. Laird* and Mexican American Education" (lesson plan), *OAH Magazine of History* 15 (Winter 2001): 28–34. Romo used the formal first names "Adolph" and "Adolpho," as well his nickname "Bebé," or "Babe." Tempe School District No. 3 in Tempe, Arizona, is known today as the "Tempe Elementary School District No. 3" or "TD3." I use the district's original name in the text, but I cite the latter. A separate district called the Tempe Union High School District No. 213, founded in 1908, manages the high schools.

2. *Romo*, Alternative Writ of Mandamus (September 24, 1925) at 2.

3. "School Year 1925-26—Enrollment to Date at Tenth St" (loose document), Minutes, Board of Trustees, Tempe Elementary School District No. 3, Tempe, Arizona (hereinafter cited as TD3 Minutes). This slip of paper shows the total enrollment for the academic year.

4. *Alvarez v. Lemon Grove School District*, Superior Court of the State of California, County of San Diego, Petition for Writ of Mandate No. 66625 (February 13, 1931); *Independent School District v. Salvatierra*, 33 S.W. 2d 790 (Tex. Civ. App., San Antonio 1930); *Francisco Maestas et al. v. Geo. H. Shone et al.* [12th Judicial District, Alamosa Combined Court, Alamosa County, Colorado, District Civil Roll No. 1 (1914)]; *Gonzalo Mendez et al. v. Westminster School District of Orange, CA, et al.*, 64 F. Supp. 544 (S.D. Cal. 1946).

5. The earliest published federal case on educational segregation in Arizona is *Gonzales et al. v. Sheely et al.*, 96 F. Supp. 1004 (D. Ariz. 1951). In this class action suit, Mexican American parents represented by lawyers, including Tempeñeño Ralph Estrada, from the Alianza Hispano-Americana, sued the Tolleson Elementary School District for segregating their children; Tolleson, Arizona, is in western Maricopa County, about a forty-five-minute drive from Tempe. The court found the segregation discriminatory and illegal on the basis of the *Mendez* holding.

The first published case on Mexican American educational segregation in the United States is the Texas appellate case, *Independent School District et al. v. Salvatierra et al.*, 33 S.W. 2d 790 (Tex. Civ. App. 1930). See Richard Valencia's discussion of the thirty-five Mexican American school desegregation cases, including *Romo*, in *Chicano Students and the Courts: The Mexican American Legal Struggle for Educational Equity* (New York: New York University Press, 2008), 7–78. For an assessment of lawyer Ralph Estrada and desegregation legal strategy, see Jeanne M. Powers and Lirio Patton, "Between *Mendez* and *Brown*: *Gonzáles v. Sheely* and the Legal Campaign Against Segregation," *Law and Social Inquiry* 33, no. 1 (Winter 2008): 127–171; and Laura K. Muñoz, "Ralph Estrada and the War Against Racial Prejudice in Arizona," in *Leaders of the Mexican American Generation: Biographical Essays*, ed. Anthony Quiroz (Boulder: University Press of Colorado, 2015), 270–299.

6. *Brown v. Board of Education*, 347 U.S. 483 (1954); Powers and Patton, "Between *Mendez* and *Brown*," 128.

7. See *Mendez*.

8. *Romo*, Exhibit A: Memorandum of Agreement (filed September 23, 1925).

9. *Arizona Republic*, September 8, 1915.

10. See *Romo*, Findings of Fact and Order (October 5, 1925).

11. Register of Non-Degree Graduates, 1887–1936, call no. 0.13, UA ASU. From 1887 to 1936, the TNS issued a two-year teaching diploma or non-baccalaureate degree that allowed graduates who passed the state certification exam to teach in Arizona and neighboring states that had negotiated "memorandums of agreement."

12. Christine Ogren, *The American State Normal School: An Instrument of Great Good* (New York: Palgrave Macmillan, 2005), 2.

13. "Arizona State Legislature College Bill, 1924–25," Arthur John Matthews, correspondence, series 7, vol. 16, Office of the President, Arizona State University Records, 1863–1981, call no. MS UM MSS 1, University Collection, UA ASU. The holiday was celebrated on March 9, 1925, and throughout the month Matthews received letters of congratulations on the four-year college designation from the U.S. Bureau of Education, the National Committee on Education, and public school administrators and university presidents from across the nation. As a result of the change from a two-year to four-year institution, the TNS officially changed its name to the Tempe State Teachers College. However, the local community continued to call it the TNS or the Normal School. Here, I use "TNS" for brevity.

14. Minutes, June 16, 1922; December 12, 1925; and June 2, 1926; Arizona Board of Regents' Minutes (hereinafter ABOR Minutes), 1885–present, call no. UE ASU 2.2 M668, UA ASU. In June 1926, the board approved the following enrollment statistics: Tempe State Teachers College, 671; Rural Training School, 190; Rohrig Training School, 79; Normal Training School (on-campus site), a kindergarten, plus the Eighth Street School, 558. In 1922, the normal school paid all of its critic teachers, except one, a full-time annual salary of $2,340.

15. ABOR Minutes, April 21, 1922; April 20, 1923. The board referenced its agreement with the Rohrig School, District No. 50 for a normal training school "under such conditions and legal procedure as provided in Title 42, chapter 4, par. 4515–18 inclusive, Revised Statutes of Arizona, 1913." These statutes allow state normal schools to operate training schools. Under this law, the Tempe Normal School operated three schools—the Tempe Normal Training School (on campus), the Rural School (at Rural and Southern), and the Rohrig School (at East University and McClintock), plus an on-campus kindergarten at the time that they negotiated use of Tempe's Eighth Street School. The normal school contracted the Rural and Rohrig schools from two different, nearby districts called "rural school districts."

16. Ariz. Rev. Stat. §§4515–18 (1913).

17. ABOR Minutes, October 23, 1924.

18. ABOR Minutes, January 16, 1925.

19. *Tempe News*, October 25, 1924; November 1, 1924; *Tempe Normal Student* (college newspaper), November 4, 1924.

20. ABOR Minutes, April 20, 1925.

21. TD3 Minutes, September 24, 1925; Waterhouse family, biographical files, Tempe Historical Museum (hereafter cited as THM), Tempe, Arizona.

22. "Tempe School Trustees Decide to Segregate Mexican Children in First Three Grades," *Phoenix Gazette*, July 21, 1915, in *An Arizona Chronology*, Vol. 2, ed. Douglas D. Martin (Tucson: University of Arizona Press, 1966), 18.

23. G. W. Persons to Gene S. Cunningham, assistant county attorney, Phoenix, Arizona (copy), February 9, 1925, TD3 Minutes. Minutes indicate that the board charged Persons with writing the letter, but the copy enclosed in the bound minute book cites "Clerk."

24. Ruby Haigler Wood's grandparents were Winchester Miller and María Sotelo, who was technically her step-grandmother by marriage. She was the daughter of Laura Ann Miller, who was Winchester's daughter from his first marriage. See "Biographical Note," Ruby Haigler Wood Photographs (CP SPC 97), AC ASU; "Ruby Olive Haigler Wood Papers, 1903–1965," UM Small Manuscripts (UN USM-178, Id. No. 69256), UA, ASU.

25. Ruby Olive Haigler Wood, "A History of Tempe" (unpublished manuscript, 1974), THM; Scott W. Solliday, "The Journey to Rio Salado: Hispanic Migrations to Tempe, Arizona" (PhD diss., Arizona State University, 1993), 106–107.

26. J. Morris Richards, "Biography of Dr. A. J. Matthews," Arthur John Matthews correspondence, 1923–1942, series 7, vol. 15, call no. 6.20 R391, Office of the President, Arizona State University Records, 1863–1981, UA ASU. Matthews was president of the Arizona State Teachers Association in 1925 (the same year as *Romo)* and he was elected vice president of the National Education Association in July 1926. Historian Gilbert González traces the history of the "Mexican Problem" in education, including some Arizona responses to it, in his seminal work, *Chicano Education in the Era of Segregation* (Denton: University of North Texas Press, 1990, repr., with new preface, 2013).

27. U.S. Department of the Interior, Office of Education, *Educational Conditions in Arizona* (Report of a Survey by the United States Bureau of Education) (Washington, D.C., 1918 [Bulletin, 1917, No. 44]).

28. Victoria-María MacDonald and Gonzalo Guzmán, "Revolution and World War I Civil Rights? Transnational Relations and Mexican Consul Records in Mexican American Educational History, 1910–1929," *Education's Histories* 4 (December 28, 2017), 26–27, available at https://scholarworks.umt.edu/eduhist/vol4/iss1/5. For examples of discussions about Spanish-speaking children in Arizona, see the editorial "Does It Pay to Educate a Mexican?" by Superintendent R. E. Somers of the Douglas City schools in the *Arizona Teacher and Home Journal* 11, no. 4 (1923): 6–8.

29. *Educational Conditions in Arizona*, 9, 12-13.

30. *Educational Conditions in Arizona*, 121-122.

31. *Educational Conditions in Arizona*, 122.

32. Historians know very little about how normal schools trained teachers to work with Mexican American children or if they differentiated training for Mexican American teachers. Notable higher education institutions that enrolled Mexican Americans as undergraduates or as training-school pupils include New Mexico's Spanish American Normal School at El Rito and Colorado's Adam State College. See Rubén Donato, *Mexicans and Hispanos in Colorado Schools and Communities, 1920-1960* (Albany: State University of New York Press, 2007); Guadalupe San Miguel Jr. and Rubén Donato, "Latino Education in Twentieth-Century America: A Brief History," in *The Handbook of Latinos and Education: Theory, Research and Practice*, ed. Enrique G. Murrillo Jr. et al. (New York: Routledge, 2010); Lynne Marie Getz, *Schools of Their Own: The Education of Hispanos in New Mexico, 1850-1940* (Albuquerque: University of Press, 1997); Ogren, *The American State Normal School*.

33. *Biennial Report of the Superintendent of Public Instruction for the Territory of Arizona, 1907-1908* (Phoenix: Arizona Department of Public Instruction, 1908), 13; "G. L. Fernández," photograph, Picadillo Yearbook (Tempe, Ariz. 1911), 10; *Bulletin of the Tempe Normal School of Arizona at Tempe, Arizona* (Tempe, Ariz., 1911-1912), 52. The TNS offered two language electives: Latin and Spanish. Fernández wrote the descriptions of the foreign-language department and these courses in the annual TNS bulletins during her tenure. By the 1920s, the Latin program was reduced to one course.

34. *Bulletin of the Tempe Normal School of Arizona at Tempe, Arizona* (1907-1908), 37.

35. *Bulletin of the Tempe State Teachers College, Tempe, Arizona* (1926-1927), 77-78.

36. *Bulletin of the Tempe State Teachers College, Tempe, Arizona* (June 1915), n.p. Training school photographs published in the bulletin emphasized farming and gardening for Mexican American boys and domestic skills for Mexican American girls.

37. Wayne McFrederick, "The Gilbert Mexican School" (a teacher's recollection), n.d., CRC ASU, 1; Maritza De La Trinidad, "The Segregation of Mexican Americans in the Tucson Public Schools," *Arizona Report* 4, no. 2 (Spring 2000): 1, 6-7; see also De La Trinidad, "Collective Outrage: Mexican American Activism and the Quest for Educational Equality and Reform, 1950-1990" (PhD diss., University of Arizona, 2008); Nona Rodee, "Americanization in the Tucson City Schools," *ATHJ* 12, no. 2 (October 1923): 9; Thomas E. Sheridan, *Los Tucsonenses: The Mexican Community in Tucson, 1854-1941* (Tucson: The University of Arizona Press, 1986), 224.

38. Helen Roberts, "Education of the Non-English-Speaking Child," *ATHJ* 5, no. 5 (October 1918): 10.

39. *Romo*, Complaint for Writ of Mandamus (September 23, 1925) at 1.

40. San Miguel and Donato, "Latino Education in Twentieth-Century America," 30-32; *Educational Conditions in Arizona*, 120.

41. Julia DeSimone, "The Tale of School Segregation" (75th Anniversary Issue), *Gilbert Independent*, 1996, ME CHI RM-166, CRC ASU.

42. "Twenty-Five Year Summary of Home Demonstration Work, 1914–1939, by Counties," Agents Reports (4-H Clubs), Arizona Annual Narrative and Statistical Reports, 1915–1944, (National Archives Microfilm Publication T847, reel 18, image 84 [p. 64]); Records of the Department of Agriculture, Extension Service, Record Group 33; National Archives at College Park, College Park, Md.

43. "Twenty-Five Year Summary of Home Demonstration Work, 1914–1939, by Counties," 64.

44. McFrederick, "The Gilbert Mexican School," 1.

45. *Arizona Republic*, May 25, 1939.

46. "Alfred Sotomayor (Image 1515)," *U.S. World War II Draft Cards Young Men, 1940-1947* [Ancestry.com database online]; The Tiger Yearbook (Gilbert, Ariz., 1941), n.p.; *Arizona Republic*, May 23, 1941; July 15, 1973. Sotomayor's registration card lists his birthday as January 27, 1921. The draft board registrar who signed Sotomayor's card was teacher María Escalante, who was in charge of the pre-primary class at the Gilbert Mexican School. Sotomayor's obituary listed his profession as grocery store clerk.

47. G. W. Persons, superintendent, Tempe Public Schools, Tempe, Arizona, to Gene S. Cunningham, deputy county attorney, Phoenix, Arizona, February 9, 1925 (loose document), TD3 Minutes.

48. Gene S. Cunningham, deputy county attorney, Phoenix, Arizona, to G. W. Persons, superintendent, Tempe Public Schools, Tempe, Arizona, February 26, 1925 (loose document), TD3 Minutes (hereafter cited as Cunningham to Persons).

49. Cunningham to Persons; "Gene Samuel Cunningham," *History of Arizona*, Vol. 4, ed. Richard E. Sloan (Phoenix, Ariz.: Record Publishing Company, 1930), 91–92.

50. Ariz. Rev. Stat. §2750 (1913); *Romo*, Finding of Facts and Order (filed October 5, 1925) at 6.

51. Cunningham to Persons, February 26, 1925.

52. Ariz. Rev. Stat. §§4515–18 (1913).

53. Victoria-María MacDonald, ed., *Latino Education in the United States: A Narrated History from 1513-2000* (New York: Palgrave MacMillan, 2004), 72–73; Ogren, *The American State Normal School*, 67–68.

54. George W. Harber, "Segregation of School Children: Mexican Children Not Embraced in Segregation Law," *Biennial Report of the Attorney General of Arizona* (Phoenix: Arizona Attorney General's Office, 1915-1916), 65.

55. Harber, "Segregation of School Children: Mexican Children Not Embraced in Segregation Law," 65.

56. For other examples of how whites and Mexicans negotiated space, *see* Cybelle Fox and Thomas Guglielmo, "Defining America's Racial Boundaries: Blacks, Mexicans, and European Immigrants, 1890-1945," *American Journal of Sociology* 18, no. 2 (September 2012): 327–379; Natalia Molina, *How Race Is Made in America: Immigration, Citizenship, and the Historical Power of Racial Scripts* (Berkeley: University of California Press, 2014).

57. Ariz. Rev. Stat. §2750 (1913).

58. Ariz. Rev. Stat. §§4515-18 (1913).

59. Ariz. Rev. Stat. §4515 (1913).

60. Ariz. Rev. Stat. §4518 (1913).

61. *Romo*, Exhibit A: Memorandum of Agreement (filed September 23, 1925).

62. *Romo*, Exhibit A.

63. Monica Muñoz Martinez, *The Injustice Never Leaves You: Anti-Mexican Violence in Texas* (Cambridge, Mass.: Harvard University Press, 2018), 27.

64. Irene Gómez Hormell, interview by Diane Matsch, February 13, 1993, interview OH-130, transcript, and interview by Scott Solliday, March 28, 1992, OH-124, transcript, Barrios Oral History Project, THM; *East Valley Tribune*, September 23, 2005; June 4, 2011.

65. Irene Gómez Hormell, in discussion with the author, October 7, 2003.

66. Santos Vega, *Mexicans in Tempe* (Charleston, S.C.: Arcadia Publishing, 2009), 46. In this picture book, Irene Gómez Hormell provided photographs of the extended Jones and Romo family members, including Alcaria Jones, her brother Francisco Monroy, her daughter Joaquina "Quina" Jones, her daughter Kate Jones, and her sons-in-law Jesus Aros Gómez and Adolpho "Babe" Romo with his brother Miguel.

67. ABOR Minutes, October 9, 1925.

68. Soto-Gómez Family Album, Hispanic Family History Albums, THM.

69. Vega, *Mexicans in Tempe*, 10-11, 13. Romo's birth is dated here as the "mid-1800s" in "Seville, Spain," even though his death certificate and other state documents note his U.S. citizenship and place of birth as California. See Adolph Romo Sr., Certificate of Death, state file no. 6434, Arizona State Department of Health, Division of Vital Statistics, dated October 15, 1956.

70. "Romo/Jones Family Album," Hispanic Family Albums, THM, https://www.tempe.gov/government/community-services/tempe-history-museum/history-and-research/hispanic-family-albums/romo-jones-family-album#ad-image-0.

71. Hormell interviews; Family No. 324 (Wilson Walker Jones and Alcaria Jones), in *Mexico/Arizona Biographical Survey*.

72. *Romo*, Finding of Facts and Order (October 5, 1925) at 1.

73. For examples of the emergent racial divisions in Arizona communities, see Katherine Benton-Cohen, "The White Man's Camp in Bisbee," in *Borderline Americans: Racial Division and Labor War in the Arizona Borderlands* (Cambridge, Mass.: Harvard University Press, 2009), 80-119; Linda Gordon, *The Great Arizona Orphan Abduction* (Cambridge, Mass.: Harvard University Press, 1999), 99-100; Bradford Luckingham, *Minorities in Phoenix: A Profile of Mexican American, Chinese American, and African American Communities, 1860-1992* (Tucson: University of Arizona Press, 1994), 25, 133.

74. Jaime R. Águila and F. Arturo Rosales, "Lost Land and México Lindo: Origins of Mexicans in Arizona's Salt River Valley, 1865-1910," in *Mexican Workers and the Making of Arizona*, ed. Luis F. B. Plascencia and Gloria H. Cuádraz (Tucson: University of Arizona, 2018), 63.

75. Edward B. Goodwin, "Founding of Salt River Valley: Civic Tasks, Murders Go Hand in Hand," *Arizona Republic*, April 9, 1941; Solliday, "The Journey to Rio Salado," 100.

76. Mrs. M. (Manuel) R. Peralta, Tempe, Ariz., to Governor George Wiley Paul Hunt, Phoenix, Ariz., January 22, 1925, RG 1, Governor's Files, Box 3, Folder 29, ASA ASLAPR ; F. Arturo Rosales, *¡Pobre Raza! Violence, Justice, and Mobilization Among México Lindo Immigrants, 1900–1936* (Austin: University of Texas Press, 1999), 5.

77. *Tempe Daily News*, July 2, 1914; Solliday, "The Journey to Rio Salado," 104–106.

78. *Tempe Daily News*, July 9, 1915.

79. Rosales, *¡Pobre Raza!*, 27.

80. Luckingham, *Minorities in Phoenix*, 29.

81. *Arizona Republic*, March 24, 1915.

82. *Arizona Republic*, September 28, 1915.

83. *Arizona Republic*, September 28, 1915.

84. *Phoenix Gazette*, July 21, 1915.

85. *Arizona Republic*, July 12, 1915; September 8, 1915.

86. Solliday, "The Journey to Rio Salado," 106–107. Although Solliday noted that the LPL faded by the mid-1920s, in 1915 its general membership exceeded 1,500 members, over half of whom resided in Maricopa County. By 1917, LPL membership had grown to 2,500. The LPL also held its annual conventions in Phoenix and Tempe during those years.

87. *Tempe Daily News*, July 9, 1915.

88. *Tempe Daily News*, July 9, 1915.

89. *Arizona Republic*, May 20, 1917.

90. Luckingham, *Minorities in Phoenix*, 29; Eric V. Meeks, *Border Citizens: The Making of Indians, Mexicans, and Anglos in Arizona* (Austin: University of Texas Press, 2007), 95–96; Herbert B. Peterson, "Twentieth-Century Search for Cibola: Post-World War I Mexican Labor Exploitation in Arizona," in *An Awakened Minority: The Mexican Americans*, 2d ed., ed. Manuel P. Servín (Beverly Hills, Calif.: Glencoe Press, 1974), 113–132; Rosales, *¡Pobre Raza!*, 138.

91. *Romo*, Exhibit A: Memorandum of Agreement (filed September 23, 1925) at 2.

92. *Romo*, Exhibit A.

93. Peralta to Hunt, January 22, 1925; Hunt to Peralta, January 23, 1925; Peralta to Hunt, January 28, 1925; Hunt to Peralta, January 29, 1925, RG 1, Governor's Files, Box 3, Folder 29, ASA ASLAPR.

94. Hormell interviews; "Arizona, U.S. Voter Registrations, 1866–1955," Ancestry .com [database online].

95. Benton-Cohen, *Borderline Americans*, 202–205; Thomas Sheridan, *Arizona: A History*, rev. ed. (Tucson: University of Arizona Press, 2012), 186–188.

96. Peralta to Hunt, June 22, 1925. I made minor punctuation edits to the quote.

97. *Arizona Republic*, August 16, 1899.

98. Sue Wilson Abbey, "The KKK in Arizona, 1921-1925," *Journal of Arizona History* 14, no. 1 (Spring 1973): 10-30.

99. Abbey, "The KKK in Arizona," 26.

100. Benton-Cohen, *Borderline Americans*, 258; Meeks, *Border Citizens*, 115-116, 173.

101. For examples, see Lozano's and Meeks's discussions on the subordination of Mexican Americans through English literacy voting requirements during and after the battle for Arizona statehood. Rosina Lozano, *An American Language: The History of Spanish in the United States* (Berkeley: University of California Press, 2018), 154-155; Meeks, *Border Citizens*, 36-43.

102. For examples of truancy court cases that resulted from Sigala's complaints, see *Maricopa County v. Feberano Martinez*, no. 37 (J.P. Crim. Ct. Ariz., Mar. 7, 1921) or *Maricopa County v. Jesus Lopez*, no. 99 (J.P. Crim. Ct. Ariz., Oct. 17, 1921).

103. Dean Smith, *Tempe: Arizona Crossroads* (Chatsworth, Calif.: Windsor Publications, Inc.), 64.

104. MacDonald and Guzmán, "Revolution and World War I Civil Rights?," 1-44. This essay explores how Mexican nationals used their consuls "to protect their children's rights in U.S. schools."

105. Benton-Cohen, *Borderline Americans,* 167-175.

106. Goodwin, "Founding of Salt River Valley; Thomas J. Goodwin (biographical note), Goodwin family, biographical file, THM.

107. Arizona lawyers had to earn bar credentials in other states prior to 1912, when the State Bar of Arizona began "official admission procedures." The Arizona Legislature did not require "mandatory membership" until 1933. See James M. Murphy, *Laws, Courts, and Lawyers: Through the Years in Arizona* (Tucson: University of Arizona Press, 1970); "History," State Bar of Arizona, https://www.azbar.org/about-us/about-the-organization/history/.

108. Goodwin, "Founding of Salt River Valley."

109. "Goodwin," *History of Arizona*. Each legislative session ran two years. Edward's oldest brother James also served in the Arizona Territorial Legislature.

110. Congress, U.S. Senate, Special Committee, *Hearings Before a Special Committee Investigating Expenditures in Senatorial Primary and General Elections*, 69th Cong., 1st sess., 30-31, October 1926, 2413. Goodwin provided testimony in this hearing conducted in Phoenix about a county campaign for Democrat Lewis Douglas. The description of Goodwin's neighborhood comes from the interviewer's question, not Goodwin's reply.

111. *Arizona Republic*, September 24, 1925.

112. *Romo*, Complaint for Writ of Mandamus (September 23, 1925) at 3-4.

113. In 1910, Mexican American parents in San Angelo, Texas, challenged the "quality of instruction" in the segregated "Mexican school" and boycotted the district in lieu of litigation. See Valencia, *Chicano Students and the Courts*, 10. See, for example, the LULAC position on white racial identity.

114. Valencia, *Chicano Students and the Courts*, 10.

115. Valencia, *Chicano Students and the Courts*, 10.

116. *Romo*, Alternative Writ of Mandamus (September 24, 1925) at 2.

117. *Romo*, Amended Alternative Writ of Mandamus (September 26, 1925) at 2.

118. *Romo*, Answer and Return of All Defendants to Alternative Writ of Mandamus (September 29, 1925).

119. *Romo*, Answer and Return of All Defendants to Alternative Writ of Mandamus, 3.

120. *Romo*, Answer and Return of All Defendants to Alternative Writ of Mandamus, 3. I have found no evidence that confirms whether the critic teachers spoke Spanish.

121. *Romo*, Answer and Return of All Defendants to Alternative Writ of Mandamus, 4.

122. *Romo*, Answer and Return of All Defendants to Alternative Writ of Mandamus, 4.

123. *Romo*, Answer and Return of All Defendants to Alternative Writ of Mandamus, 4.

124. *Romo*, Findings of Fact and Order (October 5, 1925).

125. ABOR Minutes, October 9, 1925.

126. ABOR Minutes, October 9, 1925.

127. *Dameron v. Bayless*, 14 Ariz. 180., 126 Pac. 273 (1912); Luckingham, *Minorities in Phoenix*, 133–137.

128. Chapter 67, *Arizona Session Laws* (1909), 171–172; Jared Smith, "The African American Experience in Tempe" (Tempe History Museum, 2013), 11.

129. *Wong Him v. Callahan*, 119 F. 381 (1902), *United States v. Buntin*, 10 F. 730 (1882).

130. Terry Goddard, "The Promise of *Brown v. Board of Education: A Monograph*," Arizona Attorney General's Office (March 2005), https://azmemory.azlibrary.gov/nodes/view/181609; Matthew Whitaker, "Desegregating the Valley of the Sun: *Phillips v. Phoenix Union High Schools*," *Western Legal History* 6, no. 2 (Summer 2005): 136–157.

131. *Romo*, Finding of Facts and Order (October 5, 1925) at 6, lines 6–9. Judge Jenckes's emphasis.

132. *Romo*, Finding of Facts and Order (October 5, 1925) at 6, lines 3–5; *Arizona Republic*, October 6, 1925.

133. *Romo*, Judgment (October 8, 1925).

134. *Romo*, Findings of Fact and Order (October 5, 1925).

135. TD3 Minutes, October 12, 1925.

136. TD3 Minutes, September 24, 1925.

137. TD3 Minutes, October 12, 1925.

138. TD3 Minutes, October 12, 1925.

139. Laird family, biographical files, THM.

140. *Arizona Republic*, October 16, 2021; "Hugh Laird House," Tempe Directory of Historic Buildings, Tempe Historic Preservation Office, Tempe, Arizona, available at www.tempe.gov/Home/Components/FacilityDirectory/FacilityDirectory/344/. Hugh

Laird served two terms as Tempe mayor (1928–1930 and 1948–1960); he also served on the Tempe City Council from 1930 to 1962.

141. Gene S. Cunningham, deputy county attorney, Phoenix, Arizona, to G. W. Persons, Tempe Public Schools, Tempe, Arizona (loose document), October 5, 1925, TD3 Minutes.

142. TD3 Minutes, October 12, 1925.

143. "School Year 1925-26—Enrollment to Date at Tenth St" (loose document), TD3 Minutes.

144. *Romo*, Alternative Writ of Mandamus (September 9, 1924) at 2.

145. Ian Haney López, *White by Law: The Legal Construction of Race*, rev. and updated, 10th anniv. ed. (New York, 2006), 1-7, and "Appendix A: The Racial Prerequisite Cases." These cases range from *In re Ah Yup*, an 1878 California case that held that "Chinese are not White," to *Ex parte Mohriez*, a 1944 Massachusetts case that held that "Arabians are White."

146. See case holding for *In re Rodriguez* (81 Fed. 337 [W.D. Texas 1897]) in Haney López, *White by Law*, "Appendix A," 164.

147. Haney López, *White by Law*, 1.

148. Murphy, *Laws, Courts, and Lawyers*, 179, 183.

149. *Romo*, Findings of Fact and Order (October 5, 1925).

150. John S. Goff, *Joseph H. Kibbey* (Cave Creek, Ariz.: Black Mountain Press, 1991), 55-58.

151. ABOR Minutes, June 15, 1926; Keith Crudup, "African Americans in Arizona: A Twentieth-Century History" (PhD diss., Arizona State University, 1998), 234; Luckingham, *Minorities in Phoenix*, 133-144. In 1925 (the same year as *Romo*), the TNS contracted with Dr. Moeur to be the school physician. From 1933 to 1937, he served as governor of Arizona.

152. Crudup, "African Americans in Arizona," 234-236; Richards, "Biography of Dr. A. J. Matthews," n.p.

153. Rule cited in *Romo*, Finding of Facts and Order (October 5, 1925) at 6.

154. Keith Jerome Crudup, "African Americans in Arizona," 128, 136, 323; Jared Smith, "The African American Experience in Tempe" (Tempe History Museum, 2013), 3.

155. Smith, "The African American Experience in Tempe," 11, 16, 20

156. Smith, "The African American Experience in Tempe," 11, 21.

157. ABOR Minutes, December 6, 1923; Crudup, "African Americans in Arizona," 113-162; Bob Jacobsen, "ASU Held Hope, Anguish for African Americans," *ASU Vision* 6, no. 1 (Fall 2002): n.p.; Luckingham, *Minorities in Phoenix*, 143; Whitaker, "Desegregating the Valley of the Sun," 136-137.

158. Smith, "The African American Experience in Tempe," 18-19.

159. Laura E. Gómez, *Manifest Destinies: The Making of the Mexican American Race* (New York: New York University Press, 2007), 4. Gómez's emphasis. She discusses how

these contradictory conditions replicated themselves in American law, especially in New Mexico after the Mexican-American War.

160. Gómez, *Manifest Destinies*, 4.

161. *Romo*, Exhibit A: Memorandum of Agreement (filed September 23, 1925).

162. James and Mariana Gonzales Priest were among the donors who financed the land purchase for the Territorial Normal School at Tempe. Biography of Mariana Gonzales Priest, THM, www.tempe.gov/government/community-services/tempe-history-museum/history-and-research/mariana-gonzales-priest; biography of James T. Priest, THM, www.tempe.gov/government/community-services/tempe-history-museum/history-and-research/james-t-priest.

163. Laura K. Muñoz, "Tempe Normal School," in *Latinas in the United States: A Historical Encyclopedia*, ed. Vicki L. Ruiz and Virginia Sánchez Korrol (Bloomington: Indiana University Press, 2007). Muñoz, "Appendix D: Mexican American, African American, and Asian American Alumni of the Tempe Normal School," in "Desert Dreams: Mexican American Education in Arizona, 1870–1930" (PhD diss., Arizona State University, 2006), 231n127, 334–342.

164. *Romo*, Order for Alternative Writ of Mandamus (September 23, 1925).

165. Cunningham to Persons, 6 October 1925.

166. Cunningham to Persons, 6 October 1925.

167. Haney López, *White by Law*, 88, 205n20; Luckingham, *Minorities in Phoenix*, 49–50; Powers and Patton, "Between *Mendez* and *Brown*," 138, 150; Valencia, *Chicano Students and the Courts*, 7–78; Steve H. Wilson, "*Brown* over 'Other White': Mexican Americans' Legal Arguments and Litigation Strategy in School Desegregation Lawsuits," *Law and History Review* 21, no. 1 (Spring 2003), 145–194.

168. Wilson, "*Brown* over 'Other White,'" 148.

169. *Romo*, Complaint for Writ of Mandamus (September 23, 1925) at 4.

170. My emphasis. *Romo*, Amended Alternative Writ of Mandamus (September 26, 1925) at 2.

171. *Romo*, Findings of Fact and Order (October 5, 1925) at 6; *Romo*, Judgment (October 8, 1925) at 2.

172. Harold J. Janson, Phoenix, to G. W. Persons, Tempe, October 6, 1925 (loose document), TD3 Minutes.

173. *Romo*, Notice and Motion for Modifying Findings of Fact (October 30, 1925) at 1; *Romo*, Notice and Motion for Modification of Judgment (October 30, 1925) at 2.

174. *Romo*, Amended Judgment (November 9, 1925) at 5.

175. Mae M. Ngai, *Impossible Subjects: Illegal Aliens and the Making of Modern America* (Princeton, N.J.: Princeton University Press, 2004), 26. The Johnson-Reed Act did not place quotas on immigrants from any nation in the Western Hemisphere, including Mexico.

176. Powers and Patton, "Between *Mendez* and *Brown*," 140.

177. Lillie Parra-Moraga, in discussion with the author, December 18, 2003.

178. "School Year 1925-26—Enrollment to Date at Tenth St." and "10th St. School—Mar. 1926" (loose documents), TD3 Minutes; David Ray García, "The *Romo* Decision and Desegregation in Tempe," undergraduate research paper (1993), Small Manuscripts, call no. MM CHSM-732, CRC ASU, 17.

179. *Arizona Republic*, December 6, 1925.

180. Bill Coates, "What's in a Name for Old Schools?" *Tempe Daily News*, n.d., Early Tempe Schools, file TH-611, THM.

181. "School Year 1925-26—Enrollment to Date at Tenth St.," and "Tenth St. School—Mar. 1926," ABOR Minutes, December 12, 1925. The school board approved the following enrollment statistics for December 1925: Tempe State Teachers College, 623; Rural Training School, 76; Rohrig Training School, 53; Normal Training School (on-campus site), a kindergarten, plus the Eighth Street School, 420. The enrollment total for all the training schools was 549.

182. ABOR Minutes, October 9, 1925.

183. "Children Received Special Attention in Training School," *Tempe Collegian*, May 13, 1926.

184. ABOR Minutes, June 15, 1926.

185. "TD3 Celebrates 100th Birthday," newsletter, Tempe School District No. 3, March 1, 1977, Arizona Collection, Hayden Library, Arizona State University, Tempe, Arizona; García, "The *Romo* Decision," 31-32; *Arizona Republic*, June 7, 1945.

186. "School Year 1925-26—Enrollment to Date at Tenth St." and "10th St. School—Mar. 1926" (loose documents), TD3 Minutes; García, "The *Romo* Decision," 17.

187. Hormell interviews.

188. "Pedro García de La Lama" in Manuel Gamio, *El inmigrante mexicano: La historia de su vida: Entrevistas completas, 1926-1927*, ed. Devra Weber, Roberto Melville, and Juan Vicente Palerm (Mexico, D.F.: Editorial Miguel Ángel Porrúa, 2002). De La Lama is referring to a murder of a Mexican man killed by an Anglo American, but the sentiment applies here, too.

189. Hormell interviews.

190. Hormell interviews.

Chapter 5

Epigraph: Rebecca Muñoz, "Horizons," *Mexican Voice* 2, no. 3 (1939): 1.

1. "Racial Composition of the School Population," in *Course of Study for Elementary Schools of Arizona*, Bulletin No. 1 (Phoenix, Ariz.: State Department of Education, 1932), 16; Annie Reynolds, *The Education of Spanish-Speaking Children in Five Southwestern States*, Bulletin 1933, No. 11 (Washington, D.C.: U.S. Department of the Interior, Office of Education, 1933), 38-39.

2. "Table No. 49: Pupils of Foreign Extraction Enrolled in Arizona Schools—1935-1936" and "Table No. 88: Pupils of Foreign Extraction Enrolled in Arizona High Schools—1935-1936," in *Thirteenth Biennial Report of the State Superintendent of Public*

Instruction to the Governor of the State of Arizona (Phoenix: Arizona Department of Public Instruction, 1936), 267, 294.

3. "Table No. 88: Pupils of Foreign Extraction Enrolled in Arizona High Schools—1934-1935" and "Table No. 88: Pupils of Foreign Extraction Enrolled in Arizona High Schools—1935-1936," in *Thirteenth Biennial Report of the State Superintendent of Public Instruction to the Governor of the State of Arizona, 1934-1936* (Phoenix: Arizona Department of Public Instruction, 1936), 128, 290, 294. The state counted "Mexican, Negro, Japanese, Chinese, Indian and Others" as "pupils of foreign extraction" by county. In 1935-1936, the report estimated that "of the 18,859 pupils enrolled in the high schools of the state, 2,622 or 13.9 percent were pupils of foreign extraction, 2,158 of these were Mexicans and 276 were negroes."

4. "Table No. 39: Foreign Pupils Enrolled in Arizona Schools—1933-1934," in *Twelfth Biennial Report of the State Superintendent of Public Instruction to the Governor of the State of Arizona* (Phoenix: Arizona Department of Public Instruction, 1934), 265, 267.

5. "Training Schools," *Thirteenth Biennial Report of the State Superintendent of Public Instruction to the Governor of the State of Arizona, 1934-1936* (Phoenix: Arizona Department of Public Instruction, 1936), 41.

6. *El Fronterizo*, August 4, 1936.

7. Jean Reynolds, "Mexican American Women Workers in Mid-Twentieth-Century Phoenix," in *Mexican Workers and the Making of Arizona*, ed. Luis F. B. Plascencia and Gloria H. Cuádraz (Tucson: University of Arizona, 2018), 228.

8. Mary López García, quoted in Reynolds, "Mexican American Women Workers in Mid-Twentieth-Century Phoenix," 233. Based on Jean Reynolds's interview with Mary López García, Phoenix, Arizona, March 3, 1997.

9. *Arizona Daily Star*, August 9, 1992.

10. Lydia Otero, *In the Shadows of the Freeway: Growing Up Brown & Queer* (Tucson, Ariz.: Planet Earth Press, 2019), 27-28.

11. Jean Reynolds estimates that young Mexican American domestics trained in Americanization programs offered by settlement houses, such as the Phoenix Friendly House, averaged wages of $4-$7 weekly. See Reynolds, "Mexican American Women Workers in Mid-Twentieth-Century Phoenix," 234.

12. *Arizona Daily Star*, February 2, 1947. A reporter described Urquides's classroom in this 1947 profile. She often spoke of painting the room herself or planting shade trees on her own to improve the school property.

13. "Adelante" literally means "ahead" or "going forward." In this context, it means "uplift."

14. *Arizona Daily Star*, August 9, 1982.

15. *Arizona Republic*, October 19, 1941; *Arizona Record*, June 2, 1936; *Arizona Educational Directory*, 1936-1937 (Phoenix, Ariz.: State Superintendent of Public Instruction), 110 (hereafter *AED*).

16. *AED* (1931-1932), 86.

17. *Arizona Teacher and Home Journal* 15, no. 2 (October 1926): 64 (hereafter ATHJ).

18. "Adams School/Grace Court School," Nomination Form, National Register of Historic Places, https://npgallery.nps.gov/GetAsset/b7902e57-ff49-49c0-b5fb -36d8468607cf. The Adams School was renamed in 1952 to honor principal Grace Court, who worked there from 1918 through 1952. It is now an office building in downtown Phoenix.

19. *Arizona Republic*, June 5, 1937; May 23, 1939; June 1, 1946. Bernard Carrascoso won a two-year scholarship to the University of Southern California, where he completed bachelor and doctoral degrees, before joining the U.S. Army in 1942. He later graduated Georgetown University Law School and practiced law in California. He is the brother of Josefina Carrascoso Franco, who owned the Phoenix Spanish-language newspaper, *El Sol*, from 1936 until her death in 1972.

20. Khalil A. Johnson Jr., "'Recruited to Teach the Indians': An African American Genealogy of Navajo Nation Boarding Schools," *Journal of American Indian Education* 57, no. 1 (2018): 154–176.

21. Sarah Deutsch, *No Separate Refuge: Culture, Class, and Gender on an Anglo-Hispanic Frontier in the American Southwest, 1880–1940* (New York: Oxford University Press, 1987), 196; Laura K. Muñoz, "Los Mireles and the Historical Restoration of the Mexican American Teacher in South Texas," paper delivered at American Educational Research Association, New Orleans, April 2011; Tey Diana Rebolledo, ed., *Nuestra Mujeres: Hispanas of New Mexico, Their Images and Their Lives, 1582–1992* (Albuquerque, N. Mex.: El Norte Publications, 1992), 35. See also Philis Barragán Goetz's discussion of teacher Jovita Idar in *Reading, Writing and Revolution: Escuelitas and the Emergence of a Mexican American Identity in Texas* (Austin: University of Texas, 2020), 74–80.

22. *Arizona Daily Star* (Tucson), March 20, 1936; María Urias Muñoz, "This I Remember [A Memoir]," unpublished manuscript, dated September 27, 1980, electronic copy, personal gift to the author by Rosalío U. Muñoz, 107 (hereafter Muñoz, "This I Remember").

23. *Arizona Daily Star*, November 20, 1928; *El Tucsonense*, November 20, 1928. Both newspapers ran a lengthy obituary of Hilario "Larry" Urquides.

24. Concepción Faras and Rose Faras, *AED* (1923–1924), 40–41. The directory shows that both women resided at 1006 9th Street, Douglas, Arizona.

25. Alice Buzan and Rose Buzan, *AED* (1923–1924), 121–122; *Arizona Daily Star*, June 10, 1924. The directory shows that both women resided at 493 N. Main Street, Tucson, Arizona.

26. "Maricopa County Notes," *ATHJ* 7, no. 5 (1918–1919), 30.

27. *AED* (1930–1931), 140, 151.

28. *AED* (1939–1940), 36.

29. *AED* (1940–1941), 37.

30. *AED* (1930–1931), 116–127. This figure is based on a manual count of teachers at each primary school in the district.

31. *AED* (1918-1919), 59; *AED* (1919-1920), 72.

32. *AED* (1930-1931), 118, 127; *Arizona Republic*, November 19, 1927; October 7, 1928.

33. *AED* (1930-1931), 177-187.

34. Thomas E. Sheridan, *Los Tucsonenses: The Mexican Community in Tucson, 1854-1941* (Tucson: University of Arizona Press, 1986), 218.

35. Ida Celaya also earned the master's degree from the University of Arizona in 1933.

36. *AED* (1926-1927), 125.

37. *AED* (1926-1927), 47, 49.

38. *AED* (1940-1941), 83, 104.

39. Listings for Amelia Hunt García and Dan Romero, AED (1923-1924), 4, 124.

40. Listing for Rose Oviedo, AED (1925-1926), 108.

41. Listing for Ida Celaya, María Escalante, and Raphael Estrada, AED (1923-1924), 101, 108, 114.

42. Reynolds, "Mexican American Women Workers in Mid-Twentieth-Century Phoenix," 230; Payson Smith and Frank W. Wright et al., "Education in the Forty-Eight States (Staff Study Number 1)," Report of the Advisory Committee on Education (Washington, D.C.: Government Printing Office, 1939), 99. See "Table 18. Average Salary of Teachers, Principals, and Supervisors in 24 States, by Level or Type of School and by State, 1935-1936." The report shows that in the 1935-1936 school year the average teacher salary for "elementary and kindergarten" teachers in Arizona was $1,299, while the highest paid group of "regular and vocational high" teachers earned an average of $1,741. The estimate of $3.56 a day was calculated by dividing the nine-month salary of $1,299 by 365 days.

43. Jurgen Herbst, *And Sadly Teach: Teacher Education and Professionalization in American Culture* (Madison: University of Wisconsin Press, 1989), 29.

44. Sarah Deutsch, *No Separate Refuge: Culture, Class, and Gender on an Anglo-Hispanic Frontier in the American Southwest, 1880-1940* (New York: Oxford University Press, 1987), 147.

45. Vicki L. Ruiz, *From Out of the Shadows: Mexican Women in Twentieth-Century America* (New York: Oxford University Press, 1998), 84; see also "Table 1: Occupational Distribution for Mexican Women in the Southwest, 1930-1990," 153.

46. For the history of women teachers, see Geraldine J. Clifford, *Those Good Gertrudes: A Social History of Women Teachers in America* (Baltimore: Johns Hopkins University Press, 2014); Deutsch, *No Separate Refuge*; Margaret Smith Crocco, Petra Munro, Kathleen Weiler, eds., *Pedagogies of Resistance: Women Educator Activists, 1880-1960* (New York: Teachers College Press, 1999); John Nieto-Phillips, *The Language of Blood: The Making of Spanish-American Identity in New Mexico, 1850-1940* (Albuquerque: University of New Mexico Press, 2004); Kathleen Weiler, ed., *Feminist Engagements: Reading, Resisting, and Revisioning Male Theorists in Education and Cultural Studies* (New York: Routledge, 2001); Kathleen Weiler, *Country Schoolwomen: Teaching in Rural California,*

1850–1920 (Stanford, Calif.: Stanford University Press, 1998); Kathleen Weiler and Sue Middleton, eds., *Telling Women's Lives: Narrative Inquiries in History of Women's Education* (Philadelphia: Open University Press, 1999).

47. Herbst, *And Sadly Teach*, 24–30.

48. Barry Edward Lamb, "The Making of a Chicano Civil Rights Activist: Ralph Estrada of Arizona" (master's thesis, Arizona State University, 1988).

49. Thomas E. Sheridan, "Race and Class in a Southwestern City: The Mexican Community of Tucson, 1854–1941," Renato Rosaldo Lecture Series, Vol. 4, Series 1986–1987 (Tucson: Mexican American Studies and Research Center, University of Arizona), 57.

50. "María Urquides Celebrates 25th Year as a Teacher," *Tucson Citizen*, October 28, 1952.

51. Elizabeth Quiroz Gónzalez, *The Education and Public Career of María L. Urquides: A Case Study of a Mexican American Community Leader* (PhD diss., University of Arizona, 1986), 49.

52. "María Urquides: 46-Year Teacher Ahead of Her Time," *Arizona Daily Star* [Tucson], October 16, 1983.

53. *Arizona Daily Star*, February 9, 1932; June 3, 1932. The Tucson chapter of the Young Women's Christian Association built a new center in 1934 and publicly claimed credit for it and all of its programming, including the Adelante Club. However, Urquides says she was one of the three founders of Oury Park. See *Arizona Daily Star*, November 23, 1938; February 10, 1955.

54. *Arizona Daily Star*, March 1, 1932.

55. *Arizona Daily Star*, February 9, 1932.

56. Arizona Daily Star, November 9, 1932.

57. Gónzalez, *The Education and Public Career of María L. Urquides*, 39–40.

58. *Arizona Daily Star*, January 31, 1932; April 2, 1932.

59. *Arizona Daily Star*, November 18, 1932.

60. *Arizona Republic*, January 30, 1933.

61. *Arizona Catholic Lifetime*, June 1, 1986.

62. Gónzalez, *The Education and Public Career of María L. Urquides*, 49–56.

63. "Mrs. García Passes Away," *St. Johns Herald*, November 4, 1937, A1.

64. *Arizona Republic*, January 25, 1936.

65. Madeline Ferrin Pare, *Arizona Pageant: A Short History of the 48th State* (Phoenix: Arizona Historical Foundation, 1965), 190; David King Udall and Pearl Udall Nelson, *Arizona Pioneer Mormon: David King Udall: His Story and His Family, 1851–1938* (Tucson: Arizona Silhouettes, 1959).

66. *Arizona Republic*, March 20, 1935.

67. "Amelia Hunt García," *History of Arizona*, Vol. 4, ed. Richard E. Sloan (Phoenix, Ariz.: Record Publishing Company, 1930), 484.

68. "Districts, District Clerks and Teachers," in *Biennial Report of the Superintendent of Public Instruction of the Territory of Arizona*, 1902, RG6, Box 22, Folder 346,

Secretary of the Territory, 1871–1909, ASA ASLAPR; Teacher's Certificate Register, 1905–1916, RG107 Maricopa County, Superintendent of Schools Records 1883–1931, ASA ASLAPR.

69. *St. Johns Herald*, December 9, 1909.

70. *Arizona Republic*, August 7, 1935.

71. "Amelia Hunt García," *History of Arizona*, 484; "Amelia Hunt García," microfilm, RG 91 Works Progress Administration, ASA ASLAPR (hereafter "WPA file").

72. Charlotte Whaley, *Nina Otero-Warren of Santa Fe* (Albuquerque: University of New Mexico Press, 1994). Amelia Hunt García's career also mirrored that of well-known Hispana educator Nina Otero Warren of New Mexico. Both women taught in the public schools, served as state political officials, and were strong advocates for educational access.

73. This assessment is based on my reading of the Arizona Educational Directory and other sources related to the Arizona Superintendent of Public Instruction in this period.

74. "Certificate of Appointment of Public Trustee," DS by Leandro Ortega and Monico García *et al.*, March 20, 1907; Certificates of Elections–Trustees, 1891–1900; School Records—Reports, 1886–1919, Box 2; Superintendent of Schools; Apache County, RG 100; ASA ASLAPR. García signed this document as "justice of the peace."

75. *AED* (1934–1935), 49.

76. "Appellant's Brief," *Amelia Hunt Garcia vs. Arizona*, no. 849 (January 9, 1937). This case was withdrawn from the Arizona Supreme Court by the appellant on June 21, 1937 due to financial hardship.

77. *Arizona Daily Star*, May 11, 1935.

78. *Arizona Daily Star*, May 11, 1935. Based on the U.S. Bureau of Labor Statistics' Consumer Price Index (CPI), the inflation equivalent of $150,000 in May 1935 is $3,270,000 in February 2023.

79. Initially, the law firm of Gene S. Cunningham, Charles A. Carson, and A. S. Gibbons, along with Gregorio García, represented Amelia Hunt García, but Cunningham, Carson, and Gibbons withdrew from the case in January 1936. See "Motion for Withdrawal of Attorneys," *Arizona v. Garcia*, No. 480, Apache County Superior Court (January 16, 1936).

80. *Arizona Daily Star*, May 16, 1935.

81. *Arizona Republic*, April 19, 1935; June 23, 1935. Amelia Hunt García's motion to dismiss the case was denied in June 1935.

82. *Arizona Republic*, July 31, 1935. This juror was J. D. Baca.

83. *Arizona Republic*, August 4, 1935.

84. *Arizona Daily Star*, August 5, 1935.

85. *Arizona Daily Star*, August 6, 1935.

86. *Arizona Daily Star*, August 6, 1935.

87. *Arizona Daily Star*, August 7, 1935.

88. "Motion to Quash Indictment," *Arizona v. Garcia*, No. 479, Apache County Superior Court (June 21, 1935).

89. "Motion to Quash Indictment," 2.

90. "Motion to Quash Indictment," 3.

91. Mexican American attorneys in the U.S. Supreme Court case, *Hernandez v. Texas* (1954) argued this same defense. See *Colored Men and Hombres Aqui: Hernandez v. Texas and the Emergence of Mexican-American Lawyering* (Houston, Tex.: Arte Público Press, 2006).

92. For a discussion of whiteness and early Arizona law, see James M. Murphy, *Laws, Courts, and Lawyers: Through the Years in Arizona* (Tucson: University of Arizona Press, 1970).

93. "Answer to Motion to Quash Indictment," *Arizona v. Garcia*, No. 479, Apache County Superior Court (June 21, 1935). Dodd also explained that Spanish-Americans with medical disabilities and those who no longer lived in the county due to the completion of public works projects were removed from the jury roster.

94. *Arizona Republic*, January 22, 1936.

95. Affidavit, *Arizona v. Garcia*, no. 462 (filed April 9, 1935).

96. *Arizona Republic*, January 25, 1936.

97. Cause No. 510 Reporter's Transcript, *Arizona v. Garcia*, Apache County Superior Court (July 13, 1936), 156–157.

98. Cause No. 510 Reporter's Transcript, 86.

99. *Arizona Republic*, January 26, 1936.

100. *Arizona Republic*, February 18, 1936.

101. *Arizona Republic*, February 29, 1936.

102. *Arizona Republic*, February 29, 1936.

103. Author in conversation with García family descendants, Scottsdale, Arizona, July 27, 2009 (hereafter García family descendants). James Hunt García Jr., a grandson of Amelia Hunt and Monico García, arranged for me to meet with him and his first cousins, including Charlotte "Charlie" Walker, Sandra Barnes, and Tom Hudson.

104. *Arizona Republic*, October 31, 1937.

105. *Arizona Daily Star*, October 1, 1937; *El Imparcial*, October 1, 1937

106. *Arizona Republic*, October 28, 1937; *El Imparcial*, October 29, 1937.

107. "Argument on Assignment of Error No. 2" in "Appellant's Brief," *Amelia Hunt Garcia vs. Arizona*, no. 849 (January 9, 1937), 18.

108. "Argument on Assignment of Error No. 2" in "Appellant's Brief," *Amelia Hunt Garcia vs. Arizona*, no. 849 (January 9, 1937), 19.

109. Esaú P. Muñoz, *Stories of Faith and Love: Memoirs of Esaú P. Muñoz, From the Beginnings of Evangelism in Northern Mexico* (n.p., English language version, circa 1951), Manuscript File MM CHSM-865, CRC ASU; Obituary, "Rev. Esaú Muñoz Rites Here Today," *Arizona Republic*, February 16, 1967.

110. Ross Florián Muñoz, Diploma, Master of Arts in Education, Arizona State Teachers College at Tempe, May 31, 1938, CSRC UCLA; Ross Florián Muñoz, Immigration

and Naturalization Application, U.S. Department of State, May 17, 1938 (electronic file, Ancestry.com).

111. Ross Florián Muñoz, "The Relation of Bilingualism to Verbal Intelligence and Social Adjustment Among Mexican Children in the Salt River Valley, Arizona" (master's thesis, Arizona State University, 1938).

112. H. L. Hollingworth, "Rudolph Pintner: 1884–1942," *American Journal of Psychology* 56, no. 2 (April 1943); 303–305; Rudolf Pintner, J. B. Maller, G. Forlano, and H. Axelrod, "The Measurement of Pupil Adjustment," *Journal of Educational Research* 28, no. 5 (January 1935): 334–346.

Given that one role of the American school was to prepare children to successfully enter society as contributing young adults, the pupil portrait estimated the social aptitude of students in the fourth to eighth grades, or youth nearing completion of primary school. The test results helped teachers to understand whether the student had competently developed the social skills needed beyond English language and literacy to assimilate into mainstream society.

113. Historian Gilbert González explains this reform project as "the need … to reconstruct the culture of Mexican immigrants along the lines of the American norm, in order for them to socialize effectively in the organic society." See González, *Culture of Empire: American Writers, Mexico, and Mexican Immigrants, 1880–1930* (Austin: University of Texas Press, 2004), 171; González, *Chicano Education in the Era of Segregation*, Al Filo: Mexican American Studies Series, no. 7, reprint (Denton: University of North Texas, 2013), xii–xiv.

114. González, *Culture of Empire*, 5, 18.

115. Rebecca Muñoz, "Horizons," *Mexican Voice* 2, no. 3 (1939): 1.

116. Ruiz, *From Out of the Shadows*, 94.

117. Vicki L. Ruiz and Virginia Sánchez Korrol, eds., *Latinas in the United States: An Historical Encyclopedia*, Vol. 1 (Bloomington: Indiana University Press, 2006), 5. Ahead of their time, anti-Communist redbaiting destroyed the short-lived Congreso when the Federal Bureau of Investigation began investigating its leadership.

118. Christine Marin, in conversation with Veronica Castillo (niece of Ross Muñoz Sr.), email to the author, April 27, 2021. For Spanish fantasy heritage, see Nieto-Phillips, *The Language of Blood.*

119. Interaction among Mexican American Protestant youth in Arizona, California, and New Mexico resulted in significant relationships between Los Conquistadores and the Mexican Youth Conferences (later, the Mexican American Movement), such as the marriage between Rebecca F. Muñoz and Félix J. Gutiérrez, founder of the *Mexican Voice*. Muñoz served as the Arizona correspondent to the *Mexican Voice*. After college, many youth in both organizations pursued similar vocational goals as educators and social workers in an effort to promote their vision of Mexican American self-improvement.

See Carlos Muñoz, *Youth, Identity, Power: The Chicano Movement* (New York: Verso, 1989); Christine Marin, "A Short History of 'Los Conquistadores' of Arizona State

University—Tempe," *Barriozona* (news website), June 8, 2009, https://barriozona.com/a-short-history-of-los-conquistadores-of-arizona-state-university-tempe/; George J. Sánchez, *Becoming Mexican American: Ethnicity, Culture and Identity in Chicano Los Angeles, 1900–1945* (New York: Oxford University Press, 1993), 255–269.

120. *See* "Los Conquistadores Records, 1938–1972," UM Small Manuscripts, UA ASU.

121. Rebecca Muñoz, "Personalities," *Mexican Voice* (Club Issue, n.d.): 23–25; Solomon F. Muñoz, "Arizona Spring Sports," *Mexican Voice* (Club Issue, n.d.): 25.

122. Sánchez, *Becoming Mexican American*, 256, 262; Muñoz, *Youth, Identity, Power*, 34.

123. "El Club Hispanico," *The Sahuaro* (TNS Yearbook, 1917), n.p.; Alfred J. Thomas, ed., *Arizona State University: A Documentary History of the First Seventy-Five Years, 1885–1960*, Vol. 2 (Tempe, Ariz.: Alfred Thomas, 1960), 532. Sponsored by Spanish teacher Miss Edith Salmans and founded in 1916–1917 by her students, the "Spanish Club" (its informal name) boasted 22–25 members, including senior Ida Celaya who wrote a Spanish essay featured in the club's yearbook entry. According to Thomas, the club hosted "Spanish-only" meetings with the twin goals of improving the Spanish-speaking ability of its members and of raising interest in Latin America. He says the club changed its name to Los Hidalgos del Desierto in 1924–1925.

124. Muñoz, "The Relation of Bilingualism to Verbal Intelligence," ii.

125. Castillo, "Biography of Rebecca Muñoz Gutiérrez," n.p.

126. "Spanish Club," *La Cuesta* Yearbook (Flagstaff: Northern Arizona Normal School, 1930), 128; *Arizona Daily Star*, November 28, 1925; January 30, 1935. In 1930, Amelia Vigil served as the Spanish Club president at Northern Arizona and its membership included Spanish-surnamed students Al Chacon, Adolph Orrantia, and Ysaias Flores.

127. Veronica Castillo to Christine Marin, email correspondence, March 22, 2000 (in possession of the author). Emphasis in original.

128. Quoted in Marin, "A Short History of 'Los Conquistadores' of Arizona State University," n.p.

129. *The Sahuaro* (ASTC Yearbook, 1939), n.p.

130. Marin, "Arizona Highways," 8–9.

131. Castillo to Marin, May 24, 2004; Marin, "Arizona Highways," 8–9n18.

132. Marin, "Arizona Highways," 8; Sánchez, *Becoming Mexican American*, 257.

133. Sánchez, *Becoming Mexican American*, 527.

134. Sánchez, *Becoming Mexican American*, 260; F. Arturo Rosales, *Chicano! The History of the Civil Rights Movement* (Houston, Tex.: Arte Público Press, 1996), 101.

135. Marin, "Arizona Highways," 16n30.

136. Luis H. Cordóva to "To Whom It May Concern," August 15, 1938; Albert M. García to "To Whom It May Concern," August 15, 1938; and Fred Teyechea to "To Whom It May Concern," August 16, 1938; Los Conquistadores Records, 1937–1941, Small Manuscripts UM USM-234, UA ASU. For a photo of Albert M. García, *see* Stan

Watts, *A Legal History of Maricopa County* (Charleston, S.C.: Arcadia Publishing, 2007), 37.

137. Muñoz, "This I Remember [A Memoir]," 107.

138. Muñoz, "This I Remember," 107.

139. Muñoz, "This I Remember," 98. Emphasis in original.

140. Castillo to Marin, May 24, 2004; *School Laws of Arizona as Compiled in Revised Statutes of Arizona, 1928, with New Laws and Amendments Passed by State Legislature since Revision of Code* (Phoenix: Arizona Superintendent of Public Instruction, 1929), 31. See Sec.1352, "Aliens not to be employed on public work."

141. Muñoz, "This I Remember," 111.

142. *La Cuesta* Yearbook (Flagstaff: Northern Arizona Normal School, 1930), 56; *La Cuesta* Yearbook (Flagstaff: Northern Arizona Normal School, 1931), 38.

143. Muñoz, "This I Remember," 57, 69.

144. Muñoz, "This I Remember," 93.

145. Muñoz, "This I Remember," 93. In this era, the term, "retarded" referred to students who failed, who exhibited mental slowness, or who were overage for their expected grade level.

146. Muñoz, "This I Remember," 96.

147. Muñoz, "This I Remember," 98. "E. V. "Al" Arvizu," Golden Reunion Class of 1938 Program, May 12, 1988, personal collection of the author, n.p.

148. *Arizona Republic*, April 18, 1940; AED (1940-1941), 85.

149. Castillo to Marin, May 24, 2004.

150. Marin, "Arizona Highways," 17-21.

151. Marin, "Arizona Highways," 17-21.

152. Marin, "Arizona Highways," 18.

153. Marin, "Arizona Highways," 17-21; Rebecca Muñoz, "Horizons," 1.

154. Sánchez, *Becoming Mexican American*, 260.

155. Muñoz, "The Relation of Bilingualism to Verbal Intelligence," 52-54.

156. "School teacher in grade school teaching geography. Concho, Arizona," photograph by Russell Lee, October 1940, Lot 653 (82), Farm Security Administration, Office of War Information Black-and-White Negatives, American Memory, Prints and Photographs Division, Library of Congress, https://lccn.loc.gov/2017788007.

157. "Juan Candelaria, owner of several thousand acres of land near Concho, Arizona. He is considering selling to the government for FSA (Farm Security Administration) use," photograph by Russell Lee, Lot September 1940, Farm Security Administration, Office of War Information Black-and-White Negatives, American Memory, Prints and Photographs Division, Library of Congress, https://lccn.loc.gov/2017743335.

158. *AED* (1941-1942), 37.

159. *Tucson Citizen*, June 10, 1942.

160. Office of Censorship, Washington, D.C., to Ross F. Muñoz, [Tucson, Ariz. (no address)], appointment letters dated July 27, 1942, and July 31, 1942, Ricardo Muñoz Papers, UCLA CRC.

161. Letter, Randall Jacobs, Chief of Naval Personnel (Navy Department, Bureau of Naval Personnel, Washington, D.C.) to Ross Florián Muñoz, Office of Censorship, Bisbee Field Station, Arizona, November 8, 1943, CSRC UCLA.

162. See Maggie Rivas-Rodriguez, *Mexican Americans and World War II* (Austin: University of Texas Press, 2005).

163. Ross Florián Muñoz, Honorable Discharge Certificate, United States Navy, October 5, 1945, CSRC UCLA.

164. Ross and María had five children: María Rosalía, Elvira, Ricardo, Rosalío, and Carlos. Ross also had a daughter, Margaret, from a previous marriage.

165. Coconino County Board of Social Security and Welfare, Flagstaff to Ross Muñoz, Phoenix, telegram, August 28, 1947, UCLA CRC.

166. Arlien Johnson, Dean, Graduate School of Social Work, University of Southern California, to Ross Muñoz, Flagstaff, AZ, telegram, August 29, 1947; Rosalío F. Muñoz, "Differences in Dropout and Other School Behavior between Two Groups of Ten Grade Boys in an Urban High School" (PhD diss., University of Southern California, 1957).

167. *Lincoln Heights Bulletin News* (Los Angeles), April 9, 1953, and December 20, 1951. The Muñoz and Mirabal families knew each other from the Avenue 21 PTA. Both wives served as PTA president, Muñoz in 1951 and Mirabal in 1952.

168. "Edward R. Roybal," in *Hispanic Americans in Congress, 1822-1955*, ed. Carmen E. Encisco, http://www.loc.gov/rr/hispanic/congress/roybal.html; David G. Gutiérrez, *Walls and Mirrors: Mexican Americans, Mexican Immigrants, the Politics of Ethnicity* (Berkeley: University of California Press, 1995), 168.

169. "Final Oral Examination of Ross Florián Muñoz for the degree of Doctor of Philosophy," University of Southern California Graduate School, program pamphlet (ephemera), April 1, 1957, CSRC UCLA.

170. *Los Angeles Times*, May 28, 2004; Rosalío F. Muñoz, "How Supervisors of Child Welfare and Attendance Serve Our Schools," *California Journal of Elementary Education* 22 (1953-1954), 250-252. With his sister Josefina Muñoz de Rodríguez, Muñoz also coedited three books of poetry and prose by their father, Esaú P. Muñoz.

Epilogue

1. Mario T. García, *Mexican Americans: Leadership, Ideology, and Identity, 1930-1960* (New Haven, Conn.: Yale University Press, 1989); Anthony Quiroz, ed., *Leaders of the Mexican American Generation* (Boulder: University Press of Colorado, 2015).

2. Ignacio M. García, *Viva Kennedy: Mexican Americans in Search of Camelot* (College Station: Texas A&M University Press, 2000), 66-67.

3. *Arizona Republic*, October 5, 1960; *Tucson Citizen*, October 5, 1960.

4. Maritza De La Trinidad, "Mexican Americans and the Push for Culturally Relevant Education: The Bilingual Education Movement in Tucson, 1958-1969," *History of Education* 44, no. 3 (2015): 324n28.

5. De La Trinidad, "Mexican Americans and the Push for Culturally Relevant Education," 333.

6. Bilingual Education Act of 1968 Elementary and Secondary Act Amendments, Pub. L. No. 90–247, title VII, §702, 81 Stat. 816. (1968). *See* also Carlos Kevin Blanton, *The Strange Career of Bilingual Education in Texas, 1836–1981* (College Station: Texas A&M University Press, 2004); Ofelia García and Kenzo K. Sung, "Critically Assessing the 1968 Bilingual Education Act at 50 Years: Taming Tongues and Latinx Communities," *Journal of the National Association for Bilingual Education* 41, no. 4 (2018): 318–333; Arnold H. Leibowitz, *The Bilingual Education Act: A Legislative Analysis* (Rosslyn, Va.: InterAmerica Research Associates, National Clearinghouse for Bilingual Education, 1890); Guadalupe San Miguel Jr., *Contested Policy: The Rise and Fall of Federal Bilingual Education* (Denton: University of North Texas Press, 2004).

7. *Arizona Daily Star*, May 31, 1974.

8. Yolanda Leyva, "María Luisa Legarra Urquides," in *Latinas in the United States: An Historical Encyclopedia*, vol. 3, ed. Vicki L. Ruiz and Virginia Sánchez Korroll (Bloomington: Indiana University Press, 2006), 779–780.

9. *Arizona Daily Star*, February 10, 1955. Urquides worked for the Catholic Social Services of Arizona as a case worker and, later, as a supervisor for nine years.

10. *Arizona Daily Star*, February 2, 1947.

11. De La Trinidad, "Mexican Americans and the Push for Culturally Relevant Education," 323.

12. *Arizona Daily Star*, March 26, 1944.

13. *Tucson Citizen*, April 29, 1942.

14. *Arizona Daily Star*, January 16, 1943; June 4, 1944; January 9, 1949; October 7, 1951.

15. *Arizona Daily Star*, July 1, 1948; May 4, 1951. In 1948, Urquides also served as the president of the Tucson chapter of the honorary education society, Pi Lambda Theta, which allowed her to build alliances with teachers across Pima County (*Arizona Daily Star*, November 16, 1948).

16. *Arizona Daily Star*, January 13, 1951; *Arizona Republic*, May 1, 1951.

17. *Arizona Republic*, January 7, 1949. See the public notice for the "Articles of Incorporation of Arizona Council for Civic Unity." Most histories of the CCU focus on its origins as an African American civil rights organization. See Bradford Luckingham, *Minorities in Phoenix: A Profile of Mexican American, Chinese American, and African American Communities, 1860–1992* (Tucson: University of Arizona Press, 1994), 161, 174–175; Eric Meeks, *Border Citizens: The Making of Indians, Mexicans, and Anglos in Arizona* (Austin: University of Texas Press, 2007), 178; Matthew C. Whitaker, *Race Work: The Rise of the Civil Rights in the Urban West* (Lincoln: University of Nebraska Press, 2007), 15.

18. *Tucson Daily Citizen*, October 31, 1950.

19. Urquides could have challenged issues of sexuality, but in this red-baiting era she disclosed nothing about her sexuality. Although evidence is fleeting, at least one

historian has identified her as lesbian. See Lydia Otero's memoir of Tucson, *In the Shadows of the Freeway: Growing Up Brown & Queer* (Tucson, Ariz.: Planet Earth Press, 2019).

20. *Arizona Sun*, May 4, 1951.

21. Kaye Lynn Briegel, "Alianza Hispano-Americana, 1894–1965: A Mexican American Fraternal Insurance Society" (PhD diss., University of Southern California, 1974).

22. A close parallel may have included Nina Otero Warren of New Mexico, but she had withdrawn from public work by 1950. Dr. Clotilde P. García of Texas also may have been active in her brother's American G.I. Forum, but she was completing medical school in the 1950s. Attorney Graciela Olivarez's nationally known civil rights work would follow in the 1970s. See Vicki L. Ruiz and Virginia Sánchez Korroll, eds., *Latinas in the United States: An Historical Encyclopedia*, vol. 3 (Bloomington: Indiana University Press, 2006).

23. *Arizona Daily Star*, October 29, 1950; *Tucson Daily Citizen*, October 31, 1950.

24. *Arizona Daily Star*, November 5, 1950; Luckingham, *Minorities in Phoenix*, 49, 160; Meeks, *Border Citizens*, 178.

25. *Arizona Republic*, June 18, 1934; Luckingham, *Minorities in Phoenix*, 45–45; Meeks, *Border Citizens*, 173.

26. "Contra la Segregación de Nuestros Estudiantes," *Alianza* 43, no. 10 (October 1950), 3.

27. Quote translated from Spanish. "Contra la Segregación de Nuestros Estudiantes," *Alianza* 43, no. 10 (October 1950), 3.

28. *Arizona Sun*, November 2, 1950. The front-page header also read "VOTE 318-YES—DESEGREGATE ARIZONA SCHOOLS."

29. *Gonzales v. Sheely* (1951); Jeanne M. Powers and Lirio Patton, "Between *Méndez* and *Brown*: *Gonzales v. Sheely* and the Legal Campaign Against Segregation," *Law and Social Inquiry* 33 (Winter 2008): 127–171; Richard R. Valencia, *Chicano Students and the Courts: The Mexican American Legal Struggle for Educational Equality* (New York: New York University Press, 2008).

30. Luckingham, *Minorities in Phoenix*, 49–50.

31. Cited in Powers and Patton, "Between *Méndez* and *Brown*," 127.

32. *Tucson Daily Citizen*, March 21, 1951.

33. *Arizona Daily Star*, May 16, 1951. Dunbar School became John Spring School, named for the first teacher hired at Tucson in 1871.

34. Doris Bynon McGuire, "Desegregation of the Nogales Schools," n.d., unpublished manuscript, Pimeria Alta Historical Society.

35. Terry Goddard, "The Promise of *Brown v. Board of Education*: A Monograph" (Phoenix: Arizona Attorney General's Office, 2005), 3.

36. *Baca v. Winslow*, Civ. No. 394-Pct A. (D. Ariz. 1955); *Romero v. Weakley*, 131 F. Supp. 818 (S.D. Cal. 1955); *Ortiz v. Jack* (1951).

37. Greg García, certificate of death, state file no. 5531, Office of Vital Records (Arizona Department of Health Services, Phoenix); "Murió el Ex-Presidente Supremo, Hno. García," *Alianza* 46, no. 10 (1953): 9.

38. *Arizona Republic*, March 4, 1950; *Tucson Daily Citizen*, November 20, 1951; March 19, 1952. Urquides participated in the White House Conference on Children and Youth in 1950, 1960, and 1970 under the Truman, Eisenhower, and Nixon presidential administrations, as well as on advisory committees on education and civil rights for Presidents Kennedy and Johnson.

39. *Arizona Daily Sun,* August 18, 1959.

INDEX

ACKNOWLEDGMENTS

I owe my professional success to many people, organizations, and institutions for guiding me through the academy, none more so than historians Vicki L. Ruiz, Gayle Gullett, and Asunción Lavrin. I am grateful for their resolute commitment, honesty, and expertise. Their kinship and vision continue to sustain me. Asunción, thank you for pushing me to finish the degree and for the impeccable standards you demanded of me. Gayle, thank you for working with me until the very end, for the incredible writing lessons, and to both you and Edward Escobar for treating me like your *hijada*. Vicki, I am especially thankful *con todo corazón* to you and Victor Becerra for never giving up on me and for mentoring me through my undergraduate and graduate degree programs. Thank you for being part of my chosen family. Natasha and I cannot imagine our lives without you both!

My Tejano family taught me the significance of place and of remembering. I was fortunate to know my grandparents and my great-grandparents: Gustavo M. Cantú, María "Mary" Cabrera Cantú, Alicia "Alice" Rousset Muñoz, San Juana Peña Casas, and Rosa Sánchez Rousset. They taught me ways of knowing and seeing beyond the written word. Their lessons proved critical to my work as a historian of people thought to be without history. I owe particular credit to my maternal grandmother María Cantú who put education at the forefront of our lives, when hers was curtailed as a young girl in Corpus Christi's Mexican schools. I appreciate my parents, David Rousset Muñoz and the late Alda Cantú Muñoz for valuing education and for enrolling me, at the age of six, in my first writing class at Canto Al Pueblo (the Chicano Movement literary festival). For always encouraging my academic endeavors, I thank my entire family, including my aunts, uncles, cousins, niblings, and the *compadres*, but especially my sister Audra M. Luis, my brother-in-law Martin G. Luis, my late brother David Jr., my brother Marc, my cousin Denise N. Rodriguez, and my late Aunt Frances Cabrera. For their kindness and continued daily support, I thank my in-laws

Mercedes Martínez Crawford and Weston D. Crawford. For inspiring me to write about the history of education, I thank all my family members who have worked as educators.

Many institutions and individuals invested in my scholarship. At the University of Texas at Austin, I am thankful to have studied with Mercedes de Uriarte, the late Chuck Halloran, and the late Rolando Hinojosa-Smith. At Arizona State University, thank you to Linda Britton-Farwell, Denise I. Beighe, and Vicki Krell. For significant financial support, I am indebted to the Ford Foundation Predoctoral Fellowship, the AERA/Spencer Predissertation Fellowship, and the National Academy of Education/Spencer Postdoctoral Fellowship. At Texas A&M University—Corpus Christi, I appreciated the generosity of the Joe B. Frantz Fund, and the opportunity to mentor incredible students, including my niblings Marysa G. Luis, Natalia A. Luis, Sarah L. Luis, William D. Luis, and Kara Gúzman Hays. At the University of Nebraska-Lincoln, I thank the faculty of the Institute of Ethnic Studies and the Department of History, as well as the College of Arts and Sciences and the Office of Research and Economic Development. I have been fortunate to receive direct support from incredible colleagues, especially Joy Castro, Jessica A. Coope, Dawne Y. Curry , Lory Janelle Dance, Jeannette Eileen Jones, James A. Garza, Vanessa B. Gorman, Margaret Huettl, Margaret D. Jacobs, Katrina Jagodinsky, Alice Kang, James D. Le Sueur, Amelia de la Luz Montes, Deirdre Cooper Owens, Ingrid Robyn, Luis Othoniel Rosa Rodriguez, William G. Thomas III, Victoria Smith, Ann M. Tschetter, Alexander Vazansky, Isabel Velázquez, Cynthia Willis-Esqueda, and Kenneth J. Winkle.

I owe a special debt to the fantastic archivists who helped me locate the sources to write this book. At the Arizona State Library, Archives, and Public Records, I thank former director Melanie Sturgeon and Wendi Goen, who located the *Romo v. Laird* court records. Thank you for always keeping the door open for me! I thank Jared A. Smith at the Tempe History Museum for his insight on African Americans in Tempe. I thank the entire staff of the Arizona State University Libraries, Department of Archives and Special Collections, especially Robert Spindler and Nancy Liliana Godoy. The history substantiated here also comes from the Arizona Historical Society in Tucson; the Chicano Studies Research Center Library at the University of California, Los Angeles; and the National Archives at College Park, Maryland.

This book rests on the knowledge of archivist emeritus Christine Marin and her labor of love to build ASU's Chicano Research Collection for the sole purpose of documenting the Arizonense past. She has been *amiga, tía, madrina, y curandera* on this journey! Thank you for taking me to Wicken-burg to meet the Quesada family, for the tour of Miami and Bullion Plaza School, for going with me to St. Johns to find the García court records, and for inviting me into Arizonense tradition and culture.

I also thank the many Arizonense families—especially the García, Romo, Muñoz, and Quesada descendants—who contributed their personal collec-tions to Chicano archives across the Southwest, who generously shared their knowledge and sources with me, and who always encouraged this project despite the many delays. I appreciate the time you gave me, the continued cor-respondence, and your trust in this work. I thank Kris D. Gutiérrez and her late mom Mary R. Gutiérrez of Miami, Arizona, for reading sections of this book for accuracy. Thank you specifically to Sandra Barnes, Esther Carrillo Canchola, René Díaz-Lefebvre, Pete Dimas, Tom Hudson, James Hunt García Jr., Lorraine Gutiérrez, Felix Gutiérrez, Gail Gutiérrez, Irene Gómez Hormell, Ricardo Muñoz, Rosalío U. Muñoz, Lydia Otero, the late Alice Quesada, the late Dora Quesada, the late Eugene Quesada, Joséfina Quesada Alvarez, Otto Santa Ana, Santos Vega, Charlotte Walker, and the late Wally Walker.

I am so appreciative of the leadership and consummate direction of the Penn Press editorial, production, and marketing teams who made this book possible. Series editor Stephen Pitti and senior editor Robert Lockhart are phenomenally kind and generous. I appreciate reviewers Katherine Benton-Cohen and Geraldo L. Cadava for their trusted commentary. Their thought-fulness enhanced this study, and any errors are mine alone. *¡Mil gracias!*

Thank you also to the many colleagues who read my work or listened to my ideas before publication, including Alfredo Artiles, Carlos Blanton, Roland Sintos Coloma, Maritza De La Trinidad, Rubén Donato, Manuel Espi-noza, Gonzalo Guzmán, Yndalecio Isaac Hinojosa, Patrick Hoehne, Katrina Jagodinsky, Jeannette Eileen Jones, Francesca A. López, the late Michael Oli-vas, John Nieto-Phillips, William Reese, Mario Rios Perez, Alexa Rodriguez, Guadalupe San Miguel Jr., Santos Vega, Cecelia Gutiérrez Venable, and Jon-athan Zimmerman. Their insights inspired my earlier ventures on this topic. Chapter 4 of this book is an expanded version of "*Romo v. Laird*: Mexican American School Segregation and the Politics of Belonging in Arizona," *Western Legal History* 26, nos. 1–2 (2013): 97–132. My discussion of attorney Ralph Estrada in the Introduction, Chapter 2, and the Epilogue is informed by "Ralph Estrada and the War against Racial Prejudice in Arizona," in *Lead-ers of the Mexican American Generation: Biographical Essays*, ed. Anthony Quiroz (Denver: University of Colorado Press, 2015), 277–299.

Thank you to my dearest friends—the late San Juanita Alcalá, Maricela Alexander, Luisa Bonillas (for the Nogales files!), Luis Gonzalez, Veronica Guzmán Hays, Wendy Hunt, Brooke Glenn, Lane Nevares, Martha Ruiz, Rachelle Stanley, and the late Alberto Zamora. In Lincoln, thank you to Marty Ramirez, Helen M. Montoya, and *Las Voces de Nebraska*!

I owe special recognition to my *camaradas*, the incredible Latina historians of education, Victoria-María MacDonald and Mirelsie Velázquez. Victoria-María is a kindred spirit and intellectual powerhouse, whose insight, mentorship, and friendship has buoyed me. Mirelsie's sharpness always reminds me to be fierce and keep it real, every time! ¡*Hermanas por vida*!

Finally, I thank Natasha Mercedes Crawford to whom this book is dedicated. Thank you for inviting me into your life and for your brilliance. Thank you for challenging me, for teaching me how to think like a lawyer, and for moving with me time and again so that I could do this work. You have been the greatest force of love, joy, determination, and intellect in my life!

www.ingramcontent.com/pod-product-compliance
Lightning Source LLC
Chambersburg PA
CBHW030259100426
42812CB00002B/505